AI, Ethics, and the Digital Shift in Education

Nihal Dulkadir Yaman
https://orcid.org/0000-0002-5339-7449
Kırşehir Ahi Evran University, Turkey

Fatih Yaman
https://orcid.org/0000-0002-7425-1369
Kırşehir Ahi Evran University, Turkey

IGI Global
Scientific Publishing
Publishing Tomorrow's Research Today

Vice President of Editorial	Melissa Wagner
Director of Acquisitions	Mikaela Felty
Director of Book Development	Jocelynn Hessler
Production Manager	Mike Brehm
Cover Design	Jose Rosado

Published in the United States of America by
IGI Global Scientific Publishing
701 East Chocolate Avenue
Hershey, PA, 17033, USA
Tel: 717-533-8845 | Fax: 717-533-7115
Website: https://www.igi-global.com E-mail: cust@igi-global.com

Library of Congress Cataloging-in-Publication Data

LCCN: (CIP Data Pending)
ISBN13: 9798337388571
Isbn13Softcover: 9798337388588
EISBN13: 9798337388595
British Cataloguing in Publication Data
A Cataloguing in Publication record for this book is available from the British Library.

Table of Contents

Preface ix

Chapter 1
Impact of Digital Transformation in Education Systems 1
Sanjeev Kumar, Lovely Professional University, India

Chapter 2
The Future of Artificial Intelligence in Education: An Evaluation in the Framework of Social Robots and Holograms 25
Selin Gocen, Education Faculty, Dicle University, Turkey
Gulsun Kurubacak Cakir, Ankara Haci Bayram Veli University, Turkey

Chapter 3
Artificial Intelligence and Education: Potentials and Challenges 53
Ozan Filiz, Sinop University, Turkey

Chapter 4
Artificial Intelligence in Education: From Smart Systems to Inclusive Learning 99
Betül Tonbuloğlu, Yildiz Technical University, Distance Education Application and Research Center, Turkey

Chapter 5
Exploring the Potential, Applications, and Ethical Challenges of Harnessing Artificial Intelligence in Education 159
Sohel Rana Sarkar, Hingalganj Mahavidyalaya, West Bengal State University, India
Sirajun Tahura, Kumarpukur High School, India

Chapter 6
At the Intersection of Artificial Intelligence and Giftedness: Managing Thinking Skills 189
Gülşah Avcı Doğan, Ordu University, Turkey

Chapter 7
Data Privacy and Security in Education 219
Fatma Akgün, Trakya University, Turkey
Şenay Ozan Deniz, Trakya University, Turkey

Chapter 8
Digital Transformation and Equal Opportunities: Assistive Technologies for Individuals With Special Education Needs.. 247
Özge Misirli, Eskisehir Osmangazi University, Turkey
Zeynep Şahin Timar, Karadeniz Technical University, Turkey
Geraldine Leader, University of Galway, Ireland
Merita Hoxha, University of Elbasan Aleksander Xhuvani, Albania
Gerda Sula, University of Tirana, Albania

Compilation of References 279

About the Contributors 333

Index 339

Detailed Table of Contents

Preface ix

Chapter 1
Impact of Digital Transformation in Education Systems 1
Sanjeev Kumar, Lovely Professional University, India

The digital transformation in education systems has significantly reshaped traditional learning methodologies which used innovative pedagogies tools, and innovative practices. The transformation enhances accessibility, interactivity, and personalized learning experiences, enabling students to engage effectively regardless of geographical and socio-economic barriers. Digital tools which includes; virtual classrooms, learning management systems (LMS), artificial intelligence (AI)-driven assessments, and augmented reality (AR), foster interactive and educational environments. It further addresses the challenges related to digital inequalities, privacy concerns, and teacher readiness. Findings suggest that a balanced integration of technology, supported by adequate infrastructure, professional development, and inclusive policies, maximizes educational effectiveness. The study concludes by emphasizing the importance of strategic planning and stakeholder collaboration to fully harness the potential of digital transformation in education.

Chapter 2
The Future of Artificial Intelligence in Education: An Evaluation in the Framework of Social Robots and Holograms 25
Selin Gocen, Education Faculty, Dicle University, Turkey
Gulsun Kurubacak Cakir, Ankara Haci Bayram Veli University, Turkey

Artificial intelligence technology, which has a transformative effect on learning systems, integrates with social robot and hologram technologies to bring new dimensions to the processes of learning and teaching. By providing an immersive and interactive structure to learning experiences, these technologies also contribute to increasing the retention of learning. While having considerable potential benefits, these technologies also present risks and threats that should not be ignored. In this book chapter, the definitions, development, and integration processes of artificial intelligence, hologram, and social robot technologies into education are examined within the context of their applications. The chapter also briefly addresses the ethical and legal issues that may arise during the use of these technologies.

Chapter 3
Artificial Intelligence and Education: Potentials and Challenges........................ 53
Ozan Filiz, Sinop University, Turkey

This chapter explores the transformative role of artificial intelligence (AI) in education, highlighting its vast potential alongside significant challenges. It introduces core AI principles and prompt engineering strategies that help educators engage effectively with generative AI systems. The chapter examines AI applications in content creation, personalized learning, assessment, and administrative efficiency, showing how AI can support differentiated instruction, automate feedback, and streamline tasks. It also addresses ethical concerns such as algorithmic bias, data privacy, transparency, and accountability, offering guidelines for responsible AI use. Ultimately, the chapter emphasizes that the future of AI in education depends on educators' ethical, informed choices to enhance teaching and learning while ensuring equity and trust in digital environments.

Chapter 4
Artificial Intelligence in Education: From Smart Systems to Inclusive Learning 99
Betül Tonbuloğlu, Yildiz Technical University, Distance Education Application and Research Center, Turkey

The use of AI in educational institutions is rapidly bringing changes in various aspects of learning, right from personalized learning tools, automated contents, enhanced testing methodologies, to specific help tools for physically disabled students. AI enhances classroom efficiency, accessibility, and learner focus by optimizing regular tasks, delivering real-time insights, and customizing resources to individual development. Moreover, it reduces teachers' chores by grading data and generating a lesson plan to quickly develop existing resources. However, apprehensions around student data security, latent biases in training datasets, and the ethical use of potent algorithms underscore the necessity for technology to be governed by explicit standards. This chapter juxtaposes a discussion of innovative applications with an examination of their limitations, providing educators, researchers, and school administrators with a pragmatic framework for leveraging AI.

Chapter 5
Exploring the Potential, Applications, and Ethical Challenges of Harnessing Artificial Intelligence in Education 159
Sohel Rana Sarkar, Hingalganj Mahavidyalaya, West Bengal State University, India
Sirajun Tahura, Kumarpukur High School, India

AI is rapidly transforming the educational landscape by offering innovative solutions to personalize learning, automate assessments, enhance student engagement, and improve administrative efficiency. This chapter explores the diverse applications of AI in education, focusing on adaptive learning platforms, virtual teaching assistants, predictive data analytics, and AI-enabled lifelong learning. Drawing upon empirical case studies, it illustrates both the benefits and limitations of AI integration across varied educational contexts. Ethical concerns such as data privacy, algorithmic bias, student autonomy, and digital inequality are critically examined, highlighting the urgent need for equitable, transparent, and human-centered AI systems. Looking ahead, the chapter outlines future directions including intelligent learning environments, emotional and cognitive analytics, and AI as a co-teacher. It concludes with strategic recommendations for policymakers, educators, and technologists to harness AI's full potential while safeguarding educational values and equity.

Chapter 6
At the Intersection of Artificial Intelligence and Giftedness: Managing Thinking Skills 189
Gülşah Avcı Doğan, Ordu University, Turkey

This chapter aims to develop an understanding of artificial intelligence by using high-level learning features to manage thinking skills. This draws attention to the intersection between the learning styles of gifted and talented individuals with higher-level thinking skills and machine intelligence. It presents a dual roadmap for understanding the developmental thinking styles of gifted individuals and for utilizing machine-generated information. The machines and artificial intelligence can be trained using learning and innovation skills. This relationship places meta-learners at the center of skills development. Adapting to and surviving the rapid changes predicted for the new century and beyond requires everyone to become a meta-learner. This primarily requires the reconstruction of educational programs and continuous teacher training.

Chapter 7
Data Privacy and Security in Education 219
Fatma Akgün, Trakya University, Turkey
Şenay Ozan Deniz, Trakya University, Turkey

Digital transformation in education is a process developed to create effective and efficient learning processes that meet the demands of the current era and to ensure learning. Through data collected in education, teachers can more accurately monitor student behavior, develop early intervention strategies, and create personalized learning environments. However, this data-driven approach also brings with it data security, privacy, and ethical responsibilities. While taking advantage of the opportunities offered by developing technologies, being aware of and preventing the threats they bring is a priority. This unit will address data privacy and security in education. In this context, the types of data collected in education, educational data mining, data privacy and security, basic principles of information security, security threats and risks, data protection methods, and solutions will be explained.

Chapter 8
Digital Transformation and Equal Opportunities: Assistive Technologies for Individuals With Special Education Needs.. 247
Özge Misirli, Eskisehir Osmangazi University, Turkey
Zeynep Şahin Timar, Karadeniz Technical University, Turkey
Geraldine Leader, University of Galway, Ireland
Merita Hoxha, University of Elbasan Aleksander Xhuvani, Albania
Gerda Sula, University of Tirana, Albania

The chapter "Digital Transformation and Equal Opportunities: Assistive Technologies for Individuals with Special Education Needs" explores how digital transformation promotes inclusive education by integrating assistive technologies. It discusses the opportunities and challenges of using AT to support students with special education needs, aiming to create equitable and meaningful learning experiences. The chapter highlights barriers including technological limitations, socioeconomic disparities, and pedagogical challenges. Key strategies for effective AT integration include adopting user-centered design approaches that involve students and educators, providing ongoing professional development to build teachers' digital competencies. Furthermore, the chapter emphasizes empowering students through technology to foster independence rather than dependency. Overall, it calls for coordinated efforts to bridge the digital divide and ensure all learners benefit from digital advancements.

Compilation of References 279

About the Contributors 333

Index 339

Preface

INTRODUCTION

The rapid evolution of artificial intelligence and digital technologies has brought profound changes to education systems across the globe. As classrooms become increasingly digitized and learning environments extend beyond physical boundaries, educators, policymakers, and researchers are faced with both unprecedented opportunities and complex challenges. It is within this shifting landscape that our book, *AI, Ethics, and the Digital Shift in Education*, aims to situate itself—offering critical perspectives on the pedagogical, ethical, and societal implications of emerging technologies.

Across many regions, digital transformation is reshaping how learners access information, how teachers facilitate learning, and how institutions operate. These advancements promise greater personalization, interactivity, and flexibility, enabling more inclusive learning pathways. However, they also raise pressing concerns related to data privacy, algorithmic fairness, teacher preparedness, and digital equity. Recognizing this duality is essential for ensuring that technological progress contributes positively and sustainably to the future of education.

This book brings together diverse scholars who examine these issues from multidisciplinary and international viewpoints. Each chapter highlights both the potential and the pitfalls of integrating AI and digital tools in educational settings. By presenting research-driven insights and critical evaluations, the volume seeks to support responsible innovation and to guide stakeholders toward evidence-based decisions that protect learners while enhancing educational quality.

CHAPTER OVERVIEW

Chapter 1: Impact of Digital Transformation in Education Systems

Sanjeev Kumar analyzes how digital transformation reshapes learning processes through tools such as virtual classrooms, LMS platforms, AI-driven assessments, and augmented reality. The chapter emphasizes both the pedagogical benefits and the systemic challenges—including infrastructure gaps, digital inequality, and privacy concerns. Kumar concludes that coordinated planning and capacity-building are essential for meaningful integration.

Chapter 2: The Future of Artificial Intelligence in Education: An Evaluation in the Framework of Social Robots and Holograms

Selin Gocen and Gulsun Kurubacak Cakir explore the emerging roles of social robots and hologram technologies as immersive tools that enrich learner engagement. Their chapter also addresses the ethical and legal considerations associated with these technologies, emphasizing the need for cautious and informed adoption.

Chapter 3: Artificial Intelligence and Education: Potentials and Challenges

Ozan Filiz provides a comprehensive overview of AI's expanding role in personalized learning, content generation, and assessment. The chapter balances these innovations with a discussion of risks such as algorithmic bias, transparency issues, and data governance, offering a framework for responsible and ethical use of AI in education.

Chapter 4: Artificial Intelligence in Education: From Smart Systems to Inclusive Learning

Betül Tonbuloglu examines how AI enhances classroom efficiency through automation, accessibility tools, and personalized learning systems. At the same time, the chapter highlights ethical issues related to data security and algorithmic biases, encouraging the development of standards and guidelines for safe implementation.

Chapter 5: Exploring the Potentials, Applications, and Ethical Challenges of Harnessing Artificial Intelligence in Education

Sohel Sarkar and Sirajun Tahura discuss AI applications ranging from adaptive learning platforms to predictive analytics and virtual assistants. Through empirical examples, they assess both benefits and limitations while emphasizing the importance of human-centered, equitable AI design and future-oriented policy development.

Chapter 6: At the Intersection of Artificial Intelligence and Giftedness: Managing Thinking Skills

Gülsah Avci Dogan focuses on the interplay between AI and the cognitive development of gifted learners. The chapter introduces meta-learning as a key competency for navigating technological change and argues for curriculum reforms and continuous teacher training to support higher-order thinking skills.

Chapter 7: Data Privacy and Security in Education

Fatma Akgün and Senay Deniz address one of the most critical ethical issues in today's digital education landscape: the protection of student data. Their chapter covers types of educational data, security vulnerabilities, privacy principles, and protective strategies, emphasizing the shared responsibility of institutions, educators, and policymakers.

Chapter 8: Digital Transformation and Equal Opportunities: Assistive Technologies for Individuals with Special Education Needs

Özge Misirli, Zeynep Sahin Timar, Geraldine Leader, Merita Hoxha, and Gerda Sula examine how digital transformation promotes inclusive education through assistive technologies. The chapter highlights both the opportunities for increased autonomy and accessibility, and the barriers posed by socioeconomic disparities, inadequate design, and insufficient teacher training.

CONCLUSION

The chapters within this volume collectively illustrate a rapidly evolving educational ecosystem in which AI, digital tools, and ethical considerations are inseparable. As these technologies continue to influence teaching and learning, understanding their implications becomes not merely beneficial but essential. Responsible digital transformation requires ongoing reflection, research, and collaboration across disciplines and borders.

While AI offers unprecedented potential for personalization, efficiency, and expanded access, it simultaneously demands vigilant oversight. Issues such as privacy, algorithmic fairness, digital divides, and teacher readiness must remain at the forefront of all educational innovation. The research and perspectives presented in this book underscore that technology alone cannot improve education; it must be guided by values of equity, transparency, and human-centered design.

We hope that this book serves as a meaningful resource for educators, administrators, researchers, and policymakers navigating the digital shift in education. By fostering informed conversations and encouraging ethical practices, we aim to contribute to a future in which technology enhances—not replaces—the human elements that make learning transformative.

Chapter 1
Impact of Digital Transformation in Education Systems

Sanjeev Kumar
https://orcid.org/0000-0002-7375-7341
Lovely Professional University, India

ABSTRACT

The digital transformation in education systems has significantly reshaped traditional learning methodologies which used innovative pedagogies tools, and innovative practices. The transformation enhances accessibility, interactivity, and personalized learning experiences, enabling students to engage effectively regardless of geographical and socio-economic barriers. Digital tools which includes; virtual classrooms, learning management systems (LMS), artificial intelligence (AI)-driven assessments, and augmented reality (AR), foster interactive and educational environments. It further addresses the challenges related to digital inequalities, privacy concerns, and teacher readiness. Findings suggest that a balanced integration of technology, supported by adequate infrastructure, professional development, and inclusive policies, maximizes educational effectiveness. The study concludes by emphasizing the importance of strategic planning and stakeholder collaboration to fully harness the potential of digital transformation in education.

INTRODUCTION

In modern decades, technology has become a critical driver of transformation within education systems globally. It play a different role in the education sectors and it extends beyond classroom environment effective and reshaping the new idea

DOI: 10.4018/979-8-3373-8857-1.ch001

to students and provide excessive information in term of educational content and more interaction with teachers and peers. The use of innovative tools like; "e-learning platforms, virtual classrooms, augmented reality (AR), artificial intelligence (AI), and mobile education (m-learning), technology" always plays a vital role in making learning more accessible, engaging, and personalized. The impact technology enhancing accessibility and digital platforms eliminate geographical barriers, allowing learners from remote or disadvantaged regions to participate in high-quality education (Mukul & Büyüközkan, 2023). The online courses and open educational resources (OERs) empower learners who are lacking in the educational or not have excess of ready books and other content, creating inclusive opportunities that bridge socio-economic divides. Consequently, technology democratizes education, offering an equitable learning experience to diverse populations. The advance technology significantly influences the student engagement. Interactive media, simulations, and AR create immersive environments that stimulate curiosity and motivation (Timotheou et al., 2023). The interactivity increases students' involvement, improving knowledge retention and comprehension. The AR applications also used in the science education which help to visualize complex processes, making concepts tangible and understandable (Bilyalova et al., 2020).

Personalized learning is another key benefit of educational technology which AI-driven analytics and adaptive learning systems identify individual learners' strengths and weaknesses, customizing content delivery according to student's learning pace and style. The tailored approach not only enhances academic performance but also nurtures learners' confidence and self-directed learning capabilities. On the other hand, the integration of technology in education facing the other challenges. A limited access of internet and devices where students suffering from other issues and challenges (Sych et al., 2021). Furthermore, over-reliance on digital tools also has some negative impact where students not developing the interpersonal skills, reducing face-to-face interaction and collaboration. The another negative of digital technology data privacy and security concern found major issues; now a days and these online platform quality should be improved with the help of advance technology with the collaboration of IT companies (Gillpatrick, 2020). Despite of these concerns; technology extensively improves teaching efficiency and the grading systems, real-time feedback, and digital administrative platforms streamline teachers' responsibilities, allowing more time for personalized instruction and student support. The virtual classrooms found the fast and more effective learning with the students where all the students pay more attention and show the positive interest toward the teaching. For online classroom teaching effectively harness technology's required with adequate effectively harness technology's and advance infrastructure and professional faculty and their skill should be well development and use the effective tool in the classroom to make more interesting and effective (Vachkova et al., 2022). The policymakers and educational leaders must fulfill in form of infrastructure gaps and focus on the digital literacy training with full source of technology integration. The role of technologies in education should be "transformative, enhancing accessibility, engagement, and personalization of learning experiences". There could be more challenges in the online platform but need to be balanced and intentional integration strategies and make educational systems more strong in term of leverage technology effectively for evolving digital future (Khotamov et al., 2023).

Digital Transformation and Education Systems:

The new digital transformation has significantly providing the new shape in the education systems worldwide, the new changes in the education sectors along with changes in teaching methodologies, it improve the learning environments, and administrative practices (Belousova et al., 2021). The integrating of digital technologies brings the transformation into educational frameworks which enhancing the "accessibility, flexibility, personalization, and effectiveness in educational delivery" system. The impact of digital transformation improved the accessibility of education where "online learning platforms, virtual classrooms, and digital resources" have broken geographic and socio-economic barriers in the education system (Kumar, 2023). The open educational resources (OERs) and massive open online courses (MOOCs) illustrate that how digital transformation promotes inclusivity and students learning capacity increasing day by day globally and it also minimize the cost of the institutions (Tsarapkina et al., 2021).

In addition, the digital technologies found fast learning process which also improve the "personalized learning, accommodating individual learners' diverse" needs and learning styles. The adaptive learning systems also powered by artificial intelligence (AI) which customized the educational experiences by analyzing student performance and their strengths, weaknesses, and preferred learning pathways (Kumar, 2024). These tailored approaches boost up the student engagement and enhances academic outcomes, fostering a sense of ownership and autonomy among learners. Interactive and immersive learning experiences also symbolize the benefit of digital transformation such as; augmented reality (AR), virtual reality (VR), and simulations provide dynamic, real-world scenarios, facilitating practical skill development and deeper conceptual understanding (Anisimova & Efremova, 2022). These technologies build up the confident of the students and engaging them and motivate where their knowledge increase day by day. Furthermore, digital transformation not increase the efficiency in the students but it also found more effectiveness in the administrative. Learning management systems (LMS) now a day used in the different fields like; "attendance tracking, grading, and feedback provision" allowing educators more time for personalized student interaction (Al

Hasani & Husin, 2021). The digital assessment tools provide the quick response in feedback, assessing the assignment, online evaluation and enabling educators to make data-informed instructional decisions.

Artificial Intelligence in Education: Issues and Challenges:

Artificial Intelligence (AI) has played an important role as a innovative force in the educational sector, which used various new tools and methodologies to achieve the learning outcomes. The numerous benefits the impact integration of AI in education brings various critical issues and challenges, necessitating careful consideration and strategic responses (Lim et al., 2023). Additionally, Educational institutions increasingly collect extensive data on students' behaviors, learning patterns, and personal information to facilitate personalized learning and predictive analytics (Kumar et al., 2024). On the other hand improper handling and unauthorized access lead to privacy violations, misuse and exploitation. Another notable issue identified that it loss of essential human interaction and social skills. The advanced AI-powered tools, such as "adaptive learning platforms, automated assessment systems, provide efficient and personalized educational experiences, over-reliance on technology" might reduce the value of human interactions (Ifenthaler & Schumacher, 2023). The balancing of AI integration with sufficient opportunities for social interaction is critical for holistic student development. Algorithms can inadvertently reinforce existing biases or stereotypes, potentially disadvantaging particular groups of students based on race, gender, socio-economic status, or learning differences. Furthermore, the attentiveness of educators remains a significant challenge (Singh & Kumar, 2024). It is also identified that lack adequate training in teachers and resources to effectively integrate AI tools into their pedagogical practices. Without having the professional development skill and adopting AI technologies, limiting their potential benefits and reducing overall effectiveness (Yu & Guo, 2023).

The AI offers ample of transformative opportunities in the education sectors which identifies the different challenges like; "digital divide, data privacy concerns, reduction in human interaction, algorithmic bias, and educators' preparedness". Overcoming the obstacles require change in the policy, like huge investment in robust infrastructure, ethical oversight, and targeted professional development for educators. By addressing these issues the education sector become effective in AI's technology with create more equitable, personalized, and impactful learning environments for all students (Zhang et al., 2022).

Usage of Artificial Intelligence in the Education Sector:

Artificial Intelligence (AI) play vital role in revolutionizing the education sector by transforming the way teachers teach and students learn. Personalized learning platforms found automated administrative systems where AI improving the overall efficiency and bring the modern education systems adaptability in the system where the education becomes digital and data- driven (Kumar & Bayram, 2025). AI also brings the innovation and improving the entire education system and giving the new shape the future of learning.

THE ROLE AND EFFECTS OF TECHNOLOGY IN EDUCATION

Personalized Learning

AI contributed crucial role in the education sectors which increase the ability to provide personalized learning experiences. Customary classroom teaching often one-size-fits-all approach, where all students receive positive environment and effective learning at the same pace. AI-powered systems increase the learning of every individual student and improve the performance and develop their strengths, weaknesses, learning pace, and preferences (Chen et al., 2020). There are different platforms like; Carnegie Learning, Squirrel AI, and Knewton using AI to deliver customized learning paths, enabling students to master concepts more effectively and confidently. The most significant use of AI in LMS is personalized learning paths. It customized the content and pacing. The performance, engagement, preferences, and learning styles of learners are analysed by AI algorithms and suitable content (Owoc et al., 2021). It can work on each learner's strengths and weaknesses and no one is left behind. Occurrence, a student who has trouble understanding a certain topic can be provided with extra resources, quizzes.

Intelligent Tutoring Systems

Artificial intelligent (AI)-based ITS offer one on one tutoring as well as real time feedback, hints, and explanations. These systems can tell when a student gets flustered, and when to find a work-around to solve a problem. AI tutors on the other hand can scale humans and be called on 24/7 in any part of the world, spreading access to quality education, at an affordable rate (Lin et al., 2023).

Automation of Administrative Tasks

Teachers spend much of their time on administrative work such as grading, and scheduling, and keeping student records. It's possible to standardize and automate some of these administrative activities using AI so that teachers could spend more time on instruction and interact with students (Mulyana et al., 2018). AI also has the capability to grade multiple-choice exams, judge written essays via natural language processing (NLP), and to monitor student class attendance and participation.

Predictive Analytics for Student Success

AI can analyze large datasets to **predict student outcomes**, identify those at risk of dropping out, and suggest timely interventions. This helps institutions implement personalized academic support systems and track learner progress more effectively. Predictive analytics also enable educators to make data-driven decisions and improve institutional planning.

AI in Language Learning and Translation

The rise of AI-based language apps such as Duolingo, Google Translatel, has made it possible for people to learn a new language interactively in a more adaptive manner. These are powered by AI to identify mispronunciations, suggest words that need reinforcement based on usage and give contextual feedback (Kuddus, 2022). This enables a more dynamic language acquisition, in particular in multilingual worlds.

Virtual Learning Assistants

AI-driven virtual assistants such as chatbots and voice-enabled solutions can answer questions for students, offer study resources and even remind them about assignments and deadlines." The 24/7 support systems create effective learning due to its' pay-off providing immediacy in online help and curbing the student's reliance on faculty for simple questions.

Enhancing Special Education

AI has demonstrated vast potential in aiding special-needs students. Tools such as text-to-speech, speech-to-text along with emotion AI can act as a flow instrument designed to help with those students who have challenges in visual, auditory or cognitive based.

Gamification and Engagement

AI plan an important role in gamifying educational content improve the learning and engaging the students with enjoyable. It also improves the behavior of the student and preferences, AI can adapt games to maintain interest and challenge levels, fostering motivation and sustained participation (Ab Rahman et al., 2019). The more usage of artificial intelligence in the education sector marks an example for easy handling of students by using of different methods to more "student-centered, data-driven, and technology-enabled learning environments". With ethical implementation and continuous innovation, AI holds the potential to reshape education and make it more equitable, effective, and future-ready (Alsawaier, 2018).

ARTIFICIAL INTELLIGENCE IN LEARNING MANAGEMENT SYSTEMS (LMS)

Intelligent Content Delivery and Recommendations

The artificial Intelligent in LMS platforms used "Smart Content Delivery". It can automatically recommend learning materials which includes; "articles, videos, or external courses", based on a learner's past behavior, goals, and performance analytics. This engine mimics the logic of platforms like Netflix or YouTube but tailored for educational purposes, thereby it make the learning experience more engaging and relevant (Cavus, 2010).

Automated Assessment and Feedback

Artificial intelligence tools integrated into LMS platforms are transforming how assessments are handled. These smart systems can automatically grade not just quizzes and assignments, but even written responses, thanks to natural language processing (NLP). As a result, students receive instant feedback, helping them understand where they need to improve right in the moment (Lee, 2023). For educators, this means less time spent on repetitive grading tasks and more time to focus on what truly matters: creating meaningful content and engaging directly with students.

Predictive Analytics for Student Support

AI-powered tools in Learning Management Systems (LMS) can go beyond grading they also help predict which students might be at risk of falling behind. By analyzing patterns like; "class participation, test scores, and engagement levels", the system can flag early warning signs. It allows instructors and academic advisors to step in at the right time with the right support (Khan et al., 2021). These timely interventions not only help students stay on track but also boost overall retention and academic success. Such insights enable educators to create personalized support strategies that genuinely enhance the learning experience and outcomes.

Engagement through Chatbots and Virtual Assistants

AI-powered tools like chatbots and virtual teaching assistants have become essential features in modern LMS platforms. These tools are designed to answer common student queries, guide them through course content, and even provide real-time technical support. It available 24X7 365 days, they ensure students never feel stuck no matter the time of day (Pereira et al., 2022). It continuous availability not only improves system responsiveness, but also keeps learners actively engaged, which especially valuable in online and hybrid learning environments where immediate support is often crucial.

Adaptive Testing and Learning

Artificial Intelligence transforming Learning Management Systems (LMS) more responsive educational platforms. One powerful feature adaptive testing, where the difficulty of questions changes in real-time based on how a student answers. This approach not only gives a more accurate picture of what the learner truly knows, but also creates a more personalized and less stressful assessment experience. Beyond testing, AI brings adaptability, automation, and intelligence to every corner of the LMS (Huang et al., 2009). From delivering customized learning materials and predicting student needs to offering instant support through chatbots, AI tools are helping both educators and students get more out of the digital classroom. Of course, challenges such as data privacy, access to technology, and ethical considerations still need to be addressed (Carney et al., 2018). But with thoughtful and responsible use, AI has the potential to make education more inclusive, efficient, and truly centered on the learner.

Different Tools, Application and Platforms Used in Education

Today's classrooms whether virtual or physical powered by a rich blend of digital tools that reshaping; how teaching and learning happen. Platforms like; "Moodle, Canvas, and Google Classroom" help educators organize lessons, share resources, and manage assessments seamlessly. Video conferencing tools which includes; 'Zoom, Microsoft Teams, and Google Meet" have made it possible to hold live classes, discussions, and collaborative sessions from anywhere in the world (Anghelo Josué et al., 2023). Interactive application like; "Kahoot!, Quizizz, and Duolingo" bring a fun, game-like element to learning, keeping students engaged and motivated. For learners who prefer flexibility, platforms like "Coursera, edX, and Khan Academy" provide access to high-quality courses at their own pace. Tools like Turnitin help maintain academic honesty, while AI-powered applications like "ChatGPT and Grammarly" offer writing support, research assistance, and personalized feedback (Sofi-Karim et al., 2023).

In today's digital era, education has undergone a remarkable transformation, thanks to Learning Management Systems (LMS) and smart digital tools. Platforms like; "Moodle, Canvas, Blackboard, and Google Classroom" make it easier for educators to design and deliver courses, track student progress, manage assignments, and provide timely feedback all from a single dashboard. These systems form the backbone of both online and hybrid learning models, making learning more organized and accessible while enhancing communication between students and teachers. To support live interaction, video conferencing tools such as: "Zoom, Microsoft Teams, Google Meet, and Cisco Webex" have become classroom essentials (Cortes-Camarillo et al., 2019). Whether it's a virtual lesson, a group discussion, or a parent-teacher meeting, these platforms offer features like screen sharing, breakout rooms, live chat, and recording, helping maintain the feel of a real classroom even from a distance.Learning has also become more fun and engaging with interactive tools like: "Kahoot!, Quizizz, Nearpod, Mentimeter, and Padlet". These platforms introduce games, polls, and collaborative activities that promote participation and keep students motivated. Apps like Duolingo and Photomath great examples of subject-specific support, making language learning and math more approachable through intuitive design and instant feedback (Papadakis, 2021).

Furthermore, the rise of self-paced and AI-enhanced platforms is reshaping how individuals learn and grow. Sites such as "Coursera, edX, Udemy, and Khan Academy" provide flexible access to top-quality education, encouraging lifelong learning. At the same time, tools like Turnitin help preserve academic integrity, while "Grammarly, ChatGPT, and QuillBot" assist with writing, editing, and research. AI even helps educators by automating routine tasks and offering tailored feedback based on each student's progress (Masters et al., 2024). Together, these digital innovations are building a more inclusive, personalized, and efficient learning ecosystem one that empowers both teachers and learners in powerful new ways.

Virtual Reality and Augmented Reality Applications in Digital Education Sectors

As education continues to evolve in the digital age, technologies like Virtual Reality (VR) and Augmented Reality (AR) are changing the way students learn and experience information. These tools bring lessons to life by creating immersive, hands-on environments that go far beyond textbooks and slides (Tiwari et al., 2023). Whether it's exploring the human body in 3D, conducting virtual science experiments, or walking through historical landmarks, VR and AR make learning more engaging and memorable—especially for subjects that are complex or skill-based. By blending the physical and digital worlds, these technologies help students connect theory with practice. They offer safe, interactive spaces to explore concepts and build confidence before facing real-world situations (Iatsyshyn et al., 2020). This shift from passive learning to active exploration makes education more dynamic, inclusive, and deeply meaningful. What once felt abstract or hard to visualize can now be experienced firsthand—making understanding feel natural and exciting.

Understanding VR and AR in Education

Virtual Reality (VR) and Augmented Reality (AR) are reshaping how students experience learning. VR offers a completely immersive experience when students put on a VR headset, they're transported into a 3D world where they can look around, move, and interact as if they were really there. It's like stepping inside a lesson, whether that's exploring the surface of Mars or navigating the inside of the human body (Wu et al., 2013). AR, on the other hand, adds digital elements to the real world. Instead of taking students away from their surroundings, AR layers interactive content like animations, text, or images onto what they see through a phone, tablet, or smart glasses. For example, a student could point their device at a picture in a textbook and watch it come to life with motion and sound (Radu, 2012). In concert, VR and AR make learning more exciting and hands-on, helping students understand even the toughest topics in a fun and engaging way.

Applications of VR in Education

Virtual Reality (VR) is becoming a powerful tool in education especially in subjects where hands-on experience makes a big difference. In medical training, for example, VR allows students to practice surgeries, study the human body in 3D, and interact with virtual patients without any real-life risks. Platforms like Osso VR and Medical Realities give future doctors a safe space to learn and refine their skills (Soliman et al., 2021). In fields like engineering and architecture, VR helps students explore buildings before they're even built. They can walk through structures, handle virtual machines, and view technical blueprints in 3D, making complex concepts easier to understand. Even subjects like history and geography become more vivid through VR. Instead of just reading about ancient civilizations or distant planets, students can virtually visit the pyramids of Egypt or explore the Amazon rainforest (McGovern et al., 2020). Apps like Google Expeditions turn classrooms into gateways to the world, offering virtual field trips to places many students may never have a chance to see in real life. In language learning, VR opens up virtual conversations with native speakers, helping students practice speaking and listening in real-time. This immersive experience boosts both vocabulary and cultural awareness, making learning a new language feel more natural and exciting.

Applications of AR in Education

Augmented Reality (AR) brings classroom learning to life by adding interactive digital layers to everyday materials like: "textbooks, worksheets, and activities. Imagine" a student opening a textbook and watching a 3D model of a volcano erupt or a human cell expand with labeled parts they can explore. With apps like; "Quiver, Merge Cube, and 3DBear", what was once flat and static now becomes an engaging, hands-on learning experience. In STEM subjects, AR makes tough concepts easier to grasp. Students can see how electricity flows through a circuit or how molecules react in a chemical process right on their desk (Yuen et al., 2013). It takes the guesswork out of science by letting learners see theories in action. Math lessons also become more dynamic. AR apps help students visualize shapes in 3D, rotate graphs, and interact with equations in a way that feels more intuitive and fun. It's a big step away from rote learning and toward true understanding (Bower et al., 2014). For vocational training, AR is like having a virtual mentor. It simulates real-life tools and situations, guiding students through tasks step by step whether they're learning to repair machinery, wire a circuit, or cook a recipe. This hands-on support boosts both confidence and skill retention.

Benefits of VR and AR in Digital Education

Virtual Reality (VR) and Augmented Reality (AR) changing the way students connect with what they learn making education more engaging, memorable, and hands-on. One of the biggest advantages is how these tools turn learning into an active experience. Instead of just reading or listening, students can explore, interact, and even collaborate with others in virtual or augmented environments (Neumann et al., 2022). This kind of multisensory learning is especially helpful for visual and kinesthetic learners, making lessons feel more real and exciting. These technologies also boost motivation. When students are immersed in an experience like; walking through a historical site or solving a science puzzle with classmates in AR they're more likely to stay curious and involved. Learning becomes something they want to do, not just something they have to do. Another key benefit is that VR and AR offer safe and affordable ways to simulate complex or risky scenarios. For example, instead of needing a fully equipped chemistry lab or flight simulator, students can practice safely in a virtual setting saving schools money and reducing risks (Akçayır & Akçayır, 2017). Significantly, VR and AR also support inclusive education. Students with disabilities or different learning needs can benefit from tailored, accessible content that helps them learn in a way that works best for them. In short, VR and AR are helping to create a more dynamic, inclusive, and effective learning environment one where every student can participate, explore, and thrive.

CHALLENGES AND FUTURE DIRECTIONS

While VR and AR offer exciting opportunities in education, they also come with a few hurdles. One major challenge is the cost VR headsets, AR-enabled devices, and the software needed to run them can be expensive, especially for schools with limited budgets. On top of that, setting up the right infrastructure and creating quality content requires technical expertise that not all educators or institutions currently have. There's also the human side to consider some users may feel dizzy or uncomfortable after using VR for long periods, which makes it important to balance screen time and comfort. Looking to the future, however, things are bright. The combination of AI with VR and AR, along with cloud-based platforms and faster 5G internet, is opening doors for smoother, more personalized, and real-time learning experiences. As technology becomes; "more affordable, easier to use, and widely available", we can expect these tools to become a regular part of classrooms everywhere. The goal is not just to keep up with digital trends, but to create learning environments that are more interactive, inclusive, and future-ready for every learner.

Virtual Reality (VR) and Augmented Reality (AR) are reshaping the future of education by turning learning into a truly immersive and engaging experience. These technologies bring lessons to life, spark curiosity, and help students connect with content in ways that are both meaningful and memorable. While challenges like cost, technical support, and accessibility still exist, the potential they hold is truly exciting. As more educators and institutions begin to embrace these innovations, VR and AR are set to become a natural part of how we teach and learn—making education more interactive, inclusive, and aligned with the needs of the 21st century. It's not just about using technology—it's about transforming learning into something students can see, feel, and truly experience.

THE FUTURE OF ARTIFICIAL INTELLIGENCE APPLICATIONS IN EDUCATION

Artificial Intelligence (AI) is steadily transforming how we teach and learn and its future in education holds even greater promise. As technology continues to advance, AI is set to create more intelligent, adaptive, and inclusive learning environments, turning traditional classrooms into dynamic, data-driven ecosystems. One of the most exciting developments on the horizon is hyper-personalized learning. With the ability to analyze each student's learning style, progress, strengths, and areas of struggle in real time, AI can offer tailor-made lessons that truly meet individual needs. This means learners will no longer be bound by a one-size-fits-all approach they'll receive support that fits their pace and preferences, helping them thrive. AI-powered tutoring systems are also evolving to feel more like real mentors. These intelligent assistants won't just provide answers; they'll offer meaningful feedback, guide learners through complex topics, and even detect emotions like confusion or frustration through facial expressions and tone of voice. Best of all, they'll be available anytime making learning possible beyond the boundaries of time and place. Predictive analytics will play a key role in helping educators and policymakers make smarter decisions. With AI analyzing student performance data, schools can spot those who might need extra help early on. It will also help fine-tune curricula, allocate resources more efficiently, and monitor overall progress through real-time insights.

Language and accessibility support will also grow stronger with AI. Tools like speech-to-text, real-time translation, and screen readers will make classrooms more inclusive—breaking down language barriers and supporting students with diverse learning needs. Chatbots and voice assistants integrated into LMS platforms will offer instant help with everything from assignment deadlines to test prep. AI will also make teaching easier behind the scenes by automating time-consuming tasks like generating quizzes, grading assignments, and drafting lesson plans. This frees up educators to focus on creative, student-centered teaching approaches rather than administrative duties. Of course, with all these advancements, there are important ethical considerations. Issues like data privacy, algorithmic bias, and unequal access to technology must be addressed thoughtfully. Moving forward, it's crucial that AI in education is designed with fairness, transparency, and equity at its core ensuring that every learner, no matter their background, can benefit from its full potential.

SMART CLASSROOMS AND LEARNING ENVIRONMENTS IN EDUCATION

In today's digital age, education is undergoing a powerful shift and smart classrooms are at the heart of this transformation. Gone are the days when teaching was limited to chalkboards and textbooks. Today's classrooms are dynamic, tech-enabled spaces that bring learning to life through interactive content, real-time connectivity, and powerful digital tools. A smart classroom blends technology like interactive whiteboards, tablets, projectors, high-speed internet, virtual reality (VR), artificial intelligence (AI), and Learning Management Systems (LMS) to create a more student-focused, engaging, and personalized environment (MacLeod et al., 2018). The goal isn't just to deliver lessons it's to make learning more interactive, enjoyable, and effective. Students benefit from a mix of visual, audio, and hands-on resources, while teachers gain better tools to explain complex ideas clearly and creatively. One of the biggest advantages of smart classrooms is personalized learning (Dron, 2018). AI-driven platforms and adaptive learning tools help teachers understand each student's pace, strengths, and areas that need improvement. With systems like Google Classroom, Moodle, or Edmodo, teachers can assign tasks, monitor progress, and give instant feedback. Meanwhile, students have the freedom to review recorded lessons, access materials anytime, and stay connected through online discussions even outside school hours. Gamified tools like Kahoot! and Quizizz make learning fun and boost participation by turning quizzes into games.

Smart classrooms also support collaborative learning. Students work together on projects using cloud tools like Google Docs, Padlet, or Microsoft Teams, which foster communication and teamwork—skills that are essential in today's world (Bouslama & Kalota, 2013). VR and AR take learning even further by offering immersive experiences. Imagine taking a virtual trip to the Great Wall of China, exploring the human body in 3D, or conducting a science experiment in a virtual lab. These experiences help students connect theory with real-world applications in unforgettable ways. Inclusivity is another powerful benefit. With features like screen readers, live captions, text-to-speech, and real-time language translation, students with disabilities or those from different language backgrounds can fully participate in class. Teachers, too, benefit from automation tools that reduce administrative work such as automatic grading or digital attendance giving them more time to focus on what matters most: teaching and mentoring. In essence, smart classrooms are preparing students for the future by blending technology with teaching in meaningful ways (Saini & Goel, 2020). They nurture curiosity, creativity, collaboration, and critical thinking skills vital for success in the 21st century. While challenges like cost, connectivity, and training still need to be addressed, the long-term rewards better engagement, improved learning outcomes, and greater educational access make smart classrooms a smart investment in the future of education.

DATA PRIVACY AND SECURITY IN EDUCATION

As technology becomes a core part of education, it brings incredible advantages—greater access to learning, personalized experiences, and improved efficiency. But along with these benefits come serious concerns about data privacy and security. Schools, colleges, and universities now use digital tools like Learning Management Systems (LMS), cloud storage, AI applications, and educational apps (Reidenberg & Schaub, 2018). These platforms collect a wide range of personal information from students' names and academic records to biometric data, health details, and even their communication habits. Without the right safeguards in place, this sensitive data is at risk. Cyberattacks, identity theft, and unauthorized data sharing can seriously compromise students' safety and trust. A major issue is that many institutions aren't fully prepared for this digital responsibility. Teachers and administrators often lack proper training in cybersecurity practices, which can lead to unintentional mistakes or data breaches.

Another layer of concern involves third-party educational platforms. These are often developed and managed by external companies, raising questions like: Who really controls the data? Is it being shared or sold? Could it be used unethically for targeted ads or profiling students without their knowledge? To protect everyone involved, it's vital that institutions follow strong data protection policies aligned with regulations such as the General Data Protection Regulation (GDPR) or India's Digital Personal Data Protection (DPDP) Act, 2023. Schools should clearly communicate how and why student data is collected, stored, and used. Informed consent from students or their guardians is not optional it's essential. Security tools like; "encryption, multi-factor authentication, and regular system" audits must become standard. At the same time, digital literacy should be a part of the curriculum teaching students (especially younger ones) how to stay safe online, avoid oversharing, and create strong passwords. As artificial intelligence and data analytics become more common in education, there's also a need to ensure these technologies are used ethically and fairly. Predictive tools should never lead to bias, profiling, or emotional harm. It's not just about keeping data safe it's about using it responsibly (Kamenskih, 2022).

In the end, protecting data is about protecting people. A secure and ethical digital environment builds trust, empowers students, and ensures that technology enhances education without compromising anyone's rights or wellbeing.

Gamification Increasing Student Success

In today's tech-savvy classrooms, gamification has become more than just a buzzword it's a powerful approach that is reshaping how students connect with learning. By blending game-like elements such as points, levels, badges, leaderboards, and quests into everyday lessons, educators are finding new ways to spark interest, build motivation, and help students succeed. At its heart, gamification taps into something deeply human: our natural drive for challenge, achievement, and reward. When used thoughtfully, it transforms traditional, passive learning into something more dynamic and goal-oriented. Students don't just sit and absorb—they participate, explore, and push themselves to reach the next level. And in the process, they develop confidence, resilience, and a stronger sense of ownership over their learning (Ishaq et al., 2025).

What makes gamification so effective is how well it fits into modern instructional design frameworks, such as the ADDIE model (Analyze, Design, Develop, Implement, Evaluate) and Universal Design for Learning (UDL). For example, during the design phase, teachers can align each game element with specific learning outcomes. A quest might represent a chapter goal, a badge might reward mastery of a skill, and a leader board might encourage healthy peer competition. These tools make teach more personal allowing students to progress in ways that suit their abilities. Whether a student earns points for effort or for tackling bonus challenges, everyone has a path to success. Gamification also helps with formative assessment, offering students immediate feedback so they can reflect, adjust, and improve in real time. Tools like Kahoot!, Quizizz, and Class craft make this process exciting, with colorful visuals, interactive questions, and data-driven insights that help teachers tailor instruction. Beyond that, storytelling within gamified lessons adds depth and imagination (Nevin et al., 2014). Imagine a history class where students role-play as key historical figures, making choices that shape events. This kind of activity fosters critical thinking, empathy, and a deeper understanding of content. In the bigger picture, gamification is not just about adding fun to the classroom it's about creating meaningful, motivating learning experiences. When used with care and purpose, it boosts student engagement, improves knowledge retention, and encourages a growth mindset. It fosters creativity, teamwork, and curiosity all while giving students room to explore, fail, try again, and grow. As education continues to evolve, gamification offers a fresh, learner-centered approach that turns classrooms into interactive, supportive, and exciting spaces. It's not just a trend it's a transformational strategy for making learning more human, more personal, and more powerful.

CONCLUSION

The digital transformation of education is no longer a distant concept it's a living, evolving reality that has reshaped how we teach, learn, and connect. From smart classrooms and AI-powered tools to immersive experiences using VR and AR, technology has infused education with new energy, flexibility, and possibility. Students are now able to learn in ways that are more personalized, engaging, and accessible, while educators are empowered with tools that enhance instruction and deepen their impact. However, this transformation also brings important responsibilities. Issues like data privacy, digital equity, and ethical use of AI remind us that innovation must go hand-in-hand with care, inclusivity, and thoughtful planning. The goal is not just to modernize education but to humanize it through technology, ensuring that every learner, regardless of background or ability, has a fair chance to succeed. In essence, digital transformation is not just about upgrading tools it's about reimagining the learning experience. As we move forward, it's crucial that we continue to blend innovation with empathy, building educational systems that are not only smart but also supportive, inclusive, and deeply human.

REFERENCES

Ab Rahman, R., Ahmad, S., & Hashim, U. R. (2019). A Study on Gamification for Higher Education Students' Engagement Towards Education 4.0. In Piuri, V., Balas, V. E., Borah, S., & Syed Ahmad, S. S. (Eds.), *Intelligent and Interactive Computing* (Vol. 67, pp. 491–502). Springer Singapore., DOI: 10.1007/978-981-13-6031-2_5

Akçayır, M., & Akçayır, G. (2017). Advantages and challenges associated with augmented reality for education: A systematic review of the literature. *Educational Research Review*, *20*, 1–11. DOI: 10.1016/j.edurev.2016.11.002

Al Hasani, S. H. S., & Husin, N. A. (2021). A REVIEW OF DIGITAL TRANSFORMATION OF EDUCATION IN OMAN. *Journal of Business Management and Accounting*, *11*(2), 41–59. DOI: 10.32890/jbma2021.11.2.3

Alsawaier, R. S. (2018). The effect of gamification on motivation and engagement. *The International Journal of Information and Learning Technology*, *35*(1), 56–79. DOI: 10.1108/IJILT-02-2017-0009

Anisimova, A. N., & Efremova, Yu. I. (2022). Digital Transformation of Vocational Education: Challenges of Modern Society. In Ashmarina, S. I., & Mantulenko, V. V. (Eds.), *Digital Technologies in the New Socio-Economic Reality* (Vol. 304, pp. 773–781). Springer International Publishing., DOI: 10.1007/978-3-030-83175-2_95

Belousova, M. N., Belousov, V. A., & Narkevich, L. V. (2021). Digital Transformation of the Educational Process in University in the Context of Globalization. In Popkova, E. G., Ostrovskaya, V. N., & Bogoviz, A. V. (Eds.), *Socio-economic Systems: Paradigms for the Future* (Vol. 314, pp. 1267–1277). Springer International Publishing., DOI: 10.1007/978-3-030-56433-9_133

Bilyalova, A. A., Salimova, D. A., & Zelenina, T. I. (2020). Digital Transformation in Education. In Antipova, T. (Ed.), *Integrated Science in Digital Age* (Vol. 78, pp. 265–276). Springer International Publishing., DOI: 10.1007/978-3-030-22493-6_24

Bouslama, F., & Kalota, F. (2013). Creating smart classrooms to benefit from innovative technologies and learning space design. *2013 International Conference on Current Trends in Information Technology (CTIT)*, 102–106. https://doi.org/DOI: 10.1109/CTIT.2013.6749486

Bower, M., Howe, C., McCredie, N., Robinson, A., & Grover, D. (2014). Augmented Reality in education – cases, places and potentials. *Educational Media International*, *51*(1), 1–15. DOI: 10.1080/09523987.2014.889400

Carney, P. A., Mejicano, G. C., Bumsted, T., & Quirk, M. (2018). Assessing learning in the adaptive curriculum. *Medical Teacher*, *40*(8), 813–819. DOI: 10.1080/0142159X.2018.1484083 PMID: 30106597

Cavus, N. (2010). The evaluation of Learning Management Systems using an artificial intelligence fuzzy logic algorithm. *Advances in Engineering Software*, *41*(2), 248–254. DOI: 10.1016/j.advengsoft.2009.07.009

Chen, L., Chen, P., & Lin, Z. (2020). Artificial Intelligence in Education: A Review. *IEEE Access: Practical Innovations, Open Solutions*, *8*, 75264–75278. DOI: 10.1109/ACCESS.2020.2988510

Cortes-Camarillo, C. A., Alor-Hernández, G., Sánchez-Morales, L. N., Rosales-Morales, V. Y., Rodríguez-Mazahua, L., & Sánchez-Cervantes, J. L. (2019). EduGene: A UIDP-Based Educational App Generator for Multiple Devices and Platforms. *International Journal of Human-Computer Interaction*, *35*(3), 274–296. DOI: 10.1080/10447318.2018.1459347

Dron, J. (2018). Smart learning environments, and not so smart learning environments: A systems view. *Smart Learning Environments*, *5*(1), 25. DOI: 10.1186/s40561-018-0075-9

Gillpatrick, T. (2020). Innovation and the Digital Transformation of Education. *Sınırsız Eğitim ve Araştırma Dergisi*, *5*(3), 194–201. DOI: 10.29250/sead.797372

Huang, Y.-M., Lin, Y.-T., & Cheng, S.-C. (2009). An adaptive testing system for supporting versatile educational assessment. *Computers & Education*, *52*(1), 53–67. DOI: 10.1016/j.compedu.2008.06.007

Iatsyshyn, A. V., Kovach, V. O., Lyubchak, V. O., Zuban, Y. O., Piven, A. G., Sokolyuk, O. M., Iatsyshyn, A. V., Popov, O. O., Artemchuk, V. O., & Shyshkina, M. P. (2020). *Application of augmented reality technologies for education projects preparation*. [б. в.]. https://doi.org/DOI: 10.31812/123456789/3856

Ifenthaler, D., & Schumacher, C. (2023). Reciprocal issues of artificial and human intelligence in education. *Journal of Research on Technology in Education*, *55*(1), 1–6. DOI: 10.1080/15391523.2022.2154511

Ishaq, M., Abid, K., Farooq, U., Ishaq, K., Safie, N., & Abid, A. (2025). A Framework for Designing Courses by Synergizing Project-Based Learning With Gamification. *Human Behavior and Emerging Technologies*, *2025*(1), 9915839. DOI: 10.1155/hbe2/9915839

Josué, A., Bedoya-Flores, M. C., Mosquera-Quiñonez, E. F., Mesías-Simisterra, Á. E., & Bautista-Sánchez, J. V. (2023). Educational Platforms: Digital Tools for the teaching-learning process in Education. *Ibero-American Journal of Education & Society Research*, *3*(1), 259–263.

Kamenskih, A. (2022). The analysis of security and privacy risks in smart education environments. *Journal of Smart Cities and Society*, *1*(1), 17–29. DOI: 10.3233/SCS-210114

Khan, I., Ahmad, A. R., Jabeur, N., & Mahdi, M. N. (2021). An artificial intelligence approach to monitor student performance and devise preventive measures. *Smart Learning Environments*, *8*(1), 17. DOI: 10.1186/s40561-021-00161-y

Khotamov, I. S., Umarov, E. G., Kuznetsov, V. P., Smirnova, Z. V., & Kutepov, M. M. (2023). Digital Transformation in the Modern Educational System. In Popkova, E. G., & Sergi, B. S. (Eds.), *Anti-Crisis Approach to the Provision of the Environmental Sustainability of Economy* (pp. 195–199). Springer Nature Singapore., DOI: 10.1007/978-981-99-2198-0_20

Kuddus, K. (2022). Artificial Intelligence in Language Learning: Practices and Prospects. In Mire, A., Malik, S., & Tyagi, A. K. (Eds.), *Advanced Analytics and Deep Learning Models* (1st ed., pp. 1–17). Wiley., DOI: 10.1002/9781119792437.ch1

Kumar, S. (2023). Impact of Digitalization in Higher Education and Smart Learning Techniques. In Nadda, V., Tyagi, P. K., Moniz Vieira, R., & Tyagi, P. (Eds.), *Advances in Hospitality, Tourism, and the Services Industry* (pp. 198–207). IGI Global., DOI: 10.4018/979-8-3693-0650-5.ch013

Kumar, S. (2024). Impact of Assessment on Childhood Education Theories and Practice. In Badea, M., & Suditu, M. (Eds.), *Advances in Early Childhood and K-12 Education* (pp. 84–101). IGI Global., DOI: 10.4018/979-8-3693-0956-8.ch004

Kumar, S., & Bayram, G. E. (2025). The effect on education and training. In *Greening Our Economy for a Sustainable Future* (pp. 177–185). Elsevier., DOI: 10.1016/B978-0-443-23603-7.00014-5

Kumar, S., Talukder, M. B., & Pego, A. (Eds.). (2024). *Utilizing Smart Technology and AI in Hybrid Tourism and Hospitality*. IGI Global., DOI: 10.4018/979-8-3693-1978-9

Lee, A. V. Y. (2023). Supporting students' generation of feedback in large-scale online course with artificial intelligence-enabled evaluation. *Studies in Educational Evaluation*, *77*, 101250. DOI: 10.1016/j.stueduc.2023.101250

Lim, T., Gottipati, S., & Cheong, M. (2023). *Artificial Intelligence in Today's Education Landscape: Understanding and Managing Ethical Issues for Educational Assessment*. In Review. https://doi.org/DOI: 10.21203/rs.3.rs-2696273/v1

Lin, C.-C., Huang, A. Y. Q., & Lu, O. H. T. (2023). Artificial intelligence in intelligent tutoring systems toward sustainable education: A systematic review. *Smart Learning Environments*, *10*(1), 41. DOI: 10.1186/s40561-023-00260-y

MacLeod, J., Yang, H. H., Zhu, S., & Li, Y. (2018). Understanding students' preferences toward the smart classroom learning environment: Development and validation of an instrument. *Computers & Education*, *122*, 80–91. DOI: 10.1016/j.compedu.2018.03.015

Masters, K., Correia, R., Nemethy, K., Benjamin, J., Carver, T., & MacNeill, H. (2024). Online learning in health professions education. Part 2: Tools and practical application: AMEE Guide No. 163. *Medical Teacher*, *46*(1), 18–33. DOI: 10.1080/0142159X.2023.2259069 PMID: 37740948

McGovern, E., Moreira, G., & Luna-Nevarez, C. (2020). An application of virtual reality in education: Can this technology enhance the quality of students' learning experience? *Journal of Education for Business*, *95*(7), 490–496. DOI: 10.1080/08832323.2019.1703096

Mukul, E., & Büyüközkan, G. (2023). Digital transformation in education: A systematic review of education 4.0. *Technological Forecasting and Social Change*, *194*, 122664. DOI: 10.1016/j.techfore.2023.122664

Mulyana, E., Hakimi, R., & Hendrawan. (2018). Bringing Automation to the Classroom: A ChatOps-Based Approach. *2018 4th International Conference on Wireless and Telematics (ICWT)*, 1–6. https://doi.org/DOI: 10.1109/ICWT.2018.8527810

Neumann, M. M., Keioskie, M. K., Patterson, D., & Neumann, D. L. (2022). Virtual, Augmented, and Mixed Reality: Benefits and Barriers for Early Childhood Education. *Childhood Education*, *98*(4), 68–79. DOI: 10.1080/00094056.2022.2108298

Nevin, C. R., Westfall, A. O., Rodriguez, J. M., Dempsey, D. M., Cherrington, A., Roy, B., Patel, M., & Willig, J. H. (2014). Gamification as a tool for enhancing graduate medical education. *Postgraduate Medical Journal*, *90*(1070), 685–693. DOI: 10.1136/postgradmedj-2013-132486 PMID: 25352673

Owoc, M. L., Sawicka, A., & Weichbroth, P. (2021). Artificial Intelligence Technologies in Education: Benefits, Challenges and Strategies of Implementation. In Owoc, M. L., & Pondel, M. (Eds.), *Artificial Intelligence for Knowledge Management* (Vol. 599, pp. 37–58). Springer International Publishing., DOI: 10.1007/978-3-030-85001-2_4

Papadakis, S. (2021). Tools for evaluating educational apps for young children: A systematic review of the literature. *Interactive Technology and Smart Education, 18*(1), 18–49. DOI: 10.1108/ITSE-08-2020-0127

Pereira, R., Reis, A., Barroso, J., Sousa, J., & Pinto, T. (2022). Virtual Assistants Applications in Education. In Reis, A., Barroso, J., Martins, P., Jimoyiannis, A., Huang, R. Y.-M., & Henriques, R. (Eds.), *Technology and Innovation in Learning, Teaching and Education* (Vol. 1720, pp. 468–480). Springer Nature Switzerland., DOI: 10.1007/978-3-031-22918-3_38

Radu, I. (2012). Why should my students use AR? A comparative review of the educational impacts of augmented-reality. *2012 IEEE International Symposium on Mixed and Augmented Reality (ISMAR)*, 313–314. https://doi.org/DOI: 10.1109/ISMAR.2012.6402590

Reidenberg, J. R., & Schaub, F. (2018). Achieving big data privacy in education. *Theory and Research in Education, 16*(3), 263–279. DOI: 10.1177/1477878518805308

Saini, M. K., & Goel, N. (2020). How Smart Are Smart Classrooms? A Review of Smart Classroom Technologies. *ACM Computing Surveys, 52*(6), 1–28. DOI: 10.1145/3365757

Singh, A., & Kumar, S. (2024). Effective Talent Management Practices Implemented in the Hospitality Sector. In Christiansen, B., Aziz, M. A., & O'Keeffe, E. L. (Eds.), (pp. 126–144). Advances in Human Resources Management and Organizational Development. IGI Global., DOI: 10.4018/979-8-3693-1938-3.ch008

Sofi-Karim, M., Bali, A. O., & Rached, K. (2023). Online education via media platforms and applications as an innovative teaching method. *Education and Information Technologies, 28*(1), 507–523. DOI: 10.1007/s10639-022-11188-0 PMID: 35791317

Soliman, M., Pesyridis, A., Dalaymani-Zad, D., Gronfula, M., & Kourmpetis, M. (2021). The Application of Virtual Reality in Engineering Education. *Applied Sciences (Basel, Switzerland), 11*(6), 2879. DOI: 10.3390/app11062879

Sych, T. V., Khrykov, Y. M., & Ptakhina, O. M. (2021). Digital transformation as the main condition for the development of modern higher education. *Educational Technology Quarterly, 2021*(2), 293–309. DOI: 10.55056/etq.27

Timotheou, S., Miliou, O., Dimitriadis, Y., Sobrino, S. V., Giannoutsou, N., Cachia, R., Monés, A. M., & Ioannou, A. (2023). Impacts of digital technologies on education and factors influencing schools' digital capacity and transformation: A literature review. *Education and Information Technologies*, *28*(6), 6695–6726. DOI: 10.1007/s10639-022-11431-8 PMID: 36465416

Tiwari, C. K., Bhaskar, P., & Pal, A. (2023). Prospects of augmented reality and virtual reality for online education: A scientometric view. *International Journal of Educational Management*, *37*(5), 1042–1066. DOI: 10.1108/IJEM-10-2022-0407

Tsarapkina, J. M., Anisimova, A. V., Gadzhimetova, B. D., Kireycheva, A. M., & Mironov, A. G. (2021). The impact of digital education transformation on technical college teachers. *Journal of Physics: Conference Series*, *2001*(1), 012030. DOI: 10.1088/1742-6596/2001/1/012030

Vachkova, S. N., Petryaeva, E. Yu., Milyaeva, D. A., Ageeva, N. S., & Mikhailova, S. V. (2022). *Analytical Review of Education Policies on Digital Transformation of School Education Worldwide*. 248–270. https://doi.org/DOI: 10.15405/epes.22043.23

Wu, H.-K., Lee, S. W.-Y., Chang, H.-Y., & Liang, J.-C. (2013). Current status, opportunities and challenges of augmented reality in education. *Computers & Education*, *62*, 41–49. DOI: 10.1016/j.compedu.2012.10.024

Yu, H., & Guo, Y. (2023). Generative artificial intelligence empowers educational reform: Current status, issues, and prospects. *Frontiers in Education*, *8*, 1183162. DOI: 10.3389/feduc.2023.1183162

Yuen, S. C.-Y., Yaoyuneyong, G., & Johnson, E. (2013). Augmented Reality and Education: Applications and Potentials. In R. Huang, Kinshuk, & J. M. Spector (Eds.), *Reshaping Learning* (pp. 385–414). Springer Berlin Heidelberg. https://doi.org/DOI: 10.1007/978-3-642-32301-0_17

Zhang, L., Fu, K., & Liu, X. (2022). Artificial Intelligence in Education: Ethical Issues and its Regulations. *Proceedings of the 5th International Conference on Big Data and Education*, 1–6. https://doi.org/DOI: 10.1145/3524383.3524406

Chapter 2

The Future of Artificial Intelligence in Education: An Evaluation in the Framework of Social Robots and Holograms

Selin Gocen
https://orcid.org/0000-0003-1495-7754
Education Faculty, Dicle University, Turkey

Gulsun Kurubacak Cakir
https://orcid.org/0000-0002-8068-7142
Ankara Haci Bayram Veli University, Turkey

ABSTRACT

Artificial intelligence technology, which has a transformative effect on learning systems, integrates with social robot and hologram technologies to bring new dimensions to the processes of learning and teaching. By providing an immersive and interactive structure to learning experiences, these technologies also contribute to increasing the retention of learning. While having considerable potential benefits, these technologies also present risks and threats that should not be ignored. In this book chapter, the definitions, development, and integration processes of artificial intelligence, hologram, and social robot technologies into education are examined within the context of their applications. The chapter also briefly addresses the ethical and legal issues that may arise during the use of these technologies.

DOI: 10.4018/979-8-3373-8857-1.ch002

INTRODUCTION

The educational ecosystem, one of the areas where the transformative effect of technological developments is witnessed, is increasingly moving beyond the simple integration of technology into traditional education. In other words, low-interaction digital content is giving way to immersive and highly interactive learning experiences. Personalized or adaptive learning processes, free from the constraints of time and space, have begun to be designed. The potential benefits of artificial intelligence, despite sometimes being portrayed with negative imagery, have been acknowledged, and it has started to be used more widely in educational communities. It can be argued that this acceptance has also been influenced by the fact that the potential of AI is amplified, or that it enhances the effectiveness of other technologies, when combined with them.

Artificial intelligence (AI), a technology with a deep-rooted history, is both highly comprehensive and rapidly evolving. It is utilized in numerous fields, including education, alongside the potential risks and threats it may entail. Advances in AI are impacting many technologies and being integrated into many technologies. Among these AI-powered technologies, social robots and holograms stand out. In this section, hologram and social robot technologies are evaluated together because they are thought to offer solutions to problems that may arise in learning abstract and complex concepts in the development of effective coding skills. In a discipline as inherently abstract as programming, concepts such as algorithms, loops, variables, or complex data structures can be challenging for learners. AI-powered social robots offer "concretized learning" experiences (Benitti, 2012; Bers, 2018) by transforming these abstract code commands into observable physical actions. Holograms, on the other hand, aim to reduce "cognitive load" (Leonard & Fitzgerald, 2018) by transforming complex algorithmic processes or data structures into three-dimensional, interactive models. This 'concretization' approach contributes to students learning abstract coding concepts through direct experience. In this context, this book chapter evaluates the development of AI in education, particularly its effects on coding education pedagogy, through social robots and holograms.

In this context, this book chapter evaluates the development of AI in education, taking into consideration the social robots and hologram technologies it has impacted. The chapter first examines the concept of AI and its development in education. The second part assesses the field of robotics and the use of AI-assisted robotic technologies, particularly social robots, in education. The third part explains hologram technologies and their educational applications, considering their relationship with AI. The final section briefly addresses the legal and ethical issues related to these technologies.

ARTIFICIAL INTELLIGENCE: DEFINITION, SCOPE, AND HISTORICAL DEVELOPMENT

There are different definitions in the literature regarding what AI is. According to McCarthy (2007), often called the father of AI, the concept of intelligence is considered the computational part of the ability to achieve goals in the world, which appears in various types and degrees in humans, many animals, and some machines. AI, in turn, has been defined as the science and engineering of making intelligent machines, especially intelligent computer programs. McCarthy, who defines AI as a field of science and engineering, explains this idea through the endeavor of making machines intelligent to understand human language, identify and solve problems, and achieve goals. This definition, which notes that AI is shaped on two foundations "intelligent programming" and "human-like responses" emphasizes the ability of machines/computers to perform cognitive tasks associated with human intelligence, such as reasoning, problem-solving, learning, and generalization (Arslan, 2020; McCarthy et al., 1955). On the other hand, in their work "Artificial Intelligence: A Modern Approach," Russell and Norvig (2003) modernized the definition of AI, viewing it in terms of "intelligent agents" that perceive their environment, decide what to do, and act based on their decisions. With this definition, AI began to be evaluated as a system in interaction with its environment.

AI can be thought of as a discipline with many sub-branches, whose foundations are based on and interact with numerous different disciplines such as philosophy, mathematics, logic, computer vision, physiology, biology, physics, electronics, psychology, linguistics, economics, cybernetics, neuroscience, and computer science. As an umbrella term that includes various sub-fields, AI is also used to encompass and define different methods, approaches, or technologies like machine learning, natural language processing, data mining, neural networks, and algorithms. Also defined as a branch of science that aims to understand and explain the powers and different faculties of the mind (Boden, 2014), AI is also described as the performance of human competencies such as reasoning, deriving meaning, generalizing, learning from past experiences, and self-learning by computer-controlled devices (Nabiyev, 2010). In the context of these definitions, it can be said that AI is a technology that performs algorithm-based actions such as prediction, association, diagnosis, recommendation, and evaluation.

The historical development of AI, whose theoretical foundations date back to the 1940s, can be said to be parallel to the evolution of computer science. Experiments on intelligent machines conducted by Charles Babbage in 1884 can be considered within the scope of AI's historical basis. From a theoretical standpoint, the "Boolean Circuit Model of the Brain," developed in 1943 by McCulloch and Pitts who studied how neurons in the brain work, contributed to the development of AI. In

1948, Shannon began to lay the foundation for concrete applications by arguing that computers could be used to prove theorems and play games like chess within the framework of certain algorithms. In 1949, an approach that would form the basis of learnable neural networks was established by Hebb (Arslan, 2017). In 1950, it was Alan Mathison Turing who opened AI to a comprehensive discussion based on the question, "Can machines think?" (McCarthy, 2007); he conducted studies on the cipher algorithm of the Enigma machine and proposed the idea of the Turing test. Starting from the 1950s, many other researchers joined the field of AI and began to conduct studies (Muggleton, 2014). Although the work contributing to the emergence and popularization of concrete AI applications began after the 1960s, it can be stated that the scientific acceptance of the field occurred in the 1950s. As a scientific term, "AI" was first introduced by John McCarthy at the Dartmouth Conference in 1956 (McCorduck, 1977). In the same year, the AI program "Logic Theorist," written by Allen Newell, J.C. Shaw, and Herbert Simon to solve mathematical problems, was unveiled. Meanwhile, the first neural network computer was built by Marvin Minsky and Dean Edmonds in 1951, while in 1958, John McCarthy developed the LISP programming language (Kayabaş, 2010). With the developments in the 1960s, computers began to run faster, and during this period, Joseph Weizenbaum developed ELIZA, the first example of natural language processing, at MIT's AI laboratories. Also during this time, SCHOLAR emerged as the first intelligent tutoring system. In the 1970s, the development of AI was influenced by increased interaction with other scientific disciplines, leading to a focus on designing complex systems more compatible with real-world problems or situations. The 1980s also paved the way for the development of deep learning. The goal was to analyze previously acquired, stored, or used data for application in new experiences. During the period when deep learning emerged, pioneered by John Hopfield and David Rumelhart, programs called "expert systems" structured similarly to human decision-making processes were introduced by Edward Feigenbaum (Arslan, 2020). From 1956 to the present, AI, as an umbrella concept, has developed by branching into sub-fields such as artificial neural networks, fuzzy logic, simulated annealing, expert systems, computer vision, genetic algorithms, speech recognition, chaotic modeling, and robotics (İşler & Kılıç, 2021). With the advancements in AI, it has now become an inseparable part of social life. It can be said that educational systems are among the fields where AI, whose development and impact have both increased from the past to the present, is effective. It can be assessed that the importance of AI in education has grown, particularly with the advent of expert systems.

Artificial Intelligence and Its Development in Education

The rise of AI in education continues amid the dualities of benefit and harm, opportunity and threat. Intelligent teaching systems and adaptive learning environments can provide the personalized guidance and support offered by teachers in face-to-face learning environments through technology. The ability to continuously evaluate and analyze data collected from learners, to quickly adjust content to learners' needs based on analysis results, and to provide learners with accurate and effective guidance through instant and personalized feedback contributes to the rise of AI-supported educational technologies (Prepare, 2025). Moving away from the well-known "one size fits all" education model, it is possible to focus on the individual needs of learners. These learning environments, where individuality can be offered within mass education, have a more flexible, inclusive, and egalitarian structure than traditional learning environments.

The concrete application of AI in education dates back to the 1970s, but its foundations, which could be called weak AI, date back to the 1920s. Machines that support learning, mentioned by Sidney L. Pressey but remaining at the conceptual stage due to the conditions of the time, are among the first examples of AI in education (Arslan, 2020; Lumsdaine, 1959). Pressey stated that multiple-choice tests, used to evaluate learners in a developing application, could also be used to reinforce learning (Benjamin, 1988; Skinner, 1958). Similar to Pressey, an example called the "learning machine" was developed by Skinner. This machine, which can also be considered a weak example of AI, is based on a simple algorithm. The learning machine, which is also described as the basis of intelligent teaching systems, allows the student to see the correct answer to the question and move on to the next question if the answer is correct, by writing the correct answer in a box with two windows (Skinner, 1958). Continuous and immediate feedback in learning is important for learners to see their shortcomings and advance their learning. This work by Skinner has formed the basis for different models or approaches such as personalized learning, intelligent learning/education systems, and individualized instruction. The first Intelligent Tutoring Systems developed in the 1970s can be considered the period when AI began to take shape. These systems aimed to model students' knowledge levels and provide them with personalized instructions and feedback (Carbonell, 1970; Sleeman & Brown, 1982). These systems aimed to provide a technological response to the need for individualized education, which Bloom (1984) argued was more successful for learners receiving one-on-one instruction than for those continuing their education in traditional classrooms, defining it as the "2 sigma problem" (Forsell et al., 2023). These models, referred to as intelligent tutoring systems, are classified as strong AI. The classification of weak and strong AI is made within the framework of the competencies and level of development covered by the technology. In this classification proposed by Wells (2023), the first group, referred to as weak, encompasses AI programmed to perform a single task. AI applications such as translation programs, virtual assistants, recommendation systems, health applications, and text programs, which are faster than humans but have limited reasoning abilities, are classified as weak AI. On the other hand, the strong AI class encompasses AI applications and systems that can learn on their own without human supervision and set new goals. Although Wells states that all AI applications and systems used under current conditions belong to the weak AI class, he adds that the ability of the program called Muzero to set new goals without human intervention is characteristic of the strong AI class. In addition to these two groups and classification methods, AI technology is also evaluated in three different groups: data-based, logic-based, and knowledge-based. It is explained that until the 2000s, most educational applications of AI were based on a knowledge-based approach (Arslan, 2020; Nwana, 1990; Sleeman, 1984) and that the systems of this period were called intelligent teaching systems. Today, however, logic-based and data-based systems are also used alongside knowledge-based systems. Although the approaches differ, they demonstrate that AI technology is advancing day by day.

These programs, known as intelligent teaching systems, aim to support teachers in determining what to teach, to whom, and how. These systems consist of an expert knowledge module, a learner module, a lesson module, and a user interface (Nwana, 1990). SCHOLAR, one of the first examples of intelligent educational systems (intelligent tutoring systems) and weak AI, also contributed to the emergence of dialogue-based educational systems. After SCHOLAR, various intelligent tutoring systems were developed, such as WHY, BUGGY, SOPHIE (SOPHisticated Instructional Environment), and LISP Tutor (Anderson et al., 1984; Arslan, 2020). The basic logic of intelligent tutoring systems is to present and adapt activities in a personalized way that can respond to learners' needs. Dialogue-based systems developed through the intelligent system SCHOLAR utilize fuzzy logic and are shaped entirely within the framework of a specific purpose. They are developed for different purposes such as teaching a specific topic, identifying and correcting misconceptions, and providing feedback. At this point, it can be said that dialogue-based systems are structured similarly to teacher-learner interaction in individual learning.

AI applications in education today have been classified and examined by various researchers. Taking these classifications into account, AI applications in education can be evaluated in three categories (Baker, 2016; O'Malley et al., 2005):

1. Learner-Focused AI: This category focuses on improving the learner's learning experience and includes adaptive learning environments, intelligent teaching systems, virtual assistants, and game-based learning environments.

2. Teacher-Centric AI: This category includes automatic assessment and feedback systems that support teachers in making pedagogical decisions by reducing their professional workload, learner analysis systems (learning analytics), and actions and applications related to the creation, development, and adaptation of content and learning objects.
3. System-Focused AI: This includes tools such as course schedule and resource optimization systems and registration-admission automations that facilitate, regulate, and improve administrative and institutional processes.

The widespread adoption of AI across all dimensions and aspects of education systems is fundamentally driven by technologies such as machine learning (supervised, unsupervised, and reinforcement learning), artificial neural networks, deep learning, and natural language processing. With these technologies covered by AI, systems gain the ability to improve performance by learning from data (machine learning), use neuron-like networks based on a principle similar to the human brain to process information (artificial neural networks and deep learning), and understand, interpret, and generate human language (natural language processing). (İçen, 2022; Holmes et al., 2019; Russell & Norvig, 2003; Steenis, 2025). These capabilities contribute to systems operating more quickly, effectively, and efficiently.

Since the 2010s, these competencies and capabilities that have transformed AI from rule-based systems to data-driven systems can also be considered the driving force behind the effectiveness of today's social robots and holograms in education (especially coding education). The first of these mechanisms, which can be considered as “smart” agents and interaction providers that give dynamic responses to learners' inputs, is Natural Language Processing (NLP). NLP helps machines understand, interpret, and respond to human language. In the context of social robots, this is useful in many areas, from understanding a student's complex question such as “Why isn't my robot turning?” to verbally explaining a logical error in the code they have written (e.g., ‘infinite loop’). NLP-powered dialogue systems can provide learners with instant, Socratic-style hints for coding problems, guiding them toward solutions and personalizing learning (Okonkwo & Ade-Ibijola, 2021). The second critical mechanism after NLP is called Computer Vision. This subfield of AI enables systems to interpret the visual world. Social robots can analyze learners' facial expressions or gestures using their cameras. The system can understand that the learner is “disappointed” from their frown or that they have “lost interest” from their eye contact (Michels et al., 2023). This is particularly important for identifying when the learner is struggling with a difficult task, such as coding, and for continuing the process with the right guidance and hints. Finally, Adaptive Learning Algorithms are a highly effective tool for continuously analyzing learner performance data (e.g., time taken to complete a coding task, number of errors made). Wang and Wu (2021) note that AI's ability to adapt allows it to adjust the difficulty level of learning material or the next exercise in real time based on the learner's current proficiency. In developing coding skills, AI can be effectively used in defining tasks appropriate to learners' qualities and competencies and in designing the learning process. It can be said that these AI capabilities or strengths transform social robots and holograms into pedagogical partners that understand learners, interact with them, and adapt to them, thereby increasing the effectiveness and efficiency of education systems. Furthermore, considering the intensity of cognitive activities in learning and teaching processes, the increasing need to respond quickly to individual needs, the importance of time management, and the need for continuous and instant evaluation and feedback, it can be said that AI is crucial in effectively supporting and enhancing the abilities of teachers and learners, and its importance is growing day by day. (Karsenti, 2019). Robotics, brain and computer integration, AI, and blockchain technologies will be indispensable in the educational processes of the near future; AI and blockchain technology, in particular, will be two prominent and promising tools in education systems (Sisman-Ugur & Kurubacak, 2019). Indeed, countries have begun developing content to provide AI education starting in elementary school. For example, in China, AI has been taught as an elective course in primary and secondary schools since 2019, while in Russia, AI is being integrated into school curricula. These courses, which include theoretical knowledge about AI, also feature applications that support theoretical knowledge. The main concern with integrating AI into education is that it will eliminate the need for teachers (Nabiyev & Erümit, 2020). However, the main purpose of incorporating AI into education is to make the learning process more professional and independent, responsive to individual differences, sustainable, inclusive, and enjoyable for learners. This means that the use of AI in education will not remain limited (Holmes et al., 2019) and that the use of AI in education will become even more widespread. Indeed, examples of its use in education are increasing with applications and approaches such as machine learning, deep learning, natural language processing, and data mining. For example, ProblemPal, which has Alexa skills, helps teachers automatically generate content with voice commands and provides a personalized learning experience (Trivedi, 2018). The latest NLP model developed by OpenAI, GPT-4 (Generative Pre-trained Transformer 4), and Gemini, developed by Google, are frequently used as AI and language prediction models. With these models, which possess high-level thinking and logic-based competencies like humans, it is possible to produce content and perform actions such as detecting real-time emotional states, conversing, responding, and interpreting.

These models, which can be said to have begun to be actively used in education systems, have been developed using machine learning, natural language processing, and deep learning technologies encompassed by AI. These technologies enable different applications such as analyzing, recognizing, and predicting available data, and adapting/transferring current situations to new ones, allowing them to be used in different ways such as predicting probabilities and performing supervised/unsupervised classification (Zawacki-Richter et al., 2019). These technologies, which can learn on their own and are open to development through learning, shape every area of life. In terms of education systems, these technologies ensure the reshaping, transformation, or change of the roles of the system's stakeholders (Portilla et al., 2025). These technologies, which teachers or education stakeholders in general perceive as competitive or as a force that eliminates the need for humans and human interaction, and which cause concern in this context, contribute to making the current system faster, more effective, and more efficient. From the teachers' perspective, they can be seen as collaborators that enhance their competence, save time, and simplify the process. With the use and proliferation of AI technologies in education, educators will need to take on the role of designer in addition to their roles as guides, mentors, and facilitators in learning processes. It is important for educators to have the competence to design and manage learning environments using AI tools so that learners can have a rich and interactive learning experience. Furthermore, it is stated that educators need to acquire various competencies, such as AI literacy, pedagogical integration skills, data literacy, and ethical evaluation competence, and receive training (pre-service or in-service) to gain these competencies. It is recommended that guidelines covering the principles of responsible use of AI in education, mitigation of potential risks, and design of inclusive, equitable, fair, and accessible learning environments be taken into account and that necessary regulations be implemented (Al Nabhani et al., 2025; Rasheed et al., 2025; UNESCO, 2023; Ünsal, 2024). The detailed reports prepared emphasize concerns regarding the ethical dimension in particular and provide guidance to educators and policymakers (Temur, 2025). One of these reports was prepared by the U.S. Department of Education's Office of Technology.

In a report prepared by the U.S. Department of Education in 2023, AI, which is said to advance traditional educational technologies, is defined as “relationship-based automation” due to its ability to capture data patterns and automate decisions. However, it is stated that the AI systems developed at this point may lead to bias in how patterns are detected and unfairness in how decisions are automated. It is also emphasized that it would be useful to explain the opportunities, challenges, and policy development recommendations for improving the use of AI in education. The same report states that educators closely follow technological developments, evaluate how to integrate them into learning environments while using them in their daily lives, and are also able to identify potential risks and security issues (U.S. Department of Education, 2023). Teachers' positive attitudes toward new technologies, their acceptance or adoption, contribute to accelerating the integration process, while the opposite attitude can hinder the transformation process (Azzam & Charles, 2024). In this context, it can be said that it would be beneficial to develop programs for educators that will eliminate their concerns about the use of AI in education and enable them to trust the new ecosystem.

The impact of AI technology on the education ecosystem and, consequently, on the stakeholders of the ecosystem is not limited to software or applications. With recent developments, innovative approaches are also being seen in the design of learning environments. Three-dimensional environment designs, robots capable of human-like responses, and interactive and three-dimensional holograms have initiated a completely different learning process. Social robots and holograms, which are endowed with the "intelligence" and 'interaction' capabilities of AI, can be considered technologies that fall under the category of "learner-centered AI," which can further enrich the learning experience, make it more concrete, and increase the level of interaction.

SOCIAL ROBOTS AND THEIR USE IN EDUCATION

In parallel with the ongoing developments in the field of AI, advancements are also occurring in the field of robotics. Social robots, which began to emerge in the late 1940s (Fong et al., 2003), have started to gain prominence due to factors such as developments in AI and software, the increase of technical knowledge over time, it becoming more accessible, and the growth in the amount of accessible data. AI-powered toy robots, cleaning robots, and small robots for educational and research purposes have begun to proliferate rapidly.

It is noted that it is difficult to provide a single definition for the concept of a robot, which has many varieties due to different elements like function, structure, and purpose. The International Federation of Robotics (IFR) defines robots by classifying them into two groups according to their functions: industrial and service robots. While industrial robots perform tasks where human labor is insufficient, service robots are used more for providing personal services in home or public spaces (IFR, 2017). In another definition, robots are fundamentally defined as entities that can perceive their environment, make plans, and move autonomously, with models capable of social interaction with humans being termed social robots (Steenis, 2025). However, the robots defined here are advanced robots supported by AI, which perceive their surroundings by interpreting data from their sensors, make decisions, and take action. Traditional industrial robots generally perform repetitive and programmed tasks (Thrun et al., 2005). It can be said that robotic technologies have also evolved by gaining new and comprehensive competencies through AI, and in this context, the definitions are also changing.

Social robots, the subject of this section, are defined as robots that understand human behavior, establish physical and robotic social communication (verbal and non-verbal) with people, and can adapt to their environment. Social robots are also described as autonomous or semi-autonomous robots that possess social intelligence and can fulfill specific social roles (Breazeal, 2002; Fong et al., 2003). The ability of social robots to perform these actions is made possible because they possess capabilities for human-like communication and personality development through AI algorithms. What distinguishes social robots from traditional machines is their ability to create a natural dialogue environment by using elements of social interaction such as human-specific gestures, tone of voice, and facial expressions through natural language processing technology (Steenis, 2025). Professor Cynthia Breazeal from the MIT Media Lab, considered a pioneer in the field, developed the first social robot in the late 1990s. The first social robot developed was named "Kismet," a Turkish word meaning luck and fate (Breazeal, 2002). In her work on Social Robot Design, Breazeal explained that human emotional and expressive behaviors could be modeled for robot designs to enable proper communication and interaction between humans and robots, and that robots could detect the emotional states of people from their tone of voice. Breazeal demonstrated these ideas and the method of reading emotions from facial expressions while developing the social robot Kismet.

Over time, social robots began to be able to display basic human facial expressions such as anger, resentment, surprise, fear, and sadness. The social robot designed in 2004 and named Saya is considered one of the well-known examples with these capabilities. Although the Android-based Saya is called a robot teacher, it was originally intended to be a receptionist (Arslan, 2014; Hashimoto et al., 2011). Unlike other social robots, Saya, which had a leather-like plastic placed on its face, can also make human-like gestures and facial expressions. Given a realistic human face, Saya is very successful in the non-verbal part of social communication (facial expressions). From an educational and learning perspective, this can be said to be important for attracting learners' attention and maintaining interaction throughout the learning process.

Many robots, such as Robi, iRobiQ, MentoRo, U-Robo, Cubo, and Tiro, have been designed for use in educational ecosystems (Arslan, 2014). These social robots are used in various roles, such as one-on-one teacher (tutor), peer learner, teaching assistant, and as programming tools. There are many tasks that social robots perform and can perform through the roles they undertake. They take part in performing various tasks such as patiently supporting learners, explaining lessons, helping with exercises, learning together with learners and ensuring the reinforcement of what is learned, meeting the need for social interaction, reducing the teacher's workload related to the learning process, and assisting in the preparation of learning materials

(Belpaeme et al., 2018; Mubin et al., 2013). In this context, it can be said that by undertaking these roles and performing these tasks in education, social robots have moved from a passive to an active position, becoming stakeholders in educational ecosystems and learning processes.

When the main application areas and examples of social robots in education are examined, it is seen that in addition to their potential to present or reinforce theoretical knowledge, social robots are also used in different fields such as multilingual learning, STEM, and special education (Scassellati et al., 2012). It is stated that social robots, which are very successful in language learning due to their motivation and interaction competencies, are highly effective in vocabulary acquisition by providing concrete interactions and making concepts more tangible. These claims are not based solely on potential. A neuroscientific study conducted by Alimardan et al. (2023) empirically demonstrated that interaction with robots positively affects the cognitive processes that support children's language learning. Similarly, Kanero et al. (2018) presented experimental findings showing that robots provide concrete interactions, leading to a statistically significant increase in vocabulary acquisition compared to traditional methods. Social robots, which can provide immediate feedback by assessing whether learners pronounce words correctly, enable less anxiety-inducing practice than speaking with a real person (van den Berghe et al., 2019). In this context, it can be said that social robots have the potential to solve problems that may arise in language acquisition.

Besides language learning, social robots can also be actively used in STEM education. While STEM fields are engaging, they can also be abstract and challenging for some learners. Social robots make these abstract concepts concrete on the one hand, and on the other, make the learning process engaging. Through kits such as LEGO Mindstorms or VEX Robotics, learners develop engineering and technology skills while programming robots. This process is critically important in terms of coding pedagogy, as learners can directly observe abstract concepts such as conditions, algorithms, and loops through the robot's physical movements (e.g., "if the sensor detects an obstacle, turn 90 degrees") (Benitti, 2012; Bers, 2018). This immediate physical feedback makes it easier for learners to debug their code in a concrete way and, as Papert (1980) stated in his "constructivism" theory, anchors learning in a personal and meaningful project context. In addition, while planning the robot's movements, learners also gain competencies in different fields such as mathematics and physics. This process, which is consistent with constructivist learning theory, also contributes to the development of the 21st-century skills that learners need.

Another area where social robots are used is in the education of individuals with special needs. Children with Autism Spectrum Disorder (ASD) can interact more comfortably with predictable and repetitive systems such as social robots in social interactions and communication, which they find difficult (Scassellati et al.,

2012). Robots such as NAO, developed by Aldebaran Robotics, or Milo, developed by RoboKind, are used to help children with ASD develop social skills such as making eye contact, recognizing emotions, and taking turns. Social robots that do not tire, do not judge, and patiently repeat instructions help children with ASD feel safe and easily adapt to the learning process, contributing to the development of their social life skills (Diehl et al., 2012). It is noted that the limited, consistent, and predictable structure of social robots is beneficial in creating an ideal interaction environment and developing social skills in this environment for learners with ASD who may perceive human interactions as complex, frightening, uncertain, challenging, or unpredictable. On the other hand, the fact that the studies examining these benefits are short-term and that the permanence of the acquired skills has not been sufficiently evaluated indicates that more research is needed to contribute to the literature (Kotsi et al., 2025). Robots designed for students with special needs must be based on scientific research findings and directly targeted toward their purpose. If this requirement is not considered, the potential of social robots in education may be overshadowed by risks and threats.

Providing a personalized/individualized learning experience, increasing motivation, concretization, adaptation and adjustment, reducing social anxiety, designing/adapting a learning process appropriate to the emotional state, providing rapid feedback, providing a reinforcing learning experience, encouraging collaboration, increasing interaction and participation in the learning process, supporting learners and teachers, and providing guidance. However, under current conditions, these potential benefits and advantages are accompanied by risks and threats. Access to advanced social robots may be difficult for everyone due to cost. This situation may lead to access issues, thereby creating a gap between learners and educational systems. On the other hand, attachment issues and negative psychosocial effects may be observed in younger learners. Considering that speech, behavior, posture, and decision-making skills are still developing in younger learners, it can be said that social robots must have robust and detailed recognition, perception, prediction, or foresight systems. Robots must be designed with more comprehensive capabilities than those of adults, such as the ability to correctly and completely understand the words spoken by a child, accurately analyze their posture, and recognize and evaluate uncertainties in the decision-making process. If these challenges or potential issues are not taken into account, the harm may outweigh the benefits.

Just as with AI, certain competencies must be acquired for social robots as well. There is a need for individuals with these competencies who can deal with the software, hardware, or maintenance issues of social robots. It would be beneficial for technical personnel, the teachers who will use them, and in some cases, the learners to possess these competencies. Teachers need to know how to use social robots in the learning process, how to integrate them into the learning process, and how to use them as an effective tool (Belpaeme et al., 2018). In this case, it can be said that teachers need to have both technical and pedagogical competencies related to social robots.

The use of social robots in education has positive contributions to the learning process, but it also carries potential threats and risks. It can be said that the lack of sufficient and long-term research and the difficulty of autonomous social behavior robots play an important role in the benefit-risk dilemma. Considering the potential challenges, risks, or threats, the widespread use of social robots depends on the development of detailed and careful pedagogical designs and sustainable application models.

Another transformative reflection of AI in educational ecosystems, similar to social robots, is hologram technology. It makes the learning experience more interactive by transitioning it from two-dimensional structures to three-dimensional structures. The use of hologram technology in education, which challenges the boundaries of time and space, has been briefly evaluated.

THREE-DIMENSIONAL LEARNING EXPERIENCE: HOLOGRAPHIC APPLICATIONS IN EDUCATION

Innovative technologies contribute to the transformation of experiences in traditional learning environments into interactive and immersive experiences. The limited possibilities of two-dimensional tools are expanding, and images can be created beyond the screen in three-dimensional spaces with a high sense of reality. Holography, one of these image representation technologies that allows for the visual, auditory, and tactile representation of images, is defined as the recording of light waves reflected from an object and then the reconstruction of the three-dimensional (3D) image of that object (Gabor, 1948). Unlike traditional photographs, hologram technology, which adds depth to the image by recording the intensity of light as well as the timing of the light waves, does not require additional physical devices like smart lenses or head-mounted devices, unlike other VR technologies (Yoo et al., 2022). Hologram technology, which allows for a more intense experience of reality, has been used, albeit in a limited capacity, in educational settings, and various applications have been developed.

Hologram technology is based on the wave nature of light. It was first demonstrated in 1801 by Thomas Young through a simple experiment (Gabor, 1971), but it was discovered by Dennis Garbor in 1947 (Yoo et al., 2022). Until the 1980s, hologram technology was used at a basic level, but with advances in computers, efficiency increased, and HMDs were developed that were easily accessible and applicable in educational environments (Park et al., 2020). Three different types of holograms began to be used: pseudo-holograms, analog holograms, and digital holograms. Pseudo-holograms are a type of hologram that uses 2D screens and 3D digital images to create and mimic a 3D effect. Also known as floating holograms, these holograms are frequently used in learning environments due to their simplicity and accessibility. Analog holograms encompass optical holography, which requires lenses, photographic film, and accessories. Digital holograms, which emerged in the 1980s, can be considered the advanced form of hologram technology. They offer the ability to record images in their entirety at 360 degrees and view them with the naked eye without the need for specially designed devices (Liu et al., 2013; Orcos & Magreñán, 2018; Tsang & Poon, 2016). Although it has been stated that no additional device/tool is required to utilize hologram technology, reality technology (AR, VR, MR) devices and interfaces are used to obtain real and high-quality hologram images. For this reason, the term hologram is also used to define three-dimensional virtual objects created with VR, AR, or MR technologies in a broader sense. With MR headsets like Microsoft HoloLens, users interact with digital 3D objects that are fixed or placed on top of the real world (Milgram & Kishino, 1994). In addition to HoloLens headsets, holographic images are obtained using holographic projectors, sensors, and software. The most significant development in the field encompassing reality and hologram technologies is considered to be the ability to directly project a person's life-sized 3D image into a different space. With this technology, known as holographic telepresence, geographical barriers are eliminated, and a sense of reality can be created in interactions (Bron, 2023; Petruse, et al., 2024). It can be said that this development has taken the use of hologram technology in education to another level. This technology, which transforms the ways of communicating, interacting, and collaborating by eliminating distances, can be used in the education ecosystem as well as in all areas of social life. Holograms can transform the structure of learning environments for teachers and learners. From the perspective of teachers and learners, it can be said that there are potential benefits such as minimizing time-space constraints, providing an immersive and interactive learning experience, supporting collaboration, contributing to cross-cultural integration, providing a space for learners who cannot participate in the learning process due to various barriers, and increasing opportunity equality and inclusivity in education.

It can be said that immersive technologies, which are more commonly used in teaching complex, dangerous, expensive, or abstract topics/situations, are powerful pedagogical tools. In medical education, they can be used to explain and demonstrate human anatomy without the need for cadavers, to experience surgical operations and perform repetitive applications, and to acquire surgical and medical skills (Kamphuis et al., 2014). Similar to medical education, hologram technology is also used in fields such as science, engineering, and architecture, where practical learning experiences are beneficial for acquiring skills and competencies. At the same time, in these fields, real-world applications may be difficult, dangerous, or impossible. In architecture, the full-scale structure of designed buildings; in engineering, the working principles and internal structures of engines or aircraft, or the depths of oceans, the interiors of volcanoes, and the structures of historical sites; and in science, various topics or situations such as chemical reactions and cell division can be examined in the learning environment. This learning experience, enhanced by image technology, offers unforgettable and lasting learning experiences. Beyond these uses and applications of hologram technology, the "holographic telepresence" technology we mentioned earlier can eliminate geographical barriers, enabling learning experiences through interaction with renowned surgeons, Nobel laureates, or experts in their fields, or even individuals who are no longer alive but have left their mark in various fields (Bron, 2023). Hologram technology shows even more potential with the support of AI. Static and pre-programmed 3D models can be transformed into moving and interactive entities with AI. In other words, AI enables holographic entities to become "smart" entities. AI-supported holographic entities, or AI-supported hologram technology in general, increase the immersiveness and interactivity of the learning experience. Holographic entities that recognize verbal commands with NLP support can respond or answer appropriately to commands. They can be used in various ways, such as providing feedback, personalizing or adapting the learning experience, offering guidance, providing mentorship, continuing the learning process according to the learner's needs and requirements, and ensuring that learners are active participants (Prepare, 2025). Beyond these applications, hologram technology can also be used to make the most challenging abstract concepts in programming education concrete. For example, visualizing a complex data structure such as a "linked list" or "binary tree" in 3D can help students understand how these structures work in memory. Similarly, showing the steps of a sorting algorithm (e.g., bubble sort) in a 3D interactive model transforms an abstract process into a concrete experience (Leonard & Fitzgerald, 2018). Schmuck et al. (2024) note that such enriched visualizations increase student achievement and engagement compared to traditional 2D diagrams. However, they also add that, contrary to all these potential uses and benefits, hologram technology used without careful pedagogical design will not provide any benefit in education beyond offering a visual feast and may cause cognitive load. In this context, it can be said that, as in robot technology, necessary regulations must be put in place to ensure that all stakeholders in the education ecosystem acquire the required competencies in hologram technology.

The effects of AI, social robots, and hologram technologies on the educational ecosystem, their transformative powers, the benefits they provide, and despite these benefits, the potential risks and threats have been briefly discussed. Ethical and legal responsibility, which is an important issue that needs to be considered and emphasized, can be evaluated as problems that technological innovations bring with them when integrating into any field. The integration of powerful technologies such as AI, social robots, or holograms into educational environments can bring along technical, pedagogical, legal, and ethical questions or problems (Tegmark, 2017). In this context, it can be said that caution must be exercised for these technologies to be used or implemented responsibly.

LEGAL AND ETHICAL ISSUES: RESPONSIBLE TECHNOLOGY INTEGRATION

AI systems in the education ecosystem collect and store large amounts of data. The data collected on each stakeholder in the ecosystem must be protected against cyber attacks. As a result of security vulnerabilities in the systems, data can be stolen or manipulated. Hacking of AI-supported social robot systems or holographic systems can also lead to data and privacy breaches. There are various security risks, such as the display or recording of inappropriate content, misinformation and misdirection, unauthorized commercial marketing and sale of data, unauthorized recording, unauthorized access, and use of data for purposes other than those intended. In particular, the unauthorized access of data belonging to young learners or their unwitting interaction with strangers through these technologies can cause serious problems. Legal frameworks similar to the European Union's General Data Protection Regulation can be established to protect data and ensure legal safeguards (Selwyn, 2019). Ethical and legal issues can be mitigated through various methods, such as transparent data policies, adequately informing all stakeholders in the education ecosystem, obtaining informed consent, regular and frequent monitoring, implementing explainable AI techniques to control the data that influences decision-making processes, providing technology literacy training, and developing ethical and responsible use competencies.

In addition to these potential data-related situations, algorithm-related problems can also occur. Any prejudice, stereotype, discriminatory expression, or any situation that should not be included in the learning process, found in the data sets used to train AI, can cause learners to be exposed to undesirable forms of behavior. Furthermore, the self-learning nature of AI can also lead to unexpected problems at any stage of the learning process. To eliminate these questions and problems, the use of diverse and representative data sets and the development of transparent and explainable AI mechanisms will contribute to mitigating potential risks (O'Neil, 2016). In addition to this, it would be beneficial for designers, programmers, software engineers, or developers to be competent and proficient in their fields and to have adopted ethical and moral values, to prevent AI from getting out of control or behaving in an undesirable manner during its self-learning process.

The potential questions and problems that can occur in AI can also be seen in robots and holograms, but in these technologies, problems related to privacy, social, and emotional issues may arise more frequently. Data recording occurs in reality headsets that can be used to increase the level of interaction with social robots or hologram technology. These technologies, which can record audio and video, cause concerns about privacy. Considering that social robots react by analyzing movement, speech, or gaze, they can lead to different negative situations such as emotional manipulation, incorrect analysis and consequently incorrect responses, and social isolation. Especially in younger age groups, they can cause the emergence of problems like over-attachment, alienation from real-life skills and social interaction, abuse, emotional manipulation, and a loss of the sense of reality. Furthermore, they can also cause the formation of negative psychological effects in individuals, such as anxiety, fear, a feeling of being followed, and trust issues (Ružić & Balaban, 2024). The fact that social robots are designed specifically for direct interaction with people can lead to a decrease in authentic human-human interaction if the interaction process is not managed correctly. In this regard, it can be said that for the integration of these technologies into the educational ecosystem or social life in general, it would be beneficial to adopt clear and explicit regulatory frameworks and human-centric approaches, and to prepare policy documents and guidelines at national and international levels.

CONCLUSION AND RECOMMENDATIONS

With the transformation and complexity experienced in learning systems, needs, expectations, and approaches have also changed. The responsible integration of technologies that allow learners to learn in the way, at the pace, and at the time they desire is required in learning processes. For the integration process to be managed smoothly or with minimal problems, it is thought to be important to conduct research on the use of these technologies in the educational ecosystem. In this book chapter, the reflections, effects, and potential benefits and risks of AI, social robot, and hologram technologies on the educational ecosystem have been generally evaluated.

AI, hologram, and social robot technologies are important for personalized and adaptive learning systems. They enable learners to learn together with immersive, interactive, and embodied realities. These technologies bring along various potential benefits such as the concretization of abstract concepts, enabling the experience of situations that cannot be experienced in real life, supporting cognitive learning with visual learning, and transcending the limits of time and space.

Despite their existing benefits, these technologies can also cause questions and problems in learning processes. They can lead to issues such as algorithmic bias, data breaches, security vulnerabilities, surveillance and monitoring problems, privacy issues, dependency or improper attachment in interaction, detachment from reality, and the inability to control decision-making processes. Therefore, the responsible integration of technology is important, but this responsibility covers ethical and pedagogical issues as much as it covers technical issues. For the ongoing transformation process to be successfully sustained, it is considered important that all stakeholders be trained on the responsible integration and use of technology.

In future studies on the integration of AI, social robots, and hologram technologies into learning ecosystems, it would be beneficial to conduct long-term impact studies and research with large participant groups that include maximum diversity. It would be useful to conduct studies that will focus on the subject of pedagogy, which is a part of responsible technology integration, and that will contribute to the development of new pedagogical models. Considering that each field has its own unique qualities, research that will draw attention to the integration of technologies designed to suit the needs of specific fields instead of the integration of general-purpose technologies will contribute to the development of the literature. Apart from these, it is thought that there are not sufficient studies on ethical and legal issues. It is considered important to conduct research that will especially contribute to the preparation of national and international legal and administrative policies, frameworks, and guidelines.

REFERENCES

Al Nabhani, F., Hamzah, M. B., & Abuhassna, H. (2025). The role of artificial intelligence in personalizing educational content: Enhancing the learning experience and developing the teacher's role in an integrated educational environment. *Contemporary Educational Technology*, *17*(2), ep573. DOI: 10.30935/cedtech/16089

Arslan, E. (2014). Yabancı dil öğretiminde robot öğretmenler. *Ondokuz Mayıs Üniversitesi Eğitim Fakültesi Dergisi*, *33*(1), 15–26. DOI: 10.7822/egt181

Arslan, K. (2020). Eğitimde yapay zekâ ve uygulamaları. *Batı Anadolu Eğitim Bilimleri Dergisi*, *11*(1), 71–88.

Azzam, A., & And Charles, T. (2024). A review of artificial ıntelligence in K-12 education. *Open Journal of Applied Sciences*, *14*, 2088–2100. DOI: 10.4236/ojapps.2024.148137

Baker, R. S. (2016). Stupid tutoring systems, intelligent humans. *International Journal of Artificial Intelligence in Education*, *26*(2), 600–614. DOI: 10.1007/s40593-016-0105-z

Belpaeme, T., Kennedy, J., Ramachandran, A., Scassellati, B., & Tanaka, F. (2018). Social robots for education: A review. *Science Robotics*, *3*(21), eaat5954. https://www.science.org/doi/10.1126/scirobotics.aat5954 PMID: 33141719

Benitti, F. B. V. (2012). Exploring the educational potential of robotics in schools: A systematic review. *Computers & Education*, *58*(3), 978–988. DOI: 10.1016/j.compedu.2011.10.006

Benjamin, L. T. (1988). A history of teaching machines. *The American Psychologist*, *43*(9), 703.

Bers, M. U. (2018). *Coding as a playground: Programming and computational thinking in the early childhood classroom*. Routledge.

Boden, M. A. (2014). Creativity and artificial intelligence: A contradiction in terms. *The philosophy of creativity: New essays*, 224-246.

Breazeal, C. (2002). *Designing sociable robots*. MIT Press.

Bron, D. (April 2023). *The Emergence of Holographic Telepresence: Disrupting Communication and Collaboration in the Digital Age*. https://medium.com/chain-reaction/the-emergence-of-holographic-telepresence-disrupting-communication-and-collaboration-in-the-cd3461811e

Carbonell, J. R. (1970). AI in CAI: An artificial-intelligence approach to computer-assisted instruction. *IEEE Transactions on Man-Machine Systems, 11*(4), 190–202. DOI: 10.1109/TMMS.1970.299942

Diehl, J. J., Schmitt, L. M., Villano, M., & Crowell, C. R. (2012). The clinical use of robots for individuals with autism spectrum disorders: A critical review. *Research in Autism Spectrum Disorders, 6*(1), 249–262. DOI: 10.1016/j.rasd.2011.05.006 PMID: 22125579

Fong, T., Nourbakhsh, I., & Dautenhahn, K. (2003). A survey of socially interactive robots. *Robotics and Autonomous Systems, 42*, 143–166. DOI: 10.1016/S0921-8890(02)00372-X

Forsell, K., Tibshirani, R., & Brunskill, E. (2023). *White Paper: The science behind the scootpad mastery-based adaptive learning platform.* https://learningexplorer.com/wp-content/uploads/2024/04/ScootPad-Mastery-Research-White-Paper.pdf

Gabor, D. (1948). A new microscopic principle. *Nature, 161*(4098), 777–778. https://scispace.com/pdf/a-new-microscopic-principle-2a06oi3wvh.pdf PMID: 18860291

Gabor, D. (December 1971). Holography, 1948-1971. *Nobel Lecture*, December 11, 1971. https://www.nobelprize.org/uploads/2018/06/gabor-lecture.pdf

Hashimoto, T., Kato, N., & Kobayashi, H. (2011). Development of educational system with the android robot SAYA and evaluation. *International Journal of Advanced Robotic Systems, 8*(3), 51–61. DOI: 10.5772/10667

Holmes, W., Bialik, M., & Fadel, C. (2019). *Artificial intelligence in education: Promises and implications for teaching and learning.* Center for Curriculum Redesign., http://bit.ly/AIED-BOOK

İçen, M. (2022). The future of education utilizing artificial intelligence in Turkey. *Humanities & Social Sciences Communications, 9*, 268. DOI: 10.1057/s41599-022-01284-4

International Federation of Robotics. (2017). *Executive Summary World Robotics 2017 Industrial Robots.* Retrieved from https://ifr.org/downloads/press/Executive_Summary_WR_2017_Industrial_Robots.pdf

İşler, B., & Kılıç, M. (2021). Eğitimde yapay zekâ kullanımı ve gelişimi. *Yeni Medya Elektronik Dergisi, 5*(1), 1–11. DOI: 10.17932/IAU.EJNM.25480200.2021/ejnm_v5i1001

Kamphuis, C., Barsom, E., Schijven, M., & Christoph, N. (2014). Augmented reality in medical education? *Perspectives on Medical Education*, *3*(4), 300–311. DOI: 10.1007/s40037-013-0107-7 PMID: 24464832

Kanero, J., Geçkin, V., Oranç, C., Mamus, E., Küntay, A. C., & Göksun, T. (2018). Social Robots for Early Language Learning: Current Evidence and Future Directions. *Child Development Perspectives*, *12*, 146–151. DOI: 10.1111/cdep.12277

Karsenti, T. (2019). Artificial Intelligence in Education: The Urgent Need to Prepare Teachers for Tomorrow's Schools. *Formation et Profession*, 27(1), 112-116. https://doi.org/. 2019.a166DOI: 10.18162/fp

Kayabaş, İ. (2010). *Yapay zekâ sohbet ajanlarının uzaktan eğitimde öğrenci destek hizmeti olarak kullanılabilirliği*. Anadolu Üniversitesi Sosyal Bilimler Enstitüsü Uzaktan Eğitim Anabilim Dalı, Yüksek Lisans Tezi.

Kotsi, S., Handrinou, S., Iatraki, G., & Soulis, S.-G. (2025). A Review of Artificial Intelligence Interventions for Students with Autism Spectrum Disorder. *Disabilities*, *5*(1), 7. DOI: 10.3390/disabilities5010007

Leonard, S. N., & Fitzgerald, R. N. (2018). Holographic learning: A mixed reality trial of Microsoft HoloLens in an Australian secondary school. *Research in Learning Technology*, *26*. Advance online publication. DOI: 10.25304/rlt.v26.2160

Liu, Y.-Z., Pang, X.-N., Jiang, S., & Dong, J.-W. (2013). Viewing-angle enlargement in holographic augmented reality using time division and spatial tiling. *Optics Express*, *21*(10), 12068. DOI: 10.1364/oe.21.012068 PMID: 23736427

Lumsdaine, A. A. (1959). Teaching machines and self-instructional materials. *AVCR*, *7*, 163–181. DOI: 10.1007/BF02767482

McCarthy, J. (2007). *What is artificial intelligence?* Retrieved from https://www-formal.stanford.edu/jmc/whatisai.pdf

McCarthy, J., Minsky, M. L., Rochester, N., & Shannon, C. E. (1955). A proposal for the Dartmouth summer research project on artificial intelligence. http://jmc.stanford.edu/articles/dartmouth.html

McCorduck, P., Minsky, M., & Selfridge, O. ve Simon, H. (1977). History of artificial intelligence. *IJCAI Proceedings* (951-954). https://www.ijcai.org/Proceedings/77-2/Papers/083.pdf

Michels, J. D., Ruiz, J., & Worsley, M. (2023). Computer vision in education: A survey. *IEEE Transactions on Learning Technologies*, *16*(3), 304–323. DOI: 10.1109/TLT.2023.3273898

Milgram, P., & Kishino, F. (1994). A taxonomy of mixed reality visual displays. *IEICE Transactions on Information and Systems*, *E77-D*(12), 1321–1329. https://globals.ieice.org/en_transactions/information/10.1587/e77-d_12_1321/_p

Mubin, O., Stevens, C. J., Shahid, S., Al Mahmud, A., & Dong, J. J. (2013). A review of the applicability of robots in education. *Journal of Technology in Education and Learning*, *1*(1), 1–7. DOI: 10.2316/Journal.201.2013.1.201-0002

Muggleton, S. (2014). Alan Turing and the development of Artificial Intelligence. *AI Communications*, *27*(1), 3–10. DOI: 10.3233/AIC-130579

Nabiyev, V., & Erümit, A. K. (2020). Yapay zekanın temelleri. Nabiyev, V. & Erümit, A.K. (Eds.), *Eğitimde Yapay Zeka: Kuramdan Uygulamaya* (s.2-34). Pegem Akademi.

Nabiyev, V. V. (2010). *Yapay zekâ: İnsan bilgisayar etkileşimi*. Seçkin Yayıncılık.

Nwana, H. S. (1990). Intelligent tutoring systems: An overview. *Artificial Intelligence Review*, *4*, 251–277. DOI: 10.1007/BF00168958

O'Malley, C., Vavoula, G., Glew, J. P., Taylor, J., Sharples, M., Lefrere, P., . . . Waycott, J. (2005). Guidelines for learning/teaching/tutoring in a mobile environment. *MOBIlearn*. https://hal.science/hal-00696244v1

O'Neil, C. (2016). *Weapons of math destruction: How big data increases inequality and threatens democracy*. Crown Publisher.

Okonkwo, C. W., & Ade-Ibijola, A. (2021). Chatbots in education: A systematic review. *Computers and Education: Artificial Intelligence*, *2*, 100023. DOI: 10.1016/j.caeai.2021.100023

Orcos, L., & Magreñán, A. (2018). The hologram as a teaching medium for the acquisition of STEM contents. *International Journal of Learning Technology*, *13*(2), 163–177. DOI: 10.1504/IJLT.2018.092097

Papert, S. (1980). *Mindstorms: Children, computers, and powerful ideas*. Basic Books.

Park, K., Kim, D., & Han, S. H. (2020). Usability of the size, spacing, and operation method of virtual buttons with virtual hand on head-mounted displays. *International Journal of Industrial Ergonomics*, *76*, 102939. DOI: 10.1016/j.ergon.2020.102939

Petruse, R. E., Grecu, V., Chiliban, M. B., & Tâlvan, E. T. (2024). Comparative analysis of mixed reality and powerpoint in education: Tailoring learning approaches to cognitive profiles. *Sensors (Basel)*, *24*(16), 5138. DOI: 10.3390/s24165138 PMID: 39204835

Portilla, J. E. N., Cedeño, J. K. Z., Jácome, G. O. L., & Gallegos, L. A. M. (2025). Systematic Review: Artificial Intelligence (AI) in Education 4.0. *The Journal of Educators Online*, *22*(3), n3.

Prepare, S. (2025). *Research on future of education for U.S. educators* https://skillprepare.com/research-on-future-of-education-for-u-s-educators/

Rasheed, T., Bhatti, J. A., Hashim, A., & Fauz, F. (2025). Teacher-AI collaboration: How educators can harness artificial ıntelligence without losing pedagogical control. *Review of Applied Management and Social Sciences*, *8*(2), 697–709. DOI: 10.47067/ramss.v8i2.509

Russell, S. J., & Norvig, P. (2003). *Artificial intelligence: A modern approach* (2nd ed.). Pearson.

Ružić, I., & Balaban, I. (2024). The use of social robots as teaching assistants in schools: Implications for research and practice. [*RED*]. *Revista de Educación a Distancia*, *24*(78). Advance online publication. DOI: 10.6018/red.600771

Scassellati, B., Admoni, H., & Matarić, M. (2012). Robots for use in autism research. *Annual Review of Biomedical Engineering*, *14*, 275–294. DOI: 10.1146/annurev-bioeng-071811-150036 PMID: 22577778

Schmuck, V., Spiess, T., & Ploder, C. (2024). Augmented reality glasses in class–blessing or curse. *Education and New Developments*, *2024*(2), 366–370. DOI: 10.36315/2024v2end083

Sisman-Ugur, S., & Kurubacak, G. (Eds.). (2019). *Handbook of Research on Learning in the Age of Transhumanism*. IGI Global., DOI: 10.4018/978-1-5225-8431-5

Skinner, B. F. (1958). Teaching machines. *The Review of Economics and Statistics*, *42*(3), 189–191. PMID: 13592277

Sleeman, D. (1984). *Intelligent Tutoring Systems: A Review*. https://files.eric.ed.gov/fulltext/ED257450.pdf

Sleeman, D., & Brown, J. S. (Eds.). (1982). *Intelligent tutoring systems*. Academic Press.

Steenis, van M. (2025). Social Robots in education: Should we prepare for social robots in education? *Surf Responsible Tech Reports*. https://www.surf.nl/files/2025-03/20250303-social-robots-in-education-v1.0.pdf

Tegmark, M. (2017). *Life 3.0: Being human in the age of artificial intelligence*. Alfred A. Knopf.

Temur, S. (2025). Eğitimde yapay zekâ kullanımı: Etik sorunlar ve çözümler. *Mehmet Akif Ersoy University Journal of Education Faculty*, (74), 568–595. DOI: 10.21764/maeuefd.1516576

Thrun, S., Burgard, W., & Fox, D. (2005). *Probabilistic robotics*. The MIT Press. https://docs.ufpr.br/~danielsantos/ProbabilisticRobotics.pdf

Trivedi, N. (2018). ProblemPal: Generating autonomous practice content in real-time with voice commands and amazon alexa. In *Proceedings of E-Learn: World Conference on* E-*Learning in Corporate, Government, Healthcare, and Higher Education*, (s. 80-82). https://www.learntechlib.org/primary/p/184950/

Tsang, P. W. M., & Poon, T. C. (2016). Review on the state-of-the-art technologies for acquisition and display of digital holograms. *IEEE Transactions on Industrial Informatics*, *12*(3), 886–901. DOI: 10.1109/TII.2016.2550535

United Nations Educational, Scientific and Cultural Organization [UNESCO] (2023). *ChatGPT and artificial intelligence in higher education-quick start guide*. Retrieved from https://etico.iiep.unesco.org/en/chatgpt-and-artificial-intelligence-higher-education-quick-start-guide

Ünsal, H. (2024). Yapay zekâ ve yapay zekânın eğitimin geleceğine ilişkin olası doğurguları. *Journal of Social. Humanities and Administrative Sciences*, *10*(5), 674–682. DOI: 10.5281/zenodo.13 851822

U.S. Department of Education. Office of Educational Technology, *Artificial Intelligence and Future of Teaching and Learning: Insights and Recommendations*, Washington, DC, 2023. Retrieved from https://www.ed.gov/sites/ed/files/documents/ai-report/ai-report.pdf

van den Berghe, R., Verhagen, J., Oudgenoeg-Paz, O., van der Ven, S., & Leseman, P. (2019). Social robots for language learning: A review. *Review of Educational Research*, *89*(2), 259–295. DOI: 10.3102/0034654318821262

Wells, R. E. (2023). Strong AI vs. weak AI: What's the difference? Strong AI can do anything a human can do, while weak AI is limited to a specific task. *LifeWire*. Retrieved from https://www.lifewire.com/strong-ai-vs-weak-ai-7508012

Yoo, H., Jang, J., Oh, H., & Park, I. (2022). The potentials and trends of holography in education: A scoping review. *Computers & Education*, *186*, 104533. DOI: 10.1016/j.compedu.2022.104533

Zawacki-Richter, O., Marín, V. I., Bond, M., & Gouverneur, F. (2019). Systematic review of research on artificial intelligence applications in higher education–where are the educators? *International Journal of Educational Technology in Higher Education, 16*(1), 1–27. DOI: 10.1186/s41239-019-0171-0

ADDITIONAL READING

Alnajjar, F., Bartneck, C., Baxter, P., Belpaeme, T., Cappuccio, M., Di Dio, C., & Reich-Stiebert, N. (2021). *Robots in education: An introduction to high-tech social agents, intelligent tutors, and curricular tools*. Routledge.

Belpaeme, T., & Tanaka, F. (2021). Social robots as educators. In *OECD digital education outlook 2021 pushing the frontiers with artificial intelligence, blockchain and robots: pushing the frontiers with artificial intelligence, blockchain and robots* (p. 143). OECD Publishing.

Bruno, B., Amirova, A., Sandygulova, A., Lugrin, B., & Johal, W. (2023). Culture in social robots for education. In *Cultural robotics: social robots and their emergent cultural ecologies* (pp. 127–145). Springer International Publishing.

Gupta, P., Khan, I. R., & Kurubacak, G. (Eds.). (2024). *Virtual Lifelong Learning: Educating Society with Modern Communication Technologies*. Bentham Science Publishers.

Holmes, W., Bialik, M., & Fadel, C. (2019). *Artificial intelligence in education promises and implications for teaching and learning*. Center for Curriculum Redesign.

Neumann, M. M. (2020). Social robots and young children's early language and literacy learning. *Early Childhood Education Journal, 48*(2), 157–170.

Richardson, M. J., & Wiltshire, J. D. (2017). *The hologram: principles and techniques*. John Wiley & Sons.

KEY TERMS AND DEFINITIONS

Artificial Intelligence: Multidimensional systems capable of performing actions or tasks that require human intelligence

Hologram: Next-level visualization tech

Immersive Learning: Similar to experiential learning, enabling the learner to achieve learning objectives through interactive and engaging learning design.

Social Robot: Three-dimensional virtual entities in physical life

Technology: The application of techniques, skills, methods, and processes to the aims of life or put into practical use to solve problems

Chapter 3
Artificial Intelligence and Education:
Potentials and Challenges

Ozan Filiz
https://orcid.org/0000-0001-8527-9079
Sinop University, Turkey

ABSTRACT

This chapter explores the transformative role of artificial intelligence (AI) in education, highlighting its vast potential alongside significant challenges. It introduces core AI principles and prompt engineering strategies that help educators engage effectively with generative AI systems. The chapter examines AI applications in content creation, personalized learning, assessment, and administrative efficiency, showing how AI can support differentiated instruction, automate feedback, and streamline tasks. It also addresses ethical concerns such as algorithmic bias, data privacy, transparency, and accountability, offering guidelines for responsible AI use. Ultimately, the chapter emphasizes that the future of AI in education depends on educators' ethical, informed choices to enhance teaching and learning while ensuring equity and trust in digital environments.

INTRODUCTION

The introduction of ChatGPT in November 2022 sparked worldwide interest in the effects of artificial intelligence (AI) on society and individuals. Since then, the swift progress in AI technologies has indicated significant changes in various fields, transitioning the discussion from theoretical considerations to practical applications. These innovations have led to remarkable advancements across a wide array

DOI: 10.4018/979-8-3373-8857-1.ch003

of areas, from aiding in complex surgical procedures (Benzakour et al., 2023) and enhancing clinical decision-support systems in healthcare (Haug & Drazen, 2023) to creating hypotheses that push the limits of creativity (Sourati & Evans, 2023) and speeding up scientific research (Wang et al., 2023). The broad implementation of AI in finance, agriculture, and climate modeling further underscores its transformative capabilities (OECD, 2023). Particularly noteworthy are recent projects like the partnership between OpenAI CEO Sam Altman and designer Jony Ive to create the next generation of AI hardware, illustrating the rapid changes in human-computer interaction (Inagaki et al., 2023). Among all these areas of influence, the impact of AI in education—due to its potential to influence future generations—deserves extensive and critical scrutiny.

The integration of AI into education has evolved through distinct historical stages: from early rule-based tutoring systems in the 1970s and intelligent tutoring systems in the 1980s, to data-driven adaptive-learning platforms of the 2010s. The advent of generative AI since 2022 represents a qualitative shift: for the first time, language-based systems can simulate pedagogical dialogue rather than merely analyze performance data (Luckin et al., 2016; Holmes et al., 2019). This historical continuity reveals that long-standing questions about teacher agency, equity, and data ethics continually resurface with each wave of technological innovation.

However, despite this rapid progress, a persistent gap remains between technological advancement and societies' and institutions' readiness to integrate these tools responsibly. This policy–practice divide is particularly evident in education. A recent UNESCO (2023) report found that only 10 percent of educational institutions have formal guidance for AI use, while few nations have defined curriculum objectives for AI literacy. Likewise, the OECD's (2023) Digital Education Outlook highlights that comprehensive national frameworks and teacher guidance for equitable AI adoption remain embryonic in most contexts.

In response to this global preparedness gap, nations are formulating their own roadmaps. A notable and recent example is the comprehensive strategy from the Turkish Ministry of National Education, the *Artificial Intelligence in Education Policy Paper and Action Plan (2025–2029)*, published in June 2025 (MEB, 2025). The document implicitly acknowledges that AI integration often proceeds in an unplanned and reactive manner by outlining concrete actions to manage this process, such as establishing ethics boards and designing targeted professional-development programs. Comparable moves are evident elsewhere; for instance, the European Union's forthcoming AI Act dedicates specific provisions to education, mandating transparency and robust safeguards when AI systems are deployed in classrooms (European Commission, 2024). Such national and supranational initiatives underscore the gravity with which the international community views AI's significant risks, including ethical dilemmas, algorithmic bias, data privacy concerns, and the danger of exacerbating existing educational inequities. Therefore, to fully harness the opportunities presented by this technology while mitigating its potential perils, it is imperative that education stakeholders consciously and strategically guide this transformation.

While top-down strategies such as those outlined above are essential first steps, the success of this transformation will ultimately be determined by the educators' and practitioners' capacity and confidence on the front lines. This chapter addresses this need by providing a structured overview of AI in education. It begins by demystifying the core principles of AI, followed by practical strategies for crafting effective prompts. Among these emerging competencies, prompt engineering, the ability to design purposeful prompts that effectively guide AI systems, has become a pivotal literacy skill for educators seeking to collaborate productively with generative technologies. Its inclusion marks a shift from simply using AI tools to actively shaping their pedagogical output, a theme explored further in subsequent sections. The subsequent sections explore a range of applications, such as personalized learning, and conclude by critically examining the associated ethical challenges. The overarching goal is to equip educators with the foundational competence to integrate AI into their practice effectively, ethically, and with a clear pedagogical purpose.

WHAT IS AI AND HOW DOES IT WORK?

The concept of AI continues to evolve rapidly, with its definition remaining a subject of ongoing debate and interpretation among researchers and practitioners (Wang, 2019). To ground the discussion, comparing several widely cited formulations is helpful. Russell and Norvig (2021) describe AI as "the study of intelligent agents—systems that perceive their environment and act to maximize their chances of success." Kaplan and Haenlein (2018) emphasize learning and adaptation, defining AI as "a system's ability to correctly interpret external data, learn from such data, and use those learnings to achieve specific goals through flexible adaptation." From a policy and ethical perspective, UNESCO's World Commission on the Ethics of Scientific Knowledge and Technology (COMEST) provides a more detailed characterization, describing AI as involving "machines capable of imitating certain functionalities of human intelligence, including such features as perception, learning, reasoning, problem solving, language interaction, and even producing creative work" (COMEST, 2019). Similarly, the European Commission's High-Level Expert Group on Artificial Intelligence (AI HLEG) defines AI as "systems that display intelligent behavior by analyzing their environment and taking actions—with some degree of autonomy—to achieve specific goals. AI-based systems can be purely software-based, acting in the virtual world, or embedded in hardware devices" (HLEG, 2019).

While these definitions differ in focus on agentic behavior, data-driven learning, or goal-oriented decision-making, they converge on three core elements: (1) computation, (2) learning from data, and (3) performance of tasks that historically required human intelligence. Rather than a linear process, this is best conceptualized as a continuous, cyclical learning loop, as illustrated in Figure 1.

Figure 1. The Continuous Learning Cycle of AI

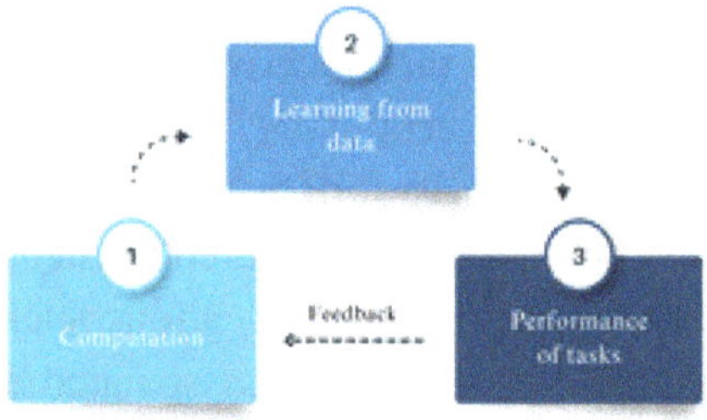

The diagram illustrates a cycle that begins with computation, progresses through learning from data, and leads to the performance of tasks. The outcomes from the performance stage serve as feedback, informing and refining subsequent cycles of computation and learning. Each stage can be described in detail as follows:

Computation: The Engine of AI

The foundation of AI is computation, the ability of computers to efficiently process large volumes of data using algorithms and mathematical operations. Unlike simple calculations, AI systems require significant computational power to analyze patterns, recognize images, or process language. The level of computation needed often depends on factors such as the data's size, the problem's complexity, and the hardware's efficiency. Recent advances in specialized hardware, such as Graphics Processing Units (GPUs) and dedicated AI chips, have made it possible to train and run AI models much more efficiently (Junaid et al., 2022; Wu et al., 2023), enabling their broader use in educational applications.

Learning from Data: Acquiring Intelligence

AI systems develop their capabilities by learning from extensive datasets, a process central to their ability to generalize and make predictions in new situations

(Adair, 2023; Russell & Norvig, 2021). This learning involves training models to adjust internal parameters based on input data, enabling the system to recognize patterns and apply knowledge to unseen cases. The quality and variety of data, including structured tables, unstructured text, images, or sensor data, directly affect the accuracy and effectiveness of AI algorithms (Budach et al., 2022).

There are three main approaches to machine learning, each with distinct educational applications:

- **Supervised Learning:** Models are trained on labeled datasets, where each example is paired with the correct output (Sen et al., 2020). In education, this approach powers automated grading platforms, which learn to assess student assignments from annotated examples, and intelligent tutoring systems that provide personalized feedback in areas such as mathematics or language learning.
- **Unsupervised Learning:** Algorithms use unlabeled data to discover patterns or groupings without predefined categories (Sarker, 2021). In educational settings, unsupervised learning can analyze student interaction data, group students by engagement patterns, or detect misconceptions in online forums.
- **Reinforcement Learning:** Systems learn by trial and error, receiving feedback as rewards or penalties (Mohammed et al., 2016). While less common in direct instruction, reinforcement learning underpins adaptive learning platforms that dynamically adjust content difficulty to optimize student engagement and challenge.

Performance of Tasks: Mimicking Human Cognition

The ultimate purpose of computation and learning in AI is to perform tasks that traditionally require human intelligence (Jordan & Mitchell, 2015; Russell & Norvig, 2021). These capabilities, realized by applying trained models to new data, encompass a broad range of cognitive functions:

- **Perception:** This involves recognizing patterns such as objects in images (computer vision) or understanding spoken language (speech recognition) (Goodfellow et al., 2016). In educational contexts, perception technologies support assistive tools like speech-to-text software for students with hearing impairments and applications that assess oral reading fluency.
- **Language:** AI systems process, understand, and generate human language through natural language processing (NLP) techniques (Jurafsky & Martin, 2024). These capabilities enable AI-driven chatbots and virtual assistants that provide real-time student support and administrative assistance.

- **Reasoning and Decision-Making:** AI analyzes complex data to solve problems and make decisions, often surpassing human performance in specific, data-intensive tasks (Silver et al., 2016). In education, AI can analyze student performance data to offer actionable insights for educators, identify students at risk, and assist in curriculum development by detecting trends and gaps.

The feedback loop depicted in Figure 1 is critical, as it transforms AI from a static tool into a dynamic, adaptive system. This iterative process of performing, receiving feedback, and re-learning underpins modern AI's evolving capabilities. Despite their advanced capabilities, AI systems do not inherently "understand" or possess consciousness in a human sense; instead, they excel at pattern recognition, prediction, and optimization based solely on the data they are trained on (Marcus & Davis, 2019; Russell & Norvig, 2021). The quality, quantity, and representativeness of this training data are paramount, as biases present in the data can be amplified and reflected in the AI's output, leading to significant ethical concerns that will be explored later in this chapter (Hong et al., 2022).

Among the diverse applications of AI, Generative AI (GenAI) represents a significant leap forward, particularly in its relevance to education. GenAI encompasses AI models capable of producing novel content, such as text, images, audio, or video, that resembles human-created output (Baïdoo-Anu & Ansah, 2023). These models are often built upon Foundation Models, which are large-scale models trained on massive, diverse datasets to learn broad patterns that can be adapted for various downstream tasks. Large Language Models (LLMs), a specific and highly prominent type of Foundation Model trained primarily on vast amounts of text data, are currently at the forefront of GenAI, enabling advanced capabilities in human-like text generation, summarization, and comprehension (Zhao et al., 2023). This new class of generative tools has profoundly impacted the accessibility of advanced AI capabilities, with significant implications for learning and teaching environments.

Modern AI, including LLMs that can understand and generate human-like text, leverages these principles to process and create information on an unprecedented scale. These advancements are profoundly transforming how we interact with knowledge and each other, particularly in educational contexts, by emphasizing the intricate interplay among AI, analytics, and human learning processes, and pointing towards the development of human–AI hybrid intelligence (Cukurova, 2025). Having outlined the fundamental operational principles of AI and its key learning paradigms, we can now transition to understanding the practical implications for educators, beginning with the critical skill of interacting effectively with these robust systems.

WRITING EFFECTIVE AI PROMPTS: FRAMEWORKS AND PRACTICAL STRATEGIES

The effective use of GenAI in education transcends a simple command-response interaction, evolving instead into a form of partnership or co-creation (Mollick & Mollick, 2024). Achieving this synergistic partnership, however, depends on mastering prompt engineering, a discipline focused on creating specific inputs to guide AI toward desired outputs (Oppenlaender et al., 2024). A high-quality prompt does not merely ask a question; it structures the entire dialogue, defining the context and constraints essential for a relevant response (White et al., 2023). This skill is paramount because of the inherent limitations of LLMs, which can produce inaccurate or nonsensical outputs, often called "hallucinations" (Ji et al., 2022). Consequently, effective prompting is an iterative dialogue, a refined skill that transforms AI from a passive tool into a dynamic pedagogical partner (Liu et al., 2022).

Recent scholarships have begun to codify this process for educators. Park and Choo (2024), for instance, analyze and incorporate practical models like the PARTS framework (Persona, Aim, Recipients, Theme, Structure) from Google (2024) into their broader IDEA framework, which guides educators through the entire prompt engineering cycle. Building on industry's best practices, such as OpenAI and Microsoft, this scholarly work highlights that successful prompting is not a single action but a multi-stage process, with the initial construction of the prompt being the most critical phase.

Drawing upon these convergent principles, this chapter proposes an organizational framework, the Foundational Prompting Framework (see Figure 2), to guide educators in this crucial first phase. The framework is illustrated below with a worked example, highlighting the function of each component.

Figure 2. Foundational Prompting Framework

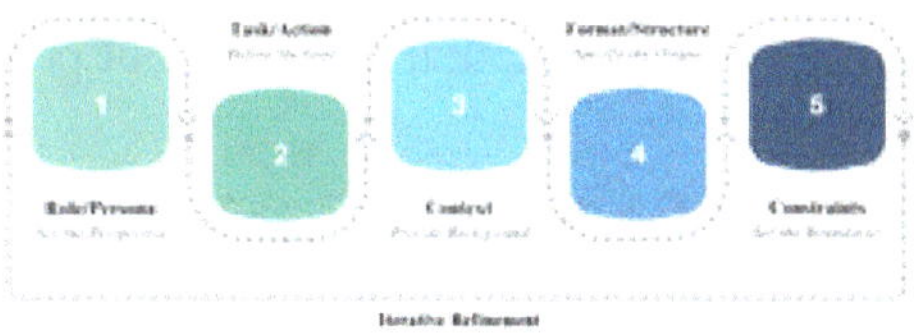

Consider the following educational scenario and the worked example prompt crafted to address it. Each component is explicitly labeled to demonstrate its function clearly:

(Role) You are an educational technology expert specializing in designing project-based learning materials for middle school students. **(Task)** Design a lesson plan draft for a 7th-grade World History class focusing on cultural exchange along the Silk Road. **(Context)** Students know the geographical location of the Silk Road and basic trade goods, but have limited knowledge about cultural interactions (religion, art, science). The goal is to foster empathy and integrate historical research. **(Format)** Present your response in a three-column table: 1. Activity Step, 2. Learning Objective, 3. Suggested Digital Tool. **(Constraints)** The project should be designed to be completed by students within two weeks and include a simple rubric draft for assessment. Avoid formal and technical language.

Each foundational component can be detailed as follows, using the worked example as a reference.

Role/Persona: Setting the Perspective

In our example prompt, the instruction begins with: "*You are an educational technology expert specializing in designing project-based learning materials for middle school students.*" This initial step is critical as it frames the entire interaction, moving it from a simple query to a professional consultation. By assigning a specific persona, we are not just asking for information; we are inviting the AI to adopt a particular mindset, tone, and level of expertise, which is a cornerstone of establishing a "partnership" with the AI rather than merely using it as a tool (Mollick & Mollick, 2024). The persona informs the AI about the implicit rules and context of the dialogue, essential for generating high-quality, relevant output (White et al., 2023).

Without this persona, a prompt like "Design a lesson plan for the Silk Road" would likely yield a generic, Wikipedia-style summary of facts, lacking the pedagogical structure and innovative project-based ideas that an "expert instructional designer" would provide. The output would be factually correct but pedagogically limited.

Task/Action: Defining the Goal

While assigning a specific persona is the first step in contextualizing the AI's response, the Task/Action component gives the interaction a clear purpose and direction. In our example, the core instruction is given with a clear action verb: "Design a lesson plan draft..." This component delineates the primary, explicit action the AI is expected to perform. It is the engine of the prompt, transforming a vague request into a specific, goal-oriented instruction. This element, termed the "Aim" in the

PARTS framework (Google, 2024), is pivotal for guiding the generation process. As Park and Choo (2024) highlight in their framework for educators, providing a clear objective is a foundational step for effective prompting. The importance of this step is echoed in engineering literature, where defining the goal is considered the necessary starting point for any subsequent iterative refinement of the AI's output (Velásquez-Henao et al., 2023). By clearly defining the task, the educator provides the AI with a precise target, essential for optimizing the output for a specific pedagogical purpose.

A prompt like "About the Silk Road for a 7th-grade class" is ambiguous without a precise task. The AI is left to guess the user's intent: Should it summarize, list facts, or create a quiz? The likely result would be a generic information dump, forcing the educator to sift through and structure the content manually. By specifying the action "Design a lesson plan draft," for example, we ensure the output has a clear pedagogical structure and immediate utility.

Context: Providing Background

While a straightforward task defines what the AI should do, the context component defines for whom and why, grounding the interaction in a specific educational reality. In our example, we provide the following context: "Students know the geographical location of the Silk Road and basic trade goods but have limited knowledge about cultural interactions (religion, art, science). The goal is to foster empathy and integrate historical research."

This component provides the AI with crucial situational awareness, preventing it from making incorrect assumptions about the learners' prior knowledge or the pedagogical goals of the task. Supplying sufficient "contextual information" is a fundamental principle of practical prompt engineering, ensuring the AI can generate a fitting response (Lo, 2023). Practical frameworks often deconstruct this broad concept into more granular elements. For instance, the PARTS framework includes "Recipients" to define the audience and "Theme" to set the style and parameters, both of which serve to contextualize the request (Google, 2024). Ultimately, providing context transforms a generic inquiry into a personalized consultation, ensuring the AI's vast knowledge is applied precisely to the educator's unique situation.

Without this context, a prompt like "You are an educational technology expert... Design a lesson plan draft for a 7th-grade class on the Silk Road" would force the AI to guess. It would likely generate a technically correct but pedagogically shallow lesson plan, unsure whether to focus on geography, economics, or culture. By specifying the students' knowledge gap (cultural interaction) and the learning goal (empathy), we direct the AI to produce a more targeted and meaningful resource, saving the educator significant time in editing and adaptation.

Format/Structure: Specifying the Output

Even with perfect context, output can be of limited utility if it is not delivered in a usable structure. This is where the Format component becomes essential. Our example explicitly defines the desired structure: "Present your response in a three-column table: 1. Activity Step, 2. Learning Objective, 3. Suggested Digital Tool." This component dictates the structural layout of the AI's response, moving beyond the content to control its presentation. Specifying the desired format is a recognized principle in prompt engineering literature, as it ensures the output meets the user's expectations of structure and style (Lo, 2023; Velásquez-Henao et al., 2023). Practical frameworks like PARTS explicitly include "Structure" as a core component, highlighting its importance in generating everything from tables and bullet points to quizzes and games (Google, 2024). For an educator, this step transforms raw information into a ready-to-use pedagogical artifact, be it a lesson plan, a rubric, or a student-facing handout.

Without a specified format, an otherwise identical prompt would likely result in a dense, narrative-style paragraph. While the content might be valuable, it would lack a structured table's scannability and immediate utility. The educator would be forced to deconstruct the text and reformat it into a usable lesson plan, defeating much of the purpose of using AI for efficiency. By preemptively defining the format, the educator ensures the output is informative and immediately actionable.

Constraints: Setting the Boundaries

Defining the format gives the output its shape, but without clear boundaries, the content within that shape can become unwieldy or irrelevant. The final component, Constraints, provides these essential guardrails. In our example, we conclude with several explicit constraints: "The project should be designed to be completed by students within two weeks and include a simple rubric draft for assessment. Avoid formal and technical language."

This component involves setting specific rules, limits, and boundaries to fine-tune the AI's output. These are the non-negotiable parameters that ensure the final product is well-structured but also practical, appropriate, and aligned with the educator's specific requirements. The principle of using "Restrictive" language to specify constraints like length, scope, and tone is a key strategy for ensuring AI-generated responses adhere to desired parameters (Eager & Brunton, 2023; Ekin, 2023). This concept is also embedded in the "Theme" component of the PARTS framework, which includes setting restrictions on voice and style (Google, 2024). In an educational partnership, setting explicit constraints is analogous to establishing clear expectations in any collaboration; it ensures both partners, the educator and the AI, work toward the same, well-defined, and achievable outcome (Mollick & Mollick, 2024).

Without these constraints, the AI might generate a lesson plan that is theoretically sound but practically infeasible, a semester-long project instead of a two-week one, or use overly academic language unsuitable for 7th graders. The educator would then be faced with the significant task of editing the plan to a manageable scope, simplifying its language, and creating a rubric from scratch, thereby diminishing the AI's value as an efficiency-enhancing partner. Constraints are the final step in transforming a powerful generative tool into a precise and reliable pedagogical assistant.

From Framework to Fluidity: The Art of Iterative Refinement

It is crucial to view the Foundational Prompting Framework not as a rigid, mandatory checklist for every interaction, but as a flexible mental model to guide an educator's thinking. An educator does not need to explicitly use all five components for a simple query, such as asking for a definition. However, for complex, high-stakes tasks, like generating the detailed lesson plan in our worked example, incorporating all five components significantly increases the likelihood of receiving a high-quality and immediately usable response.

Ultimately, the framework's most significant value lies in its role as a diagnostic tool within a continuous cycle of iterative refinement. If an AI's output is unsatisfactory, an educator can use these five components to diagnose the prompt's weakness: Was the Role unspecified? Was the Context too vague? This diagnostic process is central to the 'Evaluate and Refine' stage of prompt engineering (Park & Choo, 2024) and embodies the very nature of a human-AI partnership (Mollick & Mollick, 2024). This framework thus serves not only as a recipe for construction but as a diagnostic lens for deconstruction, allowing educators to pinpoint why a prompt failed and how to improve it methodically. Once this foundational thinking is mastered, educators can combine these components more sophisticatedly to unlock advanced reasoning from AI systems.

Beyond the Foundation: Advanced Prompting Strategies

Having established these foundational principles, we can now build upon them to explore advanced prompting strategies that unlock more complex reasoning and creativity from AI systems. While students and professionals need more prompting strategies training (Alpizar-Chacon et al., 2025), a few key techniques can significantly elevate the quality of AI-generated content (Viswanathan, 2025).

- **Chain-of-Thought (CoT) Prompting:** This technique involves instructing the AI not just to provide a final answer, but to "think aloud" by generating the intermediate reasoning steps it took to arrive at the solution (Beri & Srivastava, 2025). This is invaluable in education for modeling problem-solving processes, especially in STEM fields, and for making the AI's reasoning transparent and evaluable (Alemanno et al., 2025).
- **Few-Shot Prompting:** Instead of just describing the desired output, this strategy provides the AI with one or more examples (the "shots") of the input-output format you want it to follow (Google, 2024). This is highly effective for generating content that adheres to a specific structure, such as creating differentiated reading passages, writing test questions, or formatting bibliographic entries.
- **Prompt Chaining:** This involves breaking an enormous, complex task into a series of smaller, interconnected prompts (Viswanathan, 2025). The output from the first prompt becomes the input or context for the second, and so on. This allows for creating highly detailed and layered content, such as developing a multi-week unit plan or designing a comprehensive project-based learning module from scratch.

Table 1 provides concrete examples across various educational contexts to illustrate how these foundational and advanced strategies are implemented in practice.

Table 1. Application of Prompting Strategies Across Educational Disciplines

Discipline	Educational Goal	Example Prompt	Key Strategy
STEM (Mathematics)	Help students understand the process of solving a quadratic equation, not just the answer.	**[Role]** You are a patient and encouraging math tutor. **[Task]** Solve the equation $2x^2 + 5x - 3 = 0$ using the quadratic formula. Use the Chain-of-Thought technique to explain every step of your reasoning in simple terms, as if you were explaining it to a 9th-grade student struggling with algebra.	Chain-of-Thought Prompting
Humanities (History)	Foster historical empathy by analyzing an event from multiple perspectives.	**[Role]** You are a historical consultant. **[Task]** Generate three short, first-person diary entries (150 words each) about the Boston Tea Party. **[Context]** The entries should reflect three different perspectives: 1) a fervent Patriot who participated, 2) a loyalist merchant whose tea was destroyed, and 3) a neutral observer who is worried about the escalating conflict.	Foundational Framework (Role + Task + Context)
Language Arts (ELL)	Create differentiated reading materials for English Language Learners at varying proficiency levels.	**[Role]** You are an ESL curriculum specialist. **[Task]** Your task is to rewrite the provided paragraph for three reading levels. Here is the input and desired output structure: Input: Istanbul, straddling two continents, is a city of captivating contrasts, where ancient history and vibrant modernity coexist. The city's strategic location on the Bosphorus Strait has made it a coveted prize for empires throughout history, each leaving an indelible mark on its cultural and architectural landscape. Visitors are often mesmerized by the fusion of Eastern and Western influences, evident in everything from its cuisine to its art. Output: A three-column table labeled "Beginner," "Intermediate," and "Advanced" with the rewritten texts.	Few-Shot Prompting (One-Shot)

continued on following page

Table 1. Continued

Discipline	Educational Goal	Example Prompt	Key Strategy
Cross-Curricular (Assessment)	Generate a fair and comprehensive assessment rubric for a student project.	**[Role]** You are an expert in authentic assessment. **[Task]** Create a 4-point scoring rubric to evaluate a student's digital storytelling project. **[Context]** The project requires students to research and present a historical event as a short video. The rubric should assess three criteria: Historical Accuracy, Narrative Coherence, and Technical Production Quality. **[Format]** The output should be a well-formatted Markdown table. **[Constraints]** The language used in the rubric must be clear and student-friendly. Provide detailed descriptions for each performance level (e.g., for '4 - Exemplary', '3 - Proficient', etc.).	Foundational Framework (Full Application)
Creative Writing (Digital Storytelling)	Develop a detailed plot for a digital story through a multi-step conversation.	**[1. Initial Prompt]** I need three unique ideas for a digital story for 10th graders combining sci-fi and ancient mythology. **[2. Follow-up Prompt]** I like idea #2. Act as a professional screenwriter and expand that idea into a three-act story structure (Setup, Confrontation, Resolution). Describe the key plot points for each act.	Prompt Chaining

***Note.** Component labels (e.g., Role, Task, Context) are included here for illustrative purposes. In practice, prompts should integrate these elements seamlessly.

By integrating these foundational and advanced techniques, educators can transform their interactions with AI from simple queries into powerful pedagogical partnerships, co-creating rich, relevant, and compelling learning experiences.

LEVERAGING AI TO DEVELOP CODING SKILLS

AI has become a transformative force across the software development lifecycle, supporting developers in code generation, debugging, testing, and refactoring (Anand et al., 2024; Sergeyuk et al., 2024). LLMs such as GitHub Copilot and ChatGPT now act as intelligent collaborators that suggest, refine, and explain code with unprecedented contextual awareness (Hossain et al., 2024). This evolution positions AI as a productivity enhancer and a learning co-pilot, offering opportunities to reimagine how coding is taught and learned (Rasheed et al., 2024).

In educational contexts, AI increasingly functions as a personalized tutor, collaborative partner, and responsive debugger, adapting its feedback to learners' cognitive levels (Da Silva et al., 2024). Intelligent Tutoring Systems powered by natural language models guide students step-by-step through programming challenges, while AI-assisted code editors identify syntax errors, propose corrections, and explain logic structures—transforming debugging into an active learning experience (Hossain et al., 2024; Woodrow et al., 2024). Students can generate code snippets to solve problems and use AI explanations to strengthen conceptual understanding rather than bypass problem-solving (Arendes et al., 2024).

Practical classroom applications now demonstrate how AI-powered editors, conversational chatbots, and AI-based transition tools can scaffold learning from block-based coding (e.g., Scratch) to text-based environments like Python (Sergeyuk et al., 2024). The pedagogical benefits include greater engagement, enhanced confidence, and individualized support as students receive continuous feedback, enabling teachers to focus on higher-order thinking and creativity (Woodrow et al., 2024). However, concerns remain regarding over-reliance, disparities in access, and sustaining independent problem-solving (Rasheed et al., 2024). Cultivating AI literacy, the ability to critically assess, refine, and manage AI outputs, has become a crucial pedagogical goal. This positions these tools not as substitutes for human judgment but as supports that encourage deeper learning and reflection.

With AI becoming a co-instructor and cognitive partner in classrooms, the pedagogical conversation naturally expands beyond how students use AI to learn coding to how educators can integrate these same systems to enrich teaching more broadly. This shift from students coding with AI to teachers teaching with AI sets the stage for understanding how intelligent systems can serve as pedagogical partners across diverse subject areas and instructional contexts.

ARTIFICIAL INTELLIGENCE AND ITS USES IN EDUCATION

Building on the principles of effective prompting established in the previous section, the focus now shifts from how to communicate with AI to what these systems can help educators achieve. This section explores how advanced AI can be a pedagogical partner to enhance teaching and learning.

Students' rapid, largely unsupervised adoption of generative AI has rendered this question not just a technical curiosity, but an educational imperative of our time (Kasneci et al., 2023). Young people are already immersed in an AI-driven world, yet often lack the critical framework to navigate it effectively. A recent OECD report (2025) highlights this skills gap, noting that nearly half of young adults struggle to identify AI's shortfalls, such as its capacity to generate convincing fabrications. This finding underscores an urgent need for structured AI literacy, moving beyond mere tool use towards critical and creative application (Ng et al., 2021).

Integrating AI into education is not merely about automating tasks but augmenting human potential and intelligence (Zawacki-Richter et al., 2019). This human-centered perspective reframes the conversation around the evolving roles of both educators and learners. For teachers, the role shifts from being the primary source of information to becoming architects of learning experiences, facilitators of critical inquiry, and ethical guides who model responsible AI use. For students, the focus moves from passive knowledge consumption to active student agency, where they learn to use AI as a tool for creative exploration and problem-solving, rather than as a substitute for effort. This pedagogical rebalancing ensures that technology enhances, not diminishes, core human skills like collaboration, creativity, and critical thinking.

A significant body of research demonstrates AI's capacity to scaffold learning through personalized feedback and adaptive pathways, thereby realizing the long-held goal of differentiated instruction at scale (Ouyang et al., 2022). Furthermore, AI tools, particularly conversational agents, can serve as 'pedagogical partners,' boosting student engagement through interactive simulations and inquiry-based dialogues (Crompton & Burke, 2023). On a practical level, these technologies promise to alleviate the overwhelming administrative workloads that often divert educators' time from core teaching activities, a benefit that could significantly impact teacher retention and well-being (Mollick & Mollick, 2023). This academic potential meets a real-world demand: a 2024 study spanning several European countries, including Türkiye, revealed a significant gap between students' belief in AI's career importance and their perceived preparedness through schooling (Vodafone Foundation, 2024).

When wielded thoughtfully, AI can free educators to focus on the most human aspects of their profession: building relationships, fostering critical thinking, and inspiring a love of learning. To explore these practical applications systematically, this chapter is structured around four core domains carefully chosen to mirror the key stages of the educator's pedagogical cycle: content creation, personalized learning, assessment, and administrative efficiency. This approach allows for a coherent analysis of AI's role across the entire teaching and learning process, from initial planning to final evaluation and support.

Content Creation: The Educator as Architect, AI as Assistant

Creating high-quality, engaging, and relevant educational content is one of educators' most time-consuming and creatively demanding tasks. Before the classroom door even opens, it is often here that the "overwhelming administrative workloads" discussed previously are most keenly felt (Mollick & Mollick, 2023). The blank page of a new lesson plan or the challenge of designing a novel activity can consume significant time and cognitive energy. AI can function as a valuable assistant in this context. Handling initial drafts and structural organization allows the educator, as the architect of the learning experience, to concentrate on higher-order pedagogical design and student engagement.

This partnership manifests in several powerful ways. At its most foundational level, AI serves as an exceptional draftsman, eliminating the initial friction of content creation by producing a structured first draft of a lesson plan, a formal email, or a set of project guidelines in seconds. This capability directly addresses the challenge of cognitive load, a finding supported by experimental research showing that teachers perceive significantly lower workloads when using AI-automated systems than manual processes (Machado et al., 2025). This reduction allows educators to focus on refining the pedagogical core of the content rather than its basic structure. Beyond this foundational support, AI's most transformative role emerges in its ability to differentiate content to meet diverse learner needs instantly. An educator can provide a single text and prompt the AI to generate versions at multiple reading levels or explain a complex scientific concept using several analogies. This capacity for on-the-fly differentiation allows educators to more effectively implement the principles of Universal Design for Learning (UDL), ensuring content is not only accessible but also presented through multiple means of representation—such as converting text to audio or generating visual summaries—to match individual learners ' needs better (Saborío-Taylor & Rojas-Ramírez, 2024). Its most exciting role, however, is that of a creative muse. In this capacity, AI acts as a catalyst for pedagogical innovation, offering fresh perspectives, unconventional teaching metaphors, or gamification strategies that can break through an educator's cognitive fixedness and spark new, engaging learning experiences (Baidoo-Anu & Ansah, 2023).

The first critical step is understanding these emerging pedagogical roles: the draftsman, the differentiator, and the muse. However, translating this theoretical potential into tangible classroom materials requires a practical knowledge of the available tools and effective strategies for using them. The current landscape of AI tools for educators can be broadly categorized into three types, each suited for tasks requiring varying levels of user expertise. Table 2 provides a snapshot of this ecosystem, serving as a starting point for educators looking to integrate these assistants into their content creation workflow.

Table 2. A Categorization of AI Tools for Educator Content Creation

Tool Category	Example Tools	Primary Use Case	Required Skill Level
Specialized Education Assistants	MagicSchool AI, Curipod, Eduaide.ai	Generating lesson plans, rubrics, assessment questions, student feedback comments, and interactive presentations.	Beginner
General-Purpose Language Models	ChatGPT, Claude, Gemini	Co-writing syllabi, creating complex role-playing scenarios, drafting unique project briefs, and generating podcast scripts.	Intermediate / Advanced
Source Synthesis & Analysis	NotebookLM, Perplexity, SciSpace	Transforming research papers (PDFs) into summaries, generating study guides from class notes, and creating quizzes from uploaded readings.	Beginner / Intermediate
Multimedia & Visual Content	Canva AI, Gamma, Runway	Creating instructional videos from text, designing infographics and posters, and generating custom images for presentations or digital stories.	Beginner / Intermediate

***Note.** "Specialized" tools offer structured, education-specific templates. "General-purpose" models provide a flexible canvas requiring practical prompt engineering. "Synthesis" tools excel at processing and transforming user-provided content. "Multimedia" tools focus on converting text or ideas into visual and auditory formats.*

As Table 2 illustrates, the ecosystem of AI tools offers a rich spectrum of possibilities, from "point-and-click" assistants that generate a standards-aligned rubric in minutes to versatile models that can co-create a unique historical simulation. The key lies in selecting the right tool for the pedagogical task. A teacher might use a Specialized Assistant for daily administrative efficiencies, a General-Purpose Model for a complex, creative project, and a Multimedia Tool to design an engaging visual summary for the lesson. To move from this abstract categorization to concrete practice, we will now explore two worked examples that demonstrate how these tools can be effectively wielded in a real-world teaching context.

Worked Example 1: Creating a Historical Role-Playing Scenario with a General-Purpose LLM

This first example showcases how an educator can leverage a General-Purpose model like ChatGPT or Claude to create a dynamic and engaging role-playing activity. This moves beyond simple content delivery to crafting an immersive learning experience.

Table 3. Prompt

You are a historical fiction writer specializing in the 19th-century Ottoman Empire. Your style is to make complex historical tensions understandable and engaging for a high school audience. Create a short, two-character script for a role-playing activity. The dialogue should feel authentic to the period but be clear enough for 10th-grade students to perform. The setting is a traditional coffeehouse in Istanbul's Eminönü district, circa 1860, during the Tanzimat reform era. The characters are (1) Ahmet Bey, a young bureaucrat from the Sublime Porte, educated in Paris, passionate about Westernizing reforms he believes will save the Empire. (2) İsmail Usta, an elderly master calligrapher, sees the new printing presses and bureaucratic reforms as a threat to his art, livelihood, and the soul of the Empire. They are sharing a table. Structure the script with clear character names, dialogue, and brief, evocative stage directions in parentheses. The script should be approximately 300 words long. The dialogue must highlight the conflicting perspectives on progress and tradition during this pivotal era.

Table 4. Sample Output

Setting: A bustling Ottoman coffeehouse, low light, the aroma of roasted beans, men in fezzes and flowing robes. In a corner, beneath latticed windows, Ahmet Bey sits upright, fresh-faced, scribbling notes. İsmail Usta, gray-bearded, in ink-stained robes, carefully sips his coffee. İSMAİL USTA (setting down his cup, voice steady): Young Ahmet, you write as if notes alone can change the world. What are your thoughts today—another proposal for the Ministries? AHMET BEY (smiling, eager): Not just any proposal, Usta. Imagine an Empire where every child can read the same textbook, printed quickly, cheaply. France—where I studied—thrives on such knowledge. İSMAİL USTA (frowning, fingers tracing invisible lines on the table): Printed books—quick, yes. Cheap—certainly. But where is the soul, evladım, the beauty in ink flowing by hand? A scribe's devotion cannot be stamped by a machine. AHMET BEY (leaning forward, quietly earnest): But should beauty stand in the way of progress? If more can read, if ideas can travel farther—do we not strengthen the Empire against its enemies? İSMAİL USTA (voice rises): Strength lies in our roots! Our calligraphy, our traditions—these are not shackles, Ahmet, but the very fabric of our people. If we lose them, what remains? AHMET BEY (softly): Yet can we survive if we refuse to change, Usta? The West races ahead. I dream our children will carry both the pen and the printed word. İSMAİL USTA (sighs, looking out the window): Let us hope, Ahmet, that in your new world, there will still be room for the old ways... and for old men like me. (Both men sip their coffee, the air thick with unspoken hopes and fears.)

Note: This output was generated by a large language model (GPT-4.1) in response to the prompt. Your results may vary, but a well-structured prompt will consistently produce high-quality, relevant text in a similar style.

This worked example demonstrates how a carefully crafted prompt rooted in local history and culture can yield a rich, pedagogically purposeful output from a generative AI model. By explicitly specifying the historical context, characters, and the core tension between progress and tradition, the prompt guides the AI to create an authentic dialogue accessible to high school students and evocative of the period. The resulting script facilitates historical empathy and critical thinking. It exemplifies how prompt engineering can empower educators to design creative, culturally resonant learning materials that actively engage learners in complex topics. For classroom use, this script can serve as a reader's theater activity, a springboard for discussion, or the basis for creative writing assignments, allowing students to step into historical perspectives and debate the complexities of change and tradition. At the same time, educators should approach AI-generated scripts as dynamic drafts rather than final products. For instance, if the dialogue omits diverse perspectives or overemphasizes a single viewpoint, teachers can iterate on the prompt, adding contextual refinements or ethical considerations, to produce more balanced and inclusive outputs. This reflective revision process models the essence of prompt engineering, highlighting educators' active role in verifying, adapting, and improving AI contributions to foster critical literacy and historical accuracy.

Worked Example 2: Generating a Dialogue-Based Podcast Script with a General-Purpose LLM

Teachers increasingly seek to create engaging, contemporary learning experiences centered on complex social issues. This worked example demonstrates how a well-crafted prompt can help educators use AI to generate an age-appropriate, thought-provoking podcast script on gender equality—ready for classroom discussion or project-based learning.

Table 5. Prompt

You are an expert podcast producer and scriptwriter, creating engaging, age-appropriate content for young adults on social issues. Generate a 5-minute podcast episode script for a fictional series titled 'Voices of Change'. The episode should feature a host and a guest speaker to discuss the topic of gender equality. The target audience is high school students (10th-11th grade). The guest is 'Aisha', a 17-year-old student activist who started a 'Girls Who Code' chapter at her school. The tone should be conversational, inclusive, and empowering, avoiding a lecture-like feel. The goal is to inspire critical thinking and discussion about gender equality in students' lives. Structure the script with the following sections, clearly labeled: 1. Introduction: The Host introduces the topic and the guest. 2. Dialogue: A conversational exchange where the host asks questions and Aisha shares her perspective. 3. Personal Story: Aisha recounts a brief, specific story about a challenge she faced and overcame. 4. Closing & Call to Action: The host summarizes and poses a reflective question to the listeners. The script must use clear speaker labels (e.g., HOST:, AISHA:) and include brief, evocative stage directions in parentheses. The total spoken dialogue should be approximately 5 minutes long. Use accessible language. The dialogue must highlight the challenges and the progress related to gender equality.

Table 6. Sample Output

Introduction HOST: (Upbeat music fades in, then out) Hey everyone, welcome back to another episode of Voices of Change—the podcast where we talk about the issues that matter to you, the changemakers of tomorrow. I'm your host, Sam. Today, we're diving into a topic that's super relevant in our schools, our communities, and our futures: gender equality. I'm really excited to introduce our guest, Aisha—a 17-year-old student activist who started a 'Girls Who Code' chapter at her school. She's passionate about making sure everyone, regardless of gender, has the chance to follow their dreams. Welcome, Aisha! AISHA: Thanks so much for having me, Sam! I'm excited to be here. Dialogue HOST: (Smiling, conversational) Aisha, let's start with the basics. When you hear "gender equality," what does it mean to you? AISHA: For me, gender equality means everyone—no matter if you're a girl, a boy, or non-binary—gets the same opportunities and respect. It's about making sure no one is held back just because of their gender. HOST: That's such an important point. Do you think things are getting better for gender equality, especially in schools? AISHA: I think there's definitely been progress. More girls are joining STEM clubs, and teachers are encouraging everyone to take part in activities. But there are still challenges—like stereotypes that say coding is "for boys," or that girls shouldn't be leaders in tech. HOST: Yeah, those stereotypes can be tough to break. What inspired you to start a 'Girls Who Code' chapter? AISHA: Honestly, I noticed that in my computer science class, there were only two girls, including me. I wanted to create a space where girls could support each other, learn together, and prove that we belong in tech just as much as anyone else. Personal Story HOST: (Leaning in, interested) Can you share a specific story about a challenge and how you overcame it? AISHA: Absolutely. When I first announced the 'Girls Who Code' chapter, some people—both students and even a few teachers—said things like, "Are you sure girls are interested in coding?" or "Isn't that kind of a boys' club?" It was discouraging. But instead of giving up, I reached out to other girls who were curious but nervous. We started small—just three of us at first. We worked on a project to build a website about women in tech history. When we presented it at the school assembly, people were impressed! After that, more girls joined, and even some boys wanted to help out. It taught me that change starts with just a few people believing in themselves—and each other. Closing & Call to Action HOST: (Smiling, encouraging) That's such an inspiring story, Aisha. You showed that one person's courage can spark real change. To everyone listening: Think about your own school or community. Where do you see opportunities for more equality? What small step could you take to make things fairer for everyone? Thanks for joining us on Voices of Change. Remember—your voice matters. Let's keep the conversation going. See you next time! (Outro music fades in)

This worked example illustrates how a highly structured prompt can guide a generative AI to produce a nuanced, dialogue-based educational resource on a complex social topic. By specifying the expert (Role), the target audience and guest persona (Context), and a clear, multi-part (Format), the prompt moves the AI beyond simple text generation toward co-creating a pedagogically rich script. The resulting output is particularly effective because it features an authentic personal narrative, Aisha's story of overcoming stereotypes, which fosters historical empathy and makes abstract concepts relatable. Furthermore, including a "Call to Action" shifts the learning experience from passive consumption to active, critical reflection, empowering students to connect the topic to their lives. This demonstrates how educators can use AI to create content and craft dynamic, story-driven learning experiences that promote digital literacy and social awareness. This podcast script can be used as a model for a project-based learning unit where students research a social issue of their choice, script their own dialogue-based podcast, and record it using simple tools. This approach simultaneously develops research, writing, collaboration, and digital communication skills.

By mastering the art of prompt engineering and understanding the expanding ecosystem of AI tools, educators can reclaim their creative time, better meet student needs, and shape the future of learning in meaningful ways.

Personalized Learning and Differentiated Instruction

Personalized learning refers to the tailoring of pedagogy, curriculum, and learning environments to the individual needs, skills, and interests of each student, while differentiated instruction involves the adjustment of teaching methods and content to accommodate the varied learner profiles present in every classroom (Bernacki et al., 2021; Hardaker & Glenn, 2025). Despite the best efforts of educators, traditional "one-size-fits-all" models are consistently found to leave some learners under-challenged and others unsupported, especially as classroom diversity continues to grow (Pane et al., 2017).

Recent advances in AI have revitalized this paradigm, providing educators with scalable tools to analyze learner data and adapt instruction in real time (Halkiopoulos & Gkintoni, 2024). The literature highlights that AI enables personalized learning through several interrelated domains: intelligent tutoring, adaptive assessment, dynamic learner modeling, and expanding online and multimodal learning environments (Yilmaz et al., 2022; Kretzschmar et al., 2024). AI-powered instructional systems are now capable of delivering immediate, tailored feedback, adjusting content difficulty and presentation style, and supporting flexible pacing—enhancing both instructional quality and student engagement (Guan et al., 2020; Wang et al., 2024).

Moreover, current research emphasizes the role of AI-enabled learner modeling and predictive analytics in proactively identifying at-risk students and designing targeted interventions, thus promoting greater equity and inclusion (Dai et al., 2020). While enthusiasm for AI-driven personalization is high, scholars also underscore the importance of integrating these technologies thoughtfully alongside teacher expertise, to avoid over-individualization and to ensure that adaptive systems support, rather than replace, meaningful social and collaborative learning experiences (Bernacki et al., 2021).

Taken together, these advancements signal a clear pedagogical shift: AI is most powerful not as a substitute for the educator, but as a complementary partner—one that enables UDL, supports differentiated and accessible content delivery, and empowers every learner to achieve meaningful progress within diverse educational contexts (Halkiopoulos & Gkintoni, 2024). Building on this theoretical foundation, the following example illustrates how educators can leverage structured AI prompts and adaptive technologies to operationalize personalized learning and differentiated instruction in authentic classroom contexts.

Worked Example: Synthesizing and Adapting Text for Diverse Learners with an AI Source Analysis Tool

This example demonstrates how an educator can use a source synthesis tool, such as NotebookLM or Perplexity, to transform a complex academic text into differentiated learning materials for students of varying proficiency levels.

Table 7. Prompt

You are an expert educator skilled in adapting scholarly texts for diverse student audiences. I am preparing a lesson on the causes of climate change, and I have uploaded a scientific article ("Anthropogenic Influences on Climate: A Global Synthesis"). Please generate: 1. A 200-word summary of the article for students reading at a high school level. 2. A simplified version (100 words) for English language learners, using shorter sentences and simpler vocabulary. 3. Three discussion questions suitable for group work. Please label each section clearly.

Table 8. Sample Output

High School Summary (200 words): The article "Anthropogenic Influences on Climate: A Global Synthesis" explains how human activities such as burning fossil fuels, deforestation, and industrial production have contributed to global warming. The authors describe key evidence, including rising levels of carbon dioxide in the atmosphere and temperature records showing that the Earth is getting hotter. The article also explores how greenhouse gases trap heat, leading to changing weather patterns, melting ice, and rising sea levels. It highlights the responsibility of both developed and developing nations to take action, and concludes by discussing international efforts, like the Paris Agreement, to limit temperature increases and slow the effects of climate change. **Simplified Version (100 words):** People are changing the Earth's climate. Cars, factories, and cutting down trees add more carbon dioxide to the air. This makes the planet warmer. Scientists have measured these changes for many years. Because the Earth is warmer, the weather is different, ice is melting, and the sea is rising. All countries need to work together to fix this problem. There are big meetings, like the Paris Agreement, where leaders talk about how to keep the world safe. **Discussion Questions:** 1. What are the main ways humans have changed the Earth's climate, according to the article? 2. Why do scientists believe it is important for all countries to work together? 3. How might rising temperatures and sea levels affect your own community?

This worked example illustrates how a well-structured prompt, grounded in clear instructional goals and differentiation principles, enables a generative AI model to transform complex academic content into accessible, student-friendly learning materials. By specifying the role, task, context, and format, the prompt directs the AI to produce outputs that cater to varying proficiency levels and learning needs. The resulting materials support inclusive education by providing multiple representations of key concepts and opportunities for active engagement. For classroom use, these differentiated resources can facilitate collaborative reading, scaffold discussions, and ensure that all students, regardless of language ability or background knowledge, have meaningful entry points into complex scientific topics.

While providing differentiated content is a critical step, the true power of personalized learning is unlocked through a continuous cycle of understanding student progress and providing targeted guidance. This iterative feedback loop is the assessment domain, a process AI fundamentally reshapes by automating evaluation and amplifying feedback.

Assessment and Feedback: From Grading to Guidance

Assessment is the cornerstone of effective teaching, guiding student learning and pedagogical adjustments. Traditionally, the substantial time commitment and logistical demands of grading have often overshadowed assessment's primary purpose: to provide meaningful feedback for growth (Mollick & Mollick, 2023). AI is fundamentally reshaping this landscape, shifting the educator's role from a grader to a guide by automating evaluation processes and amplifying the quality and reach of feedback (Ouyang et al., 2023).

At its core, AI streamlines assessment by automating routine tasks, such as scoring multiple-choice questions and evaluating structured essays against rubrics (Messer et al., 2024). This efficiency frees educators from repetitive work, allowing them to reinvest time in higher-order pedagogical tasks like lesson design and direct student interaction (Cai et al., 2025). The emergence of LLMs has further enhanced this, enabling diverse question types and automated personalized feedback for open-ended responses, even boosting student confidence and engagement (Mustafa et al., 2024).

Beyond automation, AI's most transformative contribution is facilitating instantaneous, formative feedback. Decades of research affirm that timely, specific, and task-focused feedback is crucial for learning (Hattie & Timperley, 2007). AI-powered tools can deliver immediate, targeted comments—highlighting errors, clarifying misconceptions, or suggesting resources—when a student is engaged with the material (Shute & Rahimi, 2017). These systems can even leverage diverse data sources, including log data and physiological responses, to offer innovative and nuanced insights into student performance (Cai et al., 2025).

Furthermore, AI-driven assessment provides educators with powerful data-driven insights. AI can identify common misconceptions and visualize learning trends by analyzing student performance across multiple data points, allowing teachers to make evidence-based instructional adjustments (Guo et al., 2024). Within fields like STEM, AI systems perform academic performance assessment, learning status assessment, and instructional quality assessment, offering comprehensive views previously difficult to obtain (Ouyang et al., 2023). AI's predictive capabilities also enable proactive identification of at-risk students, supporting timely interventions and promoting equity (Dai et al., 2020; Pallathadka et al., 2022).

While AI offers immense potential, its integration is not without challenges, including concerns about algorithmic bias, the difficulty of evaluating creativity and nuanced critical thinking, and the vulnerability of systems to construct-irrelevant or adversarial responses, which require careful consideration (Ramesh & Sanampudi, 2022; Ouyang et al., 2023). Therefore, the most effective approach positions AI as a powerful assistant for structured evaluation, liberating the human educator to provide empathetic, holistic, and motivational guidance—a symbiotic relationship that enhances teacher efficiency, supports assessment practices, and contributes to professional development (Cai et al., 2025).

To illustrate how these principles translate into classroom practice, the following worked example demonstrates how an educator can use a structured AI prompt to automate the evaluation of student work against a rubric and generate instant, actionable feedback. This practical application shows how AI can handle the repetitive aspects of assessment, allowing teachers to focus their expertise on providing holistic guidance and support.

Worked Example: Providing Formative Feedback on a STEM Project Proposal

This example demonstrates how an AI can function as a "thought partner" or "coaching assistant" for a teacher. Instead of just grading a final product, the AI is prompted to evaluate a student's initial project idea, focusing on scientific merit and feasibility, and providing constructive feedback to guide the student toward a more robust experimental design.

Table 9. Prompt

You are an experienced high school science teacher and an expert in experimental design. I am reviewing a student's project proposal for our upcoming science fair. I need your help providing quick, formative feedback to guide the students in improving their projects before they begin. Please evaluate the following student proposal using the provided rubric. Then write an encouraging, constructive feedback message for the student that includes specific, actionable steps for improvement. **Students' Project Proposal:** "Project Title: The Urban Heat Island Effect in Our Neighborhood. Hypothesis: Darker, artificial surfaces will have higher temperatures than lighter or natural surfaces. Procedure: I will test three surface types: the asphalt of the school parking lot, the concrete sidewalk next to it, and the grass on the soccer field. Using an infrared thermometer, I plan to measure the temperature of each surface three times a day (9 AM, 3 PM, and 6 PM) for five consecutive school days. I will then calculate the average temperature for each surface type over the week to determine which is the hottest and if my hypothesis is correct." **Evaluation Rubric:** Hypothesis: Is it clear, specific, and testable? Variables: Are independent, dependent, and controlled variables clearly identified and managed? Methodology & Data Collection: Is the procedure detailed enough to be replicated? Does it account for potential confounding variables? Feasibility: Is the project practical to complete within the given timeframe and with typical school resources? **Your Task:** Provide a brief evaluation of the proposal against each point in the rubric. Write a feedback message to the student. The tone should be positive and coaching-oriented. List 3-4 straightforward, actionable suggestions for improvement.

Table 10. Sample Output

Evaluation of Student Proposal
Here is a brief assessment based on the provided rubric.
Hypothesis: Meets Expectations
The hypothesis is clear, directly testable, and establishes a logical relationship between the surface type/color and its temperature. It could be slightly more specific to the chosen surfaces, but it's a very strong start.
Variables: Needs Improvement
The independent variable (surface type) and dependent variable (surface temperature) are clearly implied. However, the proposal does not identify or plan for critical controlled variables. Factors like sun exposure, shade, and ambient weather conditions are not mentioned, and these could significantly skew the results.
Methodology & Data Collection: Needs Improvement
The procedure is a good outline but lacks the detail needed for true scientific replication and rigor. It doesn't specify how to choose the measurement spots to ensure a fair comparison (e.g., are they all in direct sun?). It also omits the crucial step of recording weather data alongside the temperature readings.
Feasibility: Exceeds Expectations
The project is highly feasible. It uses simple, accessible equipment (an infrared thermometer), common locations, and the proposed timeline of five days is perfectly manageable for a high school science fair project.

Feedback for the Student
Hello!
Thank you for submitting your project proposal. This is a fantastic and highly relevant topic! The Urban Heat Island Effect is a real-world phenomenon that impacts our daily lives, and I love that you've chosen to investigate it right here in our own neighborhood. Your hypothesis is clear, and you have a solid plan for collecting your core data. This is a great foundation for a successful science fair project.
I'm excited to help you take this from a good experiment to a great one. To make your conclusions as strong as possible, a scientist must think like a detective, looking for any other clues (or variables) that could affect the outcome. Let's refine your procedure to make sure the only major difference you're measuring is the surface type itself.
Here are a few suggestions to strengthen your experimental design before you begin.
Actionable Steps for Improvement

1. Strengthen Your Experimental Controls. To ensure you're conducting a fair test, we need to control for other factors that could change the temperature.
    - ○ Action: When you choose your three measurement spots (asphalt, concrete, grass), make sure they will have the exact same sun exposure at your measurement times. For example, choose spots in an open area away from tree or building shadows. You could even mark your precise measurement spots with a small piece of chalk to ensure you measure the identical location every time.
2. Add a Baseline Measurement. Your surface temperatures will change based on the weather of the day. A very sunny day will give different results than a cloudy one. Recording the weather helps explain these day-to-day variations.
    - ○ Action: At each measurement time, use a regular thermometer to record the ambient air temperature in the same general area (hold it in the shade for a more accurate reading). Also, make a quick note of the weather conditions: "Full Sun," "Partly Cloudy," "Light Breeze," etc. This adds a crucial layer of data to your analysis.
3. Refine Your Hypothesis for Precision. Your current hypothesis is good. You can make it even more scientific by tying it directly to the specific surfaces you've chosen to test.
    - ○ Action: Consider rephrasing your hypothesis to be more specific, like: "The dark asphalt of the parking lot will have a significantly higher average surface temperature at peak heating (3 PM) compared to the lighter-colored concrete sidewalk and the natural grass field." This makes it crystal clear what you expect to find.

You have an excellent project on your hands, and with a few tweaks to your procedure, you'll be collecting high-quality, convincing data. I'm really looking forward to seeing what you discover!

Keep up the great work,
Your Science Teacher

This example showcases the practical value of guiding AI with a clear instructional framework. By positioning AI as an expert peer in this case, an experienced science teacher, the prompt elevates its role from a simple tool to a genuine collaborator. It does not just "grade" the student's work; it interrogates the methodology, identifying the subtle flaws a seasoned educator would spot, such as the failure to account for weather conditions or the lack of precision in measurement protocols. The AI's ability to pinpoint these specific, critical details makes it a powerful asset in formative assessment.

This process fundamentally alters how a teacher can approach feedback. The AI handles much of the initial, diagnostic work—cross-referencing a submission against a rubric—which generates a consistent and thoughtful starting point for feedback. This capability is easily scaled; a teacher could quickly apply the same prompt to a single file containing an entire class's proposals to identify common misconceptions or class-wide patterns. This frees the educator to concentrate on the uniquely human aspects of teaching: fostering curiosity, engaging in motivational dialogue, and providing nuanced guidance based on the AI's analysis and their professional judgment. The result is a synergistic process that leverages the AI's speed in structured analysis and the educator's expertise in providing nuanced, contextual guidance.

By automating detailed feedback, educators improve instructional quality and reclaim valuable time. This newfound efficiency can be redirected from pedagogical tasks to the essential administrative duties that keep an educational institution running smoothly, a theme we will explore in the following section.

Administrative Efficiency: Reclaiming Time for Teaching

Beyond its direct pedagogical applications, AI is poised to revolutionize educational environments by streamlining the extensive administrative workload that consumes a significant portion of an educator's time. Teachers consistently report that non-instructional tasks—such as managing records, communicating with parents, generating reports, and organizing events—are a primary source of burnout and detract from their ability to focus on lesson planning and direct student interaction (Grissom et al., 2021). By automating these repetitive, time-intensive processes, AI can function as a powerful administrative assistant, liberating educators to reinvest their expertise where it matters most: with their students.

The scope of AI's administrative support is broad. It extends from generating routine communications and managing schedules to analyzing school-wide data for resource allocation and compliance reporting. For instance, AI-powered tools can draft personalized emails to parents about student progress, schedule parent-teacher conferences by cross-referencing multiple calendars, or even create detailed logistical plans for school events based on a few key parameters (Mollick & Mollick, 2023).

This automation saves countless hours and reduces the cognitive load of managing complex logistical details, enhancing overall professional well-being and job satisfaction (Cai et al., 2025).

Worked Example: Automating Parent Communication for a School Field Trip

This example demonstrates how an educator can use a single, comprehensive prompt to generate multiple, related administrative documents, ensuring consistency and saving significant time.

Table 11. Prompt

You are a friendly, efficient, highly organized school administrator responsible for ensuring clear parent communication. I am a 7th-grade science teacher planning a field trip and need you to generate two documents for me. Here is all the necessary information: ● **Event:** Field trip to the National Science and Technology Museum. ● **Purpose:** To supplement our unit on "Forces and Motion" with hands-on exhibits. ● **Date and Time:** Friday, October 24, from 9:00 AM to 2:00 PM. ● **Transportation:** School bus departs from the main entrance at 9:00 AM sharp. ● **Cost:** $15 per student (for museum entry and a special workshop). Payment is due by October 17. ● **Lunch:** Students must bring their own packed lunch. ● **Contact Person:** Mr. David Chen, Science Teacher. ● **Chaperones:** We are looking for three parent volunteers. **Your Task:** 1. **Document 1: Permission Slip.** Create a formal, one-page permission slip. It must include sections for student details, parental consent, emergency contact information, and a space for parents to indicate if they can volunteer as a chaperone. 2. **Document 2: Parent Email.** Write a friendly and informative email to be sent to all 7th-grade parents. The email should explain the trip's educational value, cover all the logistical details (date, time, cost, lunch), and include a call to action for both the permission slip and volunteer chaperones. Please label each document clearly.

Table 12. Sample Output

Document 1: Permission Slip
Central Middle School
7th Grade Field Trip Permission Slip
National Science and Technology Museum
Dear Parent/Guardian,
The 7th-grade science classes are planning a field trip to the National Science and Technology Museum to provide a hands-on learning experience that supplements our classroom unit on "Forces and Motion."

- Date: Friday, October 24
- Time: 9:00 AM – 2:00 PM
- Transportation: School bus, departing from the school's main entrance.
- Cost: $15.00 (covers museum admission and a special workshop).

Please complete all sections of this form and return it with payment to Mr. Chen by **Friday, October 17.**
Student Information
Student's Full Name: ____
Homeroom Teacher: ____
Parental Consent
I, the undersigned, give my permission for my child, named above, to participate in the field trip to the National Science and Technology Museum on Friday, October 24. I understand that transportation will be by school bus.
Parent/Guardian Signature: __________________________ Date: ____________
Emergency Contact Information
Parent/Guardian Name: ______________________________________
Primary Phone Number: _________________ Secondary Phone: ___________________
Please list any medical conditions, allergies, or necessary medications the school should be aware of:
____

Chaperone Volunteer
We are looking for 3 parent volunteers to help chaperone this trip. It's a wonderful opportunity to see our students engage with science. If you are interested, please check the box below.
Yes, I am available and would like to volunteer as a chaperone.
Parent/Guardian Name: __________________________
Best Contact Phone or Email: ________________________________

Document 2: Parent Email
Subject: 7th Grade Field Trip to the National Science and Technology Museum on Oct. 24
Dear 7th Grade Parents and Guardians,
I am excited to announce an upcoming educational field trip for our 7th-grade students to the National Science and Technology Museum! This trip is designed to be a fun and engaging supplement to our current science unit on "Forces and Motion," allowing students to interact with hands-on exhibits that bring these concepts to life.
Here are the key details for the trip:

- Destination: National Science and Technology Museum
- Date: Friday, October 24
- Time: 9:00 AM to 2:00 PM. The bus will depart from the main school entrance at 9:00 AM sharp and return by 2:00 PM.
- Cost: The cost is $15 per student, which covers museum admission and a special educational workshop.
- Lunch: All students will need to bring a packed lunch and a drink.

A permission slip has been sent home with your student. Please complete and return it, along with the $15 payment, no later than Friday, October 17.
We are also looking for 3 parent chaperones to join us! This is a fantastic way to experience the museum alongside the students. If you are interested in volunteering, please indicate your availability on the bottom portion of the permission slip.
We look forward to a wonderful day of learning and discovery. If you have any questions, please feel free to contact me.
Best regards,
Mr. David Chen
7th Grade Science Teacher
Central Middle School

This example highlights how AI excels at handling structured, multi-part administrative tasks. By providing all necessary information within a single, well-defined Context, the educator empowers the AI to act as a highly efficient assistant. The prompt uses a clear Role ("organized school administrator") and Task (generate two specific documents) to ensure the outputs are not only accurate but also adopt the appropriate tone for each context—one formal and one friendly.

The result is a significant reduction in the "invisible labor" of teaching. Instead of spending 30-45 minutes drafting, formatting, and proofreading these documents from scratch, the educator receives two high-quality drafts in seconds. They can then quickly review, make minor edits, and distribute the materials. This reclaimed time and mental energy can be reallocated directly to preparing engaging lessons and supporting students, demonstrating AI's potential to contribute to the sustainability of the teaching profession. However, harnessing this profound potential responsibly demands a clear-eyed assessment of the significant ethical considerations and practical challenges.

ETHICAL ISSUES AND FUTURE CHALLENGES OF ARTIFICIAL INTELLIGENCE IN EDUCATION

The integration of AI into education must be counterbalanced by a rigorous examination of its ethical dimensions. This is not a speculative concern but a matter of global consensus. A landmark meta-analysis by Corrêa et al. (2023), which synthesized 200 distinct sets of AI guidelines from public and private bodies worldwide, identified an apparent convergence around a core set of principles. These principles, also reflected in frameworks from international bodies like UNESCO, form the foundation of trustworthy AI (UNESCO, 2023).

For educators, these are not abstract ideals but essential criteria for professional practice. They provide a lens through which to evaluate AI tools and strategies before they are deployed in the classroom. This section unpacks five of these fundamental principles, reframing them as a guide for educators to navigate the complexities of AI, mitigate risks, and uphold their professional responsibilities.

Fairness and the Mitigation of Algorithmic Bias

A primary ethical challenge stems from AI models trained on data reflecting existing societal structures, often including systemic biases (Baker & Hawn, 2022). An AI system does not inherently understand fairness; it identifies and reproduces patterns. If training data correlates specific demographic or socioeconomic characteristics with lower historical academic outcomes, the AI may systematically encode and amplify these biases, potentially widening existing inequalities (Roshanaei et al., 2023). This can result in a technologically reinforced cycle of disadvantage, where the tool recommends less challenging pathways or flags certain students for intervention based on proxy indicators rather than individual potential.

Guiding Principles for Professional Practice:

- Critically vet AI tools: Before adopting a new tool, inquire about the measures developers have taken to mitigate bias in their algorithms and training data.
- Uphold professional judgment: If an AI's recommendation for a student is inconsistent with your professional assessment of that student's abilities and needs, your expertise should take precedence.
- Monitor for disparate impact: Be vigilant for any emerging patterns where an AI tool appears to consistently favor or disadvantage a particular group of students within your classroom or school, for instance, if a career exploration tool systematically recommends engineering and coding pathways more frequently to male students and humanities or care-based professions to female students, based on historical enrollment data.

Privacy and Data Protection

The efficacy of personalized AI relies on collecting and analyzing extensive student data. This practice raises critical ethical concerns regarding data privacy, security, and the potential for surveillance, which demand careful investigation (Kotsis, 2025; U.S. Department of Education, 2023). AI-powered tools often collect vast amounts of sensitive student information, and without robust safeguards, this data is vulnerable to "breaches, misuse, or unethical surveillance. Even at the national policy level, it is explicitly recognized that educational AI systems must be designed with a strong emphasis on data privacy and security and the prevention of algorithmic biases (MEB, 2025). The line between monitoring for pedagogical purposes and intrusive tracking can be thin, creating a sense of constant surveillance that can undermine the trust and psychological safety essential for a healthy learning environment.

Guiding Principles for Professional Practice:

- Demand data transparency: Institutions should require vendors to provide clear policies detailing what student data is collected, its intended purpose, storage location, and duration, and who has access to it.
- Adhere to the principle of data minimization: Only data that is strictly necessary for the stated educational objective should be collected. For example,

when you upload a scientific article to brainstorm research questions, the AI has no business asking to scan your entire cloud drive to "discover related files."

- Ensure informed consent: Ensure that consent processes for students and parents are transparent and easy to understand, and explicitly state how data will be used.

Transparency and Explainability

Many sophisticated AI models function as "black boxes," where their internal decision-making processes are opaque to the end-user. This lack of transparency makes it difficult for an educator to understand or trust an AI's output. Without insight into why a particular grade was assigned or a specific resource was recommended, the AI remains an unreliable partner. This challenge has fueled a growing demand for "Explainable AI" (XAI) in education—systems designed to provide clear rationales for their outputs, thereby fostering teacher trust and enabling more effective pedagogical integration (Khosravi et al., 2022). The increasing number of academic studies on XAI in educational contexts further underscores the urgency and importance of this issue (Türkmen, 2024).

Guiding Principles for Professional Practice:

- Advocate for XAI: Prefer tools that can provide a rationale for their outputs, allowing educators to understand the basis of a recommendation.
- Leverage AI as a catalyst for inquiry: Use AI-generated feedback not as a final verdict, but as a starting point for discussion with students, fostering critical thinking about the tool's suggestions.

Reliability and Information Security

Generative AI models are not infallible. They produce nonsensical or factually incorrect content, a phenomenon often called "hallucinations" (Athaluri et al., 2023). This poses a significant pedagogical risk, as presenting unverified AI-generated content as factual can reinforce student misconceptions and compromise academic integrity (Zawacki-Richter et al., 2019). This unreliability extends beyond simple factual errors, including the fabrication of non-existent sources and citations, making traditional verification methods insufficient (Alkaissi & McFarlane, 2023).

Guiding Principles for Professional Practice:

- Implement a verification protocol: Treat all AI-generated content, from lesson plans to assessment questions, as a preliminary draft that requires rigorous verification against reliable sources. For instance, when an LLM generates a literature review for a student's robotics project, the protocol is to check the facts and verify that the cited sources exist before accepting the summary as valid.

- Promote critical digital literacy: Model and teach students how to critically evaluate and cross-reference information generated by AI, treating it as a core competency for digital citizenship.

Accountability and Human Oversight

The distributed and complex nature of AI development and deployment often leads to a diffusion of responsibility, complicating the assignment of accountability when errors or biased outcomes arise (Rahwan et al., 2019). This challenge is particularly acute in educational contexts, where multiple stakeholders, including AI developers, educational institutions, and individual educators—interact with these systems, blurring the lines of who is ultimately answerable (Floridi et al., 2018).

Guiding Principles for Professional Practice:

- Establish clear lines of responsibility: While AI can provide invaluable support, it must not supplant the educator's professional accountability. The ultimate responsibility for instructional quality and student well-being remains firmly with the human educator (Broussard, 2018). This principle requires a clear understanding that AI can augment, not replace, the educator's expertise and ethical judgment.
- Preserve meaningful human control: The most ethical implementations of AI augment, rather than replace, professional judgment. Educators must retain the authority to override, modify, or disregard AI-generated suggestions, ensuring that pedagogy is driven by human expertise and values. For instance, if an AI plagiarism detector flags an essay for academic misconduct, the teacher must have the final say to determine if the issue is a genuine attempt to cheat or a student's struggle with proper citation skills.

By integrating these five principles into their professional practice, educators can transition from being passive recipients of technology to active, critical agents empowered to harness the benefits of AI. However, ethical practice extends beyond individual diligence to encompass systemic commitments. Safeguarding the core tenets of the profession requires advocating for equitable access to AI tools, ensuring that digital divides related to socioeconomic status, disability, or geography do not create new forms of exclusion (UNESCO, 2023; Holmes et al., 2022). Furthermore, this transition hinges on institutional investment in teacher capacity and AI literacy.

Professional development grounded in technical skill and ethical reflection is essential for transforming abstract guidelines into meaningful classroom practice (Sperling et al., 2024; Zawacki-Richter et al., 2019). Ultimately, responsible AI integration is a shared responsibility, where informed and empowered educators work within supportive systems to ensure technology serves humanistic educational goals.

CONCLUSION

This chapter provided a comprehensive framework for understanding and integrating AI into educational practice. By first demystifying AI's core mechanisms and outlining the foundational principles of practical prompt engineering, the discussion then transitioned to exploring the diverse applications of AI across key pedagogical domains: content creation, personalized learning, assessment, and administrative efficiency. Throughout this exploration, the central theme has been the evolving role of the educator—not as one replaced by technology, but as a professional whose expertise is augmented and whose practice is transformed by AI.

The practical applications detailed within this chapter illustrate how AI can serve as a powerful assistant, capable of drafting preliminary lesson plans, generating differentiated content for diverse learners, providing instantaneous formative feedback, and streamlining routine administrative tasks. This capacity to automate time-consuming processes aims to free educators' most valuable resources: their time and cognitive energy. The intention behind such integration is to allow educators to redirect their focus towards their profession's uniquely human, high-impact aspects, such as cultivating relationships, fostering critical thinking, and delivering nuanced, empathetic guidance—facets technology can support but not replicate.

However, AI's practical and responsible integration is contingent upon a clear understanding and adherence to core ethical principles. This chapter dedicated significant attention to fairness, data privacy, transparency, reliability, and accountability issues. It emphasized that without vigilant attention to these dimensions, the promising benefits of AI could inadvertently lead to unintended consequences, including the perpetuation of biases, the erosion of trust, and the compromise of academic integrity. The "Guiding Principles for Professional Practice" outlined for each ethical consideration are thus not merely recommendations but essential safeguards to ensure that AI is a tool for genuine educational progress and equity.

Ultimately, the future trajectory of AI in education is not solely determined by technological advancements but by the informed choices and ethical considerations of its human practitioners. The landscape of AI will continue to evolve, presenting new opportunities and challenges. Therefore, the ongoing cultivation of AI literacy—a blend of pedagogical expertise, technological fluency, and a strong ethical compass—is paramount for educators. This continuous learning process ensures that AI is leveraged not as an end, but as a powerful means to enhance the human capacity for teaching and deepen the student's capacity for learning, thereby contributing to a more effective, equitable, and sustainable educational ecosystem.

REFERENCES

Adair, A. (2023). Teaching and learning with AI: How artificial intelligence is transforming the future of education. *XRDS Crossroads the ACM Magazine for Students*, *29*(3), 7–9. DOI: 10.1145/3589252

Alemanno, A., Carmone, M., & Priore, L. (2025). Prompting for healthcare professionals: Enhancing clinical Decision-Making with artificial intelligence. *Infermieristica Journal*, *4*(1), 33–39. DOI: 10.36253/if-3198

Alkaissi, H., & McFarlane, S. I. (2023). Artificial hallucinations in ChatGPT: Implications in scientific writing. *Cureus*. Advance online publication. DOI: 10.7759/cureus.35179 PMID: 36811129

Alpizar-Chacon, I., & Keuning, H. (2025). Students' use of generative AI as a support tool in an advanced web development course. In *Proceedings of the 30th ACM Conference on Innovation and Technology in Computer Science Education,* Vol. 1 (pp. 312-318).

Anand, A., Gupta, A., Yadav, N., & Bajaj, S. (2024). A comprehensive survey of AI-driven advancements and techniques in automated program repair and code generation. *arXiv (Cornell University)*. https://doi.org//arxiv.2411.07586DOI: 10.48550

Arendes, K., Kerkhoff, S., & Adhikari, B. (2024). Engaging Students to Learn Coding in the AI Era with Emphasis on the Process. *Edukasiana Jurnal Inovasi Pendidikan*, *3*(2), 257–268. DOI: 10.56916/ejip.v3i2.728

Athaluri, S. A., Manthena, S. V., Kesapragada, V. S. R. K. M., Yarlagadda, V., Dave, T., & Duddumpudi, R. T. S. (2023). Exploring the boundaries of Reality: Investigating the phenomenon of artificial intelligence hallucination in scientific writing through ChatGPT references. *Cureus*. Advance online publication. DOI: 10.7759/cureus.37432 PMID: 37182055

Baïdoo-Anu, D., & Ansah, L. O. (2023). Education in the era of generative artificial intelligence (AI): Understanding the potential benefits of ChatGPT in promoting teaching and learning. *Journal of AI*, *7*(1), 52–62. DOI: 10.61969/jai.1337500

Baker, R. S., & Hawn, A. (2022). Algorithmic bias in education. *International Journal of Artificial Intelligence in Education*, *32*(4), 1052–1092. DOI: 10.1007/s40593-021-00285-9

Benzakour, A., Altsitzioglou, P., Lemée, J. M., Ahmad, A., Mavrogenis, A. F., & Benzakour, T. (2023). Artificial intelligence in spine surgery. *International Orthopaedics*, *47*(2), 457–465. DOI: 10.1007/s00264-022-05517-8 PMID: 35902390

Beri, G., & Srivastava, V. (2025). *Advanced techniques in prompt engineering for large language models: A comprehensive study*. IEEE., DOI: 10.1109/ict-big64922.2024.10911672

Bernacki, M. L., Greene, M. J., & Lobczowski, N. G. (2021). A Systematic review of research on personalized learning: Personalized by whom, to what, how, and for what purpose(s)? *Educational Psychology Review*, *33*(4), 1675–1715. DOI: 10.1007/s10648-021-09615-8

Broussard, M. (2018). *Artificial unintelligence: How computers misunderstand the world*. MIT Press.

Budach, L., Feuerpfeil, M., Ihde, N., Nathansen, A., Noack, N., Patzlaff, H., Harmouch, H., & Naumann, F. (2022). The effects of data quality on machine learning performance. *arXiv (Cornell University)*. https://doi.org//arxiv.2207.14529DOI: 10.48550

Cai, C., Zhu, G., & Ma, M. (2025). A systematic review of AI for interdisciplinary learning: Application contexts, roles, and influences. *Education and Information Technologies*. Advance online publication. DOI: 10.1007/s10639-024-13193-x

Corrêa, N. K., Galvão, C., Santos, J. W., Del Pino, C., Pinto, E. P., Barbosa, C., Massmann, D., Mambrini, R., Galvão, L., Terem, E., & De Oliveira, N. (2023). Worldwide AI ethics: A review of 200 guidelines and recommendations for AI governance. *Patterns (New York, N.Y.)*, *4*(10), 100857. DOI: 10.1016/j.patter.2023.100857 PMID: 37876898

Crompton, H., & Burke, D. (2023). Artificial intelligence in higher education: The state of the field. *International Journal of Educational Technology in Higher Education*, *20*(1). Advance online publication. DOI: 10.1186/s41239-023-00392-8

Cukurova, M. (2025). The interplay of learning, analytics, and artificial intelligence in education: A vision for hybrid intelligence. *British Journal of Educational Technology*. Advance online publication. DOI: 10.1111/bjet.13514

Da Silva, C. A. G., Ramos, F. N., De Moraes, R. V., & Santos, E. L. D. (2024). ChatGPT: Challenges and benefits in software programming for higher education. *Sustainability*, *16*(3), 1245. DOI: 10.3390/su16031245

Dai, Y., Chai, C., Lin, P., Jong, M. S., Guo, Y., & Qin, J. (2020). Promoting students' well-being by developing their readiness for the Artificial Intelligence age. *Sustainability*, *12*(16), 6597. DOI: 10.3390/su12166597

Eager, B., & Brunton, R. (2023). Prompting higher education towards AI-augmented teaching and learning practice. *Journal of University Teaching & Learning Practice*, *20*(5). Advance online publication. DOI: 10.53761/1.20.5.02

Ekin, S. (2023). *Prompt Engineering for ChatGPT: A quick guide to techniques, tips, and best practices. TechRxiv*. https://doi.org/DOI: 10.36227/techrxiv.22683919

European Commission. (2024). *Artificial Intelligence Act*. https://data.europa.eu/eli/reg/2024/1689/oj

Floridi, L., Cowls, J., Beltrametti, M., Chatila, R., Chazerand, P., Dignum, V., Luetge, C., Madelin, R., Pagallo, U., Rossi, F., Schafer, B., Valcke, P., & Vayena, E. (2018). AI4People—An Ethical Framework for a Good AI Society: Opportunities, risks, principles, and recommendations. *Minds and Machines*, *28*(4), 689–707. DOI: 10.1007/s11023-018-9482-5 PMID: 30930541

Goodfellow, I., Bengio, Y., & Courville, A. (2016). *Deep learning*. MIT Press.

Google. (2024). *Generative AI for Educators*. Grow With Google. Retrieved June 20, 2025, from https://grow.google/ai-for-educators/

Grissom, J. A., Egalite, A. J., & Lindsay, C. A. (2021). *How principals affect students and schools: A systematic synthesis of two decades of research*. The Wallace Foundation. Retrieved June 23, 2025, from http://www.wallacefoundation.org/principalsynthesis

Guan, C., Mou, J., & Jiang, Z. (2020). Artificial intelligence innovation in education: A twenty-year data-driven historical analysis. *International Journal of Innovation Studies*, *4*(4), 134–147. DOI: 10.1016/j.ijis.2020.09.001

Guo, H., Johnson, M., Saldivia, L., Worthington, M., & Ercikan, K. (2024). Human-centered AI for discovering student engagement profiles on large-scale educational assessments. *Egitimde ve Psikolojide Ölçme ve Degerlendirme Dergisi*. Advance online publication. DOI: 10.21031/epod.1532846

Halkiopoulos, C., & Gkintoni, E. (2024). Leveraging AI in e-learning: Personalized learning and adaptive assessment through cognitive neuropsychology—A systematic analysis. *Electronics (Basel)*, *13*(18), 3762. DOI: 10.3390/electronics13183762

Hardaker, G., & Glenn, L. E. (2025). Artificial intelligence for personalized learning: A systematic literature review. *International Journal of Information and Learning Technology*. https://doi.org/DOI: 10.1108/ijilt-07-2024-0160

Hattie, J., & Timperley, H. (2007). The power of feedback. *Review of Educational Research*, *77*(1), 81–112. DOI: 10.3102/003465430298487

Haug, C. J., & Drazen, J. M. (2023). Artificial intelligence and machine learning in clinical medicine. *The New England Journal of Medicine*, *388*(13), 1201–1208. DOI: 10.1056/nejmra2302038 PMID: 36988595

High-Level Expert Group on Artificial Intelligence [HLEG]. (2019). *A definition of Artificial Intelligence: Main capabilities and scientific disciplines*. European Commission. Retrieved June 19, 2025, from https://digital-strategy.ec.europa.eu/en/library/definition-artificial-intelligence-main-capabilities-and-scientific-disciplines

Holmes, W., Bialik, M., & Fadel, C. (2019). *Artificial intelligence in Education: Promises and implications for teaching & learning*. The Center for Curriculum Redesign.

Hong, Y., Nguyen, A., Dang, B., & Nguyen, B.-P. T. (2022). Data ethics framework for artificial intelligence in education (AIED). In the *2022 International Conference on Advanced Learning Technologies (ICALT)* (pp. 297–301). IEEE. https://doi.org/ DOI: 10.1109/ICALT55010.2022.00095

Hossain, S. B., Jiang, N., Zhou, Q., Li, X., Chiang, W., Lyu, Y., Nguyen, H., & Tripp, O. (2024). A deep dive into large language models for automated bug localization and repair. In *Proceedings of the ACM on Software Engineering*. (Vol. 1, Issue FSE, pp. 1471–1493). Association for Computing Machinery. https://doi.org/ DOI: 10.1145/3660773

Inagaki, K., Bradshaw, T., Murgia, M., & Garrahan, M. (2023, September 28). OpenAI and Jony Ive in talks to raise "bn from SoftBank for AI device venture. *Financial Times*. https://www.ft.com/content/4c64ffc1-f57b-4e22-a4a5-f9f90a7419b7

Ji, Z., Lee, N., Frieske, R., Yu, T., Su, D., Xu, Y., Ishii, E., Bang, Y. J., Madotto, A., & Fung, P. (2022). Survey of hallucination in natural language generation. *ACM Computing Surveys*, *55*(12), 1–38. DOI: 10.1145/3571730

Jordan, M. I., & Mitchell, T. M. (2015). Machine learning: Trends, perspectives, and prospects. *Science*, *349*(6245), 255–260. DOI: 10.1126/science.aaa8415 PMID: 26185243

Junaid, M., Arslan, S., Lee, T., & Kim, H. (2022). Optimal architecture of Floating-Point arithmetic for neural network training processors. *Sensors (Basel)*, *22*(3), 1230. DOI: 10.3390/s22031230 PMID: 35161975

Jurafsky, D., & Martin, J. H. (2024). *Speech and language processing*. Retrieved 19 June 2025, from https://web.stanford.edu/~jurafsky/slp3/

Kaplan, A., & Haenlein, M. (2018). Siri, Siri, in my hand: Who is the fairest in the land? On the interpretations, illustrations, and implications of artificial intelligence. *Business Horizons*, *62*(1), 15–25. DOI: 10.1016/j.bushor.2018.08.004

Kasneci, E., Sessler, K., Küchemann, S., Bannert, M., Dementieva, D., Fischer, F., Gasser, U., Groh, G., Günnemann, S., Hüllermeier, E., Krusche, S., Kutyniok, G., Michaeli, T., Nerdel, C., Pfeffer, J., Poquet, O., Sailer, M., Schmidt, A., Seidel, T., & Kasneci, G. (2023). ChatGPT for good? On opportunities and challenges of large language models for education. *Learning and Individual Differences*, *103*, 102274. DOI: 10.1016/j.lindif.2023.102274

Khosravi, H., Shum, S. B., Chen, G., Conati, C., Tsai, Y., Kay, J., Knight, S., Martinez-Maldonado, R., Sadiq, S., & Gašević, D. (2022). Explainable Artificial Intelligence in education. *Computers and Education Artificial Intelligence*, *3*, 100074. DOI: 10.1016/j.caeai.2022.100074

Kotsis, K. T. (2025). Issues between artificial intelligence and personal data in education. *International Review of Education*, *13*(1), 45. DOI: 10.5296/ire.v13i1.22850

Kretzschmar, V., Sailer, A., Wertenauer, M., & Seitz, J. (2024). Enhanced educational experiences through personalized and AI-based learning. *International Journal on Studies in Education*, *6*(2), 191–209. DOI: 10.46328/ijonse.206

Liu, P., Yuan, W., Fu, J., Jiang, Z., Hayashi, H., & Neubig, G. (2022). Pre-train, prompt, and predict: A systematic survey of prompting methods in natural language processing. *ACM Computing Surveys*, *55*(9), 1–35. DOI: 10.1145/3560815

Lo, L. S. (2023). The art and science of prompt engineering: A new literacy in the information age. *Internet Reference Services Quarterly*, *27*(4), 203–210. DOI: 10.1080/10875301.2023.2227621

Luckin, R., Holmes, W., Griffiths, M., & Forcier, L. B. (2016). *Intelligence unleashed: An argument for AI in education*. Pearson.

Machado, A., Tenório, K., Santos, M. M., Barros, A. P., Rodrigues, L., Mello, R. F., Paiva, R., & Dermeval, D. (2025). Workload perception in educational resource recommendation supported by artificial intelligence: A controlled experiment with teachers. *Smart Learning Environments*, *12*(1). Advance online publication. DOI: 10.1186/s40561-025-00373-6

Marcus, G., & Davis, E. (2019). *Rebooting AI: Building artificial intelligence we can trust*. Vintage.

Messer, M., Brown, N. C. C., Kölling, M., & Shi, M. (2024). Automated grading and feedback tools for programming education: A systematic review. *ACM Transactions on Computing Education, 24*(1), 1–43. DOI: 10.1145/3636515

Milli Eğitim Bakanlığı (MEB). (2025). *Eğitimde Yapay Zekâ Politika Belgesi ve Eylem Planı (2025-2029).* https://yegitek.meb.gov.tr/meb_iys_dosyalar/2025_06/17092340_egitimdeyapayzekapolitikabelgesiveeylemplani202520291.pdf

Mohammed, M., Khan, M. B., & Bashier, E. B. M. (2016). Machine learning: Algorithms and applications. In *CRC Press eBooks* (1st ed.). CRC Press., DOI: 10.1201/9781315371658

Mollick, E., & Mollick, L. (2024). Instructors as Innovators: A future-focused approach to new AI learning opportunities, with prompts. *arXiv (Cornell University).* https://doi.org//arxiv.2407.05181DOI: 10.48550

Mollick, E. R., & Mollick, L. (2023). Using AI to implement effective classroom teaching strategies: Five strategies, including prompts. SSRN *Electronic Journal.* https://doi.org/DOI: 10.2139/ssrn.4391243

Mustafa, M. Y., Tlili, A., Lampropoulos, G., Huang, R., Jandrić, P., Zhao, J., Salha, S., Xu, L., Panda, S., Kinshuk, N., López-Pernas, S., & Saqr, M. (2024). A systematic review of literature reviews on artificial intelligence in education (AIED): A roadmap to a future research agenda. *Smart Learning Environments, 11*(1). Advance online publication. DOI: 10.1186/s40561-024-00350-5

Ng, D. T. K., Leung, J. K. L., Chu, S. K. W., & Qiao, M. S. (2021). Conceptualizing AI literacy: An exploratory review. *Computers and Education Artificial Intelligence, 2*, 100041. DOI: 10.1016/j.caeai.2021.100041

OECD. (2025). *Empowering learners for the age of AI: An AI literacy framework for primary and secondary education (Review draft).* https://ailiteracyframework.org/

Oppenlaender, J., Linder, R., & Silvennoinen, J. (2024). Prompting AI Art: An investigation into the creative skill of prompt engineering. *International Journal of Human-Computer Interaction, •••*, 1–23. DOI: 10.1080/10447318.2024.2431761

Organization for Economic Co-operation and Development. (2023). OECD Digital Education Outlook 2023. In *the Digital Education Outlook.* https://doi.org/DOI: 10.1787/c74f03de-en

Ouyang, F., Dinh, T. A., & Xu, W. (2023). A systematic review of AI-driven educational assessment in STEM education. *Journal for STEM Education Research, 6*(3), 408–426. DOI: 10.1007/s41979-023-00112-x

Ouyang, F., Zheng, L., & Jiao, P. (2022). Artificial intelligence in online higher education: A systematic review of empirical research from 2011 to 2020. *Education and Information Technologies*, *27*(6), 7893–7925. DOI: 10.1007/s10639-022-10925-9

Pallathadka, H., Sonia, B., Sanchez, D. T., De Vera, J. V., Godinez, J. A. T., & Pepito, M. T. (2022). Investigating the impact of artificial intelligence in the *education sector by predicting student performance. Materials Today: Proceedings*, *51*, 2264–2267. DOI: 10.1016/j.matpr.2021.11.395

Pane, J. F., Steiner, E. D., Baird, M. D., Hamilton, L. S., & Pane, J. D. (2017). *Informing progress: Insights on personalized learning implementation and effects*. The RAND Corporation. Retrieved June 23, 2025, from https://www.rand.org/content/dam/rand/pubs/research_reports/RR2000/RR2042/RAND_RR2042.pdf

Park, J., & Choo, S. (2024). Generative AI prompt engineering for educators: Practical strategies. *Journal of Special Education Technology*. Advance online publication. DOI: 10.1177/01626434241298954

Rahwan, I., Cebrian, M., Obradovich, N., Bongard, J., Bonnefon, J., Breazeal, C., Crandall, J. W., Christakis, N. A., Couzin, I. D., Jackson, M. O., Jennings, N. R., Kamar, E., Kloumann, I. M., Larochelle, H., Lazer, D., McElreath, R., Mislove, A., Parkes, D. C., & Pentland, A. '., . . . Wellman, M. (2019). Machine behavior. *Nature*, *568*(7753), 477–486. DOI: 10.1038/s41586-019-1138-y PMID: 31019318

Ramesh, D., & Sanampudi, S. K. (2022). An automated essay scoring system: A systematic literature review. *Artificial Intelligence Review*, *55*(3), 2495–2527. DOI: 10.1007/s10462-021-10068-2 PMID: 34584325

Rasheed, Z., Sami, M. A., Waseem, M., Kemell, K., Wang, X., Nguyen, A., Systä, K., & Abrahamsson, P. (2024, April 29). *AI-powered code review with LLMs: Early results*. arXiv (Cornell University). https://doi.org//arxiv.2404.18496DOI: 10.48550

Roshanaei, M., Olivares, H., & Lopez, R. R. (2023). Harnessing AI to foster equity in education: Opportunities, challenges, and emerging strategies. *Journal of Intelligent Learning Systems and Applications*, *15*(04), 123–143. DOI: 10.4236/jilsa.2023.154009

Russell, S., & Norvig, P. (2021). *Artificial Intelligence: A Modern Approach* (4th ed.). Pearson.

Saborío-Taylor, S., & Rojas-Ramírez, F. (2024). Universal design for learning and artificial intelligence in the digital era: Fostering inclusion and autonomous learning. *International Journal of Professional Development Learners and Learning*, *6*(2), ep2408. Advance online publication. DOI: 10.30935/ijpdll/14694

Sarker, I. H. (2021). Machine learning: Algorithms, Real-world applications, and research directions. *SN Computer Science*, *2*(3). Advance online publication. DOI: 10.1007/s42979-021-00592-x PMID: 33778771

Sen, P. C., Hajra, M., & Ghosh, M. (2020). Supervised classification algorithms in machine learning: A survey and review. In *Emerging technology in modeling and graphics* (pp. 99–111). Springer.

Sergeyuk, A., Golubev, Y., Bryksin, T., & Ahmed, I. (2024). Using AI-based coding assistants in practice: State of affairs, perceptions, and ways forward. *Information and Software Technology*, *178*, 107610. DOI: 10.1016/j.infsof.2024.107610

Shute, V., & Rahimi, S. (2017). Review of computer-based assessment for learning in elementary and secondary education. *Journal of Computer Assisted Learning*, *33*(1), 1–19. DOI: 10.1111/jcal.12172

Silver, D., Huang, A., Maddison, C. J., Guez, A., Sifre, L., Van Den Driessche, G., Schrittwieser, J., Antonoglou, I., Panneershelvam, V., Lanctot, M., Dieleman, S., Grewe, D., Nham, J., Kalchbrenner, N., Sutskever, I., Lillicrap, T., Leach, M., Kavukcuoglu, K., Graepel, T., & Hassabis, D. (2016). Mastering the game of Go with deep neural networks and tree search. *Nature*, *529*(7587), 484–489. DOI: 10.1038/nature16961 PMID: 26819042

Sourati, J., & Evans, J. A. (2023). Accelerating science with human-aware artificial intelligence. *Nature Human Behaviour*, *7*(10), 1682–1696. DOI: 10.1038/s41562-023-01648-z PMID: 37443269

Sperling, K., Stenberg, C., McGrath, C., Åkerfeldt, A., Heintz, F., & Stenliden, L. (2024). In search of artificial intelligence (AI) literacy in teacher education: A scoping review. *Computers and Education Open*, *6*, 100169. DOI: 10.1016/j.caeo.2024.100169

Türkmen, G. (2024). The review of studies on Explainable Artificial Intelligence in educational research. *Journal of Educational Computing Research*. Advance online publication. DOI: 10.1177/07356331241310915

UNESCO. (2023). *UNESCO survey: Less than 10% of schools and universities have formal guidance on AI*. Retrieved June 16, 2025, from https://www.unesco.org/en/articles/unesco-survey-less-10-schools-and-universities-have-formal-guidance-ai

UNESCO World Commission on the Ethics of Scientific Knowledge and Technology (COMEST). (2019). Preliminary study on the ethics of artificial intelligence. United Nations Educational, Scientific, and Cultural Organization. https://unesdoc.unesco.org/ark:/48223/pf0000367823

U.S. Department of Education, Office of Educational Technology. (2023). *Artificial intelligence and the future of teaching and learning: Insights and recommendations*. U.S. Department of Education.

Velásquez-Henao, J. D., Franco-Cardona, C. J., & Cadavid-Higuita, L. (2023). Prompt Engineering: A methodology for optimizing interactions with AI-language models in engineering. *Dyna*, *90*(230), 9–17. DOI: 10.15446/dyna.v90n230.111700

Viswanathan, N. P. S. (2025). Prompt engineering for conversational AI systems: A systematic review of techniques and applications. *International Journal of Scientific Research in Computer Science Engineering and Information Technology*, *11*(1), 733–741. DOI: 10.32628/cseit25111276

Vodafone Foundation. (2024). *AI in European schools: A European report comparing seven countries*. Retrieved June 23, 2025, from https://skillsuploadjr.eu/docs/contents/AI_in_European_schools.pdf

Wang, H., Fu, T., Du, Y., Gao, W., Huang, K., Liu, Z., Chandak, P., Liu, S., Van Katwyk, P., Deac, A., Anandkumar, A., Bergen, K., Gomes, C. P., Ho, S., Kohli, P., Lasenby, J., Leskovec, J., Liu, T., Manrai, A., & Zitnik, M. (2023). Scientific discovery in the age of artificial intelligence. *Nature*, *620*(7972), 47–60. DOI: 10.1038/s41586-023-06221-2 PMID: 37532811

Wang, P. (2019). On defining artificial intelligence. *Journal of Artificial General Intelligence*, *10*(2), 1–37. DOI: 10.2478/jagi-2019-0002

Wang, X., Huang, R., Sommer, M., Pei, B., Shidfar, P., Rehman, M. S., Ritzhaupt, A. D., & Martin, F. (2024). The efficacy of artificial intelligence-enabled adaptive learning systems from 2010 to 2022 on learner outcomes: A meta-analysis. *Journal of Educational Computing Research*, *62*(6), 1568–1603. DOI: 10.1177/07356331241240459

White, J., Fu, Q., Hays, S., Sandborn, M., Olea, C., Gilbert, H., Elnashar, A., Spencer-Smith, J., & Schmidt, D. C. (2023). *A Prompt Pattern Catalog to Enhance Prompt Engineering with ChatGPT*. arXiv.org. https://arxiv.org/abs/2302.11382v1

Woodrow, J., Malik, A., & Piech, C. (2024). *AI teaches the art of elegant coding: Timely, fair, and helpful style feedback in a global course*. In *Proceedings of the 55th ACM Technical Symposium on Computer Science Education (SIGCSE 2024)*, Vol. 1 (pp. 1442–1448). Association for Computing Machinery. https://doi.org/DOI: 10.1145/3626252.3630773

Wu, P., Su, J., Hong, L., Ren, J., Chien, C., Chen, H., Ke, C., Hsiao, H., Li, S., Sheu, S., Lo, W., Chang, S., Lo, C., Liu, R., Hsieh, C., Tang, K., & Chang, M. (2023). A floating-point 6T SRAM in-Memory-Compute macro using Hybrid-Domain structure for advanced AI edge chips. *IEEE Journal of Solid-State Circuits*, *59*(1), 196–207. DOI: 10.1109/jssc.2023.3309966

Yilmaz, R., Yurdugül, H., Yilmaz, F. G. K., Şahin, M., Sulak, S., Aydin, F., Tepgeç, M., Müftüoğlu, C. T., & Oral, N. Ö. (2022). Smart MOOC integrated with intelligent tutoring: A system architecture and framework model proposal. *Computers and Education Artificial Intelligence*, *3*, 100092. DOI: 10.1016/j.caeai.2022.100092

Zawacki-Richter, O., Marín, V. I., Bond, M., & Gouverneur, F. (2019). Systematic review of research on artificial intelligence applications in higher education – where are the educators? *International Journal of Educational Technology in Higher Education*, *16*(1). Advance online publication. DOI: 10.1186/s41239-019-0171-0

Zhao, W. X., Zhou, K., Li, J., Tang, T., Wang, X., Hou, Y., Min, Y., Zhang, B., Zhang, J., Dong, Z., Du, Y., Yang, C., Chen, Y., Chen, Z., Jiang, J., Ren, R., Li, Y., Tang, X., Liu, Z., . . . Wen, J. (2023). A survey of large language models. *arXiv (Cornell University)*. https://doi.org//arxiv.2303.18223DOI: 10.48550

Zviel-Girshin, R. (2024). The good and bad of AI tools in novice programming education. *Education Sciences*, *14*(10), 1089. DOI: 10.3390/educsci14101089

Chapter 4
Artificial Intelligence in Education:
From Smart Systems to Inclusive Learning

Betül Tonbuloğlu
https://orcid.org/0000-0003-1542-2380
Yildiz Technical University, Distance Education Application and Research Center, Turkey

ABSTRACT

The use of AI in educational institutions is rapidly bringing changes in various aspects of learning, right from personalized learning tools, automated contents, enhanced testing methodologies, to specific help tools for physically disabled students. AI enhances classroom efficiency, accessibility, and learner focus by optimizing regular tasks, delivering real-time insights, and customizing resources to individual development. Moreover, it reduces teachers' chores by grading data and generating a lesson plan to quickly develop existing resources. However, apprehensions around student data security, latent biases in training datasets, and the ethical use of potent algorithms underscore the necessity for technology to be governed by explicit standards. This chapter juxtaposes a discussion of innovative applications with an examination of their limitations, providing educators, researchers, and school administrators with a pragmatic framework for leveraging AI.

INTRODUCTION: CONCEPTS, CURRENT TRENDS, AND SCOPE

Today's classrooms are being reshaped at breakneck speed by new technology, making lessons faster, more tailored, and easier to reach. Artificial Intelligence

DOI: 10.4018/979-8-3373-8857-1.ch004

(AI), which is defined as machines that are capable of independent thought and intelligent decision-making, is at the center of this change (Ginsberg, 2012). AI can be defined in different ways in the literature. AI can be described as a study that develops a technology that can accomplish things that would require intelligence if accomplished by humans (Minsky, 1969). Another widely accepted definition of AI is the skillful imitation of human behavior or cognition through tools or software programs (Kurzweil, 2005). Papert (1980) argued that AI offers the opportunity to study how humans learn by modeling learning processes.

Teachers and learners now enjoy tools that craft custom study paths, grade work automatically, whip up fresh materials, and track progress with little fuss. With each passing term, adding AI to schools feels less like an option and more like a must-have if the goal is richer learning, wider access, and smarter use of time and money. Research keeps showing how well AI can sift through test scores and forum posts and nudge students from just sitting and listening to wrestling with real problems, giving solid tech backup to the idea of learning that fits each person (Chang & Lu, 2019; Göçen & Aydemir, 2020; Zheng & Badarch, 2022). Systems built on this intel let kids move at their own speed, tweak lessons based on how they think, and, many times, boost grades along the way (Nguyen et al., 2024). The hope now is that, by putting AI front and center, schools will not only tailor instruction, spark imagination, and lighten teachers job lists, but also do it all at a scale never seen before (Haseski, 2019). Bayne (2015) suggests that the role of the teacher must be reimagined in light of AI developments, emphasizing the significance of virtual teaching robots. She argues that the use of automated teaching methods—such as AI instructors—within a productivity-centered approach can facilitate access to quality education for large populations. AI-powered virtual platforms promise to widen the availability of course work for students who need learning on their own schedule, letting learners from different backgrounds tap into high-quality resources (Erbaşı et al., 2023). Within smart teaching systems, such technology can act like a virtual tutor that adjusts its advice and tasks to match where each learner is in their studies (Kamalov et al., 2023).

Beyond flexible lessons and one-on-one guidance, AI has become a key helper in grading and feedback. It can generate quizzes and tests suited to each person, making classroom assessment as unique as the learning journey itself (Khademi, 2023). Automatic text-analysis tools are among the newest breakthroughs that reviewers say could reshape how teachers measure progress and give students useful, timely comments (Nair et al., 2024). Language classes, content design, and support for students with special needs also benefit from these techniques. For instance, AI can deliver words, phrases, and exercises in the learners own tongue, tailoring lessons for families with many language histories (Liu, 2023). By speeding up material creation, the same tools free teachers to spend more time on instruction and to share resource sets more broadly across schools (Bahroun et al., 2023). In special education contexts, AI tools promise more inclusive classrooms by helping teachers design lessons that fit each learner's individual needs.

Yet, along with these clear benefits, AI introduces serious worries that schools cannot afford to ignore. The applications of AI in education support and enhance learning processes from multiple perspectives, while also introducing certain limitations and risks. Concerns about student privacy, fairness, and hidden bias in recommendation algorithms still persist, and they demand careful management if the technology is to be trusted (Klímová et al., 2023). Recognizing this, the European Commission released a set of practical ethical guidelines in 2022 for primary and secondary teachers, as well as school leaders.

This book chapter aims to provide a comprehensive guide for teachers, academics, and education administrators by exploring various areas where AI can be applied in education. First, the chapter will address the historical evolution of aı in education and ıts conceptual milestones, discussing how the use of AI applications in education can be classified. Subsequently, it will address the fundamental areas of aı usage in education, such as personalized learning, intelligent teaching systems, automated assessment and testing, natural language processing applications, content creation tools, and aı in special education. Within this framework, various aı applications will be introduced, explaining their operating mechanisms and areas of effectiveness, along with their theoretical background and critical reflections. This will provide readers with a broad understanding of AI in education and practical insights into how these technologies can be integrated into teaching processes. Subsequently, teacher professional development and identity in the age of AI and long-term curriculum reforms will be discussed. Finally, the chapter will address the ethical dimensions of using AI in education and examine possible future developments.

HISTORICAL EVOLUTION OF AI IN EDUCATION AND ITS CONCEPTUAL MILESTONES

Historically, the development of AI in the educational environment has been driven by the convergence of technology development and pedagogic innovations. This can be followed by a number of key points that indicate a shift from theoretical constructs for AI to implementation that improves learning experiences and management activities associated with educational institutions.

AI's roots lie at the end of the 20th century, which was a period of increased scientific and AI technology development. This was a point where key AI pioneers such as Alan Turing and John McCarthy made seminal contributions to AI's development. Turing's imitation game, for instance, paved the way for machine imitation of human intellect and AI applications in learning institutions (Ahmad et al., 2024; Oleet and Yu, 2025). During this stage of AI's development, there was a focus on elementary computer technology and simple learning algorithms to a great extent. This representing the first theoretical studies on AI in educational settings.

In the 1980s and 1990s, a turning point was reached with the advent of intelligent tutoring systems (ITS), marking one of the biggest milestones in incorporating AI into the educational system. ITS enabled learning with customized methodologies due to algorithms that could react to learning preferences using AI (Chaudhary et al., 2024; Oleet and Yu, 2025). Conferences that centered on AI's influence on educational institutions started to take place at this stage to share scientific knowledge on AI technology's applications (Grandbastien et al., 2016). Early versions of computer-assisted learning programs for languages started to be introduced at this point to indicate AI's early applications in natural languages at that stage of technology advancement (Schulze, 2025).

Notably, there have been improvements since the turn of the 21st century, specifically with the advancement of machine learning and analytics. The development of adaptive learning systems and AI-assessment systems demonstrated the utilization of AI to optimize administrative efficiency and enable instant feedback to users, revolutionizing conventional educational systems (Begum, 2025; Hosseinkhani, 2025; Kumar et al., 2023). The Education 4.0 paradigm shift has been realized, resulting in a shift towards a data-informed educational paradigm that leverages AI for personalizing learning experiences and addressing the repertoire of educational problems, including educational access and inclusivity (Begum, 2025; Ramos and Wilson-Kennedy, 2024).

Recently, the development of new AI applications like Chat GPT has further leveraged AI technology for a more interactive learning environment and has been instrumental for developing high-level critical thinking capacities for users to assess educational problems. This demonstrates a more informed understanding of technology's impact on improving the learning environment by developing educational programs that incorporate moral perspectives and perspectives for user engagement (Babu and Suruthi, 2024; Isaacs et al., 2024). Further ahead, with innovative educational trends exploiting AI technology, specifically with the development of AI immersion technology and AI-powered educational tutors, a next-generation paradigm shift has been realized to be known as Ed Tech 5.0. This next-generation paradigm reflects a blend of AI with emotional quotient and collaborative educational learning technology to further personalize the learning environment (Dey and Sahoo, 2024; Rakshit, 2025). Historically reflecting the evolution of technology integration with AI into educational assistance programs underscores a continuous fit of educational programs to keep tapping into new AI technology innovations to not only transform existing educational programs but seek to optimize educational performance with moral perspectives for a fair learning environment.

CLASSIFICATION OF AI APPLICATIONS IN EDUCATION

Advancing AI technologies have brought significant transformations to the field of education, paving the way for the restructuring of instructional processes. Today, AI is perceived not merely as a technological tool but as a fundamental component in dynamically shaping teaching strategies, student assessment procedures, and learning environments. This transformation goes beyond improving academic performance; it has the potential to fundamentally reshape our entire perception of teaching and learning. For an understanding of the effects of AI on the economy, society, and education, it will be important to identify which jobs AI can perform by comparing it with human skills, which will then help policymakers design policies related to education according to the skills which will be in demand in the coming future (OECD, 2023).

The Application of AI in Education is tackled from various standpoints, with different studies describing the roles of AI in various aspects of learning or instructional functions in divergent classes. For an investigation of teachers' experiences using AI-supported tools in the classroom, Göçen & Aydemir (2020) identified four key functions of AI, including providing instructional aid, grading and feedback automation, encouraging student engagement, and personalized instructional design. Li & Wong (2023) identified intelligent tutoring systems as key personalization strategies in personalized learning studies, illustrating how large datasets or learning analytics can help focus intelligent tutoring systems on enhanced student outcomes. The role of AI in grading written pieces was explored by Ramesh & Sanampudi (2021), noting how natural language processing (NLP) enables the assessment of pieces according to matters of quality, organization, voice expression, and providing overall grades or written feedback on improvement. Liang & Lu (2025) narrowed their focus on generative AI, establishing how the technology enables teachers' rapid production of lesson plans, quizzes, presentations, or work sheets directly aligned with state standards, which can then be revised in real-time. Barua et al. (2022) identified another group of tools which can serve as an aid in classrooms helping students with neurodevelopmental disorders, suggesting that customized voice messages, interactive gaming interfaces, and moment-by-moment behavior tracking can increase learning autonomy. Ayeni et al. (2024) provided data on school-wide use of AI tools, connecting personalized learning with a broader application of overall educational technology. According to Holmes and Tuomi (2022), AI applications can be broadly categorized into three types that often overlap. The categories are:

- Student-centered AIED (intelligent tutoring systems; AI-powered applications (math learning; language learning); AI-powered simulations (virtual reality; augmented reality; game learning); automated essay writing; dialogue systems for tutoring; chatbots; AI-powered formative assessments)
- Teacher-centric AIED (detected plagiarism, intelligent learning material curation, class observation, automated summative assessment (autograder), AI teacher assistant, class orchestration)
- Institution-Oriented AIED (admissions (student selection), lesson planning, scheduling, timing, school security, identifying at-risk dropout students, electronic proctoring)

On the other hand, Luckin and Holmes's study (2016) highlighted the three core types of applications that can directly aid learning with regard to the application of AI technology.

1. Intelligent personal tutor for every learner (student/learner models, socratic learning, open learner models, application examples)
2. Intelligent support for collaborative learning (adaptive group formation, expert facilitation, intelligent virtual agents, intelligent moderation)
3. Smart Virtual Reality (user responsiveness, student support, virtual pedagogical agents)

An examination of these multifaceted approaches across the studies reveals that AI holds a versatile range of applications in education, from personalized learning experiences to advanced assessment techniques. Based on the contexts of use identified in the cited research, the primary areas of AI application in education can be delineated as follows:

1. Personalized learning and intelligent tutoring systems
2. Automated assessment systems
3. Natural language processing applications in education (NLP)
4. AI-supported educational content creation
5. AI in special education

In addition to these areas, AI is utilized in many other educational contexts. However, this chapter limits the discussion of AI applications in education to these key categories. The integration of these components holds the potential to redefine traditional educational methodologies and promote personalized learning experiences, thereby enhancing instructional effectiveness and increasing student engagement.

PERSONALIZED LEARNING AND INTELLIGENT TUTORING SYSTEMS

AI enhances personalized learning by tailoring educational experiences to each student, adjusting the content, resources, and pace so that nothing feels too fast or too slow for the learner. Adaptive learning platforms make lessons more engaging because they track progress in real time and shift teaching strategies on the fly, keeping the experience fresh and aligned with what the student has mastered (Begum, 2024; Ramesh, 2021). This fine-grained responsiveness is especially valuable in classrooms with mixed abilities, as it ensures that every learner, no matter how they process information, gets the guidance and challenge they need.

Intelligent tutoring systems carry this idea further by embedding AI into lesson delivery and steering teacher-student exchanges in a way that frees instructors to focus on higher-level support. These systems simulate human tutors by providing interactive and personalized support, offering real-time feedback and guidance, adjusting instruction based on student performance, and tracking engagement metrics and learning patterns to assist educators in refining their teaching methods (Ramesh, 2021). Innovative AI applications also provide data-driven insights regarding student performance and instructional effectiveness, supporting teachers' professional development (Kang et al., 2021).

Though both personalized learning and intelligent tutoring seek to match instruction to individuals, they sit on slightly different planes: the former leans on learner choice and flexible pathways, while the latter offers a structured, systematic guide that keeps students on task. Because these two models overlap, a hybrid system that marries them can draw on the strengths of each, potentially driving classroom outcomes higher than either approach alone. Table 1 lists examples of each category, giving a snapshot of the tools that schools can adopt today.

Table 1. Descriptions of Selected Intelligent Tutoring Systems and Personalized Learning AI Tools

Tool	Focus Area	Target Users	Key Features	Educational Benefit
Khanmigo	Personalized tutoring and writing support	K–12 students, teachers	GPT-4-based tutor; Socratic questioning; Writing Coach; teacher dashboards	Encourages inquiry, supports writing development, and assists teachers with planning
ASSISTments	Mathematics and formative assessment	Middle/high school students, teachers	Immediate feedback; hint system; progress dashboards	Strengthens conceptual understanding and supports data-driven instruction
Querium	Step-by-step problem solving in STEM	High school and college students	StepWise AI; adaptive problem sets; micro-analytic feedback	Promotes process-oriented learning and constructivist engagement
Squirrel AI	Adaptive learning and mastery tracking	Secondary students	Diagnostic testing; knowledge mapping; adaptive content sequencing	Provides individualized pacing and helps close achievement gaps

An example for these tools is that of Khanmigo (Figure 1), an AI teaching assistant built on the foundations of GPT-4 for the facilitation of teaching activities for teachers as well as for students. Students can pose their inquiries in the form of a conversation, for which they receive guidance in the form of responses; the Writing Coach tool helps in enhancing the capability for writing by providing ideas, composing paragraphs, and grammatical corrections in an appropriate manner. Teachers, instead, can make personalized teaching plans, make rubric systems, track student performance, and use the concept of recommendation systems with the help of the management system provided for teaching activities.

Figure 1. Screenshot of the Khanmigo

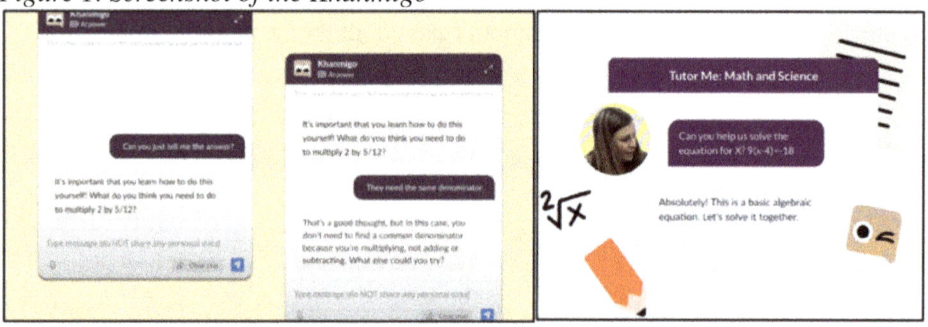

(Source: https://www.khanmigo.ai/)

ASSISTments (Fig. 2) is an open-source, artificially intelligent learning tool for mathematics in the secondary school level. Students can control their own problem-solving activities using hints, explanations, and solutions to each problem they solve. Teachers can monitor achievement levels using the control panel provided in the software, enabling tutors to make in-class interventions using reports from assignments. The software uses a formative assessment strategy in which it provides adaptive hints depending on student responses.

Figure 2. Screenshot of the ASSISTments

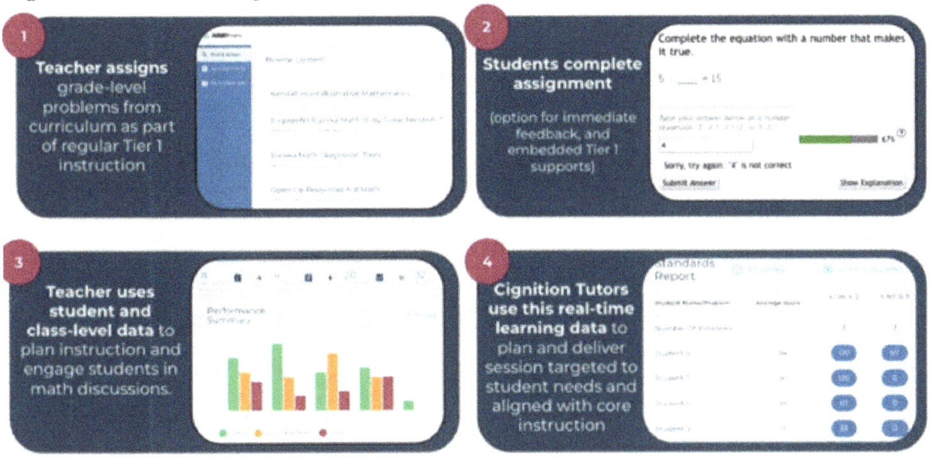

(Source: https://app.assistments.org/)

Querium (Figures 3 & 4) is an intelligent learning system that uses AI to improve conceptual knowledge in science, technology, engineering, and mathematics (STEM) among learners. The StepWise aspect of the intelligent system evaluates learners' problem-solving processes, encouraging stepwise evaluations rather than just emphasizing the correct final solution that is often provided in traditional learning systems with little consideration for the learning processes involved. Additionally, the system is able to adapt its content delivery for learners depending on their performance in the topics covered.

Figure 3. Screenshot of the Querium – 1

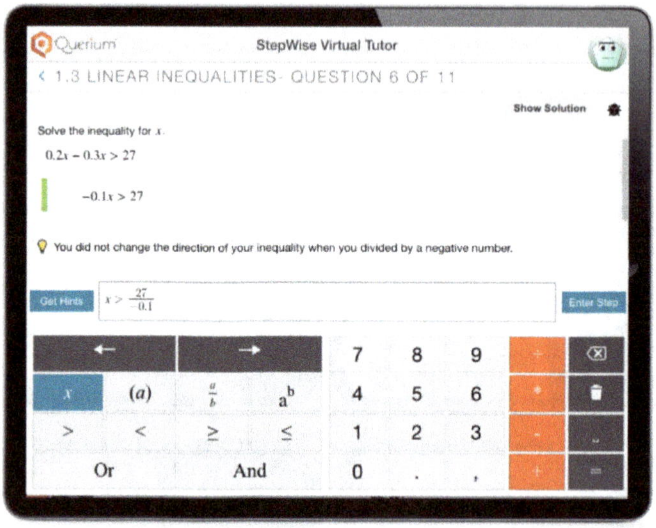

(Source: https://www.querium.com/)

Figure 4. Screenshot of the Querium- 2

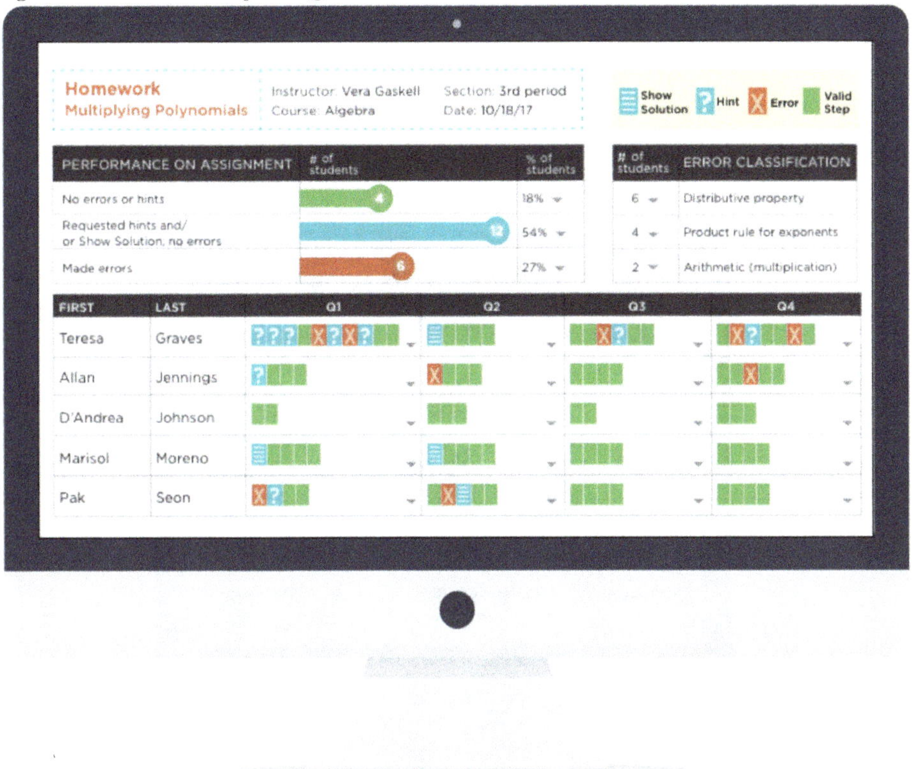

(Source: https://www.querium.com/)

Squirrel AI (Figure 5) is an intelligent tutoring system which is an AI-powered system supporting secondary education in the areas of mathematics, science, and English. The system is equipped with personalized learning pathways using pre-test exercises and nano-size knowledge nodes that evaluate the student level of knowledge. It is also designed with guiding feedback for wrong responses to exercises, reinforcement for correct responses, and graphical tracking of student progress in relation to the subject matter being taught in class. The system comprises personalized learning, intelligent tutoring, and a constructivist learning cycle for its operations.

Figure 5. Screenshot of the Squirrel AI

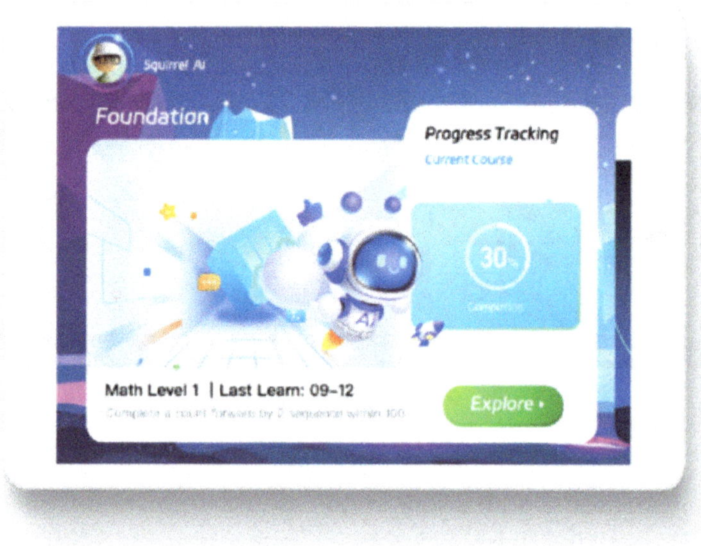

(Source: https://squirrelai.com/)

The applications for personalized learning and intelligent tutoring systems discussed in this section serve to highlight the use of AI in personalized learning processes. However, these applications mentioned in the section only represent a small aspect in the implementations of AI in personalized learning. There have been numerous personalized learning systems tailored for different learners in terms of their learning style, pacing, and needs in different implementations.

Theoretical Background

The key in AI-based personalized learning is in establishing an adaptive learning environment that leverages AI in adapting teaching content according to unique user differences (Luo, 2024; Laaziri et al., 2018). Adaptive learning systems can quickly evaluate students' strengths and weaknesses in an adaptive manner that enables immediate feedback (Laaziri et al., 2018; Pappas & Drigas, 2016). Intelligent tutoring systems rely on the use of AI in mimicking the teacher's role in personalized learning, adapting to the student's learning rhythm (Laaziri et al., 2018; Pappas & Drigas, 2016). According to Ninaus et al. (2022), the interactive aspect of AI can contribute to an enhanced learning environment in terms of adaptivity, which ultimately translates to better learning outcomes.

The category is anchored in theories of constructivism and cognitive learning, with an emphasis on engagement and reflection. The Zone of Proximal Development (ZPD), an idea from Vygotsky's theories that remains critical in the field of education, is actually the region between what an individual can actually do by themselves on their own versus with the help of someone more informed, like an instructor or another student (Khosravizadeh, 2023). The idea behind using collaboration for cognitive development is reflected in the scaffolding practices used in personalized commercial learning software, such as those provided in the systems for Khanmigo's Inquiry Learning System's guidance inquiry system, and the Hint System on ASSISTment's software.

Also, the cognitive apprenticeship approaches, as proposed by Collins (2006), highlight supporting learners in acquiring cognitive and metacognitive capabilities with the guidance of an experienced individual (''Master'') in mind. Such an apprenticeship is replicated in the personalized learning system made possible by AI, where learners get feedback on their problem-solving activities, for example, in the step-wise feedback system offered by Querium.

Conversely, from a different angle, Bloom (1968) suggested that the key to understanding achievement disparities among students is the fixed level of time dedicated to instruction and supporting students on a student-by-student basis. When feedback, extended time, and individualized help are made accessible, any student is capable of reaching high levels of mastery for subject matter. Specifically, in the area of personalized learning systems using AI, it is apparent that these systems dynamically evaluate student learning outcomes with the goal of providing instruction in areas where they need improvement as informed by their performance outcomes. Indeed, in mastery-based learning, principles embodied in its algorithms (Bloom, 1984) are implemented in adaptive learning software systems such as Squirrel AI in such a manner that each student advances only after gaining conceptual mastery in a subject area.

At the same time, the convergence between these tools and educators has spawned a blended teaching approach that leverages both the analytical prowess offered by these tools and the teaching acumen possessed by educators. The "AI Tutor + Teacher," for instance, is an exemplar of the synergy between the two factors that is required for maximizing teaching effectiveness (Wei, 2024). With their collaboration, teachers can now pursue more sophisticated teaching approaches that incorporate their own understanding derived from these tools into their teaching approaches in order to more effectively cater to the needs of their learners (Chen et al., 2020).

Critical Reflection

The integration of AI in the area of education has triggered critical debates regarding the implications associated with the use of personalized learning systems from an ethical perspective. As much as these systems have much to offer in terms of scaleability, continuous feedback provision, and motivational factors in relation to immediate feedback responses, they also pose concerns with respect to reliance on learning paths, flexibility in teaching, and simplification in learning processes (Dignum, 2021; Niu et al., 2024). Technology-based personalized systems need to allow for significant interactive function and human facilitation. Additionally, the integration of intelligent systems has to highlight teacher adaptability and soundness in teaching practice. Therefore, although tutoring systems using AI present immense opportunities for encouraging engagement and equity, long-term education outcomes also depend on careful design for these systems aligned with human-centered teaching practice. As education increasingly embraces AI technologies, it becomes crucial to address these considerations carefully to ensure that personalized learning tools enhance—rather than diminish—the educational experience.

AUTOMATED ASSESSMENT SYSTEMS

One of the most visible classroom uses of AI is automated assessment. Educators now rely on these systems to score assignments and give instant, useful feedback. Calatayud et al. (2021) called automatic grading a core AI function and pointed out that much of its work touches formative assessment. Daxenberger et al. (2023) added that AI grading is faster, more reliable, and less influenced by human bias. Liu et al. (2017) showed that AI can score English essays well, freeing teachers to focus on higher-value instruction instead of paperwork. AI-driven, adaptive testing platforms now change question difficulty on the fly, giving each student a tailor-made exam that aims to boost learning.

A variety of tools now handle parts of this smart grading work, each leaning on different AI tricks. Table 2 briefly lists a few of them.

Table 2. Descriptions of Selected AI Tools Used for Automated Assessment

Tool	Core Function	Pedagogical Basis	Strengths	Limitations / Critical View
Gradescope (Turnitin)	AI-assisted grading for written, mathematical, and mixed-format exams	Assessment for learning / Data-driven evaluation	Faster grading, consistency, LMS integration	Risk of over-reliance on automation; limited qualitative nuance
OpenEssayist	Automated formative feedback for academic writing	Constructivism / Formative assessment	Encourages reflection, self-regulation, no grading bias	Limited feedback depth; may overlook rhetorical subtleties
Peergrade	Peer assessment management and analytics	Collaborative learning / Peer feedback theory	Builds evaluative judgment, metacognitive skills	Quality depends on student engagement and rubric clarity
Formative	Real-time formative assessment with instant feedback	Learning analytics / Continuous assessment	Supports adaptive teaching, instant insights	May privilege quick responses over deep reasoning

Amongst the automation systems for evaluation is Gradescope (Figures 6 and 7), an NLP-based system for open-ended responses, handwriting recognition, and student-model-based scoring recommendations. Gradescope uses AI for the evaluation of open-ended responses, mathematical expressions, and written assignments. The tool allows for the electronic assessment of examinations, assignments, and projects for higher education institutions. Educators can upload their PDF documents with templates for evaluation, whereupon the AI-OCR technology evaluates handwritten responses for open-ended questions, providing educators with scoring recommendations for evaluation by educators for students' responses; educators can then review these scores for accuracy, with an immediate feedback system for students. The Gradescope system also enables educators to view student class performance using analytics with effortless integration into an LMS system like Canvas, Blackboard, or Moodle.

Figure 6. Screenshot of the Gradescope – 1

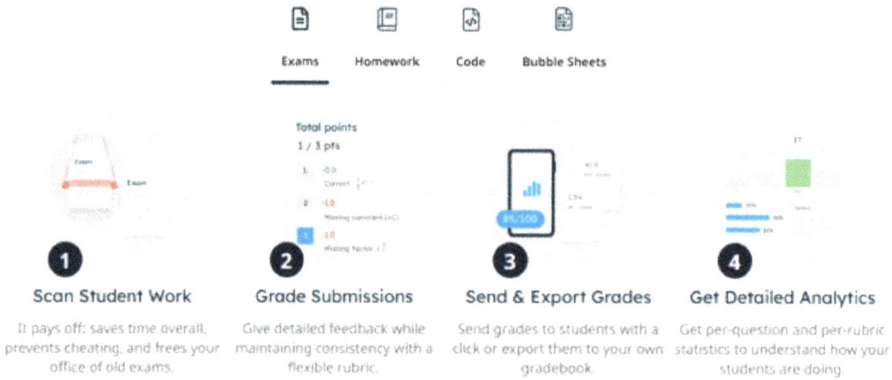

(Source: https://www.gradescope.com/)

Figure 7. Screenshot of the Gradescope - 2 (Source: https://www.gradescope.com/)

OpenEssayist (Figure 8) is an intelligent system that immediately evaluates student essays, advising according to sentence structure, the power of an argument, and essay content cohesion. OpenEssayist is appropriate for open essay questions, advising on essay content evaluation spending a significant amount of time on students' essay evaluation. That is, it is an internet-based learning technology that enables undergraduate students to upload their academic essays for immediate formative evaluation. Employing intelligent system technology with natural language processing strategies, it evaluates essay content, structure, and cohesion by highlighting key words, key sentences, and structural recommendations in an essay rather than requiring grades on correctness. OpenEssayist employs a formative evaluation strategy in enhancing essay capability.

Figure 8. Screenshot of the Essayist tool (Source: https://www.essayist.app/)

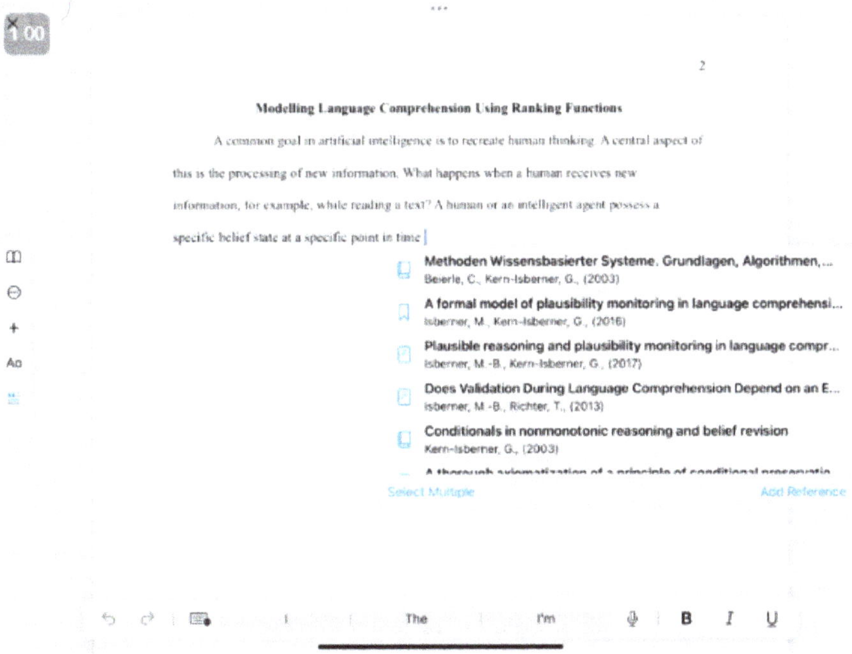

Peergrade (Figure 9) is an e-learning-based peer review system for anonymous and organized student evaluations of each other's assignments. It also comprises modules for scoring and quality assurance using AI technology. Instructors can assign tasks and set scoring criteria (rubrics), while students can submit their own assignments and appraise others' work in an anonymous manner for random assignments using the set criteria. The outcomes in terms of scores and feedback comments can be viewed by the instructor from the outcome summary dashboard. The system enables objective evaluation with anonymity and criterion-based evaluation, in addition to improving critical thinking and feedback skills for students.

Figure 9. Screenshot of the Peergrade

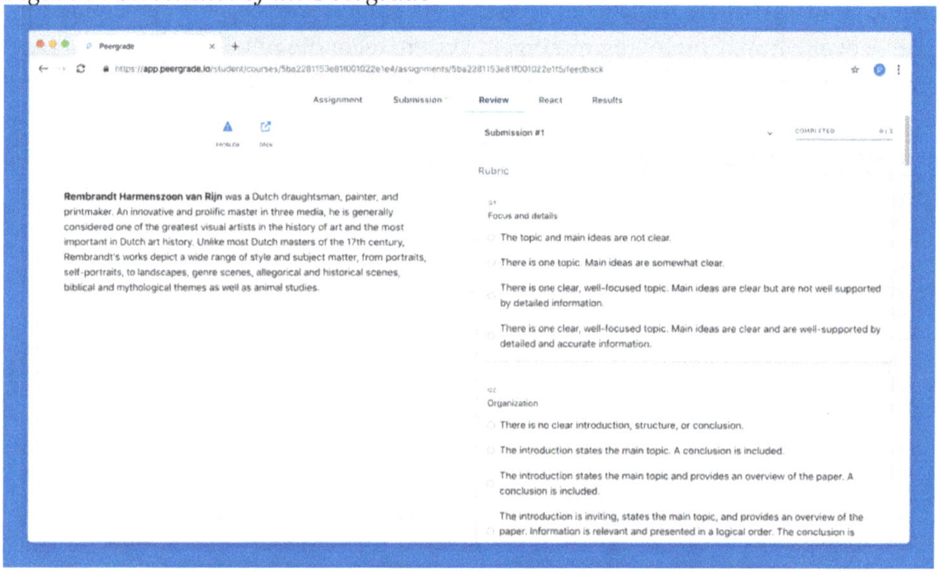

(Source: https://www.peergrade.io/)

Formative (Figures 10-11) is an interactive assessment tool that helps teachers track student progress in real-time to facilitate their engagement in the learning process effectively. The tool gives teachers instant access to view and assess student responses, hence making it easy for them to give personalized feedback to their learners. The tool is able to accommodate different forms of questioning, such as multiple choice, open-ended, short answer, matching, drawing responses, hence making it possible for teachers to evaluate different skills among their learners. Additionally, student responses appear on the teacher's screen in an instant, making it easy for the teacher to immediately identify strengths and weaknesses in his/her learners. Furthermore, the tool's feature for automatic scoring makes it efficient for teachers since it reduces their burden in scoring learners' responses, hence making it an ideal solution for teaching and learning in the classroom setting as well as in distance education opportunities.

Figure 10. Screenshot of the Formative – 1

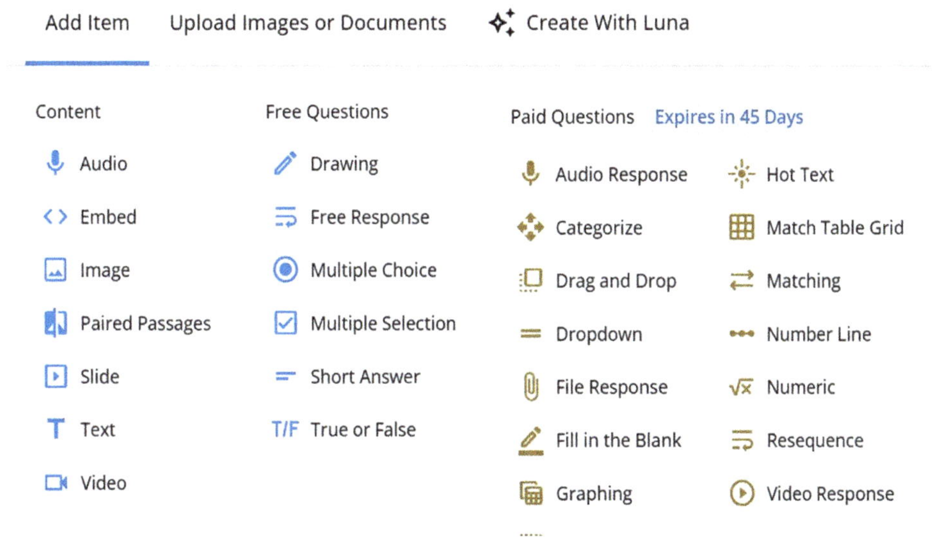

(Source: https://www.formative.com/)

Figure 11. Screenshot of the Formative – 2

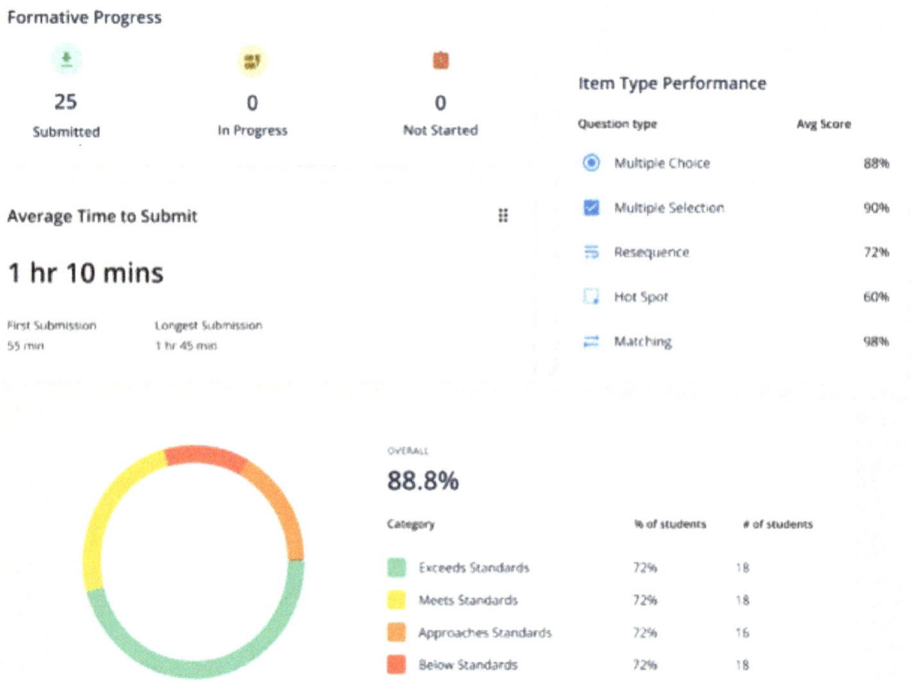

(Source: https://www.formative.com/)

The systems for the automatic evaluation discussed in this section show the different ways in which AI is used in processes for evaluation in an educational setting. The systems mentioned, however, represent only a small fraction of the different systems that already exist for automatic evaluation in areas such as written responses, performance evaluation, self-evaluation, and adaptive testing systems. There is much more to explore in terms of understanding more fully the extent to which AI is used in evaluation systems in education.

Theoretical Background

The development of these automated assessment systems also marks a shift from static testing towards learning-oriented assessment (Carless, 2007). Indeed, immediate feedback is one of the key frameworks that make possible the development of these AI-based systems for automated assessment, since it is an essential aspect in cultivating favorable learning outcomes effectively (Qian & Lehman, 2019). According to research, immediate feedback has been found to positively influence cognitive engagement and performances, in addition to aiding learners in overcoming misconceptions (Qian & Lehman, 2019). The system allows for such promptness with its algorithms able to quickly evaluate student responses, say programming exercises, with the view to providing immediate feedback on these exercises (Qian & Lehman, 2019). This is even more useful in fields such as computer science, where learners commonly exhibit conceptual misunderstandings in relation to programming (Qian & Lehman, 2019).

The cognitive apprenticeship approach proposed by Collins (2006) emphasizes the need for students to be supported in their efforts to understand complex tasks using the principles of modeling, practice, and feedback (Konishi et al., 2020). The use of AI in designing an automated assessment environment could serve to incorporate the different principles associated with cognitive apprenticeship, for example, using the system to model the activities performed by an expert while providing opportunities for students to engage with the different learning instructions dynamically (Thangaraj, 2021).

Additionally, the use of AI-based automated assessment technology is able to make use of data analytics for supporting improvement-oriented learning activities. As students engage with these systems, their results can be used to make adjustments in learning content delivery, thereby ensuring that teaching support is provided in step with the learners' levels. Gradescope and Formative are some systems that make use of the concept of learning analytics in their operations. OpenEssayist and Peergrade systems, on the other hand, make use of the principles of social constructionism in their operations by considering students as actors in the assessment environment in their own right. The incorporation of NLP technology makes it possible for self-regulation in learning to take place. By integrating an automation-human teaching model, AI-based systems for Automatic Assessment enable the conversion of an evaluation action into an interactive learning process, thus covering the gap between evaluation and engaging with education.

Critical Reflection

The first advantage to consider is its adaptability in terms of the ability to adjust the level of difficulty in questions according to the responses from individual students. By doing so, it is possible for a better representation of an individual student's capability (Kadaruddin, 2023). Another advantage is that it is able to enable immediate feedback systems, which is an essential aspect in developing reinforcement for higher levels of learning engagement (Sullivan et al., 2023).

By providing corrective feedback, it is able to stimulate a mindset for continuous learning (Sullivan et al., 2023).

Despite their numerous advantages, there also exist some challenges in implementing these systems using AI technology for automation in assessment tasks. There have been concerns over possible biases in these algorithms, possibly resulting in an unintentional advantage for certain learners over others, thereby perpetuating possible existing disparities (Zhai & Nehm, 2023). Similarly, in its critical review performed by Zawacki-Richter et al. (2019), it is emphasized that it is mandatory to critically evaluate the possible implications for ethics in these applications within the frame of education-based AI tools. Additionally, the emergence of these innovations has contributed to rising concerns with respect to academic integrity. According to Sullivan et al. (2023), these systems can present mixed ramifications with regard to student engagement and integrity. While they can be employed for authentic learning activities with personalized feedback, they also pose the risk for cheating with regard to the principles underlying academic assessment practices.

On the one hand, while automation tools such as Gradescope, Formative, etc., increase fairness and efficiency, they could potentially limit the scope of evaluation to predetermined criteria if a more nuanced understanding is not implemented. In contrast, tools like OpenEssayist, which concentrate on formative feedback, and Peergrade, which cultivates peer feedback culture, redefine feedback from an evaluative outcome to a dialogic function. However, concerns regarding the transparency of algorithms, ethics in data, bias in AI, and so on persist, particularly in light of the rising integration between evaluation data and education-related feedback in the learning landscape. The challenge in integrating these systems, therefore, is to establish a balance between the precision of technology in the operations of AI with the empathy associated with more nuanced education-related approaches in teaching. There is an immediate need for the development of ethics in the design and delivery of AI-driven self-assessment systems in these institutions. As a means for these institutions to gain the trust of their users, they need to address concerns about privacy, consent, and security with comprehensive transparency in these processes. Given the capability provided by the technology to collect personal information, especially sensitive student information, for instance, concerns have been raised with regard to consent in these processes by these institutions (Anuyahong et al., 2023).

APPLICATIONS OF NATURAL LANGUAGE PROCESSING (NLP) IN EDUCATION

Computers that actually understand words, sentences, and the little subtleties in between could completely reshape classroom and homework technologies. Educators are already putting Natural Language Processing, or NLP, to work whenever AI tools translate complex paragraphs into simpler language, or turn spoken answers into instant test scores. In language classes, for example, GPT-like algorithms pore over a learner's writing and voice recordings, grade grammar and tone, then shoot back line-by-line notes for the student and their teacher, flagging weak spots and pointing out small wins (Gyawali & Mehandroo, 2022). Those same programs now grade essays, spot errors, build quick vocabulary quizzes, and even chat with learners in real time, so the practice never stops (Yu et al., 2022). Voice assessments that judge pronunciation, rhythm, and breath control can then rewrite lessons on the fly, swapping in new exercises the instant a parent walks out of a room (Qin, 2024). Despite these contributions, as noted by Shen (2024), significant challenges such as privacy, data security, and the need for large datasets pose important obstacles to effective NLP implementation. Therefore, the contribution of NLP technologies to educational environments necessitates the effective addressing of these challenges and barriers. Table 3 provides descriptions of some of the AI tools used for natural language processing.

Table 3. Descriptions of Selected AI Tools Used for Natural Language Processing (NLP)

Tool	Core Function	Pedagogical Basis	Strengths	Limitations / Critical View
ChatGPT (OpenAI)	Conversational AI for content generation, Q&A, and writing support	Constructivism / Dialogic learning	Versatile, context-aware, promotes inquiry	Risk of misinformation; overreliance on AI feedback
Hugging Face Inference API	Open-source NLP model hub for summarization, translation, and sentiment analysis	Open education / Computational thinking	Accessibility, transparency, coding-free usability	Quality varies by model; requires human interpretation
Text Inspector	Linguistic analysis for readability, vocabulary diversity, and CEFR levels	Formative assessment / Language awareness	Objective metrics, real-time linguistic insight	Limited qualitative feedback; focuses on surface-level features
Quillbot	AI-powered paraphrasing, summarizing, and grammar correction	Process writing / Self-regulated learning	Enhances fluency, supports revision and citation skills	May hinder originality; style uniformity risk

An example of using NLP in education is ChatGPT (Figure 12), an AI app invented by OpenAI using the GPT-3.5 and GPT-4 models. As an LLM, it relies on natural language processing (NLP) for analyzing inputted text, composing appropriate responses, and engaging in other tasks involving language usage. In an academic setting, ChatGPT can be effectively used for summarizing any subject, composing texts, preparing questions for either educators or learners, translating, and explanatory activities for better understanding. Featuring an internet-based platform handy for usage, it is aptly usable for educators and learners alike, acting practically as an ordinary language model for textual practices in language learning.

Figure 12. The Use of ChatGPT in Educational Systems

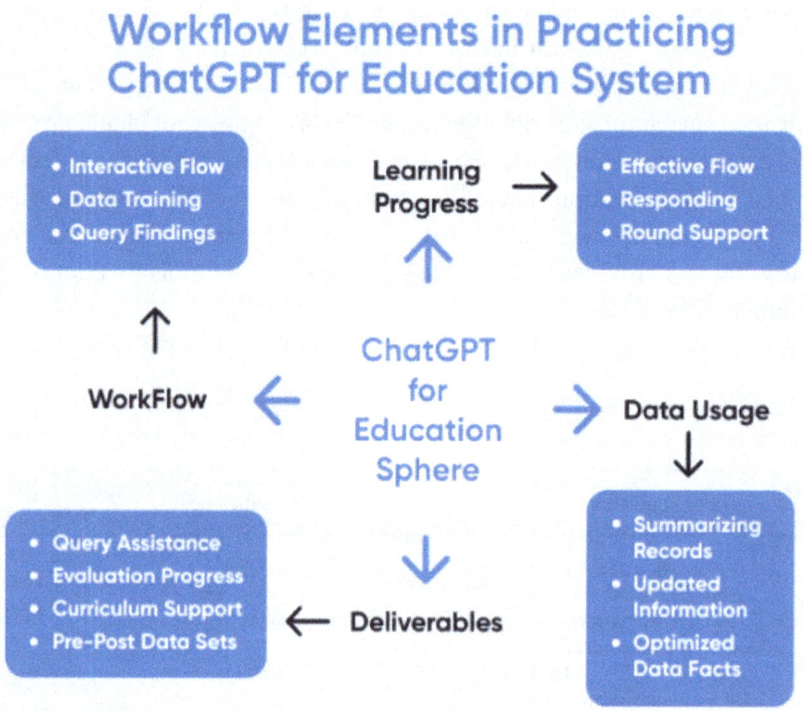

(Source: Koblyakov, 2024)

Hugging Face Inference API (Figure 13) is an open-source platform which enables users to use already existing NLP models on the platform. Some of the areas where it can be used range from summarization, sentiment analysis, translation, classification, to answering queries. It also enables users to implement NLP applications in their teaching practices in areas such as shortening lengthy texts, sentiment analysis, translating scenarios, as well as information search. Utilizing transformers for its operations, it achieves high levels of precision in understanding texts as well as their interpretation. Hugging Face Inference API is a useful tool in implementing NLP in teaching activities.

Figure 13. Screenshot of Hugging Face Inference API usage in educational systems

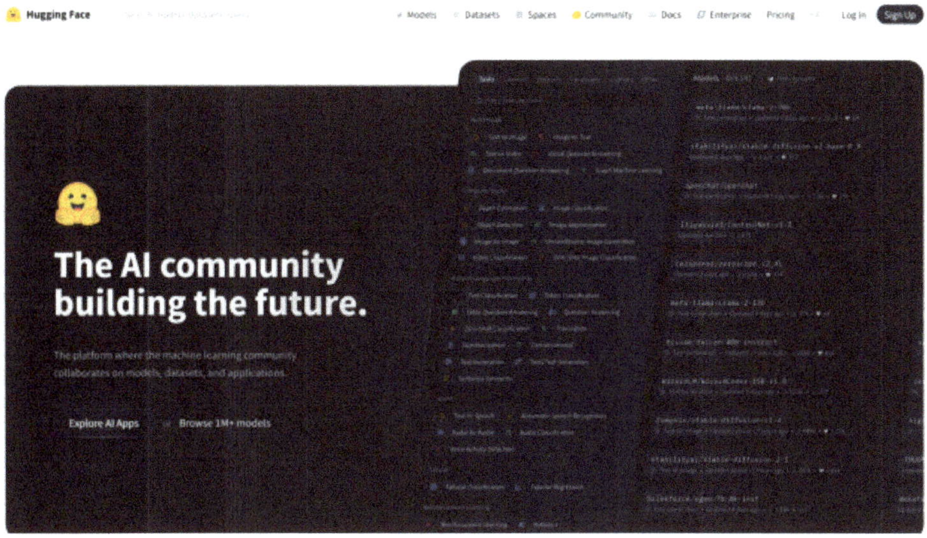

(Source: https://huggingface.co/).

Text Inspector (Figure 14) is an Internet-based NLP utility for the linguistics-driven evaluation of English-language texts. CEFR level identification, ratios for SWs, and notions of language complexity can be gleaned from these analyses, with textual inputs provided either from their websites or from uploaded documents for objective assessment in foreign languages in an academic setting with the goal of improving foreign language teaching, learning, student, and academia-related writing capabilities in students with its aid.

Figure 14. Screenshot of Text Inspecto

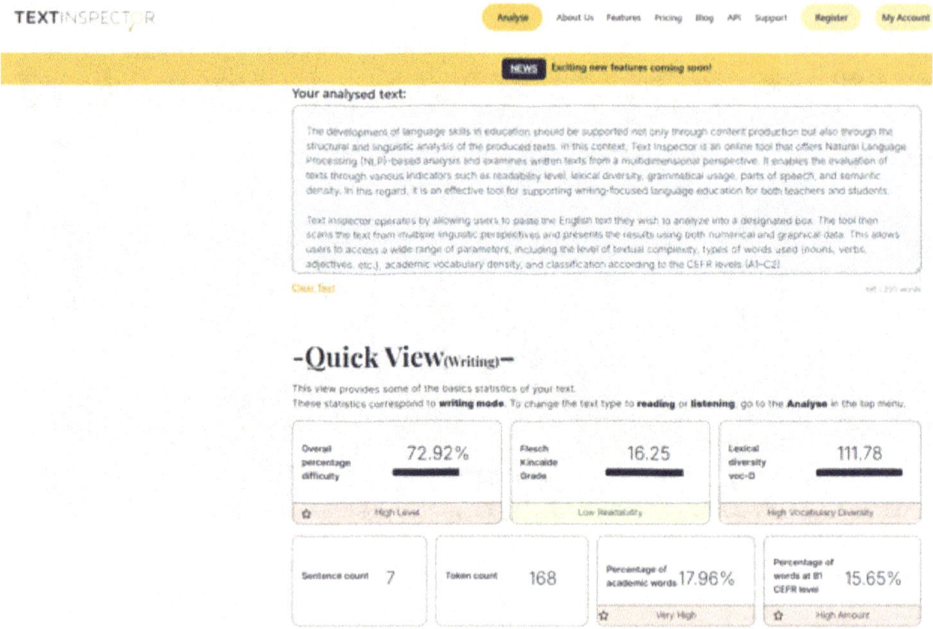

(Source: https://textinspector.com/).

QuillBot (Figure 15) is an internet-based writing assistant tool that uses AI technology with capabilities in paraphrasing, summarizing, and grammar review. The software has the ability to rephrase any kind of text provided by the user with different stylistic options (normal, fluent, formal, creative). The software's summary tool shortens any long piece of written content, has a grammar tool for language corrections, and a citation tool for making APA, MLA, or Chicago style citation lists. The software improves writing cognition for learners, making it easier for tutors to do editing work on their pieces.

Figure 15. Screenshot of Quillbot

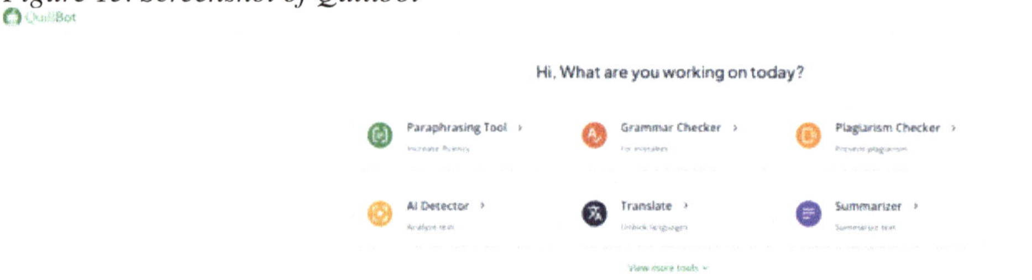

(Source: https://quillbot.com/)

The applications featuring NLP technology discussed in the research represent the incorporation of AI-based language technology in the education field in general. Nevertheless, these serve only for illustration purposes, while there is a range of other software with NLP capabilities like text analysis, auto summaries, translation, and speech recognition. Analyzing these applications helps in understanding the NLP technology applications in the education process in a more comprehensive manner.

Theoretical Background

Natural Language Processing (NLP) relies on language theories that help in the processing and interpretation of human language, thus making it possible for a more efficient relationship between computers and users (Hirschberg & Manning, 2015). Due to the improvement in methodologies from machine learning approaches, it becomes possible for NLP to train on large amounts of data in an attempt to improve their interpretation of subject matter in learning documents (Hirschberg & Manning, 2015). An example in this regard is the capability to gain valuable insights from the textual information, which is useful in determining student performance (Lukwaro et al., 2024).

The integration of NLP into education aligns with sociocultural theories, which emphasize interaction, feedback, and scaffolding, as well as constructivist educational theories, which highlight the student's role in knowledge construction. NLP facilitates personalized learning experiences through dialogue-based tutoring systems and chatbots that engage students in meaningful, adaptive conversations tailored to their individual needs (Somers et al., 2021). Such interaction also supports the development of critical thinking and problem-solving skills, which are essential for effective learning. Tools like ChatGPT operationalize dialogic pedagogy by simulating peer or instructor dialogue that promotes reflection and deeper understanding. Platforms such as Hugging Face align with Open Educational Resource (OER) principles, providing transparent access to language models for computational literacy. Tools like Text Inspector, grounded in formative assessment frameworks, encourage students to reflect on their linguistic development and support metalinguistic awareness. Similarly, Quillbot exemplifies process-oriented writing theory, offering step-by-step support that fosters drafting and revision. Collectively, these NLP applications indicate a shift toward enriched learning environments, where technology functions as a language partner and extends human communication and critical engagement with texts.

NLP instruments remain popular for supporting language learning by providing learners with an instant feedback system, thereby making it easier for learners to acquire language skills. According to research, using NLP in language learning helps make the learning process more engaging while at the same time improving understanding (Yang, 2022). Grammar checking, simplification, and vocabulary enlargement remain essential for language learners, particularly in English as a Foreign Language settings (Rayati, 2021).

Moreover, the use of NLP algorithms in auto-evaluation tools enables the evaluation of conceptual understanding from written responses, thus supporting formative evaluation (Somers et al., 2021; Smith et al., 2020). As pointed out by Smith et al., 2020, another key benefit offered by NLP is its ability to automate the evaluation for open-ended questions, thus removing time constraints for the teacher (Smith et al., 2020). By providing feedback to students on their responses, applications supported by NLP technology help students attain mastery in their domains, thus supporting mastery learning (Somers et al., 2021).

Critical Reflection

Although NLP-inspired applications add much value to the art of written expression and understanding, they also pose complex concerns for ethics and teaching practices alike. Overdependence on the use of these algorithms for written output could possibly impair critical thinking and language creativity in an individual. Additionally, the algorithms from natural language processing could end up perpetuating any existing biases in teaching-related data sets, thus leading to reinforcing disparities in teaching outcomes for different learners. Issues concerning algorithmic bias, highlighted in research on algorithms used in scoring (Beiting-Parrish & Whitmer, 2023; Johnson et al., 2022), continue to feature prominently in these situations, with perspectives provided by concerns for fairness in algorithms being underscored by Gutiérrez (2023).

Another area where the applications of NLP technology pose multiple concerns is linked to student data privacy issues. Large amounts of student personal information need to be processed in many NLP-based applications in the education field, thus raising issues associated with student personal information security (Miller, 2024). Storing student-generated information requires appropriate student personal information handling policies in learning institutions that make use of technology to offer more informed services (Kasneci et al., 2023).

Despite the progress made in NLP, the incorporation of these tools into existing teaching structures is fraught with challenges. Apps like Text Inspector considering only the grammatical correctness of an essay's structure, with little regard for its rhetorical aspect, while those from Hugging Face incorporate transparency into their systems, requiring the teacher to have appropriate digital literacy capabilities for its interpretation. Furthermore, in a technology-driven teaching structure, it is essential that these tools impart their benefits in relation to the teaching outcomes to derive any meaningful benefits (Zhu, 2023). Ultimately, NLP in education should be employed to augment human meaning-making processes rather than automate them, reinforcing critical thinking, creativity, and reflective engagement while safeguarding ethical and pedagogical standards.

AI-SUPPORTED EDUCATIONAL CONTENT CREATION

AI's growing ability to create learning materials is already changing how educators make and share content with students. By scanning curriculum guidelines alongside real-time data about learners, these algorithms can build quizzes, reading lists, and lessons aimed at each student's unique pace. Automatic-question generators, for instance, pull items straight from core materials, while adaptive platforms shape study roadmaps that shift as learners advance (Kang et al., 2021). This level of content production lightens teachers' administrative burdens and also delivers rich, context-aware resources that can scale across entire schools or systems (Kang et al., 2021). Table 4 provides descriptions of some AI tools used to create educational content.

Table 4. Descriptions of Selected AI Tools Used for Educational Content Creation

Tool	Core Function	Pedagogical Basis	Strengths	Limitations / Critical View
Curipod	Converts prompts into interactive slides, quizzes, and tasks	Student-centered learning / Constructivism	Quick content generation, interactive, Bloom's taxonomy-aligned	Reliance on AI quality; limited depth in complex topics
MagicSchool AI	Personalized lessons, progress tracking, and adaptive feedback	Personalized learning / Gamification	Accessibility-focused, real-time monitoring, automated feedback	May reduce teacher-driven nuance; AI decision opacity
Diffit	Adaptive, gamified language-learning	Adaptive learning / Motivation theory	Individualized pacing, cultural integration, gamified engagement	Overreliance may limit real-world communication practice
Conker AI (Mote)	Automated quiz and assessment creation	Formative & Summative Assessment / Efficient instruction	Fast quiz generation, multi-modal content, real-time analytics	Risk of shallow assessment; requires teacher oversight

Curipod (Figure 16), an example of an AI-based tool for the development of educational content, is an edtech tool aimed at making it easier for teachers to prepare their classes, make interactive presentations, and design activities for classes. Curipod enables teachers to prepare activities, discussion topics, and evaluation instruments for classes according to Bloom's Taxonomy domains by simply requiring teachers to type in topics for classes they teach. Students can also join interactive classes using links provided for answering questions and other interactive activities, making CuriPod an interactive tool for student engagement with enhanced teaching time with the aid of technology.

Figure 16. Screenshot of Curipod

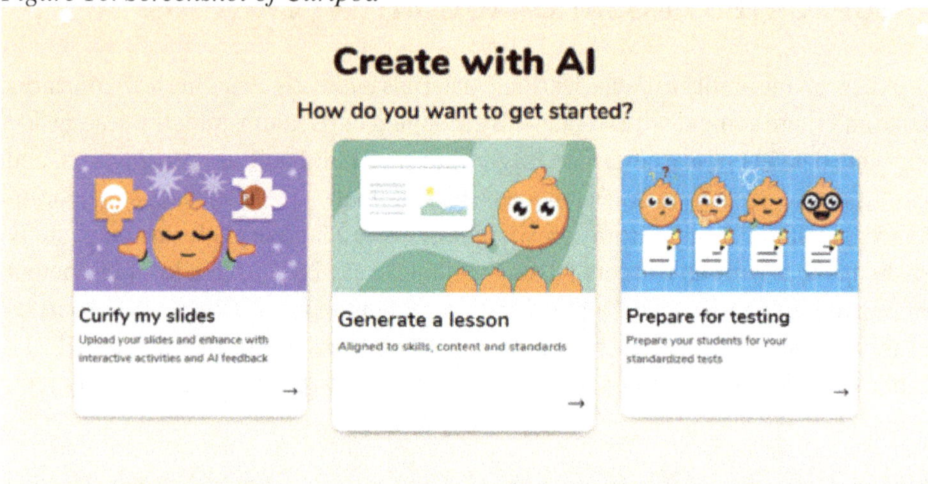

(Source: https://curipod.com/)

MagicSchool AI (Figure 17) is an AI-powered, machine learning-based personalized learning platform for students. The tool tracks the performance of each student in real time, thereby understanding their strengths and weaknesses, and creates personalized content, exercises, and feedback for each individual student accordingly. MagicSchool AI is an integrated AI-powered tool for education designed for personalized learning, improved accessibility, student-teacher interactions, learning language skills, game-based learning, accessibility, multiple languages, and more.

Figure 17. Screenshot of MagicSchool

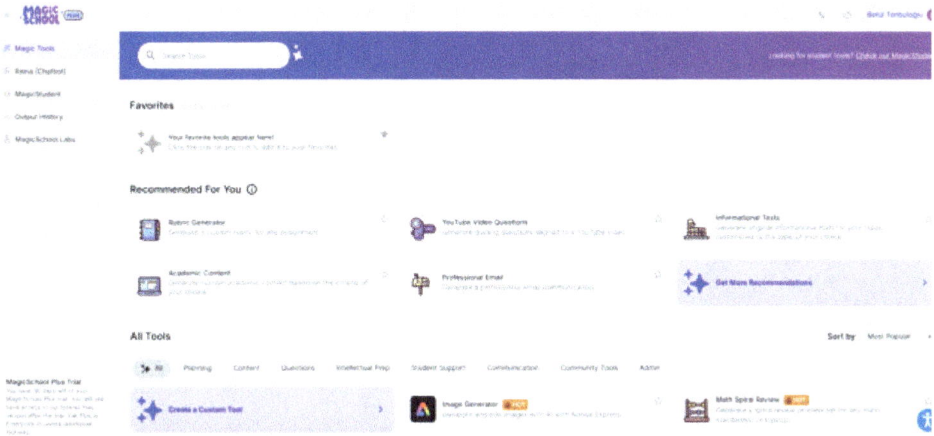

(Source: https://app.magicschool.ai/)

Diffit (Figure 18) is an AI-driven language learning platform providing personalized learning experiences on the basis of different learners' requirements. By using AI algorithms for machine learning and natural language processing, the platform evaluates learners' strengths and weaknesses in order to prepare relevant content for the learners. Educational content, immediate feedback, and engagement strategies aid in improving talking, listening, reading, and writing capabilities in different learners who belong to different countries with varying languages.

Figure 18. Screenshot of Diffit

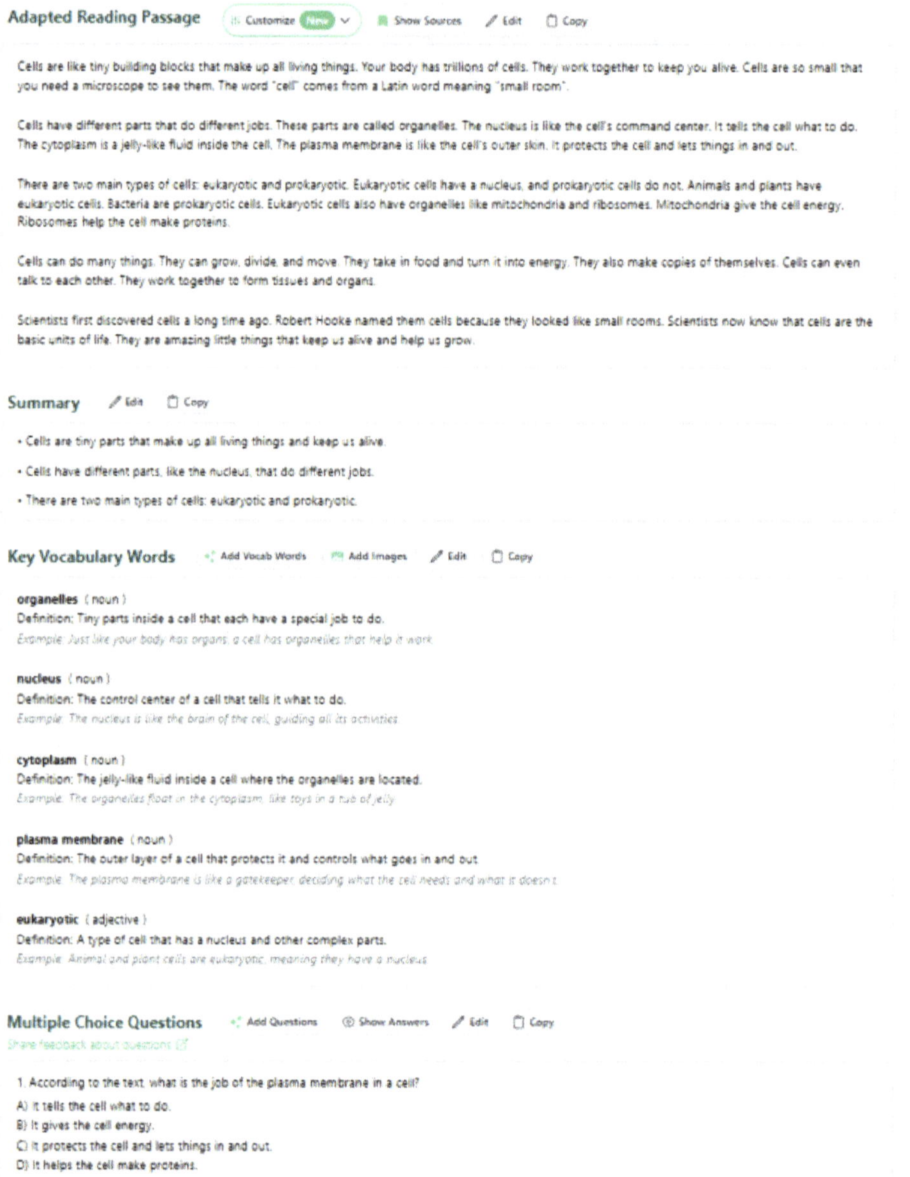

(Source: https://app.diffit.me/)

Figure 19 illustrates the system Conker AI, an educative tool for teaching that employs AI technology to allow teachers to quickly produce high-quality quizzes and Q&A exercises. The software system is able to produce multiple choice, fill-in-the-blank, and short answer questions in relation to the provided text topic, as well as allow the teacher to differentiate their questions according to cognitive level. Additionally, it allows teachers to quickly alter content, publish assignments for students, and also provides a more diversified learning experience with audio opportunities for explanations.

Figure 19. Screenshot of Conker AI

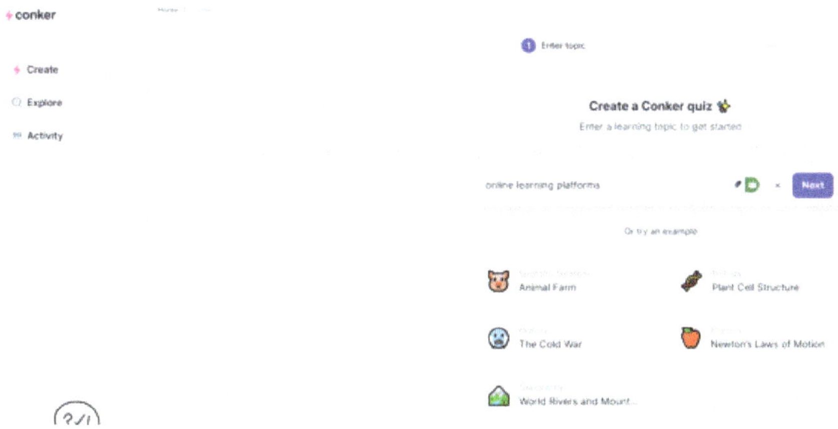

(Source: https://app.conker.ai/)

The use of AI in teaching content creation, as demonstrated in this section, is one aspect in which these applications function for instruction design purposes. Still, these applications only represent the tip of the iceberg with regards to possible usage scenarios for these systems to date. There exist a variety of other systems for the generation of textual, media, video, or even interactive content using AI in its software applications.

Theoretical Background

AI-powered content creation tools align closely with constructivist, learner-centered, and adaptive learning frameworks. These systems can support learning by generating interactive and adaptable experiences that facilitate exploration and engagement. For instance, generative AI can tailor content to individual student responses, providing customized materials that foster deeper understanding. Incorporating feedback loops within AI systems further enhances personalization in educational content, consistent with constructivist learning principles (Borocki et al., 2023). Tools like Curipod operationalize constructivist pedagogy by emphasizing active participation and cognitive interaction. Platforms such as MagicSchool AI apply personalized learning theories, dynamically adjusting content to learner needs while supporting inclusivity through accessibility features. Tools like Diffit incorporate adaptive and gamified learning principles, delivering instant feedback and motivation through rewards and progress tracking. Apps like Conker AI integrates assessment theory, offering both formative and summative evaluation tools to guide and personalize instruction. Collectively, AI-powered educational content creation tools demonstrate how AI can function as a supportive mechanism in learning environments while preserving the teacher's instructional style and subjectivity.

The integration of AI in content development also sparks debates on the changing roles of educators in the teaching profession today. With the assumed competency in content development by AI, the conventional role of teachers in providing curriculum content is transformed to act more as learning facilitators in the classroom. There is a need for professional development for teachers on integrating AI in teaching (Xu & Ouyang, 2022).

Critical Reflection

Human content creation applications with the integration of AI technology have the potential to assist teachers in their workload and increase student engagement; however, they also pose some significant challenges to teachers. As technology advances with respect to AI, it is becoming increasingly significant to incorporate ethics into the content creation practice. Despite the drastic improvement offered by the use of generative AI technology in content creation, there has been concern over the quality, accuracy, and level of validity associated with the content created by these applications (Sihite et al., 2023). There is also the potential to diminish their own teaching quality in overdependence on these algorithms for content generation. Personalized learning systems such as MagicSchool AI and Diffit need to be closely monitored in terms of their adaptability in curriculum delivery to avoid any possible biases in their systems. Curipod and others like Conker AI increase efficiency in the delivery of content; however, their capability in terms of judgment in designing tasks and assessment is yet to be completely realized for an adaptive learning system to be successful, where teachers need to act somewhat as moderators in integrating these systems with their curriculum objectives. Zhang et al. (2022) emphasize the importance of integrating AI ethics into educational curricula to prepare students for critical engagement with AI technologies. Such integration ensures that content creation aligns not only with academic standards but also with ethical considerations addressing contemporary societal challenges.

AI IN SPECIAL EDUCATION: OPPORTUNITIES AND INCLUSIVE TECHNOLOGIES

Assistive AI tools matter even more in special education, where different strengths and challenges call for flexible support. AI applications can assist students with special needs by providing adaptable resources, such as speech recognition software for hearing-impaired students or personalized learning experiences for those with learning disabilities. AI technologies offer customized instruction tailored to the specific challenges faced by students, enabling the assessment of individual barriers and learning difficulties while facilitating communication and learning (Begum, 2024). That kind of personalized support levels the playing field, so every student, no matter the need, can engage with the same curriculum. Table 5 provides descriptions of some AI tools used in special education.

Table 5. Descriptions of Selected AI Tools Used for Special Education

Tool	Core Function	Pedagogical / Accessibility Focus	Strengths	Limitations / Critical View
Seeing AI (Microsoft)	Converts visual information into spoken descriptions	Visual impairment / Assistive technology	Real-time object/ text recognition, easy interface, enhances independence	Dependent on camera quality and lighting
Google Lookout	Recognizes objects, text, currency, and surroundings	Visual impairment / Accessibility	Offline functionality, real-time guidance, intuitive interface	Limited integration with other educational systems
Voiceitt	Converts unclear speech into intelligible spoken language	Speech impairment / Communication support	Personalized speech profiles, integration with smart assistants, improves participation	Free tier limited; setup required for accuracy
Otter.ai	Live transcription of speech to text	Hearing impairment / Classroom accessibility	Speaker identification, timestamped transcripts, supports remote learning	Internet-dependent; advanced features behind paywall
Microsoft Immersive Reader	Customizable text presentation with read-aloud	Dyslexia, ADHD, reading challenges	Multimodal support (visual, auditory), interactive features, cloud-based	Limited to Microsoft ecosystem

Seeing AI (Figure 20) is an example of the usage of AI in special education, which is a mobile app from Microsoft allowing the visually impaired to recognize visually present information in the form of audible feedback. Using its computer vision technology, the app is able to read text, detect scenes and objects, identify facial expressions, and display barcode/QR code information. Having different recognition modes, it is able to detect objects, recognize products, and identify scenes in addition to others. Compatible with IOS devices and completely free, it is able to offer a rapid, reliable, and efficient user experience with little complexity in its usage, using Microsoft Azure technology.

Figure 20. Screenshot of Seeing AI (Microsoft)

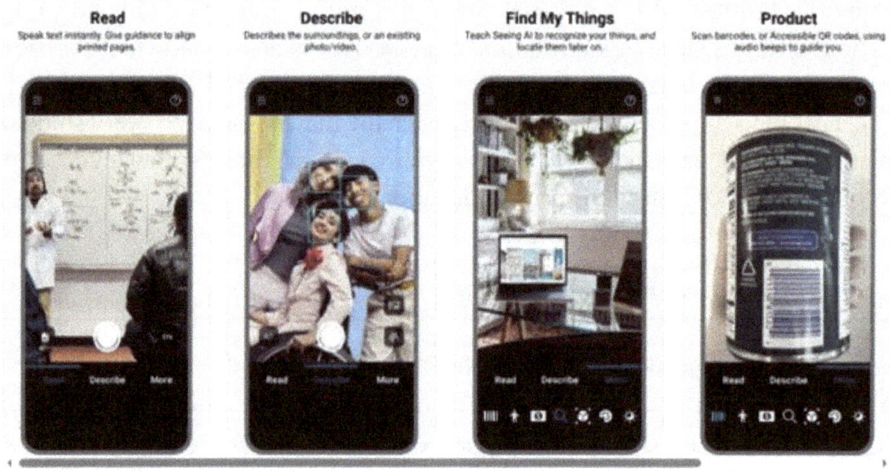

(Source: https://apps.apple.com/us/app/seeing-ai/id999062298?ign-itscg=30200&ign-itsct=apps_box_badge)

Google Lookout (Figure 21) is an Android-based mobile application using AI for visually impaired individuals to identify neighboring objects and text around them. The app makes use of computer vision and natural language processing to read back text, identify packaged goods labels, detect various currencies, and identify neighboring objects and persons. Depending on the mode, it supports different functionalities such as reading text, food labels, documents, money, and surroundings. It is an offline app with an easy-to-use interface.

Figure 21. Screenshot of Google Lookout

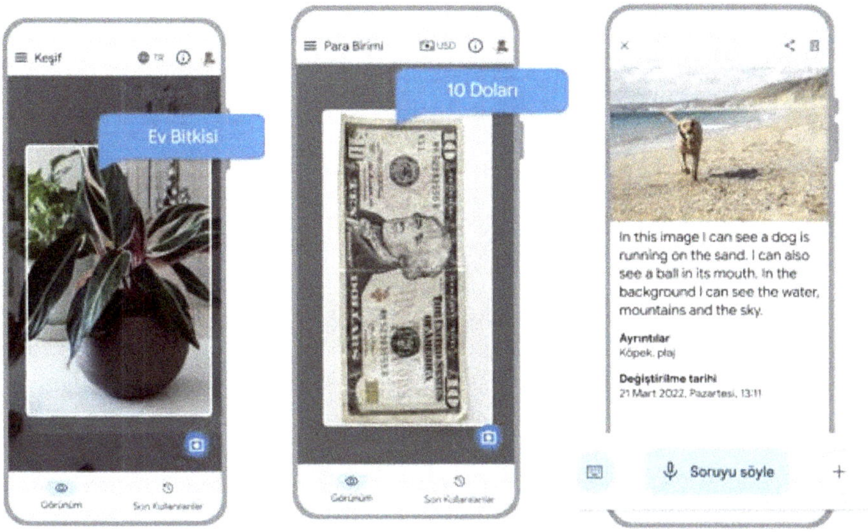

(Source: https://play.google.com/store/apps/details?id=com.google.android.apps.accessibility.reveal&pli=1)

Voiceitt (Figure 22) is an AI-powered mobile app specifically for those who have speech impairments. The app adapts to the speech impairments of the user and turns it into correct speech so that communication is possible either with an AI assistant or with other people. Common words need to be trained vocally in Voiceitt so that it forms a personalized speech pattern for the user, which is then recognized by the AI assistant for replication in voice commands. Voiceitt is compatible with an Alexa assistant, which enables execution of daily commands in a physical environment, either at home or in an education setup, using Voiceitt's basic software for free, with other versions on license fees.

Figure 22. Screenshot of Voiceitt

(Source: https://web.voiceitt.com/sign-up)

Otter.ai (Figure 23) is an AI-driven speech recognition tool for transcription purposes. It translates speech in real time into written words, presenting it in a manner organized for each speaker's specific contributions to a conversation. Otter.ai enables users to save audio files for uploading, make corrections in previous transcripts, and sync with internet-based platforms like Zoom in their paid versions. Otter.ai is applicable in an academic setting where it benefits deaf students, students with difficulty paying attention, and foreign language learners who can also record classroom discussions.

Figure 23. Screenshot of Otter.ai -1

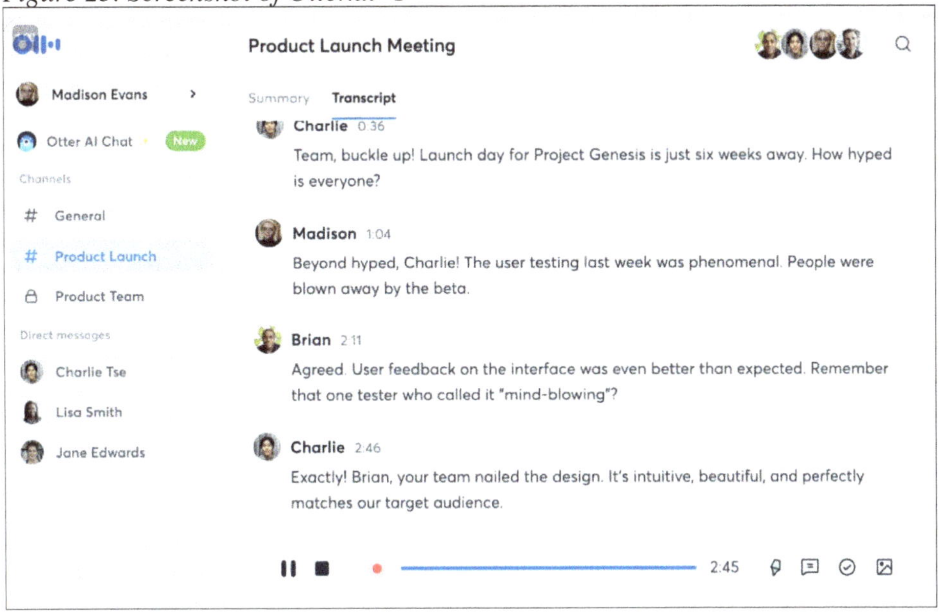

(Source: https://otter.ai/)

Microsoft Immersive Reader (Figure 24) is an electronic reading aid that employs AI algorithms for supporting its functionality by providing an enhanced reading experience for learners with dyslexia, ADHD, and other learning impairments. The tool enables readers to personalize their reading experience by varying font size, line spacing, background color, displaying reading instructions in a line-by-line manner, using synchronous text-to-speech capabilities, highlighting different types of words in reading passages, providing spelling assistance, picture dictionaries, translation capabilities, and using color semantics for an appropriate reading experience. Additionally, it is a cloud-based tool supported on Microsoft Word, OneNote, Outlook, Teams, with specific applications in learning settings for special education for improving reading, understanding, concentration, among other beneficial purposes.

Figure 24. Screenshot of Microsoft Immersive Reader

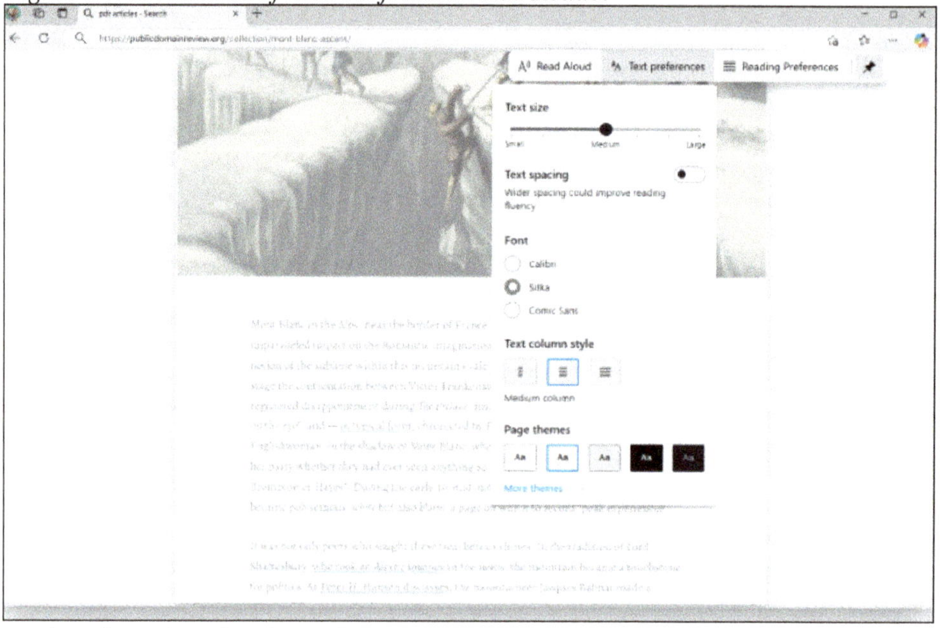

(https://www.microsoft.com/en-us/edge/features/immersive-reader?form=MA13FJ)

The applications discussed in this section give an impression of the power of AI in facilitating communication, accessibility, and personalized learning processes for special education. However, these applications only give an impression of a fraction of the technology used in special education that is presently being implemented with the aid of AI. There have been a variety of applications in the area of special education using AI technology for an assortment of disabilities.

Theoretical Background

Among the foundational paradigms for implementing AI in special education is that provided by Universal Design for Learning (UDL). UDL is informed by the notion that it is essential for the learning environment to be designed for all learners by incorporating multiple means for engagement, representation, and action & expression (McMahon & Firestone, 2024). Some ways in which AI tools can apply the principles of Universal Design for Learning is by personalizing the learning content for individual learners according to their needs, preferences, and difficulties (Chedrawi et al., 2024). AI tools can dynamically adjust the instruction content according to student engagement so that the learning experience is tailored to their specific needs (Chedrawi et al., 2024).

Additionally, the use of AI in special education encompasses the ideologies of Evidence-Based Practices in teaching, where research is employed in making teaching strategies (Li & Wong, 2023). By using their capabilities to analyze massive amounts of learning information, these systems ensure that they make informed decisions in coming up with teaching approaches for learners with disabilities (Li & Wong, 2023). By doing so, these systems make it possible for teachers to apply personalized approaches in teaching learners in their specific manner, which has been evidenced to yield positive results (Abbas et al., 2023).

Personalized learning is yet another theoretical basis for using AI in special education. Personalized learning is made possible by AI technology, where learners can progress at their own rate in mastering appropriate concepts according to their abilities. By using adaptive learning systems and intelligent tutoring systems, personalized learning for students is achieved by ensuring that no student is left behind. The ability to offer personalized learning using AI technology is disclosed in the reason for its contribution to student engagement in education (Xie, 2023). For example, applications such as Otter.ai enable inclusive access to audial content in line with inclusive assessment. Voiceitt-like applications are supportive in enabling students with speech impairments to express themselves. Other applications that incorporate AI, such as Google Lookout, implement principles linked with perception and representation by using visual stimuli to present audial input. An example is Microsoft Immersive Reader, which relies on multisensory approaches for better understanding for students with reading impairments in line with principles for compensating for impairments in cognitive independence.

Critical Reflection

An important aspect to consider in applying AI in special education is the ethics involved in its usage. The integration of AI in special education incurs an aspect of ethics whereby it encompasses concern for the rights of students in regard to the aspect of consent in regard to their data (Mpu, 2024). As different applications of AI continue to rise, their aspect in relation to ethics is supposed to be well investigated, with special concern for the rights of vulnerable learners (Hinojo-Lucena et al., 2019).

Despite the potential for democratization in quality education offered by these AI-based systems, it could also potentially worsen existing disparities within the education system. Access to technology is also not equally possible for all children, which could hamper the usefulness of these systems (Bulathwela et al., 2024). The dependency on equipment, settings, and compatibility with devices could also hinder their usefulness (Bulathwela et al., 2024). Systems like Voiceitt and transcription applications would need to be carefully set up in order to decode different accents, speech, and languages effectively.

Despite these constraints, there is immense value in using AI-driven tools for improving the equity, accessibility, and inclusivity associated with learning interfaces. Professional development for teachers on the use of AI technology is an integral starting tool for effectively incorporating these technology tools in special education environments (Pagliara et al., 2024). Teacher-student-community collaboration is essential for developing these technology tools in a manner that addresses the interests of students effectively, simultaneously countering concerns regarding bias and equity.

ETHICAL DEBATES ON THE USE OF AI IN EDUCATION

AI is seen as a game-changer in education because it can personalize learning, streamline administrative tasks, and offer new insights into student performance. Yet the same features that promise progress also raise tough ethical questions that schools, developers, and policy-makers cannot ignore. Every time an AI tool collects data to recommend resources or flag at-risk students, it touches on issues of consent, security, and fairness. To keep the focus on students and not on continuous data extraction, Akgün and Greenhow (2021) call for clear, transparent guidelines that spell out what data is collected, why it is needed, and how long it will be stored. Their proposal aligns with Dhirani et al. (2023), who assert that in the absence of robust encryption, routine audits, and clear user consent, even benevolent software can transform into a privacy catastrophe in educational settings.

Since the outputs of AI tools are shaped by the structure and scope of underlying datasets, there is a risk that biased data can perpetuate existing inequalities and lead to algorithmic bias. The possibility of such bias underscores the need for fair and ethical guidelines in both AI systems and their application in education (Karaibrahimoğlu et al., 2024; Kiemde & Kora, 2021).

Monitoring students through AI systems raises another critical ethical concern, as it has the potential to infringe upon students rights to privacy. Popenici and Kerr (2017) discuss the implications of tracking students learning behaviors and engagement levels, suggesting that while some forms of monitoring may enhance learning, they also carry risks related to over-surveillance and misuse of data. This highlights the need for policies that balance the benefits of monitoring with the protection of.

When people don't know how artificial-intelligence tools arrive at their recommendations, students, teachers, and parents naturally start to wonder whether the system is fair or even reliable. That doubt is why transparency stands out as another cornerstone of ethical AI use in schools and colleges. Jobin et al. (2019) emphasized the importance of establishing clear ethical guidelines to ensure transparent AI practices, which are necessary to build trust among users. Accountability weaves through nearly all the ethical questions surrounding AI in education. Padmaja and Lakshminarayana (2024) emphasized the need for accountability structures as AI systems increasingly play a role in decisions that affect people's lives.

The socio-economic implications of AI in education have also been explored, particularly in terms of access and equity. Anuyahong et al. (2023) addressed concerns that the use of AI may disproportionately benefit wealthier educational institutions while marginalizing schools with fewer resources. Their call for equitable AI applications underscores the obligation to ensure that all students can benefit from technological advances without facing additional barriers.

Potential ethical issues related to the use of AI in education include data privacy, algorithmic bias, student tracking, transparency, accountability and educational equity. While incorporating the benefits of AI tools in education, an encompassing framework of ethics and laws needs to be created that safeguards human rights, values, intellectual autonomy, and privacy (UNESCO, 2023). Thus, it will be possible to direct the use of AI in education in accordance with all these ethical frameworks and to inform all stakeholders of education about the conscious use of technology.

TEACHER PROFESSIONAL DEVELOPMENT AND IDENTITY IN THE AGE OF AI

In the light of technological advancements in terms of AI, the professional development needs to be transformed in the teaching profession in order to cope with the complexities arising from technological innovations. As it has been experienced with the advent of technological innovations in the form of AI in the learning paradigms, teachers need to undergo professional development in order to build positive attitudes toward the integration of AI. As highlighted by a study carried out by Aghaziarati et al. (2023), awareness on the part of teachers is an influencing factor in adopting these innovations in the teaching industry in their respective settings. Shao and Sun (2025), underscoring the multidimensional nature of teacher identity, argue that contemporary transformations necessitate a reevaluation of teachers' roles, calling for an innovative approach to both professional growth and identity formation. Moreover, teachers' familiarity with digital tools has become increasingly central to their professional identity. As AI continues to redefine roles and expectations, educators may feel pressured to reshape their professional selves to align with this new context—an issue that, if left unaddressed, can lead to feelings of insecurity or a perceived erosion of professional status (Shao & Sun, 2025; Zhao & Zhang, 2021). Therefore, professional development initiatives must support educators in navigating these shifts, enabling them to build resilient professional identities capable of adapting to future challenges.

Resilience in facing the change that technology from AI is bringing, while sticking to the core principles in education, is what is going to constitute the new normal in the professional development of teachers. Teacher education is thus to incorporate technology skills as well as professional identity building into its structure for it to be an altogether more professional endeavor in an era dominated by technology from AI (Li, 2025). However, it is also significant to identify that even if technology from AI is changing some roles in teaching, the core principles in education with the belief in the teacher's role remain unchanged (Zhao & Zhang, 2021).

LONG-TERM CURRICULUM REFORMS AND AI LITERACY

AI literacy is on the cusp of making a big impact on long-term curriculum change at different levels of education. UNESCO (2023) emphasized the need for new skills and practices in education, stating that AI and AI ethics skills should be taught alongside skills such as basic literacy, numeracy, coding, digital skills, media and information literacy. It also listed these skills as "prerequisite skills" for AI education.The reason behind such change is the need for educators and learners to be adequately informed and equipped for an upcoming future where AI-based technology surrounds every aspect of their lives.

One critical dimension in the curriculum transformation in relation to AI is improving students' long-run interest and commitment in their learning with respect to AI. According to research carried out by Chai et al. (2022), the curriculum should remain student-centric, hence bringing in long-run commitment to learning in the area of AI. By integrating the curriculum for AI in a manner that remains aligned with the interests and engagement needs in learning, the interest and commitment in the area remain long run (Chai et al., 2022). There is also the need for engaging the students in critical thinking, collaboration, and ethics in relation to AI technology.

Higher education is an area where the potential for positive transformation offered by AI is well demonstrated in its application within curriculum alignment and personalized learning experiences. Zhang et al. (2024) went on to discuss the ways in which applications of technology in the subject of asset valuation could improve effectiveness in learning, emphasizing the need for curriculum structure that employs these AI technology applications for the automation and accuracy required in these evaluations. This helps higher education systems nurture learners who possess more than theoretical knowledge – learners who understand the application of technology, in the form of AI tools, in their fields.

Another critical aspect is incorporating ethics into these frameworks in order to facilitate the integration of AI into the education system effectively. According to Grimaud and Gathu (2024), it is essential to incorporate ethics for AI into these syllabuses, mainly in areas such as medicine, where the end effects of the integration of AI would profoundly affect the lives of beneficiaries in these settings. Similarly, Zhang et al. (2022) also pointed out the importance of ethical awareness in promoting AI literacy in secondary school students. UNESCO (2023) proposed that curriculums on ethics of AI should be created on all levels of education according to national education patterns, stressing the importance of encouraging cross-domain collaboration in both training technical skills and the human-social element of AI. By providing professionals with the knowledge necessary to reap from technology in an appropriate manner, these higher learning institutions can work to make technological advancements match set standards in their ever-rapidly changing settings.

DEVELOPMENTAL PERSPECTIVES ON AI IN EDUCATION

Worldwide, educators are beginning to recognise that AI could redesign curricula, reshape assessments, and influence national policies, and this shared optimism is pushing institutions to examine how AI might offer smarter, data- driven, and more inclusive learning. Recent studies point to AI's promise in crafting flexible lesson plans that respond to individual progress and needs. Zhu (2022) argues that success demands new pedagogies and structures, especially in ideological and political education, because its insights challenge age-old assumptions about curriculum design. Similarly, Dong and Sha (2023) emphasized the integration of AI into traditional educational frameworks, suggesting that future educational curricula will be enriched with AI technologies. To realise those gains, schools must prepare students for a job market shaped by intelligent systems and therefore embed coding, ethics, and critical AI literacy into every pathway. The same intelligence fuels assessment reform, allowing faster, fairer, and more personalised evaluations.

Zawacki-Richter et al. (2019) stated that AI can be used for assessment and evaluation applications under the headings of automatic grading, feedback, assessment of student understanding, engagement and academic honesty, and evaluation of teaching, and suggested that future assessment systems can utilize AI analytics to more effectively assess student learning. Such a change could lessen the grip of one-size-fits-all standardized tests and make it easy to offer instant, personal advice to learners as they study. Another big question is how AI will shape the rules schools follow. Wang and Han (2023) argue that principals and district heads are the ones who will have to steer new courses, budget for data tools, and train staff so every classroom can go digital. They expect policies to pour money into networks, servers, and other tech, giving teachers and students the backbone they need when lessons move online. Lin et al. (2020) state that educational policies will need to include guidelines to facilitate the use of ethical AI in classrooms. Building a culture of responsible AI study now also helps future instructors show students when a tool helps and when it harms-and keep new curricula honest and grounded.

Recent research points to a growing agreement that AI is changing education in deep and far-reaching ways. From tailoring lessons to each learners pace, crafting new course materials on the fly, and grading with the speed and accuracy that pure numbers provide, schools stand on the edge of an era defined by thoughtful, purposeful use of AI tools. Education policies should also be developed to ensure equal access to AI resources and create an environment conducive to the responsible use of these powerful tools.

CONCLUSION AND RECOMMENDATIONS: A ROADMAP FOR INTEGRATING AI INTO EDUCATION

The examples and classifications presented in this chapter clearly demonstrate the diversity and potential of applications of AI in education. In the light of the concepts and trends defined in the introduction, it is seen that AI-supported systems touch almost every aspect of education, ranging from teaching processes to assessment, content production to special education applications.

In the field of personalized learning, examples such as Khanmigo, ASSISTments, Querium and Squirrel AI offer student-centered, flexible and adaptive learning environments. Grading tools like Gradescope, OpenEssayist, Peergrade, and Formative lighten teachers workloads by providing faster, data-rich, and more consistent evaluations. Meanwhile, natural-language systems such as ChatGPT, Hugging Face, Text Inspector, and Quillbot help polish reading and writing skills for teachers and learners alike. AI-driven content creation tools like Curipod, MagicSchool AI, Diffit, and Conker AI ease the burden on teachers by speeding up lesson prep and adding fresh methods to classrooms. Accessibility apps such as Seeing AI, Google Lookout, Voiceitt, Otter.ai, and Immersive Reader open doors so students with disabilities can fully participate alongside their peers. Together, these innovations show that AI can boost learning while also honoring the twin pillars of accessibility and inclusivity. Keeping this promise in mind, the following actions are offered as practical guideposts for teachers, school leaders, and policy makers:.

- While integrating AI into the teaching process, educators should choose tools that are compatible with pedagogical goals, support students' cognitive development, and use AI in a supportive role, especially in content production, evaluation and individualization processes.

- Administrators should organize in-service trainings for teachers to use these technologies effectively and ethically, and establish school-based policy and guidance mechanisms on security, data privacy and digital literacy.
- Policymakers should develop inclusive digital strategies to ensure that AI does not undermine the principle of equal opportunity and create systematic support to ensure access to these technologies, especially for disadvantaged groups.

The ethical integration of AI into education involves many considerations such as data privacy, algorithmic bias, student tracking, transparency, accountability and educational equity. Furthermore, it should be emphasized at all levels that AI should be used as a supportive tool, not a decision-making tool.

AI is not only a technological innovation in education, but also a strategic force with the potential to transform the quality of teaching. However, for this transformation to take place effectively and ethically, it requires a multi-actor approach supported by a strong vision, continuous professional development and comprehensive digital policies.

REFERENCES

Abbas, N., Ali, I., Manzoor, R., Hussain, T., & Hussain, M. H. A. i. (2023). Role of artificial intelligence tools in enhancing students' educational performance at higher levels. *Journal of Artificial Intelligence. Machine Learning and Neural Network*, (35), 36–49. DOI: 10.55529/jaimlnn.35.36.49

Aghaziarati, A., Nejatifar, S., & Abedi, A. (2023). Artificial intelligence in education: Investigating teacher attitudes. *AI and Tech in Behavioral and Social Sciences*, *1*(1), 35–42. DOI: 10.61838/kman.aitech.1.1.6

Ahmad, W., Shokeen, R., & Raj, R. (2024). Artificial intelligence. *Advances in Educational Technologies and Instructional Design*, •••, 459–520. DOI: 10.4018/979-8-3693-5538-1.ch017 PMID: 38274052

Akgün, S., & Greenhow, C. (2021). Artificial intelligence in education: Addressing ethical challenges in k-12 settings. *AI and Ethics*, *2*(3), 431–440. DOI: 10.1007/s43681-021-00096-7 PMID: 34790956

Anuyahong, B., Rattanapong, C., & Patcha, I. (2023). Analyzing the impact of artificial intelligence in personalized learning and adaptive assessment in higher education. *International Journal of Research and Scientific Innovation*, *X*(IV), 88–93. DOI: 10.51244/ijrsi.2023.10412

Ayeni, O. O., Hamad, N. M. A., Chisom, O. N., Osawaru, B., & Adewusi, O. E. (2024). Ai in education: A review of personalized learning and educational technology. *GSC Advanced Research and Reviews*, *18*(2), 261–271. DOI: 10.30574/gscarr.2024.18.2.0062

Babu, C. V. S., & Suruthi, G. (2024). Unravelling the evolution of generative ai in communication education. *Advances in Educational Technologies and Instructional Design*, •••, 55–71. DOI: 10.4018/979-8-3693-0831-8.ch003

Bahroun, Z., Anane, C., Ahmed, V., & Zacca, A. (2023). Transforming education: A comprehensive review of generative artificial intelligence in educational settings through bibliometric and content analysis. *Sustainability*, *15*(17), 12983. DOI: 10.3390/su151712983

Barua, P. D., Vicnesh, J., Gururajan, R., Oh, S. L., Palmer, E. E., Azizan, M. M., & Acharya, U. R. (2022). Artificial intelligence enabled personalised assistive tools to enhance education of children with neurodevelopmental disorders—A review. *International Journal of Environmental Research and Public Health*, *19*(3), 1192. DOI: 10.3390/ijerph19031192 PMID: 35162220

Bayne, S. (2015). Teacherbot: Interventions in automated teaching. *Teaching in Higher Education, 20*(4). Advance online publication. DOI: 10.1080/13562517.2015.1020783

Begum, I. U. (2024). Role of artificial intelligence in higher education- an empirical investigation. [IRJAEM]. *International Research Journal on Advanced Engineering and Management*, *2*(03), 49–53. DOI: 10.47392/irjaem.2024.0009

Begum, R. (2025). A systematic literature review on how artificial intelligence (AI) is revolutionizing education 4.0. *Journal of Scientific Reports*, *9*(1), 60–79. DOI: 10.58970/jsr.1096 PMID: 39747217

Beiting-Parrish, M., & Whitmer, J. (2023). Lessons learned about evaluating fairness from a data challenge to automatically score naep reading items. https://doi .org/DOI: 10.35542/osf.io/j9c5g

Bloom, B. S. (1968). *Learning for mastery. Evaluation Comment*, 1(2), 1–12. University of Chicago, Department of Education. https://eric.ed.gov/?id=eD053419

Borocki, J., Jovanović, A., Vekić, A., Đaković, V., & Cović, M. (2023). Empowering content creation with generative ai in metaverse. *19th International Scientific Conference on Industrial Systems,* 554-559. https://doi.org/DOI: 10.24867/is-2023-vp1.1-14_07941

Bulathwela, S., Pérez-Ortiz, M., Holloway, C., Cukurova, M., & Shawe-Taylor, J. (2024). Artificial intelligence alone will not democratise education: On educational inequality, techno-solutionism and inclusive tools. *Sustainability*, *16*(2), 781. DOI: 10.3390/su16020781

Calatayud, V. G., Espinosa, M. P. P., & Vila, R. R. (2021). Artificial intelligence for student assessment: A systematic review. *Applied Sciences (Basel, Switzerland)*, *11*(12), 5467. DOI: 10.3390/app11125467

Carless, D. (2007). Learning-oriented assessment: Conceptual bases and practical implications. *Innovations in Education and Teaching International*, *44*(1), 57–66. https://www.tandfonline.com/doi/abs/10.1080/14703290601081332

Chai, C. S., Chiu, T. K. F., Wang, X., Jiang, F., & Lin, X. (2022). Modeling chinese secondary school students' behavioral intentions to learn artificial intelligence with the theory of planned behavior and self-determination theory. *Sustainability*, *15*(1), 605. DOI: 10.3390/su15010605

Chang, J., & Lu, X. (2019, August). The study on students' participation in personalized learning under the background of artificial intelligence. *In 10th International Conference on Information Technology in Medicine and Education (ITME)* (pp. 555-558). IEEE

Chaudhary, N., Jain, P., & Sharma, C. (2024). From traditional to technological. *Advances in Educational Marketing, Administration, and Leadership*, •••, 79–108. DOI: 10.4018/979-8-3373-1692-5.ch004

Chedrawi, C., Kazoun, N., & Kokkinaki, A. (2024). The role of ai agents in fostering inclusivity for heis' students with special needs against backdrops of the accreditation trend. *Quality Assurance in Education*, *32*(4), 582–596. DOI: 10.1108/qae-01-2024-0010

Chen, L., Chen, P., & Lin, Z. (2020). Artificial intelligence in education: A review. *IEEE Access : Practical Innovations, Open Solutions*, *8*, 75264–75278. DOI: 10.1109/access.2020.2988510

Collins, A. (2006). Cognitive apprenticeship. In Sawyer, R. K. (Ed.), *The Cambridge Handbook of the Learning Sciences* (pp. 109–127). Cambridge University Press.

Daxenberger, F., Deußing, M., Eijkenboom, Q. L., Gust, C., Thamm, J., Hartmann, D., & Sattler, E. (2023). Innovation in actinic keratosis assessment: Artificial intelligence-based approach to lc-oct pro score evaluation. *Cancers (Basel)*, *15*(18), 4457. DOI: 10.3390/cancers15184457 PMID: 37760425

Dey, S., & Sahoo, B. B. (2024). Ai integration in education 5.0. *Advances in Educational Technologies and Instructional Design*, •••, 77–92. DOI: 10.4018/979-8-3693-8191-5.ch003

Dhirani, L. L., Mukhtiar, N., Chowdhry, B. S., & Newe, T. (2023). Ethical dilemmas and privacy issues in emerging technologies: A review. *Sensors (Basel)*, *23*(3), 1151. DOI: 10.3390/s23031151 PMID: 36772190

Dignum, V. (2021). The role and challenges of education for responsible ai. *London Review of Education*, *19*(1). Advance online publication. DOI: 10.14324/lre.19.1.01

Dong, Z., & Sha, N. (2023). Research on the current situation and countermeasures of cultivating talents in recreational sports under the perspective of artificial intelligence. *Applied Mathematics and Nonlinear Sciences*, *9*(1). Advance online publication. DOI: 10.2478/amns.2023.2.00161

Erbaşı, Z., Tural, B., & Çoşkuner, İ. (2023). The role and potential of artificial intelligence and gamification in education: The example of vakıf participation bank. *Orclever Proceedings of Research and Development*, *3*(1), 243–254. DOI: 10.56038/oprd.v3i1.329

European Commission Directorate-General for Education Youth Sport Culture. (2022). Ethical Guidelines on the Use of Artificial Intelligence (AI) and Data in Teaching and Learning for Educators. *Publications Office of the European Union* https://op.europa.eu/en/publication-detail/-/publication/d81a0d54-5348-11ed-92ed-01aa75ed71a1/language-en

Ginsberg, M. (2012). *Essentials of artificial intelligence*. Morgan Kaufmann Publishers.

Göçen, A., & Aydemir, F. (2020). Artificial intelligence in education and schools. *Research on Education and Media*, *12*(1), 13–21. DOI: 10.2478/rem-2020-0003

Grandbastien, M., Luckin, R., Mizoguchi, R., & Aleven, V. (2016). Preface to the ijaied 25th anniversary issue. *International Journal of Artificial Intelligence in Education*, *26*(1), 1–3. DOI: 10.1007/s40593-015-0092-6

Grimaud, L. M., & Gathu, C. (2024). Integrating artificial intelligence ethics education into the undergraduate medical curriculum - a scoping review. (preprint). https://doi.org/DOI: 10.2196/preprints.57746

Gutiérrez, L. (2023). Artificial intelligence in language education: Navigating the potential and challenges of chatbots and nlp. *Research Studies in English Language Teaching and Learning*, *1*(3), 180–191. DOI: 10.62583/rseltl.v1i3.44

Gyawali, Y. P., & Mehandroo, M. (2022). Artificial intelligence in english language teaching: Navigating the future with emerging perspectives. *Journal of Language and Linguistics in Society*, *26*, 21–27. DOI: 10.55529/jlls.26.21.27

Haseski, H. I. (2019). What do Turkish pre-service teachers think about artificial intelligence? *International Journal of Computer Science Education in Schools*, *3*(2). Advance online publication. DOI: 10.21585/ijcses.v3i2.55

Hinojo-Lucena, F., Díaz, I. A., Reche, M. P. C., & Rodríguez, J. M. R. (2019). Artificial intelligence in higher education: A bibliometric study on its impact in the scientific literature. *Education Sciences*, *9*(1), 51. DOI: 10.3390/educsci9010051

Hirschberg, J., & Manning, C. D. (2015). Advances in natural language processing. *Science*, *349*(6245), 261–266. DOI: 10.1126/science.aaa8685 PMID: 26185244

Holmes, W., & Tuomi, I. (2022). State of the art and practice in AI in education. *European Journal of Education*, *57*(4), 542–570. DOI: 10.1111/ejed.12533

Hosseinkhani, N. T. (2025). Evaluating the economic impact, equity implications, and long-term prospects of AI-powered personalized learning in education by mid-century. https://doi.org/DOI: 10.31219/osf.io/j8kh4_v1

Isaacs, M., Majeed, A. P. P. A., Moussa, K. H., & Shodipo, D. (2024). Design and implementation of an ethical ai-based teaching assistant for iot security education. *African Journal of Inter/Multidisciplinary Studies, 6*(1). https://doi.org/DOI: 10.51415/ajims.v6i1.1586

Jobin, A., Ienca, M., & Vayena, E. (2019). The global landscape of ai ethics guidelines. *Nature Machine Intelligence, 1*(9), 389–399. DOI: 10.1038/s42256-019-0088-2

Johnson, M., Liu, X., & McCaffrey, D. F. (2022). Psychometric methods to evaluate measurement and algorithmic bias in automated scoring. *Journal of Educational Measurement, 59*(3), 338–361. DOI: 10.1111/jedm.12335

Kadaruddin, K. (2023). Empowering education through generative ai: Innovative instructional strategies for tomorrow's learners. *International Journal of Business, Law, and Education, 4*(2), 618–625. DOI: 10.56442/ijble.v4i2.215

Kamalov, F., Calonge, D. S., & Gurrib, I. (2023). New era of artificial intelligence in education: Towards a sustainable multifaceted revolution. *Sustainability, 15*(16), 12451. DOI: 10.3390/su151612451

Kang, Y., Forkan, A. R. M., Jayaraman, P. P., Wieland, N., Kolliasl, E., Du, H., . . . Li, Y. (2021). An ai-based solution for enhancing delivery of digital learning for future teachers. *arXiv preprint*. https://doi.org//arxiv.2112.01229DOI: 10.48550

Karaibrahimoğlu, A., İnce, F., Hassanzadeh, G., Alizadeh, A. M., Bagheri, K., Yucel, I., & Shariat, A. (2024). Ethical considerations in telehealth and artificial intelligence for work related musculoskeletal disorders: A scoping review. *Work (Reading, Mass.), 79*(3), 1577–1588. DOI: 10.3233/wor-240187 PMID: 39093108

Kasneci, E., Seßler, K., Küchemann, S., Bannert, M., Dementieva, D., Fischer, F., & Kasneci, G. (2023). Chatgpt for good? on opportunities and challenges of large language models for education. https://doi.org/DOI: 10.35542/osf.io/5er8f

Khademi, A. (2023). Can chatgpt and bard generate aligned assessment items? a reliability analysis against human performance. *Journal of Applied Learning &Amp. Teaching, 6*(1). Advance online publication. DOI: 10.37074/jalt.2023.6.1.28

Khosravizadeh, O. (2023). Analysis of the impact of vygotsky's collaborative learning theory on the development of group skills. *Journal of Study and Innovation in Education and Development, 3*(1), 1–14. DOI: 10.61838/jsied.3.1.1

Kiemde, S. M. A., & Kora, A. D. (2021). Towards an ethics of ai in Africa: Rule of education. *AI and Ethics, 2*(1), 35–40. DOI: 10.1007/s43681-021-00106-8

Klímová, B., Pikhart, M., & Kacetl, J. (2023). Ethical issues of the use of AI-driven mobile apps for education. *Frontiers in Public Health*, *10*, 1118116. DOI: 10.3389/fpubh.2022.1118116 PMID: 36711343

Koblyakov, P. (2024). ChatGPT in the Educational Landscape: A Comprehensive Guide.

Konishi, E., Saiki, T., Kamiyama, H., Nishiya, K., Tsunekawa, K., Imafuku, R., & Suzuki, Y. (2020). Improved cognitive apprenticeship clinical teaching after a faculty development program. *Pediatrics International*, *62*(5), 542–548. DOI: 10.1111/ped.14095 PMID: 31834972

Kumar, D., Haque, M. A., Mishra, K., Islam, F., Mishra, B. K., & Ahmad, S. (2023). Exploring the transformative role of artificial intelligence and metaverse in education: A comprehensive review. *Metaverse Basic and Applied Research*, *2*, 55. DOI: 10.56294/mr202355

Kurzweil, R. (2005). The singularity is near. In *Ethics and emerging technologies* (pp. 393–406). Palgrave Macmillan UK., https://link.springer.com/chapter/10.1057/9781137349088_26

Laaziri, M., Khoulji, S., Benmoussa, K., & Kerkeb, M. L. (2018). Outlining an intelligent tutoring system for a university cooperation information system. *Engineering, Technology &. Applied Scientific Research*, *8*(5), 3427–3431. DOI: 10.48084/etasr.2158

Li, K. C., & Wong, B. T. M. (2023). Artificial intelligence in personalised learning: A bibliometric analysis. *Interactive Technology and Smart Education*, *20*(3), 422–445. DOI: 10.1108/itse-01-2023-0007

Liang, Y., & Lu, J. (2025). How school support influences the content creation of pre-service teachers' instructional design. *Behavioral Sciences (Basel, Switzerland)*, *15*(5), 568. DOI: 10.3390/bs15050568 PMID: 40426346

Lin, P., Brummelen, J. V., Lukin, G., Williams, R., & Breazeal, C. (2020). Zhorai: designing a conversational agent for children to explore machine learning concepts. Proceedings of the *AAAI Conference on Artificial Intelligence, 34(*09), 13381-13388. https://doi.org/DOI: 10.1609/aaai.v34i09.7061

Liu, M. (2023). Exploring the application of artificial intelligence in foreign language teaching: challenges and future development. *SHS Web of Conferences,* 168, 03025. https://doi.org/DOI: 10.1051/shsconf/202316803025

Liu, M., Wang, Y., Xu, W., & Liu, L. (2017). Automated scoring of chinese engineering students' english essays. *International Journal of Distance Education Technologies*, *15*(1), 52–68. DOI: 10.4018/ijdet.2017010104

Luckin, R., & Holmes, W. (2016). Intelligence unleashed: An argument for AI in education. https://www.pearson.com/content/dam/corporate/global/pearson-dot-com/files/innovation/Intelligence-Unleashed-Publication.pdf

Lukwaro, E. A. E., Kalegele, K., & Nyambo, D. G. (2024). A review on nlp techniques and associated challenges in extracting features from education data. *International Journal of Computing and Digital Systems*, *15*(1), 961–979. DOI: 10.12785/ijcds/160170

Luo, Y. (2024). Innovative research on ai-assisted teaching models for college english listening and speaking courses. *Applied and Computational Engineering*, *69*(1), 155–160. DOI: 10.54254/2755-2721/69/20241493

McMahon, D., & Firestone, J. B. (2024). Remixing special education practices with artificial intelligence: Udl, ebp, and hlps. *Journal of Special Education Preparation*, *4*(2), 66–76. DOI: 10.33043/3dq2d32d

Miller, W. T. (2024). Adapting to ai: reimagining the role of assessment professionals. Intersection: *A Journal at the Intersection of Assessment and Learning*, *5*(4). https://doi.org/DOI: 10.61669/001c.121439

Minsky, M. (Ed.). (1969). *Semantic information processing*. The MIT Press.

Mpu, Y. (2024). *Bridging the knowledge gap on special needs learner support: the use of artificial intelligence (ai) to combat digital divide post-covid-19 pandemic and beyond – a comprehensive literature review*. Education and Human Development., DOI: 10.5772/intechopen.113054

Nair, B. R., Loon, J. v., Lierop, M. v., & Govaerts, M. (2024). Leveraging narrative feedback in programmatic assessment: The potential of automated text analysis to support coaching and decision-making in programmatic assessment. *Advances in Medical Education and Practice*, *15*, 671–683. DOI: 10.2147/amep.s465259 PMID: 39050116

Nguyen, A., Kremantzis, M., Essien, A., Petrounias, I., & Hosseini, S. (2024). Enhancing Student Engagement Through Artificial Intelligence (AI): Understanding the Basics, Opportunities, and Challenges. *Journal of University Teaching & Learning Practice*, *21*(06). Advance online publication. DOI: 10.53761/caraaq92

Ninaus, M., & Sailer, M. (2022). Closing the loop – the human role in artificial intelligence for education. *Frontiers in Psychology*, *13*. Advance online publication. DOI: 10.3389/fpsyg.2022.956798 PMID: 36092115

Niu, W., Zhang, W., Zhang, C., & Chen, X. (2024). The role of artificial intelligence autonomy in higher education: A uses and gratification perspective. *Sustainability*, *16*(3), 1276. DOI: 10.3390/su16031276

OECD. (2023), AI and the Future of Skills, Volume 2: Methods for Evaluating AI Capabilities, Educational Research and Innovation, OECD Publishing, Paris, https://doi.org/DOI: 10.1787/a9fe53cb-en

Oleet, J. B., & Yu, C. (2025). Ai and the future of education. *Advances in Computational Intelligence and Robotics*, •••, 407–440. DOI: 10.4018/979-8-3693-7873-1.ch015

Padmaja, C. V. R. and Lakshminarayana, S. (2024). The rise of ai: a comprehensive research review. *IAES International Journal of Artificial Intelligence (IJ-AI), 13*(2), 2226. https://doi.org/DOI: 10.11591/ijai.v13.i2.pp2226-2235

Pagliara, S. M., Bonavolontà, G., Pia, M. G., Falchi, S., Zurru, A. L., Fenu, G., & Mura, A. (2024). The integration of artificial intelligence in inclusive education: a scoping review. https://doi.org/DOI: 10.20944/preprints202410.1386.v1

Papert, S. (1980). *Mindstorms: Children, computers, and powerful ideas*. Basic Books.

Pappas, M. A., & Drigas, A. (2016). Incorporation of artificial intelligence tutoring techniques in mathematics. [iJEP]. *International Journal of Engineering Pedagogy*, *6*(4), 12. DOI: 10.3991/ijep.v6i4.6063

Popenici, Ş., & Kerr, S. (2017). Exploring the impact of artificial intelligence on teaching and learning in higher education. *Research and Practice in Technology Enhanced Learning*, *12*(1). Advance online publication. DOI: 10.1186/s41039-017-0062-8 PMID: 30595727

Qian, Y., & Lehman, J. D. (2019). Using targeted feedback to address common student misconceptions in introductory programming: A data-driven approach. *SAGE Open*, *9*(4). Advance online publication. DOI: 10.1177/2158244019885136

Qin, L. (2024). Adaptive system of english-speaking learning based on artificial intelligence. *Journal of Electrical Systems*, *20*(6s), 267–275. DOI: 10.52783/jes.2637

Rakshit, S. (2025). Edtech 5.0: The role of immersive technologies and ai tutors in shaping future classrooms. *International Journal of Recent Innovations*, *01*(01), 24–31. DOI: 10.63665/ijri.v1i1.04

Ramesh, D., & Sanampudi, S. K. (2021). An automated essay scoring systems: A systematic literature review. *Artificial Intelligence Review*, *55*(3), 2495–2527. DOI: 10.1007/s10462-021-10068-2 PMID: 34584325

Ramesh, S. (2021). Unleashing the future: The dynamic impacts of artificial intelligence on education. *Journal of Artificial Intelligence. Machine Learning and Neural Network*, (12), 27–31. DOI: 10.55529/jaimlnn.12.27.31

Ramos, J. G., & Wilson-Kennedy, Z. S. (2024). Promoting equity and addressing concerns in teaching and learning with artificial intelligence. *Frontiers in Education*, *9*. Advance online publication. DOI: 10.3389/feduc.2024.1487882

Rayati, M. (2021). Neuro-linguistic programming and its applicability in efl classrooms: Perceptions of nlp-trained english teachers. *Language Teaching Research Quarterly*, *24*, 44–64. DOI: 10.32038/ltrq.2021.24.03

Schulze, M. (2025). Icall and AI: Seven lessons from seventy years. *Insights Into AI and Language Teaching and Learning,* 11-31. https://doi.org/DOI: 10.29140/9781763711600-02

Shao, J., & Sun, S. (2025). Teacher identity in the era of intelligence. *Journal of Educational Theory and Practice*, *2*(1). Advance online publication. DOI: 10.62177/jetp.v2i1.141

Shen, S. (2024). Application of large language models in the field of education. *Theoretical and Natural Science*, *34*(1), 147–154. DOI: 10.54254/2753-8818/34/20241163

Sihite, M. R., Meisuri, M., & Sibarani, B. (2023). Examining the validity and reliability of chatgpt 3.5-generated reading comprehension questions for academic texts. *Randwick International of Education and Linguistics Science Journal*, *4*(4), 937–944. DOI: 10.47175/rielsj.v4i4.835

Smith, G., Haworth, R., & Žitnik, S. (2020). Computer science meets education: Natural language processing for automatic grading of open-ended questions in ebooks. *Journal of Educational Computing Research*, *58*(7), 1227–1255. DOI: 10.1177/0735633120927486

Somers, R., Cunningham, S., & Boles, W. (2021). Applying natural language processing to automatically assess student conceptual understanding from textual responses. *Australasian Journal of Educational Technology*, *37*(5), 98–115. DOI: 10.14742/ajet.7121

Sullivan, M., Kelly, A., & McLaughlan, P. (2023). Chatgpt in higher education: Considerations for academic integrity and student learning. *Journal of Applied Learning & Teaching*, *6*(1). Advance online publication. DOI: 10.37074/jalt.2023.6.1.17

Thangaraj, J. (2021). Automated assessment & feedback system for novice programmers. *Proceedings of the 26th ACM Conference on Innovation and Technology in Computer Science Education* v. 2, 672-673. https://doi.org/DOI: 10.1145/3456565.3460021

UNESCO. 2023. *Recommendation on the ethics of artificial intelligence.* Retrieved from https://www.unesco.org/en/articles/recommendation-ethics-artificial-intelligence

Wang, D., & Han, Y. (2023). Exploration of the path for school principals to promote the construction of artificial intelligence curriculum – based on case study. *Fuzzy Systems and Data Mining, IX.* Advance online publication. DOI: 10.3233/faia231092

Wei, S. (2024). Research on the disruptive transformation and future development of american teaching models in the context of intelligent transformation. *Advances in Economics. Management and Political Sciences, 72*(1), 201–210. DOI: 10.54254/2754-1169/72/20240696

Xie, X. (2023). Influence of ai-driven inquiry teaching on learning outcomes. [iJET]. *International Journal of Emerging Technologies in Learning, 18*(23), 59–70. DOI: 10.3991/ijet.v18i23.45473

Xu, W., & Ouyang, F. (2022). The application of ai technologies in stem education: A systematic review from 2011 to 2021. *International Journal of STEM Education, 9*(1). Advance online publication. DOI: 10.1186/s40594-022-00377-5

Yang, Z. (2022). Natural language enhancement for english teaching using character-level recurrent neural network with back propagation neural network based classification by deep learning architectures. *JUCS -. Journal of Universal Computer Science, 28*(9), 984–1000. DOI: 10.3897/jucs.94162

Yu, Y., Han, L., Du, X., & Yu, J. (2022). An oral english evaluation model using artificial intelligence method. *Mobile Information Systems,* •••, 1–8. DOI: 10.1155/2022/3998886

Zawacki-Richter, O., Marín, V. I., Bond, M., & Gouverneur, F. (2019). Systematic review of research on artificial intelligence applications in higher education – where are the educators? *International Journal of Educational Technology in Higher Education, 16*(1). Advance online publication. DOI: 10.1186/s41239-019-0171-0

Zhai, X., & Nehm, R. H. (2023). ai and formative assessment: The train has left the station. *Journal of Research in Science Teaching, 60*(6), 1390–1398. DOI: 10.1002/tea.21885

Zhang, C., Zheng, X., & Wan, J. (2024). Research on the construction of a curriculum system of asset appraisal major under the background of artificial intelligence. *International Journal of Education and Humanities*, *15*(3), 357–360. DOI: 10.54097/e7yprc40

Zhang, H., Lee, I., Ali, S., DiPaola, D., Cheng, Y., & Breazeal, C. (2022). Integrating ethics and career futures with technical learning to promote ai literacy for middle school students: An exploratory study. *International Journal of Artificial Intelligence in Education*, *33*(2), 290–324. DOI: 10.1007/s40593-022-00293-3 PMID: 35573722

Zhao, N., & Zhang, J. (2021). The "change" and "constancy" of teacher's role in the age of artificial intelligence. *Proceedings of the 6th International Conference on Education Reform and Modern Management (ERMM 2021)*. https://doi.org/DOI: 10.2991/assehr.k.210513.098

Zheng, R., & Badarch, T. (2022). Research on applications of artificial intelligence in education. *American Journal of Computer Science and Technology*, *5*(2), 72. DOI: 10.11648/j.ajcst.20220502.17

Zhu, C. (2022). Reflections on the reform of curriculum ideological and political teaching mode in the era of artificial intelligence. *International Symposium on Robotics, Artificial Intelligence, and Information Engineering* (RAIIE 2022), 114. https://doi.org/DOI: 10.1117/12.2660041

Zhu, Q. (2023). Natural language processing in teacher training: A systematic review. *Lecture Notes in Education Psychology and Public Media*, *18*(1), 83–90. DOI: 10.54254/2753-7048/18/20231293

KEY TERMS AND DEFINITIONS

Accessible Technology: Technologies designed in accordance with accessibility standards that enable individuals with disabilities to fully participate in digital content and learning environments. AI-powered accessibility tools (e.g., Voiceitt, Seeing AI) fall into this category.

AI Literacy for Educators: The ability of educators to understand, evaluate, and effectively use AI. As part of digital pedagogical competencies, it involves integrating AI tools into teaching for pedagogical purposes.

AI-generated Educational Content: The automatic creation of learning materials (e.g., questions, activities, lesson plans) by AI tools. These resources facilitate teachers' preparation processes and increase the diversity of instructional materials.

Artificial Intelligence (AI): A general term for computer systems that simulate human-like cognitive processes such as learning, reasoning, and problem-solving. In the context of education, AI is used in areas such as personalized learning, content generation, and assessment.

Automated Assessment: The use of AI or algorithms to automatically evaluate student performance. It draws on multiple data sources, including exams, written responses, and interaction data.

Ethical AI in Education: Focuses on the ethical principles (transparency, fairness, data security, autonomy) that must be upheld in the use of AI in education. This includes protecting student data and ensuring the use of unbiased algorithms.

Inclusive Education: An educational approach aiming for the equal participation of all students in shared learning environments, while respecting individual differences. AI plays a significant role in inclusive education through personalization and support services.

Intelligent Tutoring Systems (ITS): AI-based digital instructional systems that provide students with personalized feedback and guidance. These systems adapt to student performance through real-time data analysis.

Natural Language Processing (NLP): A subfield of AI focused on processing and interpreting human language. In education, it is used in applications such as text analysis, simplification, automatic summarization, and speech recognition.

Chapter 5
Exploring the Potential, Applications, and Ethical Challenges of Harnessing Artificial Intelligence in Education

Sohel Rana Sarkar
https://orcid.org/0000-0003-4237-672X
Hingalganj Mahavidyalaya, West Bengal State University, India

Sirajun Tahura
https://orcid.org/0009-0008-4172-9611
Kumarpukur High School, India

ABSTRACT

AI is rapidly transforming the educational landscape by offering innovative solutions to personalize learning, automate assessments, enhance student engagement, and improve administrative efficiency. This chapter explores the diverse applications of AI in education, focusing on adaptive learning platforms, virtual teaching assistants, predictive data analytics, and AI-enabled lifelong learning. Drawing upon empirical case studies, it illustrates both the benefits and limitations of AI integration across varied educational contexts. Ethical concerns such as data privacy, algorithmic bias, student autonomy, and digital inequality are critically examined, highlighting the urgent need for equitable, transparent, and human-centered AI systems. Looking ahead, the chapter outlines future directions including intelligent learning environ-

DOI: 10.4018/979-8-3373-8857-1.ch005

ments, emotional and cognitive analytics, and AI as a co-teacher. It concludes with strategic recommendations for policymakers, educators, and technologists to harness AI's full potential while safeguarding educational values and equity.

INTRODUCTION

Artificial Intelligence (AI) has emerged as a pivotal force reshaping modern education. From personalized learning platforms to automated assessments, from intelligent tutoring systems to data-driven decision-making tools, AI is transforming every facet of educational experience. It promises to enhance accessibility, increase efficiency, and elevate learning outcomes. However, with these opportunities come significant challenges—ethical, pedagogical, and infrastructural—that demand careful deliberation.

This chapter offers a comprehensive exploration of the multifaceted role of AI in education. It begins by analyzing the immense potential of AI technologies to personalize learning, optimize instructional design, and support student engagement across diverse contexts. Drawing on both theoretical frameworks and empirical studies, the discussion highlights how AI-driven innovations such as adaptive learning systems, predictive analytics, and virtual teaching assistants are influencing contemporary classrooms and educational management systems.

The chapter also provides an in-depth review of real-world applications through global case studies that illustrate both the benefits and the limitations of AI implementation. These examples underscore the critical importance of equity, transparency, and cultural relevance in deploying AI systems effectively and ethically.

Further, the narrative critically evaluates the ethical challenges posed by AI integration in education. Issues such as data privacy, algorithmic bias, the evolving role of teachers, student autonomy, and the digital divide are discussed in detail. It advocates for an ethical framework grounded in human rights, inclusivity, and participatory design.

Looking toward the future, the chapter examines evolving trends such as emotional and cognitive analytics, intelligent learning environments, AI-assisted lifelong learning, and AI-enabled career guidance. It emphasizes the role of AI as a co-educator—augmenting rather than replacing human teachers—and calls for a harmonious partnership between human insight and machine intelligence.

The chapter concludes with a robust set of recommendations for educators, policymakers, and developers on how to integrate AI responsibly and equitably. In doing so, it presents AI not just as a tool for innovation, but as a catalyst for reimagining education in more inclusive, ethical, and transformative ways.

POTENTIALS OF AI IN EDUCATION

Artificial Intelligence (AI) holds immense transformative potential for education, particularly in personalizing learning, enhancing engagement, improving instructional delivery, and enabling lifelong skill development. This section explores the major dimensions in which AI is reshaping educational opportunities and outcomes, including personalized learning experiences, predictive data analytics, instructional enhancement, and AI-facilitated upskilling in underserved communities.

AI-Driven Personalized Learning Experiences

AI-driven personalized learning experiences significantly improve student outcomes in diverse educational settings by tailoring instructional content to individual cognitive needs. These systems leverage machine learning algorithms, real-time analytics, and behavioral data to build customized pathways for learners, thereby fostering active engagement, boosting motivation, and closing learning gaps. By continuously assessing student performance, these technologies adjust content difficulty, pacing, and feedback dynamically, promoting mastery-based progression.

AI enhances student engagement by delivering learning activities suited to individual styles and preferences (Iman et al., 2024; Zaharuddin et al., 2024). Students using AI-adaptive platforms report heightened interest and interactive participation, leading to notable gains in academic achievement. These systems support differentiated instruction—critical for accommodating learning diversity and ensuring inclusive education—by identifying learner strengths, weaknesses, and progress patterns (Sari et al., 2024; Iman et al., 2024).

Furthermore, AI enables a more learner-centric pedagogical model. Traditional classrooms often adopt a one-size-fits-all approach, which may disengage learners at both ends of the academic spectrum. AI personalizes the pacing and sequencing of instruction, ensuring that advanced learners are sufficiently challenged, while students needing additional support receive scaffolded content.

However, personalized learning environments also necessitate a cultural shift in classroom dynamics. Teachers must act more as facilitators or learning designers than as sole knowledge providers. This change in role requires significant training and capacity building. Moreover, there are technological constraints, such as equitable access to infrastructure and quality digital content, especially in low-resource settings. Challenges such as algorithmic bias and data misinterpretation can lead to misclassification or inappropriate learning recommendations, highlighting the importance of human oversight (Y et al., 2024; Gupta, 2024).

AI-Driven Data Analytics in Education

AI-powered data analytics are revolutionizing how educators understand, monitor, and support student learning. Through intelligent dashboards and real-time reporting, AI provides granular insights into learning behaviors, academic trends, and performance anomalies. These systems not only diagnose learning gaps but also enable early intervention, personalized recommendations, and predictive modeling to support timely instructional decisions.

Adaptive algorithms assess student engagement levels and personalize content accordingly (Silva et al., 2024). Predictive analytics identify at-risk learners by analyzing historical and behavioral data, enabling educators to implement targeted support strategies before academic failure occurs (Ghosh, 2024; Murwaningsih et al., 2024). AI also enhances personalized feedback by evaluating student submissions and delivering tailored suggestions for improvement (Vashishth et al., 2024).

Additionally, the power of AI to integrate data from multiple sources—including assessment results, behavioral logs, attendance records, and demographic information—allows for a comprehensive learner profile. These profiles support teachers in designing inclusive lesson plans and allocating resources where they are needed most. Institutions can use aggregated analytics to inform policy decisions, curriculum design, and teacher professional development.

Yet, ethical considerations around data privacy, surveillance, and consent become more urgent with increased data collection. Students and educators must be aware of how their data is collected, stored, and used. Transparent data governance policies and algorithmic audits must be in place to ensure fairness and accountability (Silva et al., 2024; Ghosh, 2024).

Enhancing Instructional Quality Through AI Feedback Tools

AI-powered feedback systems not only support student learning but also enhance instructional quality. These tools automate grading, track performance metrics, and generate analytics that inform teaching strategies. For educators, this translates into less time spent on administrative tasks and more time for instructional design and student mentorship.

AI enables timely, individualized feedback, allowing students to act on recommendations without delay (Lee & Moore, 2024). It also supports teachers with data visualizations and diagnostics that reveal class-wide learning trends and individual anomalies (Vetrivel et al., 2024). Tools customized for language support and instructional clarity are especially helpful for teachers from non-dominant language backgrounds (Pang et al., 2024).

Moreover, AI can facilitate instructional innovation by offering real-time suggestions for pedagogical strategies based on student performance data. For example, a teacher might receive recommendations to shift from direct instruction to project-based learning for a specific group of learners based on their interaction patterns.

At the same time, concerns around the mechanization of assessment and depersonalization of feedback remain valid. Automated grading tools may misinterpret creative or nuanced responses, particularly in humanities subjects. Thus, AI-based feedback tools should be seen as augmentative—not replacement—mechanisms. Their implementation should be accompanied by capacity-building programs and opportunities for teachers to adapt tools to their professional judgment (Karmakar & Das, 2024).

AI-Enabled Lifelong Learning and Workforce Readiness

AI plays a crucial role in enabling lifelong learning and preparing learners for the evolving job market, especially in underserved communities. Adaptive systems support continuous education by curating content aligned with user goals, progress, and interests. Personalized platforms deliver upskilling opportunities to learners with limited access to traditional education, addressing global skills shortages and promoting inclusive development.

AI creates customized learning paths and provides intelligent tutoring systems that deliver instant feedback and adaptive assessments (Aggarwal, 2023; Oberdieck & Moch, 2024). It also facilitates scalable STEM education and digital literacy programs crucial for workforce development (Kumar et al., 2024; Muhtar, n.d.).

Additionally, AI-enabled micro-credentialing and modular learning allow professionals to gain job-relevant skills in short, flexible formats. Platforms can recommend learning pathways based on labor market trends and individual competency gaps. This dynamic responsiveness can be particularly transformative for displaced workers, those returning to education, and learners in geographically isolated regions.

Nevertheless, critical issues remain. The risk of digital exclusion looms large, as access to devices, internet connectivity, and culturally relevant content remains uneven. Moreover, concerns around surveillance, algorithmic bias in career recommendations, and dependency on proprietary platforms must be addressed (Oberdieck & Moch, 2024; Kumar et al., 2024; Muhtar, n.d.).

Expanding Horizons: Beyond Cognitive Gains

While academic performance remains a central metric, the potential of AI extends to emotional intelligence, creativity, and soft skill development. Platforms that analyze emotional cues and behavioral data can detect student disengagement, stress, or confusion and respond with interventions such as motivational prompts or alternative resources. These AI emotional analytics tools foster more compassionate and responsive learning environments.

AI is also contributing to the development of social-emotional learning (SEL) frameworks. Systems embedded with sentiment analysis and facial recognition technologies are being piloted to monitor classroom climate and student well-being. While promising, these applications raise serious ethical concerns around student surveillance, consent, and emotional manipulation.

Collaborative learning is another domain being enhanced through AI. Algorithms can form balanced student groups based on interaction data, recommend peer tutors, and mediate discussions. AI-driven forums and chatbots are supporting social interaction and community building in virtual learning environments.

Summary of Potentials

The integration of AI into educational systems opens up unparalleled opportunities for improving access, personalizing instruction, and ensuring continuous learning. As outlined above, AI's core strengths lie in its:

- Capacity to deliver real-time, data-informed personalization.
- Ability to automate and enhance the efficiency of assessment and feedback.
- Role in expanding educational access and equity, particularly in underserved contexts.
- Support for lifelong learning, professional development, and skills acquisition.
- Enhancement of teacher agency and instructional decision-making.
- Contribution to the development of soft skills, creativity, and collaboration.

To fully realize these potentials, a hybrid approach must be embraced—one where technology augments human-centered teaching, safeguards learner dignity, and promotes holistic development. The challenge for the future lies not only in advancing AI technologies but in aligning them with inclusive pedagogical values and ethical educational visions.

APPLICATIONS OF AI IN EDUCATION

Artificial Intelligence has revolutionized the educational landscape by embedding itself into various components of teaching, learning, assessment, and administration. The practical applications of AI extend beyond personalization; they encompass adaptive learning platforms, AI-driven virtual assistants, smart assessment tools, language learning enhancements, and streamlined institutional management. This section critically examines these applications in detail, drawing on empirical evidence and contemporary research.

Adaptive Learning Platforms

Adaptive learning platforms represent a cornerstone of AI's application in education. These systems utilize AI algorithms to adjust content and pacing based on individual learner profiles, ensuring a personalized educational experience. These platforms continually assess a student's mastery of content and adapt learning pathways in real time.

AI algorithms analyze student data—including quiz scores, engagement patterns, and behavioral cues—to dynamically alter instructional content (ME et al., 2024). This continuous feedback loop enhances learning efficacy by ensuring content difficulty is calibrated to the learner's zone of proximal development (Gupta, 2024).

The benefits of adaptive learning are profound. Research indicates that learners using adaptive systems demonstrate improved academic outcomes, higher test scores, and increased knowledge retention (Gligorea et al., 2023). These platforms shift learners from passive recipients to active participants by integrating interactive elements, gamified challenges, and peer collaboration (Rumbaugh et al., n.d.).

However, the widespread adoption of adaptive systems faces challenges. The sophistication of AI technologies can introduce systemic inequalities where students in low-resource environments may lack access to devices or connectivity. Furthermore, the complexity of algorithms and the risk of non-transparent personalization may lead to ethical concerns regarding fairness and bias (Gligorea et al., 2023). Continuous pedagogical integration and ethical audits are necessary to ensure these systems remain student-centered and inclusive (Gupta, 2024).

AI-Based Virtual Assistants

AI-driven virtual assistants have emerged as essential tools for academic support and administrative optimization. These AI-powered entities assist students by answering queries, providing concept explanations, scheduling tasks, and delivering real-time feedback. Their capacity to operate around the clock enhances accessibility, particularly for asynchronous and distance learners.

Virtual assistants tailor study plans based on individual learning data and help clarify complex topics, thereby boosting student motivation and performance (Singh et al., 2024). They use machine learning to track performance trends and customize interventions for struggling learners. Curriculum adjustments and real-time feedback further personalize the learning process (Nagy et al., 2024).

From the educators' perspective, virtual assistants alleviate administrative burden by automating repetitive tasks such as grading, attendance, and scheduling (Singh et al., 2024). This enables teachers to focus more on pedagogical strategy and individualized instruction (Bah, 2024).

In collaborative learning environments, virtual assistants support team-based activities through real-time communication tools, file sharing, and interactive simulations, fostering digital cooperation even across geographic distances (Nagy et al., 2024).

Nevertheless, ethical considerations, especially around data privacy and the need for professional development, must not be overlooked. The deployment of virtual assistants still requires refinement, as many tools remain in experimental phases and demand continuous user feedback to improve accuracy and responsiveness (Bah, 2024; Pereira et al., 2022).

AI-Enhanced Educational Assessment

AI is transforming assessment practices by improving accuracy, timeliness, and personalization. Through automated grading systems, adaptive testing, and formative analytics, AI is optimizing how student learning is measured and how educators make informed interventions.

Automated grading reduces bias and error by applying consistent scoring criteria across assessments (Giri, 2024; Apetorgbor et al., 2024). This efficiency also accelerates feedback loops, enabling students to immediately adjust learning strategies based on real-time performance data (Apetorgbor et al., 2024; Vetrivel et al., 2024).

AI-driven data analytics identify learning patterns, allowing for individualized instruction and targeted remediation (Mahamuni et al., 2024). Adaptive testing dynamically calibrates the difficulty of questions based on student responses, leading to more accurate evaluations of ability and comprehension (Mahamuni et al., 2024; Vetrivel et al., 2024).

Furthermore, AI tools generate individualized feedback reports that clarify strengths and areas for improvement, enhancing metacognitive awareness (Owan et al., 2023; Giri, 2024). This supports a growth mindset and encourages self-directed learning.

Despite these advancements, the ethical deployment of AI in assessments is critical. Concerns regarding student surveillance, data misuse, and digital access must be proactively addressed to prevent widening the achievement gap (Mahamuni et al., 2024; Apetorgbor et al., 2024).

AI-Powered Language Learning Tools

Language education has been significantly enhanced by AI through platforms that utilize natural language processing (NLP), speech recognition, and real-time feedback. These tools personalize the language acquisition journey by adapting content to learners' unique linguistic capabilities and preferences.

AI tools dynamically adjust lessons based on individual progress in pronunciation, grammar, and vocabulary (Zhong, 2024). Learners benefit from self-paced learning environments that allow them to focus on areas of difficulty while bypassing mastered topics, improving learning efficiency.

Moreover, these platforms accommodate diverse learning styles. Visual, auditory, and kinesthetic learners benefit from multimodal content presentation (Goh & Rahman, 2024). Interactive simulations and chatbot-based conversation practice foster communicative competence and lower language anxiety (Ismoilovna, 2025).

Continuous feedback and performance tracking allow educators to identify areas where learners need support, enabling differentiated instruction (Ismoilovna, 2025). The 24/7 accessibility of AI platforms is particularly beneficial for learners with irregular schedules or those in remote locations (Abernathy, 2024).

However, the overuse of automated systems may reduce human interaction, which is essential for cultural immersion and pragmatic competence. Ethical concerns regarding speech data usage and equitable access must also be addressed.

AI in Educational Administration and Institutional Management

AI is playing an increasingly central role in educational administration by optimizing decision-making, forecasting trends, and managing institutional resources. Key applications include intelligent scheduling, predictive enrollment analysis, and digital resource management.

AI-driven scheduling systems automate the allocation of time slots, instructors, and physical resources, improving efficiency and minimizing conflicts (Ajuwon et al., 2024). These tools reduce administrative burdens, enabling leaders to focus on strategic objectives (Deri et al., 2024).

Predictive analytics help institutions forecast enrollment fluctuations and adapt accordingly. By analyzing historical data, AI systems identify demographic shifts and enrollment trends, enabling institutions to plan for future capacity and curriculum needs (Ajuwon et al., 2024; Domingo-Alejo, 2024; Kayyali, 2025).

Digital resource management systems powered by AI streamline access to learning materials, monitor usage trends, and allocate budgets more effectively. This data-driven governance ensures that educational institutions remain agile and responsive to evolving learner needs (Domingo-Alejo, 2024; Kayyali, 2025).

While these innovations have led to operational gains, successful implementation depends on adequate faculty training, transparent policy frameworks, and institutional buy-in. Ethical issues—such as decision-making transparency and algorithmic accountability—must be embedded in governance protocols (Ajuwon et al., 2024; Kayyali, 2025).

ETHICAL CHALLENGES OF AI IN EDUCATION

While Artificial Intelligence offers transformative potential across educational domains, its integration also presents profound ethical concerns. These challenges are not peripheral but central to the future of AI-enabled learning. At stake are the core values of autonomy, equity, transparency, and accountability in education. This section explores the most pressing ethical challenges arising from AI implementation and outlines actionable strategies to address them.

Data Privacy and Information Security

AI systems in education thrive on data. From tracking student performance to customizing instructional paths, these systems collect and process massive amounts of sensitive information. However, this data dependency raises critical questions about privacy, consent, and institutional responsibility. Students often have limited awareness or control over how their data is collected, shared, or stored. Unauthorized access to personal data, data breaches, and misuse for commercial or non-educational purposes are persistent risks (Farooqi et al., 2024; Salloum, 2024).

Ensuring compliance with international data protection regulations such as the General Data Protection Regulation (GDPR) is essential. Institutions must develop and enforce data governance frameworks that include clear protocols for consent, anonymization, data minimization, and breach response. Without such frameworks, trust in AI and its role in education will erode.

Algorithmic Bias and Discrimination

One of the most widely discussed challenges in AI ethics is the problem of bias. If training data reflects existing societal inequities—be it gender, racial, linguistic, or socioeconomic—AI models risk perpetuating these biases. In education, biased algorithms may misidentify students' needs, disproportionately recommend remedial interventions for certain groups, or unjustly prioritize specific learning profiles over others (Singh & Thakur, 2024; Leta & Vancea, 2023).

This becomes particularly problematic in high-stakes environments such as automated assessments or admissions systems. Transparency in algorithm development, rigorous bias testing, and inclusive datasets are critical to preventing AI from reinforcing educational inequalities. Stakeholders must demand "explainable AI" that allows both technical and non-technical users to understand how decisions are made.

Student Autonomy and Over-Reliance on Automation

While personalized learning pathways can enhance academic outcomes, excessive reliance on AI risks undermining student autonomy and critical thinking. There is a fine line between guided learning and algorithmic control. AI-driven systems may unintentionally limit intellectual curiosity by presenting only what the system deems optimal, thereby reducing opportunities for exploratory learning, ambiguity, and failure—all vital components of education (Salloum, 2024; Singh & Thakur, 2024).

Balancing automation with opportunities for student choice, self-reflection, and collaborative learning is essential. Education must remain a process of discovery, not mere optimization. AI should support—not replace—students' agency to question, debate, and construct knowledge actively.

The Changing Role and Agency of Educators

As AI takes on more instructional, evaluative, and administrative functions, the professional identity of educators is in flux. Teachers may feel disempowered or displaced, particularly when AI is introduced without adequate consultation or training. Resistance to AI integration often stems from perceived threats to teacher autonomy, reduced relational engagement with students, or increased dependency on opaque systems (Farooqi et al., 2024; Gaur et al., 2024).

To address these concerns, institutions must invest in robust professional development programs. Teachers should be positioned as co-designers of AI systems, contributing their pedagogical expertise to ensure meaningful integration. Recognizing the irreplaceable human role in mentoring, empathy, and contextual understanding is vital to a balanced education ecosystem.

Equity, Accessibility, and the Digital Divide

Perhaps the most pressing challenge is ensuring that AI does not exacerbate existing educational disparities. Access to AI-powered resources often depends on infrastructure—reliable internet, modern devices, and digital literacy—that remains unevenly distributed across regions and populations. Marginalized groups, including rural learners, low-income families, and students with disabilities, face heightened barriers to benefiting from AI (Gaur et al., 2024; Leta & Vancea, 2023).

The digital divide is not just a technological problem—it is an ethical and political one. Inclusive technology policies, public-private partnerships, and government investments are needed to ensure equitable access to AI-enabled education. Solutions must be co-created with affected communities to ensure they are contextually relevant and culturally appropriate.

Ethical Strategies for Responsible AI Deployment

Ethical AI in education cannot be an afterthought. It must be embedded from the outset in the design, deployment, and evaluation of AI systems. The following strategies provide a framework for responsible and ethical implementation:

Data Governance and Transparency

Developing comprehensive data governance protocols is non-negotiable. These should include guidelines for data acquisition, user consent, retention, deletion, and anonymization (Contreras & Jaimes, 2024). Institutions must commit to transparency in how algorithms are trained, what data they use, and how they make decisions (Leta & Vancea, 2023).

Algorithmic Accountability and Audits

Explainable and interpretable AI models allow educators and students to understand the rationale behind AI outputs. Establishing independent auditing mechanisms, impact assessments, and mechanisms for grievance redress will foster accountability and public trust (Contreras & Jaimes, 2024; Saylam et al., 2023).

Professional Development and Teacher Involvement

Training educators in the ethical and pedagogical use of AI is essential. This includes understanding how to interpret AI recommendations, recognizing limitations, and exercising professional judgment. Teachers should have a voice in selecting and evaluating AI tools (Singh & Thakur, 2024).

Student Empowerment and Digital Literacy

Students must be taught not only how to use AI tools but also how to critically engage with them. Digital literacy programs should include discussions about AI ethics, privacy, surveillance, and bias, encouraging learners to be active participants in shaping their educational futures (Saylam et al., 2023).

Inclusive Design and Accessibility

Inclusive design principles ensure AI tools are accessible to all students, regardless of ability, language, or geography. AI solutions must be tested with diverse user groups to ensure usability and fairness. Participatory design, where marginalized voices are central, is essential for ethical innovation (Gaur et al., 2024).

Conclusion: Toward a Human-Centered AI Future

Ethical challenges are not roadblocks but signposts directing us toward more thoughtful, inclusive, and equitable AI systems. If left unaddressed, these challenges threaten to undermine the very goals of education—empowerment, equity, and transformation. But when actively engaged, ethics can enhance innovation and ensure that AI serves as a force for good.

The future of AI in education must be human-centered. This requires collaborative governance, cross-sector partnerships, and an unwavering commitment to justice, transparency, and inclusion. By embedding ethics at the heart of technological advancement, we can ensure that the promise of AI is realized—not only efficiently, but ethically and equitably.

CASE STUDIES AND EMPIRICAL EVIDENCE

Real-world examples are crucial for understanding both the transformative potential and the practical complexities of integrating AI into education. Case studies offer insights into how AI tools and systems operate in different educational settings, revealing their strengths, limitations, and ethical implications. This section draws upon empirical evidence to highlight successful implementations of AI in education, as well as critical challenges that have emerged in the process.

AI-Powered Tutoring Systems: Enhancing Learning Outcomes

One of the most impactful applications of AI in education is the use of AI-powered tutoring systems. In a middle school initiative in Southeast Asia, personalized math instruction delivered through an AI-driven tutoring platform significantly improved learning outcomes for students struggling with core numeracy skills. The AI system dynamically adapted instructional content based on each student's pace and accuracy, offering targeted interventions when a learner failed to master a concept (Leong et al., 2025).

The implementation revealed that AI can personalize learning at scale, enabling differentiated instruction even in under-resourced classrooms. Teachers reported a noticeable increase in student confidence and participation, while standardized test scores saw measurable improvement over one academic term. However, the case also highlighted the need for teacher training in interpreting AI-generated data and integrating it into pedagogical practices (Trivedi, 2023).

Adaptive Learning Platforms in Rural Education

Another compelling case comes from rural education initiatives in South Asia, where AI-powered adaptive learning platforms were introduced to bridge gaps in instructional quality and access. These platforms provided students in remote areas with interactive lessons, quizzes, and automated feedback in local languages. Importantly, the platforms adjusted content difficulty based on real-time learner analytics, ensuring that students could learn at their own pace (Kaur et al., 2024).

Evaluation studies found that learners using the platform demonstrated higher retention and comprehension levels than their peers in conventional classrooms. Moreover, teachers in rural schools—many of whom lacked formal training—benefited from AI-generated teaching aids and structured lesson plans. However, the deployment faced hurdles, including unreliable internet connectivity, limited device access, and concerns over the cultural neutrality of AI content (Zaman, 2024).

AI-Based Essay Grading: A Double-Edged Sword

In higher education, the use of AI for grading written assignments has sparked both enthusiasm and criticism. A large public university in Europe adopted an AI-based essay grading tool to manage increasing class sizes and administrative burdens. The system was able to provide immediate feedback on grammar, structure, and argument coherence, significantly reducing turnaround time for evaluations (Sumbera, 2024).

While many students appreciated the quick responses, some raised concerns about the system's inability to recognize creativity, cultural nuance, and rhetorical style—elements central to disciplines such as literature and philosophy. Faculty members echoed these concerns, stressing that AI lacked the contextual understanding required to assess complex human expression. This case underscores the importance of maintaining human oversight and using AI as a support tool rather than a full replacement for human judgment.

Blended Classrooms with AI Assistants: Augmenting Human Teaching

In an experimental program implemented in Scandinavian secondary schools, AI-powered classroom assistants were integrated into blended learning environments. These assistants helped with administrative tasks, answered factual questions during lessons, and facilitated group projects by organizing digital resources and timelines.

The results were promising: students reported feeling more supported and autonomous, while teachers found more time to engage in one-on-one mentoring. The AI assistants enabled a shift from content delivery to personalized guidance. However, the program also faced resistance from educators who felt their authority was being undermined by the presence of an "always-on" AI co-instructor. Addressing these perceptions through collaborative design and transparent role delineation proved essential.

Predictive Analytics for Dropout Prevention

In a pilot program at a large urban university in Latin America, predictive analytics were employed to identify students at risk of dropping out. The AI system analyzed variables such as attendance, grades, engagement on learning platforms, and socio-economic background. Based on these inputs, the system issued risk scores and recommended specific interventions, such as counseling sessions or academic tutoring.

After one year, the dropout rate decreased by 12%, and more than half of the flagged students successfully continued their studies. Importantly, the success of this program hinged on the human follow-up—counselors who used AI insights to tailor their approach, not replace it. Still, ethical debates emerged around student surveillance, data privacy, and the implications of profiling students based on sensitive data.

Cross-Cultural AI in Multilingual Contexts

A case study from sub-Saharan Africa explored the use of AI tools in multilingual classrooms. In regions where students spoke indigenous languages but instruction occurred in English or French, language learning AI platforms played a vital role. These tools translated lessons, provided vocabulary support, and used speech recognition to help students practice pronunciation.

Teachers noted marked improvement in comprehension and student participation. However, concerns were raised about the AI tools' limited understanding of regional dialects and cultural references. This highlighted the importance of training AI models with locally relevant data and involving communities in content development to prevent epistemic marginalization.

Key Insights and Implications

Across these diverse case studies, several key insights emerge:

- **Human-AI synergy is crucial**: The most successful implementations occur when AI complements rather than replaces educators.
- **Context matters**: Local infrastructure, culture, and curriculum design play a significant role in determining AI effectiveness.
- **Ethical oversight is essential**: From privacy concerns to algorithmic fairness, ethical implications must be addressed from the outset.
- **Capacity building is non-negotiable**: Teachers, administrators, and students must be trained to effectively use and interpret AI tools.

These cases demonstrate the promise of AI in enhancing education but also reinforce the need for thoughtful, inclusive, and contextually sensitive deployment strategies. By learning from both successes and setbacks, future initiatives can build systems that are not only intelligent but also just and humane.

FUTURE DIRECTIONS FOR AI IN EDUCATION: A COMPREHENSIVE OVERVIEW

As Artificial Intelligence continues to evolve, its application in education is poised for profound transformations that extend far beyond current use cases. The next frontier of AI in education envisions not just personalized learning, but deeply intelligent, emotionally aware, inclusive, and lifelong learning ecosystems. This section explores the emerging directions in which AI is heading, focusing on intelligent learning environments, emotional analytics, equitable access, collaboration with teachers, and ethical regulation.

Intelligent Learning Environments

The future of education will likely be defined by Intelligent Learning Environments (ILEs)—AI-driven ecosystems that dynamically respond to each learner's needs, behaviors, and emotions. These environments integrate real-time data analysis, learner modeling, and natural language processing to adapt instructional strategies on the fly. By doing so, they aim to create highly responsive and immersive learning experiences that mirror the adaptiveness of one-on-one human instruction (Xiao et al., 2025; Msambwa et al., 2025).

These environments do not merely deliver content; they simulate dialogue, observe learning behavior, detect signs of confusion or disengagement, and suggest remedial actions. Virtual tutors within ILEs can interpret both verbal and non-verbal cues to better guide students through complex problem-solving processes. Integrated collaboration tools further enable learners to engage in peer-to-peer learning regardless of geographical barriers, cultivating social-emotional skills and global competence (Fortino et al., 2025; Nagy et al., 2024).

Adaptive Learning Systems

Building on the success of current AI-based customization, future adaptive systems will be even more granular, employing multi-modal data inputs such as keystroke analysis, facial recognition, and biometric feedback to refine learning trajectories. These systems will adjust not only what is taught but how it is taught—altering modality, tone, sequence, and support levels in response to the learner's micro-behaviors (Taşkın, 2025; Y et al., 2024).

Such systems will continuously calibrate challenge levels to maintain students within their optimal learning zones, preventing both frustration and boredom. They will function as diagnostic, prescriptive, and formative tools, enabling educators to intervene more effectively while freeing them from routine monitoring tasks. In time, these systems may serve as the backbone for fully automated, scalable micro-credentialing and modular education programs.

Emotional and Cognitive Analytics

The next wave of educational technology is expected to incorporate emotional and cognitive analytics as core features. Through AI-driven sentiment analysis and emotion recognition, platforms will detect learners' affective states in real time, enabling dynamic adaptation of content and instructional approaches. These technologies will help identify anxiety, burnout, boredom, and disengagement early, making it possible to deliver targeted interventions (Msambwa et al., 2025; Mishra, 2024).

Cognitive analytics, on the other hand, will map higher-order thinking processes such as inference, synthesis, and evaluation. By doing so, AI can scaffold metacognitive strategies, helping learners become more aware of how they think and learn. This will not only enhance academic performance but also promote self-regulation and lifelong learning skills. Educators will benefit from dashboards summarizing both emotional and cognitive indicators, providing a fuller picture of student progress (Yılmaz, 2024).

Enhancing Student Engagement and Motivation

AI will play a critical role in reimagining engagement strategies, particularly through gamification, interactive storytelling, and social simulations. These tools will be customized through AI to match individual learner preferences, ensuring maximum cognitive and emotional investment. By blending instructional content with game mechanics and social contexts, learners will experience education as both meaningful and enjoyable (Msambwa et al., 2025; Hamdi, 2024).

Future platforms will increasingly use reinforcement learning models to identify which engagement strategies are most effective for specific students over time. AI will also track engagement patterns, providing real-time feedback to educators and enabling adaptive pacing. This personalized, data-informed approach will help reduce dropout rates and cultivate intrinsic motivation.

Expanding Access in Underserved Regions

AI's potential to bridge educational inequities is immense, particularly in resource-constrained settings. Future AI platforms will be designed to function across low-connectivity environments and multiple languages, enabling students in remote regions to access high-quality instruction. Locally trained models will ensure contextual relevance and cultural sensitivity (Zhang, 2024; Vootukuri & Jyothi.V, 2024).

Initiatives will increasingly focus on building AI-powered educational content that aligns with regional curricula and is delivered through mobile-first platforms. Partnerships between governments, NGOs, and tech companies will drive large-scale implementation. Through modular content and intelligent feedback, these tools will help elevate learning outcomes for marginalized populations while supporting local teachers with tailored guidance (Yadav, 2024).

Mobile and Offline Accessibility

Given that many learners globally still lack reliable internet, the future of AI in education must be mobile and offline-friendly. Developers are working on compressed models and edge computing solutions that enable AI tools to function with limited connectivity. Offline learning modules, coupled with AI-based local data storage and synchronization, will ensure continuity of learning regardless of location (Zhang, 2024; Vootukuri & Jyothi.V, 2024).

Battery-efficient apps, text-to-speech functionality, and localized content will make learning more inclusive. These tools will empower students to learn asynchronously and affordably, expanding the scope of educational opportunity to those historically left behind.

Collaborating with Teachers

AI is increasingly being viewed not as a replacement but as a partner to educators. Future AI tools will function as intelligent teaching assistants, offering real-time analytics on student progress, automating assessments, and providing pedagogical suggestions based on data trends. Teachers will be able to refine lesson plans based on insights generated by AI while preserving their professional autonomy (Abbas, 2024; Kaiser & Kaiser, 2024).

AI will also support professional development by recommending personalized learning paths for educators, tracking instructional effectiveness, and highlighting growth areas. This collaborative approach will redefine the educator's role—from information provider to facilitator, mentor, and data-literate learning architect.

AI as a Co-Teacher

In future classrooms, AI systems will assume responsibilities traditionally managed by teaching assistants. These include content delivery, formative assessment, monitoring group dynamics, and providing individualized feedback. As AI systems become more conversational and context-aware, they will engage with students in meaningful ways, responding to questions, prompting deeper thought, and adjusting learning environments in real time (Zhang, 2024; Y et al., 2024).

This AI-human co-teaching model allows educators to focus on emotional connection, creative instruction, and ethical leadership—domains where machines still lag behind. Meanwhile, AI can ensure that no learner is left unsupported, even in large or asynchronous classes. Together, AI and teachers will co-create enriched learning experiences.

Lifelong Learning and Upskilling

In the future, AI will be a catalyst for lifelong learning by enabling just-in-time learning modules that respond to career shifts and industry demands. These platforms will assess individual competencies, recommend personalized upskilling paths, and track progress through intelligent assessments (Mishra, 2024).

From displaced workers to retirees seeking enrichment, AI will facilitate accessible, flexible, and affordable learning. Micro-credentialing, digital portfolios, and blockchain-secured certificates will be managed and recommended by AI systems aligned with global job market trends. This democratization of continuous education will redefine what it means to be an "active learner."

Tailored Learning Pathways

Future AI systems will synthesize diverse data streams—including academic records, psychometric profiles, and learner preferences—to create highly customized learning journeys. These systems will go beyond content delivery, supporting holistic learner development by integrating socio-emotional learning, career planning, and cognitive skill-building (Taşkın, 2025).

Learners will engage with dynamic content that adjusts not just difficulty but also modality (video, text, simulation) based on real-time feedback. AI will guide learners toward certifications, electives, or experiential opportunities that align with both their capabilities and aspirations.

Skill Development and Simulation Environments

AI will be instrumental in cultivating both hard and soft skills through immersive environments. Simulated work scenarios will allow learners to practice decision-making, leadership, collaboration, and technical execution in low-stakes, high-feedback contexts (Xiao et al., 2025).

Using reinforcement learning algorithms, these platforms will tailor difficulty and narrative complexity to learner progress. Instructors will receive rich analytics on skill acquisition, allowing for personalized coaching. These simulation-driven learning environments will help students transition from theory to practice with greater confidence.

Career Guidance and Forecasting

Career readiness will be increasingly supported by AI tools capable of integrating psychometric data, academic performance, and job market trends. These systems will recommend fields of study, internships, and extracurricular opportunities that align with future workforce needs (Zhang, 2024; Kaiser & Kaiser, 2024).

AI will map pathways between current competencies and desired career outcomes, identifying gaps and suggesting targeted learning experiences. By forecasting skill demands and offering dynamic re-skilling options, AI will support a more agile and prepared workforce.

Navigating Ethical and Technological Challenges

The advancement of AI will not be without obstacles. Issues of algorithmic opacity, bias, surveillance, and ownership of learning data must be addressed through multi-stakeholder governance. Transparency and explainability will be essential to maintain user trust and institutional credibility (Choi et al., 2025).

Moreover, equitable access to the necessary infrastructure—devices, electricity, connectivity—must be prioritized. Without careful planning, AI could deepen the digital divide rather than bridge it. Public policy must support inclusive technological ecosystems that ensure AI enhances, rather than replaces, human potential.

Ethical Frameworks for AI Integration

AI in education must be guided by ethical principles that safeguard human dignity, autonomy, and equity. Future systems must be designed with built-in accountability mechanisms, audit trails, and opt-out options for users. Institutions must disclose how algorithms function, what data is used, and what implications these decisions carry (Abbas, 2024).

Ethical frameworks should encourage participatory design, particularly from vulnerable or marginalized populations. Learners should retain control over their data and be empowered to make informed choices about algorithmic interventions. AI must serve as an empowering tool—not a deterministic force.

The future of AI in education is filled with promise—but also responsibilities. If thoughtfully designed and inclusively implemented, AI can catalyze a more personalized, equitable, and lifelong learning ecosystem. However, its potential will only be realized if grounded in ethical governance, human collaboration, and a commitment to justice and inclusion.

CONCLUSION AND RECOMMENDATIONS

The integration of Artificial Intelligence (AI) into education stands as one of the most transformative developments of the 21st century. From personalized instruction and intelligent tutoring systems to administrative optimization and real-time emotional analytics, AI is reshaping not only what is taught, but how, when, and to whom it is delivered. This chapter has comprehensively explored the potentials, applications, ethical challenges, empirical insights, and future directions of AI in education. As this technological evolution accelerates, it is essential to draw clear conclusions and offer forward-looking recommendations to guide stakeholders toward responsible, inclusive, and impactful implementation.

Summary of Key Findings

- **Personalization at Scale**: AI enables tailored learning experiences that adapt in real time to each learner's strengths, needs, and pace. This personalization has been shown to increase engagement, improve learning outcomes, and bridge achievement gaps.
- **Efficiency and Innovation in Assessment**: Automated grading, predictive analytics, and adaptive testing offer faster and more accurate assessment methods. These innovations allow educators to focus on interpretation and strategy rather than data collection.
- **Augmented Teaching and Learning**: AI serves as a powerful complement to human educators, taking on routine tasks and enabling deeper, more relational teaching practices. Intelligent assistants and co-teaching models have already begun to transform classroom dynamics.
- **Equity and Access Challenges**: Despite its benefits, AI risks amplifying existing inequalities. Barriers related to digital infrastructure, language, socioeconomic status, and algorithmic bias require systemic attention.
- **Ethical Imperatives**: Issues such as data privacy, transparency, student autonomy, and educator agency must be addressed head-on. Ethics must not be an afterthought but an integral part of AI system design and deployment.
- **Lifelong and Inclusive Learning**: AI's potential extends beyond the classroom. It promises to facilitate lifelong learning through mobile, modular, and adaptive systems, serving learners of all ages and backgrounds.

Recommendations for Policy and Practice

1. **Develop Inclusive Digital Infrastructure**: Governments and educational institutions must invest in broadband access, device availability, and multilingual support systems, especially in underserved regions. Without these foundations, AI in education cannot achieve its inclusive potential.
2. **Embed Ethics in Design**: AI tools must be designed with fairness, accountability, transparency, and privacy as core principles. Ethical audits, participatory

design processes, and algorithmic impact assessments should become standard practices.

3. **Train Educators in AI Literacy**: Teachers should be equipped with both the technical understanding and pedagogical strategies to effectively and ethically use AI. Continuous professional development and peer learning networks will be vital.
4. **Support Student Agency and Digital Literacy**: Learners must be empowered to understand and question AI systems. Education in data ethics, algorithmic awareness, and critical digital engagement should be integrated into curricula.
5. **Foster Multi-Stakeholder Collaboration**: The successful deployment of AI in education requires collaboration among policymakers, technologists, educators, learners, and communities. Open communication and shared governance models are crucial for trust-building.
6. **Invest in Research and Development**: Ongoing research should focus on improving AI's effectiveness across diverse educational contexts. Attention must also be given to the long-term effects of AI on learning, cognition, social development, and mental health.
7. **Balance Automation with Human Values**: AI must not replace the human touch in education. Systems should be built to support—not supplant—human relationships, creativity, and empathy. The goal should be a harmonious human-machine partnership.
8. **Ensure Scalability with Sensitivity**: Scaling AI systems should not come at the cost of cultural, linguistic, and contextual appropriateness. Local adaptations and user-centered customization are essential for equitable and sustainable impact.
9. **Institutionalize Accountability Mechanisms**: Educational institutions must establish clear policies for the use, monitoring, and review of AI tools. Mechanisms for addressing errors, grievances, and unforeseen consequences must be readily accessible.

Looking Ahead

The road ahead for AI in education is both promising and challenging. It holds the potential to redefine learning experiences, democratize knowledge access, and enhance educational equity worldwide. However, this promise will only be realized through intentional, inclusive, and ethically grounded actions.

The future belongs not to technology alone, but to those who wield it with care, vision, and a deep commitment to human flourishing. AI in education is not merely a tool—it is a mirror reflecting our educational values and aspirations. As we shape its development, we must ensure that it, in turn, shapes us toward a more just, enlightened, and empowered society.

REFERENCES

Abbas, H. A. (2024). Transforming education: The role of Artificial Intelligence. *Studies in Engineering and Exact Sciences*, *5*(3), e12579. DOI: 10.54021/seesv5n3-041

Abernathy, P. C. (2024). *AI Tools as Supplementary Support in Language Acquisition*. https://doi.org/DOI: 10.20944/preprints202407.2213.v1

Aggarwal, D. (2023). Exploring the Scope of Artificial Intelligence (AI) for Life-long Education through Personalised & Adaptive Learning. *Journal of Artificial Intelligence. Machine Learning and Neural Network*, *41*, 21–26. DOI: 10.55529/jaimlnn.41.21.26

Ajuwon, O. A., Animashaun, E. S., & Chiekezie, N. R. (2024). *Integrating AI and technology in educational administration: Improving efficiency and educational quality*. Open Access Research Journal of Science and Technology., DOI: 10.53022/oarjst.2024.11.2.0102

Apetorgbor, M., Narad, S., Akpabio, E., Dhawale, C., Konto, A., & Verma, P. (2024). *Leveraging Artificial Intelligence for Effective Assessment and Evaluation in Education: A Comprehensive Review*. 1–6. https://doi.org/DOI: 10.1109/idic-aiei61867.2024.10842940

Choi, W. C., Choi, I. C., & Chang, C. (2025). *The Impact of Artificial Intelligence on Education: The Applications, Advantages, Challenges and Researchers' Perspective*. https://doi.org/DOI: 10.20944/preprints202501.1420.v1

Deri, M. N., Singh, A., Zaazie, P., & Anandene, D. (2024). Leveraging Artificial Intelligence in Higher Educational Institutions: A Comprehensive Overview. *Revista de Educación y Derecho*, *30*. Advance online publication. DOI: 10.1344/reyd2024.30.45777

Domingo-Alejo, J. (2024). *AI Integrated Administration tool design with ML Technology for Smart Education System*. *42*, 1423–1428. https://doi.org/DOI: 10.1109/icacite60783.2024.10616455

Farooqi, M. T. K., Amanat, I., & Awan, S. M. (2024). Ethical Considerations and Challenges in the Integration of Artificial Intelligence in Education. *Systematic Reviews*, *3*(4), 35–50. DOI: 10.69565/jems.v3i4.314

Fortino, G., Mangione, F., & Pupo, F. (2025). Intersezione tra intelligenza artificiale generativa e educazione: Un'ipotesi. *Journal of Educational. Cultural and Psychological Studies*, *30*. Advance online publication. DOI: 10.7358/ecps-2024-030-fort

Gaur, A., Sharan, H. O., & Kumar, R. (2024). *AI in Education*. IGI Global., DOI: 10.4018/979-8-3693-2964-1.ch003

Ghosh, M. (2024). *Using AI for Student Success*. 236–243. https://doi.org/DOI: 10.1201/9781032694375-13

Giri, A. K. (2024). Revolutionizing Student Evaluation. *Advances in Educational Technologies and Instructional Design Book Series*, 333–362. https://doi.org/DOI: 10.4018/979-8-3693-6170-2.ch012

Gligorea, I., Cioca, M., Oancea, R., Gorski, A., Gorski, H., & Tudorache, P. (2023). *Adaptive Learning Using Artificial Intelligence in e-Learning: A Literature Review*. Neveléstudomány., DOI: 10.3390/educsci13121216

Goh, Y., & Abdul Rahman, N. A. (2024). Personalized Language Learning With AI for Pedagogical and Andragogical Approaches. *Advances in Educational Technologies and Instructional Design Book Series*, 153–174. https://doi.org/DOI: 10.4018/979-8-3693-6130-6.ch007

Gupta, T. R. (2024). Adaptive Learning Systems: Harnessing AI to Personalize Educational Outcomes. *International Journal For Science Technology And Engineering*, *12*(11), 458–464. DOI: 10.22214/ijraset.2024.65088

Hamdi, M. (2024). *How AI is Transforming and Shaping the Future of Education*. 000115–000116. https://doi.org/DOI: 10.1109/ines63318.2024.10629089

Iman, M. Z., Asis, A. A., & Rahma, A. U. Z. (2024). Enhancing Personalized Learning: The Impact of Artificial Intelligence in Education. *Edu Spectrum.*, *1*(2), 101–112. DOI: 10.70063/eduspectrum.v1i2.55

Kaiser, G., & Kaiser, S. (2024). AI in Education. *Advances in Educational Technologies and Instructional Design Book Series*, 241–260. https://doi.org/DOI: 10.4018/979-8-3693-6130-6.ch010

Karmakar, S., & Das, T. K. (2024). *Effect of artificial intelligence on education*. 198–211. https://doi.org/DOI: 10.1201/9781003536796-8

Kaur, S., Budhraja, K., Pahuja, A., Nayyar, V., & Saluja, S. (2024). Leveraging Artificial Intelligence in Education. *Advances in Marketing, Customer Relationship Management, and e-Services Book Series*, 125–140. https://doi.org/DOI: 10.4018/979-8-3693-6660-8.ch010

Kayyali, M. (2025). AI in Higher Education. *Advances in Educational Technologies and Instructional Design Book Series*, 31–62. https://doi.org/DOI: 10.4018/979-8-3693-7949-3.ch002

Kumar, J., Jieyao, Z., & Soeiro, J. D. (2024). *Empowering Lifelong Learning*. IGI Global., DOI: 10.4018/979-8-3693-6955-5.ch003

Lee, S. S., & Moore, R. L. (2024). Harnessing Generative AI (GenAI) for Automated Feedback in Higher Education: A Systematic Review. *Online Learning : the Official Journal of the Online Learning Consortium*, *28*(3). Advance online publication. DOI: 10.24059/olj.v28i3.4593

Leong, W. Y., Leong, Y. Z., & Leong, W. S. (2025). Artificial Intelligence in education. *IET Conference Proceedings.,* 2024(22), 183–184. https://doi.org/DOI: 10.1049/icp.2024.4341

Leta, F. M., & Vancea, D.-P. (2023). Ethics in Education: Exploring the Ethical Implications of Artificial Intelligence Implementation. *Ovidius University Annals: Economic Sciences Series*. https://doi.org/DOI: 10.61801/ouaess.2023.1.54

Leta, F. M., & Vancea, D.-P. (2023). Ethics in Education: Exploring the Ethical Implications of Artificial Intelligence Implementation. *Ovidius University Annals: Economic Sciences Series*. https://doi.org/DOI: 10.61801/ouaess.2023.1.54

Mahamuni, A. J., & Tonpe, S. S. (2024). Enhancing Educational Assessment with Artificial Intelligence. *Challenges and Opportunities.*, *112*, 1–5. DOI: 10.1109/ickecs61492.2024.10616620

Mishra, S. (2024). Transformative Impact of AI on Education: Personalizing Learning and Addressing Challenges. *International Journal For Science Technology And Engineering*, *12*(8), 1183–1189. DOI: 10.22214/ijraset.2024.63891

Mishra, S. (2024). Transformative Impact of AI on Education: Personalizing Learning and Addressing Challenges. *International Journal For Science Technology And Engineering*, *12*(8), 1183–1189. DOI: 10.22214/ijraset.2024.63891

Msambwa, M., Wen, Z., & Kangwa, D. (2025). The Impact of <scp>AI</scp> on the Personal and Collaborative Learning Environments in Higher Education. *European Journal of Education*, *60*(1). Advance online publication. DOI: 10.1111/ejed.12909

Muhtar, F. (n.d.). Navigating AI Integration for Inclusive Development: A Case Study of Sabah's Socio-Economic Landscape. *Social Science Research Network*. https://doi.org/DOI: 10.2139/ssrn.4807268

Murwaningsih, T., Rahardjo, S. S., Suwandi, S., Saddhono, K., & Nurhasanah, F. (2024). *A Well Structured Strategy Development via AI Integrated Analytics Systems to Improve Performance of Education*. 873–878. https://doi.org/DOI: 10.1109/icacite60783.2024.10617260

Nagy, E., Sík, D., Biczó, Z., Zimányi, K., Pörzse, G., & Molnár, G. (2024). *Advanced Digital and Artificial Intelligence-Based Solutions for Interactive, Collaborative Learning Support.* 103–108. https://doi.org/DOI: 10.1109/cando-epe65072.2024.10772869

Oberdieck, T., & Moch, E. (2024). Lifelong learning with artificial intelligence: Potentials, challenges and future perspectives. *International Journal of Advanced Research, 12*(06), 545–555. DOI: 10.21474/ijar01/18915

Owan, V. J., Idika, D. O., & Bassey, B. A. (2023). Exploring the potential of artificial intelligence tools in educational measurement and assessment. *Eurasia Journal of Mathematics, Science and Technology Education, 19*(8), em2307. Advance online publication. DOI: 10.29333/ejmste/13428

Pang, T. Y., Kootsookos, A., & Cheng, C.-T. (2024). Artificial Intelligence Use in Feedback: A Qualitative Analysis. *Journal of University Teaching & Learning Practice.* Advance online publication. DOI: 10.53761/40wmcj98

Rojas Contreras, M., & Portilla Jaimes, J. O. (2024). *AI Ethics in the Fields of Education and Research: A Systematic Literature Review.* 1–6. https://doi.org/DOI: 10.1109/icacit62963.2024.10788651

Rumbaugh, D., King, J. E., Berman, M. L., Washburn, D. A., Gould, K., Kornell, N., Scaturo, D. J., Haig, B., Schvaneveldt, R., Barton, B. K., Ulrich, T. A., Robinson, P., Schuelke, M. J., Day, E. A., Chase, H. W., Carayannis, E. G., Flemming, T. M., Mitchelmore, M., White, P., … Reznikova, Z. (n.d.). *Adaptive learning.* https://doi .org/DOI: 10.1007/978-1-4419-1428-6_3075

Salloum, S. A. (2024). *AI Perils in Education: Exploring Ethical Concerns.* Springer International Publishing., DOI: 10.1007/978-3-031-52280-2_43

Sari, H., Tumanggor, B., & Efron, D. (2024). Improving Educational Outcomes Through Adaptive Learning Systems using AI. *International Transactions on Artificial Intelligence, 3*(1), 21–31. DOI: 10.33050/italic.v3i1.647

Saylam, S., Duman, N., Yildirim, Y., & Satsevich, K. (2023). *Empowering education with AI: Addressing ethical concerns.* London Journal of Social Sciences., DOI: 10.31039/ljss.2023.6.103

Silva, G., Godwin, G., & Jayanagara, O. (2024). *The Impact of AI on Personalized Learning and Educational Analytics.* https://doi.org/DOI: 10.33050/itee.v3i1.669

Singh, G., & Thakur, A. K. (2024). *AI in Education.* IGI Global., DOI: 10.4018/979-8-3693-2964-1.ch002

Sumbera, B. G. (2024). The Ethical Use of AI in Education. *Advances in Educational Technologies and Instructional Design Book Series*, 175–210. https://doi.org/DOI: 10.4018/979-8-3693-6130-6.ch008

Taşkın, M. (2025). Artificial Intelligence in Personalized Education: Enhancing Learning Outcomes Through Adaptive Technologies and Data-Driven Insights. *Human-Computer Interaction*, *8*(1), 173. DOI: 10.62802/ygye0506

Trivedi, N. B. (2023).. . *AI in Education-A Transformative Force.*, *1*, 1–4. DOI: 10.1109/idicaiei58380.2023.10406541

Vashishth, T. K., Sharma, V., Sharma, K. K., Kumar, B., Panwar, R., & Chaudhary, S. (2024). *AI-Driven Learning Analytics for Personalized Feedback and Assessment in Higher Education.* IGI Global., DOI: 10.4018/979-8-3693-0639-0.ch009

Vetrivel, S. C., Vidhyapriya, P., & Arun, V. P. (2024). The Role of AI in Transforming Assessment Practices in Education. *Advances in Educational Marketing, Administration, and Leadership Book Series*, 43–70. https://doi.org/DOI: 10.4018/979-8-3693-5443-8.ch003

Vootukuri, N. S. R., & Jyothi, J. (2024). Harnessing the potential of AI applications in Education: Opportunities, challenges, and future directions. *Magna Scientia Advanced Research and Reviews*, *11*(2), 405–410. DOI: 10.30574/msarr.2024.11.2.0139

Xiao, N., Pei, Y., Yuan, C., Bu, Y., & Cai, Z. (2025). Transforming Education with Artificial Intelligence: A Comprehensive Review of Applications. *Challenges, and Future Directions.*, *2*(1), 337–356. DOI: 10.70693/itphss.v2i1.211

Y, M. N., H, L. P., & N, S. (2024). Revolutionizing Education: Harnessing AI for Personalized Learning Pathways and Student Success. *International Journal For Multidisciplinary Research*. https://doi.org/DOI: 10.36948/ijfmr.2024.v06i05.28371

Yadav, S. (2024). Advancing Education With AI-Driven Education for Diverse Learners. *Advances in Educational Technologies and Instructional Design Book Series*, 49–80. https://doi.org/DOI: 10.4018/979-8-3693-6130-6.ch003

Yılmaz, Ö. (2024). *Personalised learning and artificial intelligence in science education: current state and future perspectives*. Educational Technology Quarterly., DOI: 10.55056/etq.744

Zaman, B. U. (2024). *Transforming Education Through AI Benefits Risks and Ethical Considerations*. https://doi.org/DOI: 10.20944/preprints202407.0859.v1

Zhang, C. (2024). AI in Education: Opportunities, Challenges, and Pathways for Equitable Learning. *Journal of Education. Humanities and Social Sciences*, *45*, 723–728. DOI: 10.54097/kfgp6j07

Zhang, Q. (2024). Harnessing Artificial Intelligence for Personalized Learning Pathways: A Framework for Adaptive Education Management Systems. *Applied and Computational Engineering*, *82*(1), 167–172. DOI: 10.54254/2755-2721/82/20241102

Zhong, W. (2024). Adaptive System of English-Speaking Learning Based on Artificial Intelligence. *Journal of Electrical Systems*. https://doi.org/DOI: 10.52783/jes.2637

Chapter 6
At the Intersection of Artificial Intelligence and Giftedness:
Managing Thinking Skills

Gülşah Avcı Doğan
https://orcid.org/0000-0002-9733-3228
Ordu University, Turkey

ABSTRACT

This chapter aims to develop an understanding of artificial intelligence by using high-level learning features to manage thinking skills. This draws attention to the intersection between the learning styles of gifted and talented individuals with higher-level thinking skills and machine intelligence. It presents a dual roadmap for understanding the developmental thinking styles of gifted individuals and for utilizing machine-generated information. The machines and artificial intelligence can be trained using learning and innovation skills. This relationship places meta-learners at the center of skills development. Adapting to and surviving the rapid changes predicted for the new century and beyond requires everyone to become a meta-learner. This primarily requires the reconstruction of educational programs and continuous teacher training.

INTRODUCTION

The quest for understanding and making sense of what has begun today leads to a similar quest to understand a new thinking system and to make sense of the knowledge produced. The knowledge and experiences gained in the process of

DOI: 10.4018/979-8-3373-8857-1.ch006

finding meaning lead people to new knowledge and experiences. As the "Tabula Rasa (Blank Slate)" symbolized by John Locke fills up, brand new discoveries lead to the opening of new blank slates. This shows that knowledge multiplies as it multiplies and that there is no limit to it. Locke explains knowledge as emerging in the case of understanding the dependence and compatibility or contrast and incompatibility between ideas. He states that knowledge cannot go further than human ideas, and that even if the ideas are simple or complex, the field of knowledge is narrow when the connection between them is not known. In today's counterpart of these 17th century hypotheses, Türker Kılıç (2021) puts forward the argument that every system that processes information eventually produces intelligence with his proposal of connectivity through the thought generation process of the brain. In his proposal, he argues that all systems that process information produce minds and that the building blocks of life are not atoms but information.

Although individuals have high intelligence scores, they may not have sufficient skills in using information effectively. In recent years, with the need for education of thinking skills, skills that have developed in parallel with the new world working order and are classified as 21st century skills are emerging. While the skills that stood out in the previous century were hardworking, fast, good at collaborative work, able to take and follow instructions, and able to think at a professional level, 21st century priorities include being able to produce and process information, follow scientific and technological developments, and apply these developments to one's own life (Hamarat, 2019). New century skills expect individuals to be able to keep up with change under rapid and continuous change and offer the necessary skills to teach and develop them (Partnership for 21st Century Skills, P21, 2019). Practices are carried out by integrating all areas related to social sciences in the context of teaching and evaluation. At the international level, organizations such as the World Economic Forum (WEF) or Program for International Student Assessment (PISA) prioritize various skills. These, in turn, provide information about the level of development of countries. Common skills include basic literacy, reading comprehension, numeracy skills, using knowledge and skills in real life, using technology-supported skills, and problem solving. In its various reports, WEF (2015) states that there is a need for qualified manpower and recommends various skills for education programs in the acquisition of skills based on 21st century requirements. These are given in Figure 1.

Figure 1. 21st Century Key Skills

Basic Literacies

- Reading and writing
- Numeracy
- Scientific literacy
- Information and communication technologies literacy
- Financial literacy
- Cultural and civic literacy

Competencies

- Critical thinking/problem-solving
- Creativity
- Communication
- Collaboration

Character Qualities

- Curiosity
- Initiative
- Persistency/grit
- Adaptability
- Leadership
- Social and cultural awareness

(WEF, 2015)

The current WEF 2025 occupations report includes the occupations and skills needed for the period until 2030. Of course, in parallel with technological developments, artificial intelligence and information processing, robotics and automation, energy production, storage and distribution are prominent job groups. Skills related to artificial intelligence and big data, networks and cybersecurity, and technology literacy will be in demand and will be the fastest growing. Complementing technology-related skills, analytical and creative thinking, resilience, flexibility and agility, motivation and self-awareness, curiosity and lifelong learning, and skills management skills are expected to continue to grow in importance in the 2025-2030 period. As these are not yet integrated into the content of education and training programs, the classification in this section is based on 2015 basic skills.

New generation skills or 21st century skills are reflected in all learning and teaching processes. However, while the first quarter of the century is still being completed, updates in these skills are expected to accelerate with the age of artificial intelligence. Although the learning processes of artificial intelligence, i.e. machine intelligence, seem to be very fast, it needs to be guided by human-specific skills. In this bidirectional interaction, humans need to learn to use their intelligence effectively and control the machine intelligence that produces information quickly.

For the learning processes underlying the interaction, it is important that education systems teach the use of knowledge, not the transfer of knowledge. There is a need to provide students with the competencies to cope with uncertainty and adapt to changing situations. These skills will become the strongest shield of individuals against machine intelligence. In the learning process, individuals need guides in unlocking their potential.

Cahit Arf (1959) shared his propositions on the question "Can the machine think and how can it think?" in a conference he gave in Türkiye when there were emerging ideas that could be seeds for machine learning. Arf emphasized the language used by the machine with the machine's reaction against the effect, that is, output against input, and gave examples through the working principles of alarm clocks and telephones. He then develops this idea and shares the learning and working principles of a machine in the subjects of calculation and inheritance. After comparing machines with the human brain, Arf emphasizes that although machines can do some tasks much faster than the human brain, their biggest shortcoming is that they do not have the ability to make decisions on their own. Compared to human beings, machines remain as they were originally built and can become as competent as their programs allow them to be. Here, Arf emphasizes that machines cannot make decisions for the solution of a problem beyond the programs loaded on them, that is, they cannot act as an autonomous being.

The idea of likening the functioning of a machine to artificial brains assumes the transformation of effects into reactions, as in the human brain. The transformation work in machines takes place when an object produced by a human being becomes operational with its programs. In a study conducted by HaeJin and colleagues (2025), it was demonstrated that an AI-supported educational tool helps students more accurately predict their own learning and adjust their learning behaviors accordingly. The findings of the study indicate that AI can have a direct effect on the development of metacognitive skills. A study examining artificial intelligence applications in educational sciences has indicated that adaptive learning systems, intelligent teaching systems, and artificial intelligence-supported learning analytics provide personalization and efficiency in learning processes, while also presenting ethical and practical challenges (Akyel and Tur, 2024). Research on the use of artificial intelligence in lifelong learning indicates that personalized learning platforms, intelligent educational assistants, customized recommendation systems, and adaptive testing systems can be effective in developing individuals' metacognitive skills (Yeşilbaş, Özenç and Başaran, 2024). Such technologies support individuals' abilities to manage, monitor, and evaluate their own learning processes. Artificial intelligence-supported learning environments, learning analytics, personalized feedback mechanisms, cognitive coaching applications and the assessment of individual differences are tools and methods that contribute to the development of students' metacognitive awareness, self-regulated learning and self-management skills.

The relationship between the use of artificial intelligence and metacognitive skills enables us to better understand artificial intelligence. At this point, utilizing the thinking patterns of gifted individuals, who are superior meta-learners, offers a sound approach. At the confrontation of machine intelligence and human intelligence or the intersection of the two, the thinking and learning styles of individuals defined as gifted come to the fore. In this book chapter, firstly, based on 21st century skills, the thinking styles of gifted individuals and their higher-order thinking skills are examined. The aim of the chapter is to provide a roadmap for understanding and developing higher-order thinking skills and to offer suggestions for effective use of artificial intelligence.

BACKGROUND

In defining and categorizing 21st century skills, universally needed human qualities were considered. The Partnership for 21st Century Learning-P21 (2019) identifies the knowledge and skills to be embedded in education programs in the context of the human qualities required by the periods. The learning framework presented in Figure 2 consists of skills and supporting systems in the themes and core subjects required for all students.

Figure 2. P21 Framework for 21st Century Learning

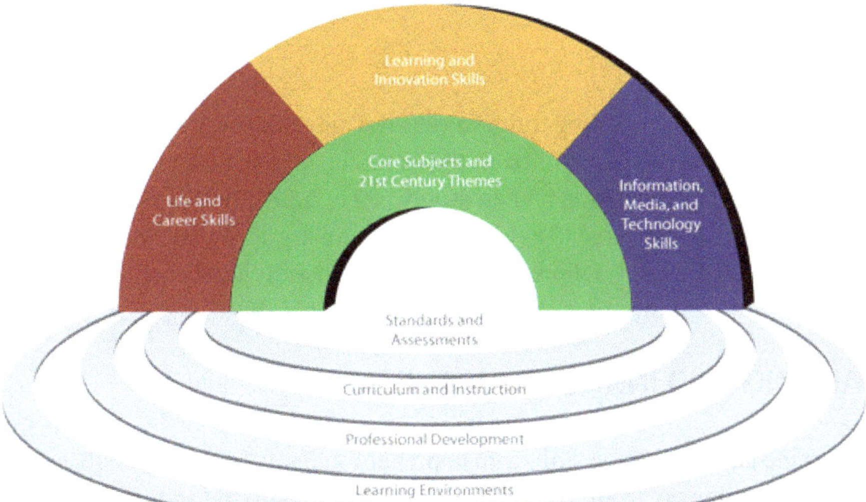

(2019, p.1)

The core subjects of the P21 learning framework include English, linguistics, reading, mathematics, science, history, geography, economics, world languages, management and citizenship. It is recommended to integrate literacy skills in the areas of global awareness, economics, financial, vocational entrepreneurial, health, environment and citizenship for higher level development in education and students in the core subjects. For this purpose, skills within the new learning paradigm are grouped into life and career skills, learning and innovation skills, information, media and technology skills (Figure 3).

Figure 3. 21st Century Skills according to the P21 Framework

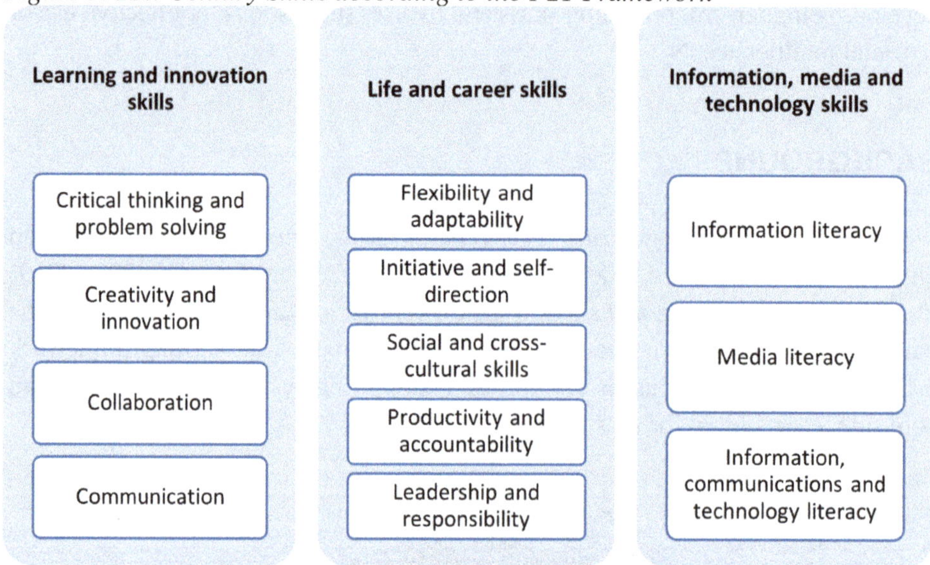

At the center of the learning framework is learning and innovation skills, with an emphasis on the core skills defined as the 4Cs. The 4Cs stand for critical thinking, communication, collaboration and creativity (P21, 2008). In this book chapter, 4C skills, which are also referred to as higher order thinking skills, and the management of these skills based on the thinking styles of gifted individuals are discussed.

LEARNING AND INNOVATION SKILLS

Learning and innovation skills aim to prepare students for increasingly complex living and working environments in the 21st century. With the acquisition of skills, students who are ready for change will turn into individuals who can survive at the point where those who are not ready are separated. The learning and innovation skills examined in the P21 framework focus on creativity, critical thinking, communication and collaboration. The importance of these skills in preparing students for the future is emphasized.

There are also intersections between 21st century skills and ICT-related skills. An international organization (International Society for Technology in Education [ISTE], 2017) lists seven standards that students should have in using information technologies: Empowered learner, digital citizen, knowledge maker, innovative designer, computational thinker, creative communicator, global collaborator.

In this section, the skills within the scope of learning and innovation, which focus on learning processes within the framework of 21st century skills, are examined. It is aimed to focus on the intersection or combination of the relevant skills with different skill areas as well as the skills that are intended to be integrated into education programs.

Critical Thinking

Exercise: "This chapter provides you with all the information you need about critical thinking."

After reading this statement, do you immediately start reading what is written or do you ask yourself some questions?

If your answer is the latter, you are at the point where you really start to understand critical thinking!

What questions did you ask yourself after reading the first sentence?

For example:

- Really?
- Just by reading this passage?
- Is there no other information?
- Is there any evidence of this?
- If it is such short information, why are there so many publications?

At the point where we start to think by asking ourselves questions before immediately believing the information we hear, read or watch, our critical thinking journey begins. Critical thinking is briefly the ability to question why, how and how true it is in the process of acquiring information. Critical thinking includes the ability to focus on elaborating and revealing deficiencies, deep thinking, problem solving, careful thinking, logical thinking, independent thinking, comprehending principles, hypothesizing, evaluating prejudices, assumptions, inconsistencies, ideas and other questionable sources of information, presenting ideas by showing reasons, and making decisions based on criteria or evidence.

Although critical thinking has emerged as a discipline based on a way of thinking, it is one of the survival skills in today's complexity order. In a world of rapid information flow and change, it is necessary to distinguish the information that accumulates in almost breathing time. The process of selecting, analyzing and using the necessary information can be managed with critical thinking skills. Critical thinking skill is a skill that individuals can learn and develop. Although it is aimed to include the development of critical thinking skills based on the integration of 21st century skills in the content of education programs, it has not yet been effective and sustainable.

Allen and Rott shared various principles for critical thinking in their research, the framework of which they put forward in 1969. Although it may seem surprising that these principles have not changed in almost half a century, it reminds us once again that the real issue is in using information rather than accessing it. The principles on critical thinking are as follows (Allen and Rott, 1969):

- Evaluation of inferences
- Evaluation of the justification for a claim
- Verifying the reliability and accuracy of information
- Following reasoning in logically valid ways
- Identifying missing parts of the argument
- Recognizing the content of objections
- Identification of appropriate outcomes

As educators, the first thing that probably comes to our minds when reading these principles is not how to teach them, but how to use them. A person may not be able to manage the flow of thought with his/her students if he/she is not successful in using it himself/herself. In order to manage the flow of individual thinking, we can start from the principle of machine thinking. Nowadays, many of us use artificial intelligence tools either to help us in our daily lives (e.g., What should I cook today?) or to catch changes in professional development (e.g., Which method can I use to develop creative writing skills?). But which of the information they provide do we trust completely and use without questioning? The answer to this question is given in the exercise at the beginning of this topic. For detailed answers, we can think in line with the Allen et al.'s principles listed above.

Self-monitoring our own thinking process is not an easy skill. There are, of course, various strategies for its development. In order to understand the critical thinking skill in the flow of thinking, an example given by artificial intelligence is given in the text box.

Scenario: "Miracle Cream" Going Viral on Social Media

Ada comes across an advertisement while browsing social media. It promotes a new product called "Miracle Cream". The ad claims the following:

- "Eliminates all skin blemishes in just one week!"
- "Makes your skin 10 years younger, completely erases wrinkles!"
- "All natural ingredients and no side effects!"
- A video clip of a famous actress saying "This cream changed my life!" is shown.
- There are hundreds of positive comments and "before-and-after" photos.

Ada has a little problem with skin blemishes, and this ad sounds great. Just as she is about to order, she starts thinking. She comes to her conclusion by finding the answers to the following steps:

- Questioning the claims (Is it true?)
- Examine the source and evidence (Is it reliable?)
- Seek alternative/detailed information (Different perspectives)
- Conclusion

Conclusion: After all this questioning, Ada concludes that the promises of the "Miracle Cream" are unrealistic, the evidence is dubious, and the marketing tactics are manipulative. She decides that it would be much safer and wiser to consult a dermatologist rather than risk damaging her skin.

Inference of the AI agent: In this example, Ada protects herself from potential harm by actively questioning information, comparing different sources, recognizing logic errors and potential manipulation, rather than simply believing an advertisement and acting quickly. Critical thinking is an indispensable mental shield for making the right decisions in today's age of information overload.

Some common characteristics are shared for people with critical thinking skills (Beyer, 1991; Facione, 1990). These include being a good listener, being prudent, being skeptical, speaking thoughtfully, acting moderately rather than reactively, being open to new ideas, respecting openness and accuracy, considering different perspectives, seeking necessary explanations in conversations/examinations, striving to find the truth, recognizing logical relationships, making generalizations and inferences, striving to reach reliable information when making important decisions, reading and writing critically, and trying to recognize their strengths and weaknesses.

Critical thinking is a process and can become a habit of thinking through thought exercises and repetition. For this reason, it is recommended that educators use strategies for teaching critical thinking and developing skills starting from the first learning levels. As a practical way for educators, it is suggested that they make use of Bloom's taxonomy levels, which are the building blocks of curricula. The taxonomy starts at the bottom with the cognitive domain of knowledge and comprehension - remembering and understanding in the revised taxonomy- upward to the level of evaluation, which is associated with original production (Anderson and Krathwohl, 2021). Many educators state that they spend most of their time at the first two levels, knowledge and comprehension, and that even if they move up to the other levels, they do so not with a designed content but in the flow, sometimes without realizing it. In the Delphi report of similar skills covering the higher levels of the taxonomy, the six skills related to critical thinking are listed as follows (Facione, 1990): analysis, interpretation, self-regulation, inference, explanation and evaluation. In order to use, support and develop higher-order thinking skills, there is a need to move towards the higher levels of the taxonomy and to do so with conscious awareness. Educators should aim to move up to higher levels in addition to the first levels of the lesson plans. Unfortunately, these processes are often overlooked because they cannot be carried out properly in terms of teaching students higher-order thinking skills that educators often do not have. Therefore, it is imperative that educators first put developing higher order thinking skills among their professional development goals. Otherwise, they will only remain as skills that are included in the programs under the name of 21st century skills, but which do not have implementation and sustainability.

As the content of the curricula moves to higher levels, the use of higher order thinking skills will naturally come along with it. There are resources on the names and application forms of frequently used strategies. Some of these strategies are Socratic questioning, mapping, concept and mind mapping, role playing, active learning strategies, scaffolding, De Bono thinking technique, Lipman philosophy for children.

There are various difficulties in both teaching and assessing critical thinking. Teachers who are obliged to complete the content in certain class hours are not lucky enough to allocate the flexible time needed for the development of higher-level skills. Therefore, the teacher needs to include it in the program with good planning. Because there will be a need for a processual evaluation after the teaching of higher-level skills. Students should use knowledge not at the level of recall and concept, but at the level of analysis and synthesis. This may sometimes cover a semester and sometimes a year. Another possible problem with assessment is the differences in assessment criteria. Evaluation based on processual development requires the teacher to follow up and evaluate without subjectivity. As a precaution, teachers can concretize the evaluation criteria before the teaching process and share them with students. With this measure, both the criteria will be objective, and the students will know what they will be evaluated according to. The categories suggested by some researchers in the field of evaluation of critical thinking skills to be used in evaluation are compiled by Ünal and Davis (2023) presented in Table 1.

Table 1. Critical Thinking Categories

First Order	**Second Order**
Clarifying the thesis, problem or issue	Reformatting/transformation
	Summarizing
	Questioning
	Defining concepts
	Identifying and challenging assumptions
Inference and interpretation	Deduction
	Induction
	Imagining and exploring alternatives
	Transferring to other states
Supporting inferences and interpretations	Using reliable sources
	Using personal observations
Making value judgments	Assessing the validity and interpretability of the source or supplementary material
	Evaluating observation reports
	Considering the adequacy of the solution, inference or interpretation
	Re-evaluate when new evidence, perspectives or research tools emerge, and change the current position when the evidence and reasons are sufficient to do so

Source: Ünal and Davis, 2023

The categories in Table 1 can be utilized in the creation and evaluation of educational content.

Creativity

When the definitions and classifications of creativity are examined, attention is drawn to the multidimensional and dynamic structure of the concept. Creativity approaches, definitions and characteristics of creative people may vary according to the field of study and cultures. In the development of creativity definitions, it is seen that creativity focuses on the product or process rather than the person. A general definition of creativity emphasizes any action, idea or product that changes an existing field or transforms an existing field into a new field (Csikszentmihalyi, 1996). In a study compiling the common elements of definitions of creativity, common characteristics such as being new and useful, being product-based and being part of a process are shared (Batey and Furham, 2006). A product is considered creative according to the criteria of novelty (originality) and appropriateness (usefulness-effectiveness-efficiency) (Csikszentmihalyi, 1996; Mumford, 2003; Sternberg and Lubart, 1995). In the innovation criterion, the characteristics sought in the product are being unusual and unpredictable. In problem solving, a solution that does not come to mind when it is first thought of is put forward. It is also important to be able to see different ways of solution and to continue the solving stages. It will only fail if it proposes an original solution and fails to reach the result. In the criterion of appropriateness, a product or idea should be effective, useful and efficient along with its originality. A product that is considered to be original is expected to have use value, utility or impact potential. The impact of relevance here should not be expected to be a worldwide impact. A product with a small impact but a large benefit to a problem of the time can also be considered creative. Creativity in the context of the product can be summarized as the product being useful, meeting a need, providing use value or inspiring the emergence of new ideas or products (Sak, 2014).

Exercise: Let's Think of a Creative Product

In line with the characteristics of a creative product, think of a product that first comes to your mind in your daily life and evaluate it according to whether it meets the criteria.

Example: Let's ask AI?

Let's analyze the first response of an AI chat tool when asked for an example of a creative product from daily life.

Foldable and Portable Mat

It offers a practical and innovative solution to a problem we face in daily life (flasks take up a lot of space in a bag or are bulky even when empty). It is an example of a simple but highly creative product that emerges by rethinking the basic design of a product in line with user needs.

- Now evaluate the example given by artificial intelligence in terms of creativity criteria.

While it is possible to get an idea about the characteristics of creative people in relation to the creative products they produce, it will not be possible to group them under general characteristics.

The cognitive and personality characteristics of creative people may differ according to the field, time and culture in which they work. In any field/discipline, period or culture, common characteristics can be listed along with differences. Individuals with creative personality traits are sensitive to social problems, have leadership skills, are aware of their own potential and have confidence in their abilities, are open to new experiences, curious, highly motivated, mentally flexible, and have the ability to work independently (Csikszentmihalyi, 1996; Runco 2007). In terms of prominent cognitive characteristics, creative people are defined as finding/generating problems, developing many and new solutions for existing problems, not avoiding complexity and being willing to develop solutions, putting forward original ideas, being original in establishing unestablished relationships (Tardif and Sternberg, 1988).

Kaufman and Beghetto (2009), who propose a classification based on the "major" and "minor" effects of creativity, explain it with the Four C model. In this classification, it is seen that the level of creativity is taken into account. The creativity levels in the mini-c, little-c, Pro-c and Big-C classes, as can be understood from their names and letter characters, include an order from small to large. The mini-c level is inherent in learning and has a processual effect on the development of product. The mini-c effect can be mentioned in the context of creative products exhibited by students in classes, activities and projects at educational levels. Little-c level refers to the point after which personal development begins to progress. The person is provided with appropriate guidance and feedback. The pro-c level indicates that the person has moved to the professional level. The area where creativity is recognized and supported has now turned into an area where creative products are produced. At the Big-C level, products that meet the criteria of novelty and appropriateness are expected to emerge as innovative products at the social level. A career journey product emerges on the foundations of one's entire working life.

Teachers' understanding of the levels and patterns of creativity is essential for students' development. As a first step, teachers are expected to recognize and accept that nurturing creativity is part of the learning process. They should remember that a process that starts with a small light can turn into great creativity when supported. It is important to recognize and support the value of creativity at all levels. If students' creativity is not appreciated and nurtured, it can have a negative impact on the world and deprive them of new inventions. There are several examples of how recognizing creative talents is not always easy (Rimm, Siegle and Davis, 2018). These are:

- Albert Einstein spoke at the age of 4, started reading at the age of 7, and was an academic failure.
- Pablo Picasso barely learned to read by the age of 10 and did not have a bright educational life.
- Bill Gates attended Harvard University but did not continue his studies.

- Enrico Caruso's music teacher told him, “You have no voice, you cannot sing.”

It can be inferred from the examples that not every creative individual can be discovered at an early age, but it can also be inferred that teacher should try to understand the “difference” in these students and support them. For teachers to ensure student development, it is imperative that they accept that creativity can be developed and that they have professional competence in the development of creative thinking skills.

There are many effective variables in the development of creative thinking skills. Since creativity is multifaceted, its development also depends on these dimensions. These can be analyzed as cognitive, emotional, attitudinal, interpersonal and environmental components (Plucker, Runco and Hegarty, 2011). Cognitive dimensions include information processing, transfer, storage, metacognitive skills and problem-solving skills. Strategies that can be used in educational institutions for the development of creative thinking skills on the basis of cognitive characteristics are suggested. Some of these can be brainstorming, analogical thinking, selective thinking, contrastive thinking, SCAMPER technique, plural thinking and various problem-solving methods. Emotional traits are essentially effective in the good functioning of cognitive traits. Therefore, although cognitive traits are in the foreground, there is a need for supportive emotional traits in the background. Characteristics such as motivation (intrinsic-extrinsic), curiosity, persistence are among the characteristics that an individual should have in the development of creativity. Positive attitudes are needed to support the extraordinary ideas of the creative individual. The attitude dimension is also intertwined with the environmental dimension. The attitude, tolerance and expectations of the environment in which the individual lives are effective in supporting creativity. Of course, the richness of environmental resources is also important for the development of creativity. The richness of resources is nourishing both for inspiration at the beginning of creativity and for producing creative products. One aspect of the interpersonal dimension is again related to the environment. There should be people around the individual whose creativity is accepted and who can value the creative product. Otherwise, the individual will either stop producing or attempt to change the environment in which he/she lives within his/her means. The other aspect of the interpersonal dimension consists of the creative individual's friends who are willing to work together. As a matter of fact, the way of working, which is also included under the title of collaboration, is among the features that increase innovation and are sought after in businesses in recent years.

There are several skills that are widely accepted in the assessment of creativity. The skills that first appeared in Torrance (1998) creativity assessment studies have been expanded with the increase in measurement tools. Some of the skills frequently used in creativity assessment are as follows:

Fluency: The ability to generate ideas to find an answer to an open-ended question or problem. There is no limit or end to ideas. The student is left free to think and is expected to produce as many answers as possible.

Flexibility: It is the ability to use different categories of ideas or to see a situation from different perspectives in order to solve a problem. It is expected that the answers produced freely by the student are not repetitive.

Originality: It is the ability to be unique, to think outside the box. In this skill, which is less likely to be encountered in student responses than the first two skills, the student is expected to think of something that no one else has thought or seen before.

Elaboration: It is the ability to add details to a specific idea, develop and apply it. Students are expected to think about the ideas they produce in detail or they are encouraged to think in detail during the in-class activity.

Collaboration

Learning and innovation skills may at first glance seem to focus on higher order thinking skills, but they draw attention to a wide range of skills that serve to move learning forward. Even if an individual is as creative as he or she can be on his or her own, if he or she is unable to work in a good collaborative team, the result may be less successful than expected. Although the solitude of the individual glorifies individual success, it also implies long hours of work and a work management process that has not been thought through in every aspect. The new world working order demands maximum quality output in minimum time. This is based on a collaborative working process with an effective team. At all levels of educational environments, students are encouraged to work in groups in order to channel individual talents and work together with different talents.

Cooperative work has influenced the organization of educational programs with 21st century skills and then passed into the literature as a method. Cooperative learning is a learning and teaching approach. It aims to gain skills such as effectiveness in working in groups, management of students, problem solving, decision making, and confidence building. In addition, the development of cognitive development together with affective characteristics is supported. Johnson et al. (1990) explain some basic building blocks in the implementation of the cooperative learning-teacher approach. These are:

- Group members depend on each other to achieve a common goal,

- Group members are responsible for playing their part in the implementation process (Individual accountability),
- Although there is task-oriented individual work in group work, group members are together and the work is carried out in an interactive process,
- Build confidence in each other by supporting the appropriate use of collaborative skills when students are given the opportunity,
- It is the evaluation of the performance of group members as a team, even if they work individually.

In the cooperative learning process, if students form a random group and the groups are not guided, it will not yield successful results. In order for the method to achieve its purpose, it is recommended to make homogeneous or heterogeneous groupings according to the subject of study and to guide the process by the teacher. It is necessary for students to talk together within the framework of the study topics, to listen to each other, and to consider the suggestions on the way to a solution.

The cooperative learning method benefits students in terms of academic and social-emotional development. The method contributes to students' character development and social development by supporting cognitive and affective development. Students have the opportunity to recognize and develop each other's and their own strengths and weaknesses, increase academic success, and develop a sense of confidence. It is known that the method is effective in developing their interest and curiosity about the subjects of study, making connections between what they have already learned and new information, eliminating misconceptions, communicating with their friends or completing their deficiencies (Webb, 1982). In cooperative learning environments, students gather around a common goal and must stick to it. Fulfilling individual tasks is insufficient to achieve success and the learning process should be planned together; group members should help and support each other. If a student is very successful in his/her individual studies, fulfilling the tasks in the group will not make him/her successful, and the group will be successful only if his/her peers fulfill their tasks and become successful as well. It is precisely this purpose that fulfills the intention of cooperative learning.

This method, which is based on group work, allows the use of many methods and techniques in the implementation process. Methods such as questioning, discussion, small and large group discussions, brainstorming, problem solving, creative thinking, critical thinking are frequently used. In addition to these, some of the methods and techniques recommended in cooperative learning are cooperative learning, peer learning, student teams-achievement sections, team games, group research, combined cooperative reading and writing, let's ask together, let's learn together, merging techniques. Although these are methods and techniques whose effectiveness has been demonstrated by research, taking into account the individual learning styles of each student, making groupings according to the subject of study, choosing methods and techniques appropriate to the subject of study and student characteristics, and following the process by the teacher and supporting it with guidance are points that will increase efficiency.

Communication

The process in which the passage of emotion and thought between living beings is defined is known as communication. Although it has been a discipline that has been studied for many years, it remains up to date due to the diversity and rapid development of communication channels. Communication channels and tools also affect the form of communication. These leads living beings to search for different ways of communicating. Communication skills, like many other skills, are among the skills that need to be developed in educational environments.

Communication skills and language skills are considered together. Although there are non-linguistic channels of communication, language is the primary communication channel. Language skills are considered as the main tool of communication skills. These skills play an important role in the personal and social development of individuals. Although it may seem possible to communicate without speaking the same language, a common language depends on a common culture and cultural codes are part of communication. Language and communication skills include the ability of individuals to convey their feelings, thoughts, attitudes and values, to understand others, to exchange information and ideas, to express opinions, desires, needs, fears and concerns (Council of Europe, 2016). Language and communication skills are analyzed under three sub-skills: communication in mother tongue and foreign languages, negotiation and effective listening skills (Council of Europe, 2016).

The technological literacy demanded by the technological age has given birth to a new form of communication in the next stage. There are many areas where communication in the digital age has an impact. Here, the aspect affecting education is briefly mentioned. The digital age has moved people's basic habits, lifestyles, relationships, ways of accessing information and forms of communication to another platform. With technological communication channels, it is easy and fast to reach information, institutions and people in many parts of the world and has developed a common language. This change has caused life to accelerate and our first means of communication to be technological tools. One of these tools, the writable web (Web 2.0), is an internet-based tool. It is a digital communication technology that provides writable, readable, updatable, fast and low-cost sharing of content produced by users, leading in economic, social and technological fields. Web 2.0 technology is also a new way of thinking. A new form of communication has emerged with social media channels and new media platforms that are part of this technology.

Codes of communication and interaction between people have been rewritten and socialization experiences have become different. This has led to the reconstruction of private and public life spaces. Unabated technological developments have continued with Web 3.0, defined as the third-generation web technology since 2006. It aims to accelerate the flow of information between various web applications and utilizes various data sets (big data sets) for this purpose. Web 3.0 technology has replaced user-controlled management with machine-to-machine interaction. It was the beginning of the era when machines/computers could share data with each other, which we can see as the birth of today's artificial intelligence (Hendler, 2009).

Technological tools and communication with them have intervened between teacher-student communication in the direction of affecting education. With Web 2.0 applications, course content is produced, organized and shared with multiple users at the same time. Tools that facilitate the sharing of information, emotions, thoughts and ideas have caused differentiation in dimensions such as educational content, process and educational environments. In fact, with the transition to the digital age, it is not possible to follow the innovations in this age in the wind of rapid change. While new ways of communication are being sought in the digital age, issues related to privacy and the protection of personal data have also emerged.

Communication tools continue to evolve rapidly. What is important here is to raise individuals who possess technological literacy skills, who can understand and critically evaluate these tools. Technologically literate individuals will not see technology merely as a tool but will also act by analysing its potential social impacts, ethical dimensions, and risks. Although the ways of using information may vary for individuals with higher-order thinking skills who can access accurate and reliable information, positive outcomes will be achieved through the proper management of the process. Therefore, in preparing students for a rapidly changing future, it is essential not only to equip them with the ability to use today's technological tools but also to prepare them with the skills to adapt to the unknown aspects of the future.

GIFTED AND TALENTED STUDENTS AND THEIR CHARACTERISTICS

The term of gifted and talented student means that "Children, or youth who give evidence of high achievement capability in such areas as intellectual, creative, artistic, or leadership capacity, or in specific academic fields, and who need services or activities not ordinarily provided by the school in order to fully develop those capabilities." for United States of America (USA) Federal Primary and Secondary Education Act. Various definitions of giftedness have been proposed. What is striking about the definitions is that giftedness is a social construct created by societies (Pfeiffer, 2012).

Sak (2014) defines giftedness as extraordinary achievement or performance in areas that are fundamental to human life. According to Tannenbaum (2003), gifted individuals are those who have the potential for productivity in physical, moral, social, emotional, and intellectual areas. Giftedness is a state of being at an advanced level in all mental areas or of being motivated and disciplined in working towards a goal. Giftedness corresponds to advanced development in various areas. As can be understood from the definition given in the introduction, it encompasses advanced development in areas such as art, sports, and leadership, in addition to the cognitive domain. In this content, advanced cognitive development characteristics are examined, and similarities between gifted intelligence and machine intelligence are explored through the development and management of skills.

Certain common characteristics observed in gifted individuals from infancy onwards have been identified (Clark, 2002; Davis, 2006; Sak, 2014; Rimm, Siegle and Davis, 2020). It should be noted that all of these characteristics may be present in the gifted individual, or none of them may be present. Some of the characteristics identified or observed in the researches are listed in Table 2.

Table 2. Characteristics of the Gifted and Talented

Domain	Skills
Intellectual	Early developed language skills An extensive vocabulary Fast information processing High memory capacity Logical thinking Early mathematic/arithmetic skills Early art and music skills Advanced-level interests Higher-order thinking skills (problem-solving, analytical-critical thinking, metacognitive skills, etc.) Being attentive and curious High awareness and self-awareness Intellectual hypersensitivity
Social-emotional	Motivation Persistence and determination Personal adaptation or maladaptation Independence Emotional oversensitivity Self-esteem and self-control Self-discipline Personal preferences in learning Advanced sense of humor High levels of moral thinking, fairness, and empathy Perfectionism Asynchronous development
Psychomotor	High energy Constant need for stimulation Intense physical activity Impulsivity Being out of fix
Creativity	General creativity Creativity in writing Creativity in reading Domain-specific creativity (mathematic, scientific, artistic) Multi talents

The characteristics given in Table 2 are generally classified according to intellectual, social-emotional and psychomotor characteristics according to areas of development. Creativity has also been included. Creativity skills have been added to examine them within the framework of 21st-century skills and to understand the relationship between intelligence and creativity. Research has shown that there is a positive linear relationship between creativity and intelligence up to a certain point. However, the 'threshold' theory emphasizes the necessity of a basic intelligence capacity for creative productivity and claims that there is no meaningful relationship between intelligence levels measured above this threshold and creativity (MacKinnon, 1978). Various studies continue to be conducted to test the threshold theory.

Various skills are included in the structure referred to as higher-order thinking. In general, the skills examined at a higher level are described as problem solving, creative thinking, critical thinking, analytical thinking, evaluative thinking, and metacognitive skills. Higher-order thinking is the process of using cognitive skills at the highest level necessary to solve complex problems.

Solving complex and abstract problems/issues requires the use of mental skills at a high level, as well as establishing connections and making inferences beyond the use of knowledge. In addition to the use of skills, Güneş (2012) also includes the use of metacognitive skills in higher-order thinking. The individual's awareness of their own thinking processes is based on controlling and improving these processes. King, Goodson, and Rohan (1998) explain the process based on three assumptions:

1. Thinking and learning levels cannot be separated from each other. Thinking and learning are two interconnected concepts. They have components and levels.
2. Whether thinking can be learned without subject content is purely theoretical. Regardless of the outcome of theories, in real life, students learn in both social and academic environments. The knowledge students have previously acquired will form the basis for both higher-level thinking and the knowledge they will learn later.
3. Higher-level thinking involves various thinking processes that are applied to complex situations and have multiple variables.

Features, assumptions, etc. related to higher-level thinking processes are shared to demonstrate that these skills can be taught and developed. This is because early research claimed that these skills were hereditary, which posed an obstacle to their development. However, with the increase in brain-based learning studies, it has been demonstrated that these skills can be developed and taught, and that it is important to begin teaching them at an early age (Resnick and Klopher, 1989).

Here are some suggestions for teachers to develop higher-order thinking skills in the classroom. Students' readiness levels are a prerequisite for reaching a high level. Students should have basic knowledge of the subject, understand the information, and be ready to apply what they know. Therefore, the information must be taught first. In order to develop higher-order thinking skills, it is important for teachers to create a learning environment that encourages students to think, to be role models for students in the process, to guide them, and to support them. Focusing on subject-specific knowledge, clarifying the structure of the subject, using strategies appropriate to the subject and the student, and facilitating the process by serving as a role model or through direct instruction is necessary when teaching complex and challenging skills. Implementing metacognitive strategies in educational settings can enhance learning for students of all abilities (Preckel et al., 2020). Teachers play a crucial role in incorporating these strategies into their teaching, which can make the learning process more efficient and effective for gifted students. Although metacognitive strategies are particularly beneficial for gifted students, it is important to recognize that they can also be adapted for students with different abilities. Using metacognitive strategies universally can foster a more inclusive and supportive learning environment that benefits a diverse range of learners. Many specialized or general strategies can be used in teaching higher-order thinking skills. This chapter also lists some of the names of the relevant skills. How to use the strategies is more critical than what they are. Anyone can access the strategies from the sources and even learn how to use them from videos of educators explaining them and sharing their applications on social media accounts. Unfortunately, even when these strategies are learned, they are not immediately put into practice. This is because, even if the strategy is the same, your students are different. In fact, each learning environment, physical surroundings, and resources are also different. In this context, differentiation in instruction has been included to provide teachers with a roadmap.

Differentiation

Educational programs prepared with a universal design approach are designed according to the needs arising from individual differences such as age, learning style, and language characteristics (Hitchcock and Stahl, 2003). These arrangements, based on universal design principles, are expressed in the literature as 'differentiated instruction'. Differentiation refers to instructional arrangements that provide students with meaningful learning experiences in line with their individual learning characteristics and interests, giving them the opportunity to demonstrate what they have learned. Differentiation in teaching is recommended for all students in general education classrooms who differ from their peers in terms of learning speed and capacity. The purpose of this chapter is not to explain how to differentiate for the specified student groups. However, the inclusion of higher-order thinking skills in the program is also a type of differentiation. Therefore, the aim is to understand the basic elements of the program and the philosophy of differentiation.

Differentiation can be achieved by adapting at least one of the program elements—outcomes, content, process, product/assessment, and learning environment—to the needs of gifted students. The way to differentiate instruction begins with adapting the learning outcomes of the relevant course and progresses with adaptations made in one or more of the fundamental dimensions of the program, namely content, process, product/assessment, and learning environment (Maker and Schiever, 2010; Tomlinson, 2001).

- Learning outcomes are the characteristics that students are expected to acquire.
- Content is the set of topics, principles, concepts, rules, facts, etc. necessary to achieve the specified goals. This dimension addresses the question, 'What will be taught?'
- Process refers to the methods and techniques used to teach the content. This dimension addresses the question, 'How will it be taught?'
- Learning environment is the ideal environment and physical arrangements necessary for learning to take place. This dimension seeks to answer the question 'Where will it be taught?'
- Product/assessment; the level of achievement of program objectives. Assessment can be results-oriented or process-oriented.

Through program dimensions, teachers can plan well where and how to incorporate the higher-order thinking skills they aim to achieve. Differentiation, an important approach to increasing efficiency and effectiveness in learning, is student-centered. As intended by 21st-century skills, it is an approach that supports students in discovering their own learning styles, problem-solving, critical and creative thinking, and teaching them to collaborate, rather than being based solely on knowledge transfer. By supplementing the traditional gifted program with artificial intelligence instruction, an example is presented that supports students' autonomy and participation while also offering educators opportunities for differentiation (Ecker, Eckert and Cummings, 2025). Through the systematic integration of artificial intelligence tools, recommendations are made to provide more personalized, challenging and engaging learning experiences that better meet the accelerated development needs of gifted students in modern educational environments.

SOLUTIONS AND RECOMMENDATIONS

The approach to designing thinking skills training and teaching individuals' skill management based on the thinking patterns of gifted individuals is outlined in this chapter. Gifted students access information, understand it, and take action to directly acquire skills and use information. This is where the thinking/learning patterns of gifted students and the working principle of machine intelligence show similarities. This similarity cannot explain the flow exactly, but it highlights the importance of the control mechanism that machines do not have but that is possible with human intelligence. Skill management increases the effectiveness of utilizing the information that machines have and can access quickly.

Preparing and working on 21st century skills is a necessity not only for individuals but also for schools. Education in schools is curriculum-based. Today, the changes that need to be made in educational environments should be based on this curriculum, which also includes education in schools. Fadel and colleagues (2015) suggest that curricula should be based on four main dimensions. These are knowledge, skills, character, and meta-learning. These four dimensions should function in an intertwined manner in educational environments. The knowledge dimension seeks answers to the question, 'What do we know and understand?'; the skills dimension seeks answers to the question, 'How do we use what we know?'; and the character dimension seeks answers to the question, 'How do we behave and interact in the world?' The meta-learning dimension completes the foundation of these dimensions. The question 'How do we reflect and adapt?' essentially targets the learning and management of all skills, with an emphasis on metacognition and growth mindset.

These skills also include those presented within the framework of P21. However, it offers a practical approach to educational environments and defines the 21st century learner. What sets this person apart is their ability to manage their metacognitive skills through meta-learning.

Figure 4. Skills Management Satellite

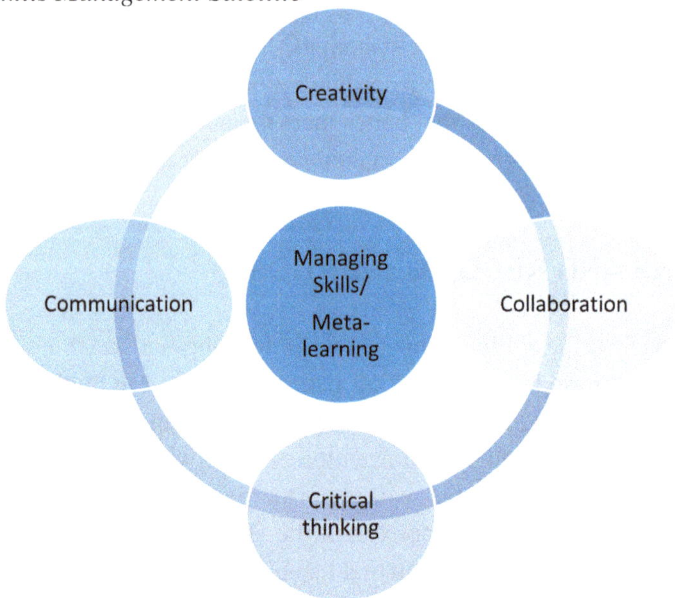

The P21 framework and the characteristics of gifted individuals are defined in Figure 4. In the figure, the person who can manage skills is at the center of the orbit, and the skill method is as effective as the skills they possess.

The process invites us to think not about choosing between people or machines, but about how good integration can increase equality, creativity, and complexity in the education of gifted individuals. A series of publications on gifted individuals and artificial intelligence research has clearly called for action: Educator training programs, research institutions, and school systems should invest not only in technology but also in the professional capacity to use it wisely (Buchanan and Farrell, 2025).

CONCLUSION AND FUTURE RESEARCH DIRECTIONS

Within the established skills framework, acquiring and developing these specific competencies is deemed critical to ensuring the effective and proficient utilization of artificial intelligence. Without these skills, the use of artificial intelligence tools will serve only to repeat existing knowledge or present it in different forms. This will result in unoriginal, non-innovative production. Therefore, it is recommended that the transition to the trainability of artificial intelligence be based on the thinking and learning styles of gifted individuals.

The use of digital communication technologies does not require separate skills. It depends on the effective use and control of higher-level thinking skills. Education in educational institutions should also be structured with programs that integrate these skills. In this context, the first recommendations will be for teachers and teacher candidates. This is because education can be designed with competencies aimed at developing the relevant skills. Teachers or teacher candidates possess these skills as personal competencies but teaching them requires knowledge and application of different strategies, methods, and techniques. In this context, it is recommended that training be provided during or before the service period for the relevant professional groups. It is also very important that this training be not only theoretical but also application based. Various studies have shown that teachers use technological tools in their teaching processes and try to keep up with developments. However, the pandemic period has revealed that these competencies are actually lacking and insufficient. It is emphasized that post-pandemic teacher education programs should include the integration of technology into education and teaching programs (Linder and Webb, 2022).

REFERENCES

Akyel, Y., & Tur, E. (2024). Prospects, challenges, and future directions in the research and investigation of artificial intelligence's potential and applications in educational sciences. *Ahi Evran Üniversitesi Kırşehir Eğitim Fakültesi Dergisi, 25*(1), 645–711. DOI: 10.29299/kefad.1322341

Allen, R. R., & Rott, R. K. (1969). *The nature of critical thinking*. Report from the Concepts in Verbal Argument Project. Theoretical Paper No. 20.

Anderson, L. W., & Krathwohl, D. R. (Eds.). (2021). *A Taxonomy for Learning, Teaching, and Assessing: A Revision of Bloom's Taxonomy of Educational Objectives*. Addison Wesley Longman, Inc.

Arf, C. (1959). *Makine düşünebilir mi ve nasıl düşünebilir?* [Can machines think, and how do they think?]. [Conference session]. Atatürk Üniversitesi 19581959 Öğretim Yılı Halk Konferansları (1), 91-103.

Batey, M., & Furnham, A. (2006). Creativity, intelligence, and personality: A critical review of the scattered literature. *Genetic, Social, and General Psychology Monographs, 132*(4), 355–429. DOI: 10.3200/MONO.132.4.355-430 PMID: 18341234

Beyer, B. K. (1991). *Teaching thinking skills: A hand book for secondary school teachers*. Allyn and Bacon.

Buchanan, M. B., & Farrell, S. J. (2025). The editorial word: Binary balancing the binary—AI, expertise, and the future of gifted education. *Journal of Advanced Academics, 36*(4), 593–600. DOI: 10.1177/1932202X251373093

Clark, B. (2002). *Growing up gifted: Developing the potential of children at home and at school* (6th ed.). Pearson College Div. Council of Europe (2016). *Competencies for democratic culture: Living together as equals in culturally diverse democratic societies*. Council of Europe. https://rm.coe.int/16806ccc07

Csikszentmihalyi, M. (1996). *Creative aging*. Harper Collins.

Davis, G. A. (2006). *Gifted children and gifted education*. Grest Potential Press.

Ecker, J., Eckert, G., & Cummings, E. (2025). Augmenting gifted education through artificial intelligence: A four-dimensional framework for AI tutoring integration. *Journal of Advanced Academics, 36*(4), 879–896. DOI: 10.1177/1932202X251356326

Facione, P. A. (1990). *Critical thinking: A statement of expert consensus for purposes of educational assessment and instruction*. The California Academic Press.

Fadel, C., Bialik, M., & Trilling, B. (2015). *Four dimension education. The competence learner need to succeed.* The Center For Curriculum Redesign.

HaeJin., L., Frank, S., Ruohan, Z., Hannah, V., Dong, W., & Nigel, B. (2025). *Learning behaviors mediate the effect of AI-powered support for metacognitive calibration on learning outcomes.* In CHI Conference on Human Factors in Computing Systems (CHI '25), April 26–May01, 2025. https://doi.org/DOI: 10.1145/3706598.3713960

Hamarat, E. (2019). *21.yüzyıl becerileri odağında Türkiye'nin eğitim politikaları* [Türkiye's education policies focused on 21st century skills]. Seta Analiz. https://www.setav.org/assets/uploads/2019/04/272A.pdf

Hendler, J. (2009). Web 3.0 emerging. *Computer, 42*(1), 111–113. DOI: 10.1109/MC.2009.30

Hitchcock, C., & Stahl, S. (2003). Assistive technology, universal design, universal design for learning: Improved learning opportunities. *Journal of Special Education Technology, 18*(4), 45–52. DOI: 10.1177/016264340301800404

ISTE. (2017). *ISTE Standards.* International Society for Technology in Education. https://www.iste.org/standards

Johnson, D. W., Johnson, R. T., & Holubec, E. J. (1990). *Cooperation in the Classroom.* Interaction Book Co.

Kaufman, J. C., & Beghetto, R. A. (2009). Beyond big and little: The four c model of creativity. *Review of General Psychology, 13*(1), 1–12. DOI: 10.1037/a0013688

Kılıç, T. (2021). *Yeni bilim: Bağlantısallık – Yeni kültür: Yaşamdaşlık: "Beyin Nedir?"den, "Yaşam Nedir?"e bir bilim serüveni* [New science: Interconnectedness – New culture: Coexistence: A scientific journey from 'What is the brain?' to 'What is life?']. Ayrıntı Yayınları.

Linder, A. L., & Webb, C. L. (2022). Educational technology: A systematic review of the literature. In Webb, C. L., & Linder, A. L. (Eds.), *Preparing pre-service teachers to integrate technology in K-12 classrooms: Standards and best practices* (pp. 1–45). IGI Global., DOI: 10.4018/978-1-6684-5478-7.ch001

MacKinnon, D. W. (1978). *In search of human effectiveness.* Creative Education Foundation.

Maker, C. J., & Schiever, S. W. (2010). *Curriculum development and teaching strategies for gifted learners.* Pro.ed An International Publisher

Mumford, M. D. (2003). Where have we been, where are we going? Taking stock in creativity research. *Creativity Research Journal*, *15*(2-3), 107–120. DOI: 10.1207/S15326934CRJ152&3_01

Partnership for 21st Century Skills. (2019). *P21 framework definitions.* https://files.eric.ed.gov/fulltext/ED519462.pdf

Pfeiffer, S. I. (2012). *Serving the gifted: Evidence-based clinical and psychoeducational practice*. Routledge.

Plucker, J. A., Runco, M. A., & Hegarty, C. B. (2011). Enhancement of creativity. In Runco, M. A., & Pritzker, S. R. (Eds.), *Encyclopedia of creativity* (2nd ed., pp. 456–460). Academic Press., DOI: 10.1016/B978-0-12-375038-9.00090-X

Preckel, F., Golle, J., Grabner, R., Jarvin, L., Kozbelt, A., Müllensiefen, D., Olszewski-Kubilius, P., Schneider, W., Subotnik, R., Vock, M., & Worrell, F. C. (2020). Talent development in achievement domains: A psychological framework for within- and cross-domain research. *Perspectives on Psychological Science*, *15*(3), 691–722. DOI: 10.1177/1745691619895030 PMID: 32196409

Resnick, L. B., & Klopher, L. E. (1989). *Toward the thinking curriculum: Current cognitive research.* ASCD Yearbook. Association for Supervision and Curriculum Development.

Rimm, S. B., Siegle, D., & Davis, G. A. (2018). *Education of the gifted and talented* (7th ed.). Pearson.

Runco, M. (2007). *Encouraging creativity in education.* Creativity a Handbook for Teachers. Stallion.

Sak, U. (2014). Üstün zekâlılar: Özellikleri, tanılanmaları, eğitimleri [Giftedness: Characteristics, identification, education] (4th ed). Vize Yayıncılık.

Sternberg, R. J., & Lubart, T. I. (1995). *Defying the crowd: Cultivating creativity in a culture of conformity*. Free Press.

Tannenbaum, A. J. (2003) Nature and nurture of giftedness. In Colangelo, N. & Davis, G. A. (Eds.) *Handbook of gifted education* (3rd ed.), 45-59. Pearson Education.

Tardif, T. Z., & Sternberg, R. J. (1988). What do we know about creativity? In Sternberg, R. J. (Ed.), *The nature of creativity. Contemporary psychological perspectives* (pp. 429–440). Cambridge University.

Tomlinson, C. A. (2001). *How to differentiate instruction in mixed-ability classrooms*. Pearson Education.

Torrance, E. P. (1998). *The Torrance Tests of Creative Thinking Norms—technical manual figural (streamlined) forms* (Vol. A & B). Scholastic Testing Service.

Ünal, N. E., & Davis, G. (2023). Eleştirel düşünme becerilerinin geliştirilmesine yönelik stratejiler. In B. B., & N. N. Ateşgöz (Eds.) *Üst düzey düşünme becerilerini geliştirme stratejileri* (pp. 88-139). Anı Yayıncılık.

Webb, N. M. (1982). Student interaction and learning in small groups. *Review of Educational Research*, *52*(3), 421–445. DOI: 10.3102/00346543052003421

World Economic Forum. (2015). *The skills needed in the 21st century.* https://widgets.weforum.org/nve-2015/chapter1.html

World Economic Forum. (2025). *Future of jobs report.* https://reports.weforum.org/docs/WEF_Future_of_Jobs_Report_2025.pdf

Yeşilbaş Özenç, Y., & Başaran, R. (2024). Lifelong learning and artificial intelligence. *Sinop Üniversitesi Eğitim Fakültesi Dergisi*, *1*(1), 101–125.

KEY TERMS AND DEFINITIONS

Artificial Intelligence: High-level and fast imitation of human thought processes by machines.

Creativity: The ability to establish original connections between things that have not been established before.

Critical Thinking: The ability to question, analyze and evaluate information in the process of preparing it for use.

High Intelligence-Gifted and Talented: The individuals who show advanced development in cognitive processes compared to individuals who show typical development.

Higher Order Thinking: It is a thought control system that requires control of an individual's thinking capacity.

Innovation: “Surprise me” production.

Meta-Learning: The ability to control and regulate learning process.

Chapter 7
Data Privacy and Security in Education

Fatma Akgün
https://orcid.org/0000-0002-9728-7516
Trakya University, Turkey

Şenay Ozan Deniz
https://orcid.org/0000-0003-1300-5225
Trakya University, Turkey

ABSTRACT

Digital transformation in education is a process developed to create effective and efficient learning processes that meet the demands of the current era and to ensure learning. Through data collected in education, teachers can more accurately monitor student behavior, develop early intervention strategies, and create personalized learning environments. However, this data-driven approach also brings with it data security, privacy, and ethical responsibilities. While taking advantage of the opportunities offered by developing technologies, being aware of and preventing the threats they bring is a priority. This unit will address data privacy and security in education. In this context, the types of data collected in education, educational data mining, data privacy and security, basic principles of information security, security threats and risks, data protection methods, and solutions will be explained.

INTRODUCTION

Technological developments are currently taking place that will cause fundamental changes in many areas. Technologies such as virtual reality, augmented reality, cloud technologies, mobile technologies, Web 3.0, big data, the Internet of Things,

DOI: 10.4018/979-8-3373-8857-1.ch007

wearable technologies, 3D printers and artificial intelligence have brought about major changes, and will continue to do so. Indeed, artificial intelligence technology is at the heart of these changes, alongside the innovations taking place today. These technologies offer many opportunities, which are being utilised to produce solutions to existing problems or to ensure development and improvement. Conversely, needs are diversifying in all areas during this process and, consequently, the skills and competencies expected of individuals are evolving, as are social needs. Given the evolving technology and updated social needs, it is clear that fundamental changes are required in education to provide effective solutions to these needs. Digital culture and digital competencies have brought the use of evolving technologies in educational and teaching environments to the forefront, emphasising activities aimed at acquiring, developing and enhancing digital skills.

DIGITAL TRANSFORMATION IN EDUCATION

Digital transformation in education is a comprehensive change process involving the integration of emerging technologies into educational and teaching environments, the use of these technologies throughout the process, and the fundamental restructuring of educational and teaching methods and learning processes. Digital transformation in education has been developed to create effective and efficient learning processes that align with the requirements of the modern age and guarantee learning outcomes. Those who will experience learning are individuals who use these technologies at every turn in their lives. At the same time, society expects individuals who can use these technologies effectively and efficiently, and who possess critical thinking and problem-solving skills. Technological advances increase efficiency by overcoming the limitations of traditional educational approaches. Integrating developing technologies into learning and teaching processes increases individual motivation and ensures the success of the learning process. The absence of place and time constraints in the learning process, the ability to offer various learning environments tailored to individuals' characteristics, and the adaptability of these environments are key to creating a successful, student-centred learning environment. Teachers and administrators can manage learning processes more effectively and carry out measurement and evaluation quickly. This transformation enables teachers to move beyond traditional teaching methods and enhance the learning experience. There are many important elements to this process of change and transformation. Among these, data-driven decision-making processes stand out as a significant factor.

DATA COLLECTED IN EDUCATION AND EDUCATIONAL DATA MINING

The power behind the opportunities provided by digital transformation lies in large data sets. Big data is a term used to describe data that is high-volume, high-speed and highly diverse (Mills et al., 2012). It refers to data sets that are difficult to obtain, store, manage and process, and which appear complex and meaningless at first glance. In the field of education, big data consists of personal information stored in digital environments, biometric data, data related to academic achievement, and behavioural data. Personal information about students, teachers and parents is recorded and stored in institutional databases. This personal information is also recorded alongside data related to academic performance. Biometric and behavioural data can be obtained from online learning environments, learning management systems, e-learning environments and distance education platforms, as well as social media. Recording every action in databases leads to the accumulation of large amounts of data that can be used to draw various inferences about students. Learning processes conducted in online environments also result in learners leaving digital traces, creating big data (Bozkurt, 2016). Learning management systems allow for the detailed monitoring of learners' interactions with content, other learners and instructors within online learning environments. In educational environments that integrate emerging technologies, all learner interactions can be recorded. This includes learners' grades, the amount of time spent on materials, progress made, correspondence with other learners and instructors, and submitted assignments. Social networks are among the environments where learning interactions are most intense and individuals are most active. Learners communicate primarily with each other in these environments and are influenced by these interactions (Fırat, 2015). The interactions, comments and statements made by individuals in online communities within these environments are accessible to all and form part of large data sets. These data generally consist of metrics such as the types of content users browse, how much time they spend on different types of pages, how many clicks there are, how many e-evaluations there are, how many user-user (student-student/student-instructor) interactions there are, and so on. This big data is processed using educational data mining to extract valuable information that improves the learning process and enhances learning. This comprehensive interaction data is referred to as 'big data' in the literature (Siemens, 2013).

Educational Data Mining is an emerging discipline, concerned with developing methods for exploring the unique and increasingly large-scale data that come from educational settings and using those methods to better understand students, and the settings which they learn in (The International Educational Data Mining Society, 2025). In this context, big data is highly valuable in the field of education. Data mining in education involves analysing and utilising the rapidly growing amount of stored data in educational processes (Kurniawan & Halim, 2013). It can be defined as a new discipline involving the development of methods for discovering unique data types in educational environments, with the aim of improving student understanding (Baker & Yacef, 2009). Narli, Aksoy and Erciyes (2014) define educational data mining as 'a field of research that emerges from the application of data mining methods to data obtained from educational databases for educational purposes'. Educational data mining provides information that enables many developments in education. This information is used to improve and understand learning and teaching processes. As a result, schools can gain insight into students' current situations and make predictions about their future ones (Bienkowski et al., 2012). This analysis can identify students' academic achievements and the factors influencing their success (Abbasoğlu, 2020; Hottoman, 2020). The quality of education can be determined and students experiencing learning difficulties can be identified more easily. This reveals characteristics affecting success, such as emotional and behavioural traits (Meng & Meng, 2014). Indeed, educational data mining is used to determine student characteristics, group and model students, predict performance, identify undesirable behaviours and provide feedback and support to educators (Romero & Ventura, 2013). The information obtained from educational data mining is important for educators, students and administrators when making decisions about solving educational problems and improving educational environments. However, this data-driven approach also raises data security, privacy and ethical issues. While the integration of digital technologies into education offers significant opportunities, safeguarding data privacy and security is paramount for fostering a secure learning environment. It is also necessary to strike a balance between the opportunities offered by technology and the risks it poses to achieve a healthy digital transformation in education.

Accurate data collection, secure processing and ethical use have become key factors in determining the sustainability and quality of education systems. The protection of personal data and student privacy, as well as transparent data usage, are among the main elements that should not be overlooked in the digital transformation process. A good balance must be struck between the opportunities technology offers to enable a healthy digital transformation in education and the risks it brings. To avoid issues when collecting, processing and storing data in educational environments, it is important to have the necessary knowledge and skills in data privacy and security. While benefiting from the opportunities offered by developing technologies, it is essential to be aware of and prevent the associated threats.

DATA PRIVACY AND SECURITY CONCEPTS (CIA TRIANGLE)

Data privacy and security are highly sensitive issues in the field of education, where personal data is involved. The data used in educational data mining comes from educational environments and individuals receiving educational services. It consists entirely of personal data and can be referred to as educational data. In this context, protecting educational data and storing it securely should be prioritized. It is necessary to ensure the privacy and security of educational data and the information obtained as a result of educational data mining. At this point, it is important to explain the concepts of data, information, and knowledge in order to understand the subject and the authors' approach to it. These concepts are often used interchangeably and perceived as the same. However, there are differences in their content. Zins (2007) states that "Data are sets of characters, symbols, numbers, and audio/vi-sual bits that are represented and/or encountered in rawforms." According to Kalseth and Cummings (2001: 166), "data is transformed into information through the addition of value via summarization, correction, calculation, classification, and content processing". "Knowledge involves both data and the relationships amongdata elements or their sets. This organization of data basedon relationships is what enables one to draw generalizationsfrom the data so organized, and to formulate questions aboutwhich one wishes to acquire more data" (Zins, 2007). Data alone does not convey meaning and is in its raw form. However, it is the foundation of information and knowledge. Information is obtained by processing data. Knowledge is obtained through the processing and organisation of information. There are two conversion processes: the first involves converting data into information by organising it according to a specific formula, and the second involves converting information into knowledge (Jensen, 2005).

The difference between data and information relates to their usefulness and functionality rather than their structure (Yılmaz, 2009). Although data, information and knowledge are closely related concepts, there are some differences between them. When discussing privacy and security issues, these concepts can be evaluated under the same heading. It could therefore be argued that data and information privacy and security issues are no different to knowledge privacy and security issues, and that the same theories apply to all three concepts. In this context, data privacy and security issues are explained by the basic principles of information security.

Basic Principles of Information Security

The three main elements of these principles are confidentiality, integrity and availability (Bayrakcı & Koçman, 2023; Değirmenci & Demiral, 2023; Farid et al., 2023; Fussel, 2005; Gültekin & Özel, 2023; McCumber, 2005; Radanliev, 2024;

Sevinç & Avcı, 2024; Tekerek, 2008). These principles provide a framework through which institutions and organisations can protect their data and information assets, and manage risks.

Figure 1. Basic principles of information security

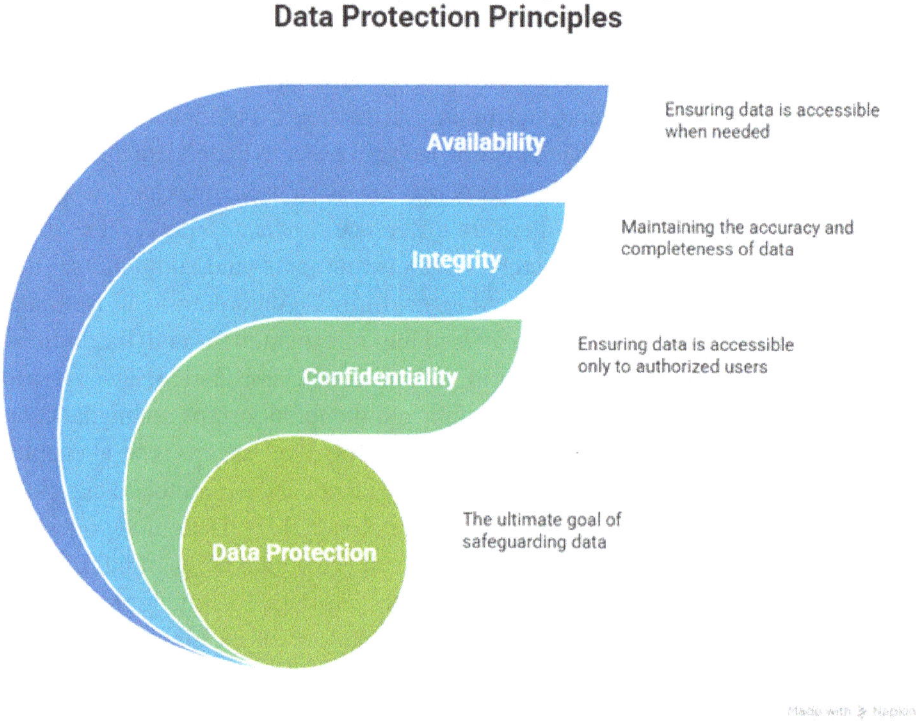

Confidentiality: Information is confidential if it cannot be accessed or fall into the hands of unauthorized persons, or if it can be prevented from doing so (Akseki et al., 2023). It ensures that information is accessible only to authorized individuals. One of the most important elements of information security is protecting sensitive information from unauthorized access. However, it also refers to situations where information is not disseminated to unauthorized persons, processes or devices (Fussel, 2005). The principle of confidentiality involves maintaining authorized controls over access and disclosure, as well as implementing protective measures (Farid et al., 2023). Protecting personal information and individual rights is one of the most comprehensive privacy topics (Değirmenci & Demiral, 2023). According to Güler and Fırat (2022), the principle of privacy is shaped by two fundamental concepts: data security and privacy. Data security ensures that private or confidential information is not disclosed to unauthorized persons. Privacy, on the other hand, enables individuals to control or influence what information about themselves can be collected and stored, and who can disclose this information (Stallings & Brown, 2015, p. 13).

Integrity: Integrity is the prevention of unauthorized deletion, alteration, or damage to information. It refers to the transmission of information from the source to the destination without any external interference and without any changes such as deletion, addition, or editing. Integrity means ensuring that information is accurate and complete. Integrity is ensured by delivering the information to the recipient in its entirety, as it was sent by the sender (Fussell, 2005). Summarization algorithms are used to ensure the integrity of data during information transfer (Tekerek, 2008). The principle of integrity also protects information from being altered or destroyed by unauthorized persons who do not have access to it. Protecting information from unauthorized changes ensures the accuracy of decision-making processes and operational efficiency. It also aims to maintain the non-repudiability and authenticity of information (Farid et al., 2023).

Availability: Availability means ensuring that authorized users can access information when they need it. It refers to the ability of authorized individuals to access information when it is needed. Unlike confidentiality, availability is not concerned with who can access information, but rather with whether the information is accessible or not. In short, it is about ensuring that information is available when and where it is needed (Çetin, 2014). System accessibility can be affected by factors such as errors in computer software, the use or configuration of the system by biased, uninformed, or untrained personnel, or natural disasters (Fussell, 2005). The continuous availability of systems and data ensures the uninterrupted continuity of business processes.

Information security should be considered in terms of confidentiality, integrity and availability as a whole. It is not possible to ensure information security by considering these principles in isolation. Some researchers may also consider the concept of availability to be synonymous with usability (Bayrakcı and Koçman, 2023; Değirmenci and Demiral, 2023; Maconachy et al., 2001; McCumber, 1991). Similarly, like accessibility, usability is an area of information security that requires services and components to be continuously available to the user community. Indeed, failure to use a service or component means that the principles of confidentiality and integrity cannot be evaluated (Fussel, 2005). Protecting information systems against unauthorised access or changes to information during storage, processing or transmission, and denying service to unauthorised users refers to the necessary measures to detect, document and counter such threats (Maconachy et al., 2001). McCumber (1991) addressed the fundamental principles and subcomponents of information security in relation to the state of information, its source, and security measures. He created the Information Security Model, shown in Figure 2. This model highlights the interconnectedness of confidentiality, integrity, and availability (CIA) in ensuring system security.

Figure 2. Information security model

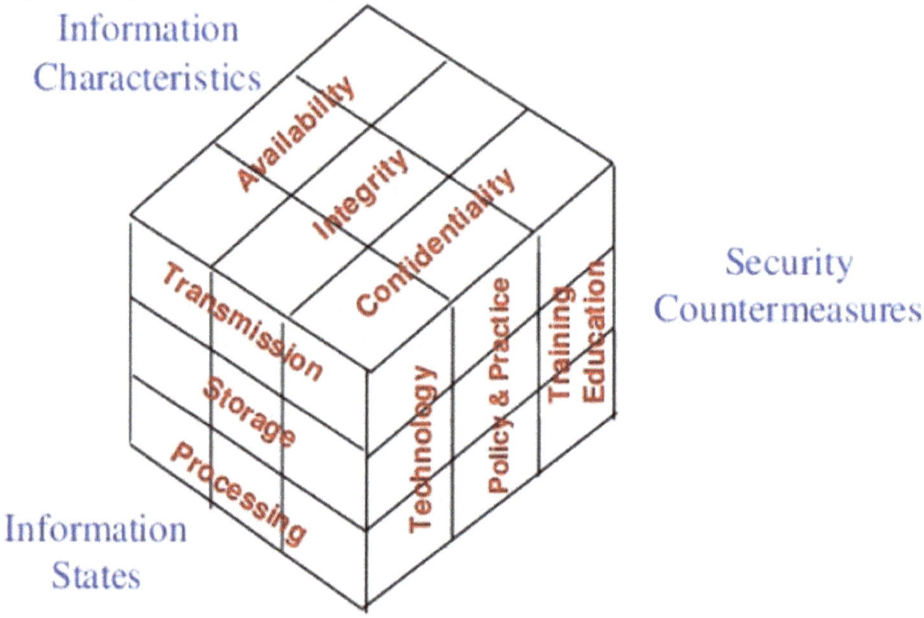

The Information Security Model, developed by John McCumber, is a comprehensive framework designed to ensure and enhance the security of information and communication systems within organisations. Also known as McCumber's Cube, it is a multidimensional framework designed to systematically address information security risks and solution strategies. It is a comprehensive approach to understanding and managing the complexity of information security. It consists of three main dimensions:

- Information States: This represents the different states that information is in throughout its lifecycle.
- Information Components: These represent the various ways in which information is stored, processed or transmitted.
- Security Measures: These represent the various security controls implemented to protect information assets.

The intersection of these three dimensions forms a matrix that is used to analyse information security risks and determine appropriate security measures. The

McCumber Information Security Model is a valuable tool for addressing information security risks and developing solution strategies systematically. It provides a comprehensive framework for identifying and implementing the security measures necessary to protect an organisation's information assets.

SECURITY THREATS AND RISKS

Intensive use of information and communication technologies by users can give rise to various security risks. Some of these risks may be caused by user errors, while others may be carried out by malicious individuals (attackers) who gain unauthorised access to the system. Given that the internet is used for a variety of purposes (work, personal life, education, banking, communication, health, etc.) and by users of all ages, it is reasonable to assume that the number of users encountering such security risks is also increasing (Boston Consulting Group, 2022; Velki & Romstein, 2018). In particular, users can be exposed to many security threats due to malware and/or attacks such as phishing.

Malicious Software

In terms of information security, it is critically important for users not to download files from untrustworthy websites, open spam emails or run files attached to such emails. Software developed with the intent of damaging users' personal computers is referred to as malware (malicious software). Malware refers to small software programs developed for various malicious purposes, such as disrupting the operation of a computer, crashing the system, rendering network resources unusable or gaining unauthorised access.

Virus: Computer viruses typically reach their targets via files, programs, USB sticks or external disks, with the aim of damaging a system. They typically infect executable files or the boot sector of the target system. They have no direct effect on the system unless they are executed. Viruses can also spread through files that are shared unwittingly or sent via email. Once activated, they can result in data loss, including the corruption or deletion of files and folders, and can also prevent the system from functioning properly.

Worm: Worms are malicious software that can replicate themselves using computer networks to infect other systems. Although worms share similar structural characteristics with viruses, the most significant difference between the two lies in their infection methods: worms can spread automatically over networks without requiring human intervention or a host program because they have their own transmission mechanisms. They can spread without user interaction, slow down the system and increase network traffic.

Trojan horses: Trojan horses are malicious software that allows attackers to gain unauthorised access to user systems. They typically infiltrate systems by hiding within programs, activating when the program is run, and performing malicious activities on the device. These programs spread through attractive content such as online games, internet-based applications or media files and can replicate themselves, steal confidential data or damage the system.

Backdoors: Backdoors are malicious programs that allow individuals with malicious intent to gain unauthorised access to the target system without the user's knowledge. They can bypass authentication mechanisms to connect to the system, enabling the attacker to delete files, run programs or take complete control of the system. They are often spread through a worm mechanism and can enable the attacker to gain permanent remote access to the system.

Spyware: Spyware is malicious software that secretly collects personal data, such as bank and credit card information, passwords and online browsing habits. It then transmits this information to third parties. It can infiltrate a target system via Trojan horses embedded in legitimate software and operate in the background without the user's knowledge.

Adware: Adware is malicious software installed on users' devices without their knowledge that creates unwanted pop-up ads. It displays ads integrated into the content of visited websites and some types also track users' online activities, collecting their personal data and transmitting it to third parties. This can lead to privacy violations and negatively affect device performance.

Keyboard and screen loggers (keyloggers/screenshots): These are software or hardware applications that capture and store all keystroke information entered on the keyboard. Screen loggers are software applications that periodically record the user's screen activity in image or video format. Both can be exploited by attackers for malicious purposes, collecting personal information such as passwords, usernames, social media or email accounts, and credit card information without the user's knowledge.

Distributed Denial of Service Attacks (DDoS): These cyber attacks overload the resources of the target system or network with intense traffic flow created from multiple sources, causing services to slow down or stop completely. The goal of this type of attack is to make the service inaccessible to legitimate users. Attacks typically aim to temporarily disable online services while concealing the attacker's identity.

Figure 3. Types of malware and their effects

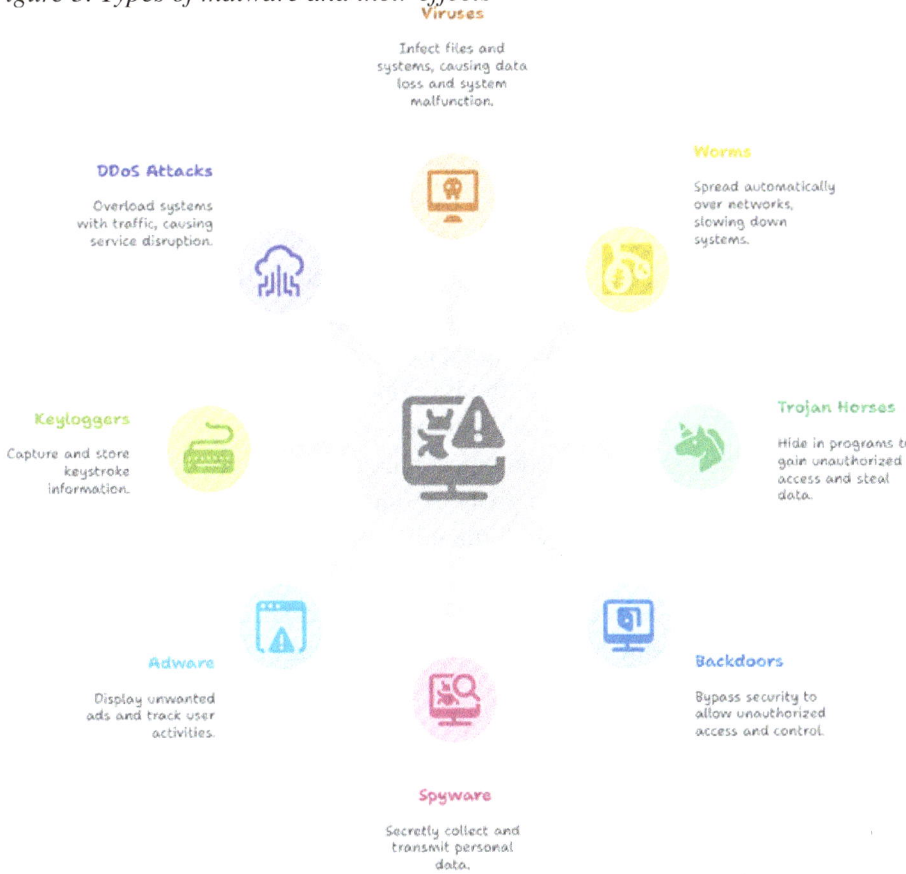

Cyber Security Threats and Information Theft

In today's digital world, cyber security threats and information theft can target individual users, institutions, and organisations. Attackers aim to manipulate users in order to obtain their information or that of the institution or organisation they belong to, which can pose a security threat if used maliciously. These threats are intended to cause harm to institutions or individuals. As information and communication technologies have developed and become more widely used, users have become exposed to various cyber threats in the virtual world. Data theft is one such threat and can be defined as the unauthorised acquisition of personal data, corporate information and intellectual property rights by unauthorised persons. Data theft is one of the most critical security threats and can cause serious economic and security problems. Social engineering and phishing attacks are the most common of the malicious applications that cause various financial and reputational losses and hinder the functioning of the system.

Social engineering: Attacks of this kind are considered to be among the most dangerous types of attack on information systems because they allow critical information to be obtained through persuasion alone, without the need for technical knowledge (Hekim, 2015). When it is not possible to infiltrate a system with no security vulnerabilities, attackers resort to social engineering. It is defined as a manipulative form of attack that directs employees to disclose confidential information or perform actions that threaten institutional security (Grassegger & Nedbal, 2021). Today, social engineering attacks pose the greatest threat to cybersecurity (Salahdine & Kaabouch, 2019). According to the European Union Agency for Cybersecurity (ENISA), social engineering is defined as 'performing an illegal transaction or sharing data with others without the user's permission'. In this common type of attack, attackers apply psychological pressure to users to gain unauthorised access to a system and achieve their goals (Aydın, 2022). This type of attack is one of the threats that have emerged with the intention of damaging information and communication technologies. In recent years, many users have been at risk due to social engineering (Birthriya et al., 2025a; Krombholz et al., 2015). One of the most notable and effective methods of social engineering attack is the phishing attack.

Phishing attack: A phishing attack is derived from the combination of the words 'password' and 'fishing'. It aims to steal personal data, such as passwords or credit card information, by directing internet users to fake links. This common type of attack relies on deceiving users and gaining their trust. Phishing is typically carried out via fake emails, impersonated websites and social engineering techniques, thereby exposing users to online fraud. In phishing attacks, attackers attempt to deceive specific individuals or organisations by posing as trusted entities to obtain sensitive information or gain unauthorised access to systems (Birthriya et al., 2025b). Although user awareness and education are considered the most effective solutions for safeguarding against such attacks, corporate-level security policies are also recognised as playing a significant role in mitigating risk (Borate et al., 2024).

DATA PROTECTION METHODS AND SOLUTIONS

In today's information age, information and communication technologies are available to users in every field. While digitalisation offers many opportunities, it also poses risks depending on how it is used. Security risks include unauthorised access to data, theft, alteration or deletion of information, and other malicious uses. Therefore, information security has become a critical priority at both individual and corporate levels. To ensure information security, it is important to encrypt information, implement access control with identity verification, use firewalls and internet security software, perform regular backups and establish security policies.

Authentication systems: Authentication is the process of verifying the identity of an individual or object. During this process, the authentication mechanism uses the identity information provided to determine whether the person or object in question has the claimed identity (Authentication, 2017). This involves verifying the information provided by the user to prove their identity (Suleski et al., 2023). It is a critical service in both network-based and physical security systems and various techniques are employed, including smart cards, one-time passwords, biometric methods and multi-factor authentication. There are three basic identity verification applications that can be used in this process. The first is knowledge-based authentication, such as passwords or unlock patterns. The second is physical or behavioural authentication, such as fingerprints, eye or facial features, finger or hand movements, voice or gait. The third is two-factor or multi-factor authentication, such as software tokens or the physical address of the device (Wang et al., 2020).

Multi-factor authentication: Single-factor authentication (SFA), such as a password or PIN, is widely used but considered one of the weakest methods due to the possibility of it being shared and compromised. However, two-factor authentication (2FA) has emerged as an alternative, combining representative data, such as usernames and passwords, with ownership factors, such as smart cards or phones. Users consider information factors such as passwords or usernames that they know, ownership factors such as cards or smartphones that they possess, and biometric factors such as physical or behavioural characteristics that are unique to them to be important for reliable authentication. A high level of security can be achieved with Multi-Factor Authentication (MFA) by using two or more identity information factors/categories (Ometov et al., 2018). MFA adds an extra layer of security to user accounts. Instead of logging in with just a password, a one-time code sent to an email address or mobile phone may also be required. Thus, at least two different verifications are required to log in (Suleski et al., 2023).

Figure 4. Evolution of authentication methods from SFA to MFA

(Ometov et al., 2018)

Data encryption and anonymisation: Encryption is one of the measures that can be employed to ensure information security. Its purpose is to prevent unauthorised individuals from understanding the information/data. Encryption is one of the fundamental concepts of cryptology and involves rendering text or images unintelligible. Cryptographic algorithms, which apply various mathematical techniques, are used in the encryption process. Data encrypted using these algorithms can only be decrypted using the keys and algorithms available to the sender and recipient. Decrypting encrypted text is called decryption. This converts the encrypted text into plain text. Wireless communication is considered more vulnerable than wired communication because it transmits information via frequencies rather than through a physical medium. Indeed, wireless short-range networks (Wi-Fi, Bluetooth, Zigbee, NFC, etc.) and cellular networks (GSM, 3G, 4G/LTE, 5G, etc.) transmit information through the air, which makes it easy for third parties to intercept (eavesdrop on or 'sniff') or even alter the signal using an antenna or Wi-Fi adapter. To ensure the security of communications on mobile devices, transmitted information such as conversations, images and video files is encrypted using algorithms within the phones, and is transmitted in an encrypted form between phones and base stations, as well as between the base stations themselves. Similarly, Wi-Fi devices that we use in cafés or at home must be encrypted using a reliable protocol such as WPA2 or WPA3 instead of WEP or WPA, in order to protect against attacks. Alternatively, data transmission can be encrypted using tunnelling methods such as a VPN (Virtual Private Network) or IPSec (Internet Protocol Security). To find out which security protocol wireless devices in shared areas are using, click on the Wi-Fi icon in the taskbar, then select the network you are connected to. Check the security type in this network's properties section. If no security protocol is specified and it says 'open' or 'none', the network is not encrypted, which can create a major security vulnerability. Indeed, due to the intensive use of technology, data sets have become extremely important. To protect the personal information contained within them, the European Union General Data Protection Regulation (GDPR) and Turkey's Personal Data Protection Law (KVKK) No. 6698 have been introduced. Under these laws, certain methods must be used when sharing data and some data must be kept confidential. While sharing personal data without consent is generally prohibited, in commercial situations, some information may be shared after being anonymised (Gümüş & Eyüpoğlu, 2022). Data anonymisation involves using personal or identifying information after it has been concealed or altered. Data anonymisation can be achieved using data masking methods, such as replacing real names with random names, or using age ranges instead of specific ages, or only using the year instead of the full date of birth. However, even though the data is anonymised in the process, certain information and existing old data can be revealed through comparison. This allows the data to be used for research or analysis while maintaining privacy and confidentiality.

Use strong passwords: When accessing social media platforms, email accounts, banking transactions, personal websites and cloud computing services in a virtual environment, encryption-based operations are generally performed to ensure security and privacy. However, users' preference for simple passwords (e.g. their name, date or place of birth) means that attackers can crack them in a short time using various methods, resulting in a significant security risk. For this reason, many websites and online platforms encourage users to create strong passwords and do not accept passwords that do not comply with certain rules, such as having a minimum of eight characters and using a combination of upper- and lower-case letters, numbers, and special characters. They also request that users generate new passwords. Users must ensure password security by following the recommended steps and using different passwords for different applications.

Secure data backup: Backup processes play a critical role in ensuring the security of information systems and maintaining business continuity. They also help to prevent potential data loss. Backup operations are essential for restoring the system in the event of data loss. During the backup process, users can perform system and file backups manually or automatically. The most commonly used types of backup today are local backup, cloud backup and hybrid backup. Local backup involves storing data on local disks, external drives, or NAS (Network-Attached Storage) devices, whereas cloud backup ensures that data is protected in cloud-based storage services. Hybrid backup combines both approaches to provide greater security, flexibility and sustainability.

Firewall and security software: A firewall is the first line of defense that ensures security by preventing any external attacks on computer systems. Firewalls act as a filter between internal traffic and external traffic, which is generally considered less secure, protecting the system and network from external attacks and risks, while allowing authorized users to access the system (Anwar et al., 2021). Antivirus software, which is among security software, is a basic security tool developed to protect computer systems and smart devices against malicious software (malware). This software performs the functions of detecting, blocking, neutralizing, and, when necessary, removing malicious software from the system. Computer viruses typically infect data files on the system they infect and multiply, potentially compromising data integrity in the process. Antivirus software can detect and clean such malicious code and restore files to their previous state. However, in some cases, malicious software cannot be directly cleaned and is placed in quarantine. The quarantine process isolates the file from the system, preventing the spread of malicious software and contributing to maintaining system security. Antivirus software primarily detects and removes malicious software, but it can also perform other security tasks according to user preferences.

Internet security software: Internet security is a subcategory of computer security that focuses on safeguarding online transactions and preventing attacks on networks, browsers, applications and operating systems (Pea-Assounga et al., 2024). Concerns relating to internet security include malware, adware, spyware, phishing software, keyloggers/screen recorders, viruses and Trojan horses. Unlike antivirus programs, which focus on detecting malware in files or programs, internet security software aims to ensure the security of online activities. It enables users to safely carry out activities such as online shopping, using social media, conducting online banking transactions, accessing emails and tracking news. These software solutions automatically detect and block online risks and threats, offering features such as real-time protection, web content filtering, email security, file and network traffic encryption (VPN – Virtual Private Network).

Access control and authorization: Authorization regarding which users can access and use which resources and for what purposes is carried out through access control. The aim here is to prevent unauthorized persons from accessing the system and/or data, thereby preventing security vulnerabilities. Users often confuse the concepts of access control and authorization. Access control determines which users can access what, while authorization determines which operations an authenticated user can perform. Authorization can include operations such as reading, writing, deleting, or modifying, while role- and department-based authorization for work units (e.g. accounting, production or R&D) and conditional authorization for specific times (hours and days) and specific devices (e.g. firewalls, routers, switches or servers) can also be implemented. Additionally, identity verification processes are carried out to identify users within the scope of access control. In identity verification processes, in addition to simple verification methods such as passwords, stronger identity verification techniques based on physical and behavioral characteristics (such as fingerprint recognition, iris recognition, and voice verification) can be used.

Physical security measures: In addition to virtual security measures, physical security measures are important for safeguarding information and communication technologies. The security of the physical environment plays a critical role in protecting an organisation's IT infrastructure and valuable assets. It is crucial to implement robust physical security measures in all premises housing buildings, offices, system rooms, and/or critical software and hardware. Various threats to physical security, such as unauthorised access, theft, sabotage and natural disasters, must be considered (Kınacı et al., 2023). Premises requiring security should be continuously monitored by cameras and various identity verification methods (such as passwords, facial recognition, iris recognition, voice recognition, and palm scanning) should be used to access such environments. Access to devices located in system rooms should be via secure channels such as VPN or IPSec with multi-factor authentication. Recovery scenarios should be organised to restore information systems and critical business processes to their original state as soon as possible in the event of cyber sabotage, fire, flooding or other disasters. To implement this plan and process, referred to as disaster recovery, the institution or organisation must implement regular and secure backup strategies. For this process, daily and weekly backups can be taken and the 3-2-1 rule implemented. Under this rule, three copies (one primary and two backups), two different environments (disk and cloud systems) and one copy in a different location (outside the building) can be used as a solution. Additionally, the disaster recovery plan should be continuously monitored and tested, and should not be left to chance.

Internal cybersecurity protocols and crisis plans: Information security and finding solutions to this issue are among the most important items on the agenda for institutions and organisations. Therefore, developing strategies, designing action plans and establishing policies on information security are fundamental issues in this context. Indeed, protecting critical infrastructure services, ensuring cybersecurity within the scope of national security and guaranteeing the security of public information are of vital importance to countries (Yıldırım, 2024). Both public institutions and the private sector should adopt information security as an institutional culture, and awareness-raising activities in this area should be supported. Additionally, a robust relationship must be established between strategic management and institutional information security processes, and information security governance must be mandated in public institutions (Güngör, 2015). Technology managers in institutions must also make decisions that are appropriate for the technological ecosystem in order to ensure business continuity and establish the most efficient business models as part of the institutional culture within the new order (Korucu, 2021). Technology managers must establish cybersecurity protocols, such as access control and authorisation, to regulate employee access to the system. Alongside technical measures such as using up-to-date security software for system management, data encryption and communication with security protocols, various policies should be implemented to raise security awareness, such as providing internal training. Furthermore, competence in ensuring business continuity is necessary, involving the management of various crisis plans such as determining and preventing the type of attack, preventing data breaches, isolating the system to prevent the spread of the attack, informing employees and restoring the system.

Policies specific to educational institutions: As with all institutions, educational environments hold large amounts of data. This data is collected, processed and stored by systems with different technological infrastructures. In order to ensure the confidentiality and security of this data, certain rules must be established to determine the conditions under which it will be stored, who will have access to it, which actions can be performed with which permissions, and the conditions under which it can be shared. It is especially important for educational institutions to act in accordance with specific policies regarding data confidentiality and security, particularly when it comes to sensitive personal data. The processing of personal data is therefore subject to regulations. Data security is a key aspect of personal data protection law, and ensuring data security is one of the fundamental responsibilities of educational institutions as data controllers. A review of the literature reveals that there are no regulations that directly apply to educational institutions. However, it is believed that regulations established for other institutions can guide educational institutions in terms of data and information security.

ISO 27001 is a worldwide Information Security Management Systems (ISMS) standard that is becoming increasingly mandatory in many areas. It explains to organisations how they can generally achieve information security. At the same time, countries are enacting legal regulations for data security. The European Union, for example, has established a legal regulation called the General Data Protection Regulation (GDPR) to regulate the processing and protection of personal data (European Commission, 2023). In our country, the processing and protection of personal data has been regulated by the Personal Data Protection Law (KVKK) since 2016. To comply with KVKK requirements, institutions must obtain explicit consent from data owners, establish data security policies and report data breaches to the relevant authorities. It can be said that most of the data held by educational institutions belongs to children. Notably, a legal regulation governing children's personal data exists in the United States (US). The Children's Online Privacy Protection Act (COPPA) came into force in the US in 2000. COPPA requires companies to establish procedures to protect the privacy, security and integrity of personal information collected from children. It also stipulates that children's personal information may be transferred to third parties who can protect such information and guarantee its privacy, security and integrity, and that companies must take reasonable steps to ensure this (Fırat Güner, 2021). While COPPA directly targets children, the United Nations Convention on the Rights of the Child (UNCRC) indirectly protects their data. In its General Report No. 25, published in 2021, the European Commission emphasised the right to privacy of children and the necessity of this right in digital environments (Unicef, 2021). According to this report, children's personal data may only be processed for the purpose of providing them with education, healthcare and other benefits. Children's privacy rights also apply in legal situations, such as criminal cases, for the sake of their dignity and safety.

DISCUSSION AND CONCLUSION

Technology permeates every aspect of life, both individually and institutionally, and is used in many areas, including education, health, trade, tourism, daily life and business. Information and communication technologies provide users with greater convenience and efficiency in terms of speed, access, time and space. Mobile technologies, in particular, have become widespread due to their ease of use and portability. Their widespread use has not only changed social life and communication patterns, but also work processes and learning experiences. These technologies are known to be used most frequently by children and young people in society (Bianchi & Phillips, 2005; Küçükvardar & Tıngöy, 2018; Özünlü Pekyavaş et al., 2020) and are used for various purposes, such as sharing information and using social media. These technologies have become indispensable to users and have paved the way for new concepts such as big data and cloud computing. However, considering the unlimited transfer of information in an unlimited virtual world, various security risks may arise in this information pool. Therefore, while information and communication technologies offer users unlimited possibilities, they may also be exposed to attacks from malicious individuals. In this context, the most important solutions are implementing all possible security measures on the system and educating users about information security and privacy to raise their awareness in this regard.

Information Security Awareness

A lack of knowledge among users about how to use the technologies they possess and how to ensure their security may pose a risk of unauthorized external intervention. Raising awareness among individuals about the safe use of technology is the solution to eliminating or minimising these risks (Costa et al., 2017; Gültekin & Özel, 2023; Gündüzalp, 2021; Karayel & Akbıyık, 2023; Öztezcan & Çetinkaya, 2018; Radanliev, 2024; Yılmaz et al., 2015; Yılmaz et al., 2016). Information security awareness is defined in the literature as "a situation in which users in an organisation are aware of security objectives — ideally, they are committed to these objectives" (Hwang et al., 2021). User awareness training is also important in this context. Examining information security research reveals that it has traditionally focused on technologies and products. However, Zeng and Koutny (2019) have defined human behaviour and information security awareness as critical factors in determining the effectiveness of security measures. Indeed, in their bibliometric analysis study examining 4,252 articles on information security and cybersecurity conducted between 1980 and 2021, Karayel and Akbıyık (2023) emphasised the importance of the social dimension of security, including "information security management", "information security policies", "information security culture" and "information security awareness".

Although software and hardware are used to ensure information security, the human factor is widely regarded as the most vulnerable aspect of this security (Parsons et al., 2017; Suvacı & Yamacı, 2024; Tseng et al., 2022). If we accept that the human factor is indeed the weakest link in the security chain, it is crucial to recognise and address potential errors and violations arising from this factor, and to prioritise their elimination (Karaoğlan Yılmaz et al., 2014). Astakhova (2020) also emphasises the importance of raising public awareness of information security, which has become a major societal issue due to the increasing demand for digital technologies. She notes that theoretical and experimental studies on this subject are on the rise. Brantly (2017) highlights that the public lacks sufficient knowledge of the tools and techniques for ensuring digital security, emphasising the need for training to improve security. Similarly, Keser and Güldüren (2015) emphasise that technical security measures alone are insufficient to ensure the security of corporate and personal information. They argue that it is important for institutions and employees to be security-conscious and for people to be educated on this issue and gain the necessary skills to use the required security technologies at the right time and place.

User Awareness Training

In the digital world, various security measures are employed behind the scenes for information exchange and storage, as well as for all kinds of operations. However, it cannot be said that individuals in society have fully acquired the necessary knowledge and skills in this area. Nevertheless, a closer examination reveals that almost everyone utilises technology in many areas of their lives, including education, social interactions, professional activities, banking transactions, economic spending, healthcare services and government services. As information is stored electronically, developing robust and reliable strategies to protect it is of great importance. Teoh and Mahmood (2017) have emphasised the importance of devising security strategies to address cybersecurity issues and implement security measures in the virtual world. They also highlight the importance of public awareness, research and development, and international cooperation in this regard. One of the most important components of an effective digital security strategy is educating users about potential dangers and threats (Radanliev, 2024). Indeed, many studies emphasise that human-related threats are the most important factor threatening the security of information and communication systems, and that the human factor is at the forefront of the measures that can be taken (Yılmaz et al., 2015; Yılmaz et al., 2016). Regarding this issue, Zwillinga et al. (2022) emphasised that users should be aware of all types of cyber threats and the measures taken to prevent them, in order to raise awareness of information security risks. Similarly, Birthriya et al. (2025b) emphasise that preventing security threats depends not only on technological solutions, but also on users' ability to identify potential threats and increase their awareness in this regard.

In order to ensure security in all applications using information and communication technologies, one of the most fundamental tasks is to raise security awareness among members of society (Astakhova, 2020; Avcı & Oruç, 2020; Brantly, 2017; Teoh & Mahmood, 2017; Yılmaz et al., 2015). Wagner and Brooke (2007) emphasise that the key element in the security of information and communication technologies is human-related. Although this is known by many IT specialists, organisations focus on technology to ensure security. To increase users' awareness of information security, solutions such as creating strong and unique passwords, requiring multi-factor authentication and conducting security awareness tests (by sending fake emails to determine awareness levels) and surveys (to measure pre- and post-training levels) can be employed, as well as short videos and posters to keep users informed. Users can also be provided with theoretical knowledge on information security training topics (e.g. data protection methods, network attack risks and threats) at specific intervals, and their awareness can be increased through interactive training based on real attack examples.

REFERENCES

Abbasoğlu, B. (2020). Predicting academic achievement of secondary school students using educational data mining methods. *Data Science*, *3*(1), 1–10.

Akseki, B., Meydaneri, S., & Taşdemir, C. (2023). Cyber security and information securıty studies in Turkey. [Smart Journal]. *Social Mentality and Researcher Thinkers Journal*, *9*(73), 3902–3909. DOI: 10.29228/smryj.70755

Anwar, R. W., Abdullah, T., & Pastore, F. (2021). Firewall best practices for securing smart healthcare environment: A review. *Applied Sciences (Basel, Switzerland)*, *11*(19), 9183.

Astakhova, L. V. (2020). Issues of the culture of information security under the conditions of the digital economy. *Scientific and Technical Information Processing*, *47*(1), 56–64. https://link.springer.com/article/10.3103/S0147688220010062

Authentication. (2017). In *Guide to Computer Network Security* (pp. 207–225). Springer.

Avcı, Ü., & Oruç, O. (2020). Investigation of the students' personal cyber security behaviour and information security awareness. İnönü University Journal of the Faculty of Education, 21(1), 284-303. doi: DOI: 10.17679/inuefd.526390

Aydın, Ö. (2022). *Security and privacy in computer systems*. Efeakademi Press.

Baker, R. S. J. D., & Yacef, K. (2009). The state of educational data mining in 2009: A review and future visions. *Journal of Educational Data Mining*, *1*(1), 3–17.

Bayrakcı, E., & Koçman, M. A. (2023). Information security and electronic warfare. [NEUSBF]. *Journal of the Faculty of Political Science*, *5*(Special Issue), 184–206. DOI: 10.51124/jneusbf.2023.56

Bianchi, A., & Phillips, J. G. (2005). Psychological predictors of problem mobile phone use. *Cyberpsychology & Behavior*, *8*(1), 39–51. DOI: 10.1089/cpb.2005.8.39

Bienkowski, M., Feng, M., & Means, B. (2012*). Enhancing teaching and learning through educational data mining and learning analytics: an issue brief.* https://files .eric.ed.gov/fulltext/ED611199.pdf

Birthriya, S. K., Ahlawat, P., & Jain, A. K. (2025). a. A comprehensive survey of social engineering attacks: Taxonomy of attacks, prevention, and mitigation strategies. *Journal of Applied Security Research*, *20*(2), 244–292.

Birthriya, S. K., Ahlawat, P., & Jain, A. K. (2025). b. Detection and prevention of spear phishing attacks: A comprehensive survey. *Computers & Security, 104317.* Advance online publication. DOI: 10.1016/j.cose.2025.104317

Borate, V., Adsul, A., Dhakane, R., Gawade, S., Ghodake, S., & Jadhav, M. P. (2024). A comprehensive review of phishing attack detection using machine learning techniques. *International Journal of Advanced Research in Science* [IJARSCT]. *Tongxin Jishu*, *4*(3).

Boston Consulting Group. (2022, September). *Why children are unsafe in cyberspace.* https://web-assets.bcg.com/ec/76/4d06204a4f8e9f90428a3d992373/bcg-why-children-are-unsafe-in-cyberspace-sep-2022.pdf

Bozkurt, A. (2016). Learning analytics: E-learning, big data and personalized learning. *Journal of Open Education Applications and Research*, *2*(4), 55–81.

Brantly, A. (2017). Innovation and adaptation in jihadist digital security. *Survival Global Politics and Strategy*, *59*(1), 79–102. DOI: 10.1080/00396338.2017.1282678

Çetin, H. (2014). Personal data security and determination of its users' awareness level. *Akdeniz İİBF journal, 14*(29), 86-105. https://dergipark.org.tr/en/pub/auiibfd/issue/32333/359291

Costa, C., Sousa, C., Rogado, J., & Henriques, S. (2017). Playing digital security: Youth voices on their digital rights. [IJGBL]. *International Journal of Game-Based Learning*, *7*(3), 11–25. DOI: 10.4018/IJGBL.2017070102

Değirmenci, N., & Demiral, D. G. (2023). Research on information security awareness among university students. *BlackSea Journal of Social Sciences*, 15(29), 613-635. https://dergipark.org.tr/en/pub/ksbd/article/1347428

European Commission. (2023). Proposal for a Regulation laying down additional procedural rules relating to the enforcement of GDPR. https://commission.europa.eu/publications/proposal-regulation-laying-down-additional-procedural-rules-relating-enforcement-gdpr_en

Farid, G., Warraich, N. F., & Iftikhar, S. (2023). Digital information security management policy in academic libraries: A systematic review (2010–2022). *Journal of Information Science*, •••, 1–15. DOI: 10.1177/01655515231160026

Fırat, M. (2015). A new field in educational technology research: learning analytics. *Mersin University Faculty of Education Journal, 11(*3), 870-882

Fırat Güner, D. (2021). Protection of children's personal data. (Unpublished doctoral dissertation). Istanbul Bilgi University.

Fussell, R. S. (2005, October). Protecting information security availability via self-adapting intelligent agents. In *MILCOM 2005-2005 IEEE Military Communications Conference* (pp. 2977–2982). IEEE.

Grassegger, T., & Nedbal, D. (2021). The role of employees' information security awareness on the intention to resist social engineering. *Procedia Computer Science, 181*, 59–66. DOI: 10.1016/j.procs.2021.01.103

Güler, C., & Furat, F. (2022). The contribution of records management and archival practices to information security principles. *Turkish Librarianship, 36*(1), 74–89.

Gültekin, V., & Özel, N. (2023). Information security awareness of university students: Example of ankara university. *Journal of International Management, 6*(2), 310–331. https://dergipark.org.tr/tr/pub/by/issue/81900/1366855

Gümüş, H. T., & Eyüpoğlu, C. (2022). Anonymization techniques and attack types in big data: Application examples. *İstanbul Commerce University. Journal of Science, 21*(42), 422–441.

Gündüzalp, C. (2021). University employees' awareness of digital data and personal cyber security (a case study of IT departments). *Journal of Computer and Education Research, 9*(18), 598–625.

Güngör, M. (2015). *National information security: Strategy and institutional structuring*. Republic of Turkey Ministry of Development.

Hekim, H. (2015). *Phishing attacks*. Retrieved from academia: http://www.academia.edu/35136881/Oltalama_Phishing_Saldirilari

Hwang, I., Wakefield, R., Kim, S., & Kim, T. (2021). Security awareness: The first step in information security compliance behavior. *Journal of Computer Information Systems, 61*(4), 345–356.

Jensen, P. E. (2005). A Contextual Theory of Learning and the Learning Organization. *Knowledge and Process Management, 12*(1), 53–64.

Kalseth, K., & Cummings, S. (2001). Knowledge management: Development strategy or business strategy? *Information Development, 17*(3), 163–172.

Karaoğlan Yılmaz, D. F. G., Yılmaz, D. R., & Sezer, B. (2014). Secure information and communication technology usage behavior of university students and an overview to information security training. *Bartın University Journal of Faculty of Education, 3*(1), 176–199. DOI: 10.14686/BUEFAD.201416213

Karayel, T., & Akbıyık, A. (2023). A global perspective of cybersecurity research: Publication trends and research directions. *Journal of Information Technology*, *16*(3), 221–235. https://dergipark.org.tr/en/pub/gazibtd/issue/79101/1291783

Keser, H., & Güldüren, C. (2015). Development of information security awareness scale. *K.U. Kastamonu Education Journal*, *23*(3), 1167–1184. DOI: 10.17051/io.2016.27218

Kınacı, B. F., Güven, E. Y., Seyyarer, E., Biçek, E., Kına, E., Ayata, F., & Yiner, Z. (2023). *Information and information systems security*. Nobel Academic Publishing.

Korucu, O. (2021). Effects of the new normal world order to cyber and information security. *Journal of Management Information Systems, 7*(1), 2021, 44-60, Issn: 2148-3752

Krombholz, K., Hobel, H., Huber, M., & Weippl, E. (2015). Advanced social engineering attacks. *Journal of Information Security and Applications*, *22*, 113–122.

Küçükvardar, M., & Tıngöy, Ö. (2018). Investigation of technology addiction based on symptoms. AJIT-e. *Online Academic Journal of Information Technology*, *9*(35), 111–123. DOI: 10.5824/1309-1581.2018.5.008.x

Kurniawan, Y., & Halim, E. (2013). *Data Warehouse and Data Mining to Predict Student Academic Performance in Schools: A Case Study (Perspective Application and Benefits).* 2013 IEEE International Conference on Teaching, Assessment and Learning for Engineering (TALE), Kuta/Indonesia.

Maconachy, W. V., Schou, C. D., Ragsdale, D., & Welch, D. (2001, June). A model for information assurance: an integrated approach. In *Proceedings of the 2001 IEEE workshop on information assurance and security* (Vol. 310, pp. 5-6). United States Military Academy, West Point. IEEE.

McCumber, J. (1991, October). *Information systems security: a comprehensive model. 14th National Computer Security Conference*, Baltimore, MD, Washington D.C.

McCumber, J. (2005). *Assessing and managing security risk in IT systems*. CRC Press.

Meng, L., & Meng, L. Q. (2014). Application of Big Data in Higher Education. *2nd International Conference on Teaching and Computational Science*. Shenzhen/ China.

Mills, S., Lucas, S., Irakliotis, L., Ruppa, M., Carlson, T., & Perlowitz, B. (2012). Demystifying big data: A practical guide to transforming the business of government. Available at http://breakinggov.com/documents/demystifying-big-data-a-practical -guide-to- transforming-the-bus/

Ometov, A., Bezzateev, S., Mäkitalo, N., Andreev, S., Mikkonen, T., & Koucheryavy, Y. (2018). Multi-factor authentication: A survey. *Cryptography*, *2*(1), 1.

Öztezcan, B. A., & Çetinkaya, A. (2018). A research on information security awareness: The example of Marmara University. *National Multidisciplinary Refereed Journal of Social Sciences and Research*, 56-71. doi: DOI: 10.17373/MSBAD.2017.1.3

Özünlü Pekyavaş, N., Yürük, Z. Ö., & Saygılı, F. (2020). Pain syndrome caused by increased mobile technology use: "Text Neck". *Adnan Menderes University Journal of Health Sciences*, *4*(3), 251–257. DOI: 10.46237/amusbfd.713569

Özünlü Pekyavaş, N., Yürük, Z. Ö., & Saygılı, F. (2020). Pain syndrome that occurs with increased usage of mobile technology: "text neck". *Journal of Adnan Menderes University Health Sciences Faculty*, *4*(3), 251–257. doi: DOI: 10.46237/amusbfd.713569

Parsons, K., Calic, D., Pattinson, M., Butavicius, M., & McCormac, A., & Zwaans, T. (2017). The human aspects of information security questionnaire (HAIS-Q): Two further validation studies. *Computers & Security*, *66*, 40–51. DOI: 10.1016/j.cose.2017.01.004

Pea-Assounga, J. B. B., Yao, H., Bahizire, G. M., Bambi, P. D. R., & Ngapey, J. D. N. (2024). Effect of financial innovation and stakeholders' satisfaction on investment decisions: Does internet security matter? *Heliyon*, *10*(6).

Radanliev, P. (2024). Digital security by design. *Security Journal*, 1–40. DOI: 10.1057/s41284-024-00435-

Romero, C., & Ventura, S. (2013). Data mining in education. *Wiley Interdisciplinary Reviews. Data Mining and Knowledge Discovery*, *3*(1), 12–27.

Salahdine, F., & Kaabouch, N. (2019). Social engineering attacks: A survey. *Future Internet*, *11*(4), 89.

Sevinç, M., & Avcı, İ. (2024). Analysis of security vulnerabilities caused by human error in iot devices. *Journal of Engineering Sciences and Design*, *12*(2), 403–415. doi: DOI: 10.21923/jesd.1231326

Siemens, G. (2013). Learning analytics: The emergence of a discipline. *The American Behavioral Scientist*, *57*(10), 1380–1400.

Stallings, W. & Brown, L. (2015*). Computer security: Principles and practice* (3. bs.). Pearson Education, Inc.

Suleski, T., Ahmed, M., Yang, W., & Wang, E. (2023). A review of multi-factor authentication in the Internet of Healthcare Things. *Digital Health*, *9*, 20552076231177144.

Suvacı, B., & Yamacı, A. (2024, February). *Bibliometric analysis of thesis studies on knowledge security*. International AEGEAN Conferences On Social Sciences & Humanities IX, İzmir, Türkiye.

Tekerek, M. (2008). Information Security Management. *KSÜ Journal of Natural Sciences, 11*(1), 132-137. https://dergipark.org.tr/en/pub/ksudobil/issue/35406/393310

Teoh, C. S., & Mahmood, A. K. (2017). National cyber security strategies for digital economy. *Journal of Theoretical and Applied Information Technology*, *95*(23), 6510–6522. doi: DOI: 10.1109/ICRIIS.2017.8002519

The International Educational Data Mining Society. (2025, 10 August). Educational Data Mining. Retrieved August 10 from https://educationaldatamining.org/

Tseng, E., Sabet, M., Bellini, R., Sodhi, H. K., Ristenpart, T., & Dell, N. (2022, April). *Care infrastructures for digital security in intimate partner violence*. In *Proceedings of the 2022 CHI Conference on Human Factors in Computing Systems* (pp. 1-20).

Unicef (2021). Convention on the Rights of the Child. General comment No. 25 (2021) on children's rights in relation to the digital environment. https://www.unicef .org/bulgaria/en/media/10596/file

Velki, T., & Romstein, K. (2018). User risky behavior and security awareness through lifespan. *International Journal of Electrical and Computer Engineering Systems*, *9*(2), 53–60.

Wagner, A. E., & Brooke, C. (2007). Wasting time: The mission impossible with respect to technology-oriented security approaches electronic. *Journal of Business Research Methods*, *5*(2), 117–124. https://academic-publishing.org/index.php/ejbrm/ issue/view/147

Wang, C., Wang, Y., Chen, Y., Liu, H., & Liu, J. (2020). User authentication on mobile devices: Approaches, threats and trends. *Computer Networks*, *170*, 107118.

Yıldırım, A. (2024). Analysis of turkey's cyber security policy through action plans. *Journal of Organization and Management Sciences*, *16*(1), 23–47.

Yılmaz, E., Şahin, Y. L., & Akbulut, Y. (2015). Development of the digital data security awareness scale. *AJIT-e: Academic Journal of Information Technology, 6*(21), 23-40. https://dergipark.org.tr/en/pub/ajit-e/article/740906

Yılmaz, E., Şahin, Y. L., & Akbulut, Y. (2016). Digital data security awareness of teachers. *Sakarya University Journal of Education*, 6(2), 26-45. https://dergipark .org.tr/tr/pub/suje/issue/24692/261095

Yılmaz, H. (2014). Establishment of information security management system and information security risk analysis within the scope of TS ISO/IEC 27001 information security management standard. *Denetişim*, (15), 45–59.

Zeng, W., & Koutny, M. (2019). Modelling and analysis of corporate efficiency and productivity loss associated with enterprise information security technologies. *Journal of Information Security and Applications*, *49*, 102385.

Zins, C. (2007). Conceptual approaches for defining data, information, and knowledge. *Journal of the American Society for Information Science and Technology*, *58*(4), 479–493.

Zwilling, M., Klien, G., Lesjak, D., Wiechetek, Ł., Cetin, F., & Basim, H. N. (2022). Cyber security awareness, knowledge and behavior: A comparative study. *Journal of Computer Information Systems*, *62*(1), 82–97.

Chapter 8
Digital Transformation and Equal Opportunities:
Assistive Technologies for Individuals With Special Education Needs

Özge Misirli
https://orcid.org/0000-0002-6135-6815
Eskisehir Osmangazi University, Turkey

Zeynep Şahin Timar
https://orcid.org/0000-0002-7696-6237
Karadeniz Technical University, Turkey

Geraldine Leader
University of Galway, Ireland

Merita Hoxha
https://orcid.org/0009-0006-0464-7057
University of Elbasan Aleksander Xhuvani, Albania

Gerda Sula
https://orcid.org/0000-0001-7977-3249
University of Tirana, Albania

ABSTRACT

The chapter "Digital Transformation and Equal Opportunities: Assistive Technologies for Individuals with Special Education Needs" explores how digital transformation promotes inclusive education by integrating assistive technologies. It discusses the

DOI: 10.4018/979-8-3373-8857-1.ch008

opportunities and challenges of using AT to support students with special education needs, aiming to create equitable and meaningful learning experiences. The chapter highlights barriers including technological limitations, socioeconomic disparities, and pedagogical challenges. Key strategies for effective AT integration include adopting user-centered design approaches that involve students and educators, providing ongoing professional development to build teachers' digital competencies. Furthermore, the chapter emphasizes empowering students through technology to foster independence rather than dependency. Overall, it calls for coordinated efforts to bridge the digital divide and ensure all learners benefit from digital advancements.

INTRODUCTION

The technological advancements that influence day-to-day life have introduced changes and evolutions in the field of education, just as they have influenced most other sectors. Nowadays, subject matters of digital technology lead us to think about artificial intelligence, which has entered our lives only recently; however, it must be considered that the process of transformation has been escalating at an exponential level ever since the origin of digital data and the usage of the internet. The rapid development of technology improves accessibility through decreased technological equipment and/or infrastructure costs on one hand, and at the same time changing the needs of individuals on the other. Also, the presence of information from multiple sources, changes in access speed (Alakoç, 2003), and accelerated distribution and usage of information are the major benefits of digital transformation.

The evolution of assistive technologies in education occurs within a broader framework of international accessibility standards and regulatory instruments that increasingly shape implementation practices. The United Nations Convention on the Rights of Persons with Disabilities, through its comprehensive provisions on accessibility and inclusive education, establishes fundamental principles that guide how nations approach assistive technology adoption (United Nations, 2006). These international frameworks work in concert with technical standards such as the Web Content Accessibility Guidelines and ISO accessibility specifications to create a normative environment that influences not merely product development, but fundamentally shapes institutional policies, procurement decisions, and implementation strategies across educational contexts. According to the ISO/IEC Guide 71, understanding this standards landscape becomes essential for comprehending both the opportunities and challenges inherent in assistive technology integration (ISO/IEC, 2014).

Transformation is a process that entails change and enhancement. As Bozkurt et al. (2021) outline, digital transformation is the process of generating new value and possibilities through leveraging digital technologies, thereby enhancing social structures and enabling them to be more effective. Digital transformation will thus be viewed from this perspective in this chapter, as it offers a more fitting perspective with regard to assistive technologies (AT).

The process of digital transformation in education entails the deliberate uptake of information and communication technologies (ICT) for enhancing both the learning and teaching processes and the general management of learning institutions (Dermatini et al., 2020). This end-to-end change incorporates digital content, pedagogical methods, management systems, and stakeholder communication to deliver more interactive, flexible, and personalized learning experiences. Such settings are especially advantageous for individuals with varied learning needs and styles, including those who use assistive technology.

The integration of digital technology in education has precipitated new modes of teaching and scholarship. In this regard, thus, digital transformation presents education with prospects that are more individualized to address the specific needs of each student (Al Husaeni & Wahyudin, 2023). It is arguable that special needs students are the category that will benefit most from heterogeneous classrooms. This is where innovation has transformed learning, and it has made special education needs children more accessible and inclusive. Special education needs constitute a wide set of learning difficulties or disabilities that have a significant impact on children's learning capacity compared to their age mates. The category includes, but may not be limited to, challenges such as autism spectrum disorder (ASD), intellectual disability, sensory impairment, speech and language difficulty, and learning disorders including dyslexia and attention deficit hyperactivity disorder (ADHD). There have been great technological advancements and innovations that have made technology within reach for these individuals, allowing them to engage in learning processes on a more equitable basis with their counterparts. Technological Devices such as screen readers and adaptive learning systems play a significant role in guaranteeing independent learning, encouraging participation, and making learning environments more inclusive. Thus, it has become essential to represent the place of technology in the lives of children with special education needs, reveal the primary challenges, and suggest ways of better integration and creation of technical solutions in this field.

Digital transformation impacts every part of our lives - from the way we live to how we work and play (UNESCO, n.d). As play is an integral part of learning and education, it is pivotal to consider the role of AT for individuals with special education needs so that inclusion does not remain just a buzz word. The European Accessibility Act, approved in 2019, marks a significant shift in the EU market mandating that a range of products and services comply with accessibility requirements for persons with disabilities (AccessibleEU / European Commission, 2025). This means that the Act and the guidelines provided, will also influence the general approach towards the use of AT in education. While digital policy initiatives and awareness on the use of AT grow, it becomes essential to equip educators and practitioners with the skills and tools they need to effectively use Ats, ensuring that the educational systems are inclusive and supportive (Ara, J. et al., 2024).

A critical yet often overlooked dimension in the development and implementation of assistive technologies concerns the systematic integration of end-user perspectives throughout the entire technology lifecycle. The voices and experiences of individuals with disabilities themselves remain insufficiently represented in many design and evaluation processes, despite growing recognition that their insights are fundamental to creating truly effective solutions. This participatory approach moves beyond traditional models where technologies are developed for users to one where they are developed with and by users, ensuring that the resulting tools address genuine needs rather than assumed requirements. When individuals with special education needs actively contribute to design decisions, testing protocols, and iterative refinement processes, the technologies produced demonstrate markedly improved usability, adoption rates, and educational outcomes. Moreover, such involvement transforms users from passive recipients of technological solutions into active agents in shaping the tools that will support their learning journeys, fostering a sense of ownership and empowerment that extends well beyond the immediate educational context.

While most of the existing literature focuses on the design or functionality of assistive technologies, fewer studies investigate how these tools are used in real life by individuals with specific needs. This section addresses this gap by attempting to reveal the interaction between technology use, contextual challenges, and supportive or restrictive policy frameworks. By bringing these dimensions together, it enables a more comprehensive understanding of the factors that enable or hinder digital participation. It thus seeks to demonstrate the applicability of technological innovations in the educational process for children with special educational needs, helps identify key barriers, and offers recommendations for greater integration and creation of technological innovations in this field. The organization of the chapter was set to give a complete and analytical review of the complex interplay between assistive technologies and inclusive education for children with special education needs.

The chapter is organized into three complementary and related parts, each of which deals with a distinct but connected aspect of the subject. In the first section, we discuss the current state of AT integration in educational settings. This involves looking into how AT tools and systems are being adopted and utilized in various types of schools, ranging from typical public schools to special education settings.

Specific attention is paid to the heterogeneity of implementation practices, which tend to reflect wider systemic inequalities, including neoliberal infrastructural availability, institutional priorities, and socio-economic contexts. Additionally, we address the degree to which assistive technologies are integrated into pedagogical practice, curriculum development, and wider efforts towards the digitalization of education. The next part examines the key obstacles to effective and equitable integration of assistive technologies into educational settings. These obstacles consist of chronic accessibility obstacles—both in physical spaces and virtual learning environments—that restrict the inclusion of children with special education needs. Further, this part considers the continuous requirement for extensive teacher training and professional development to cultivate the skill sets necessary for the effective utilization of assistive devices.

We also address concerns with technology advancements, more precisely the discrepancy between the fast pace of technology change and the slow rate of institutional change. The conversation further identifies resource-based limitations, including deficiencies in funding, absence of technical assistance, and disjoined policy application, that persist significantly in perpetuating digital divides among and within education systems. The final part of the book offers a forward-looking perspective by offering strategic suggestions to enhance accessibility through the integration of assistive technologies. This involves discussion of how AT can facilitate greater autonomy and agency in students, allow for personalized and differentiated learning pathways, and support inclusive pedagogical approaches.

Strong focus is given to the necessity of policy directives in applying accessibility standards, harmonizing multi-stakeholder collaboration, and guaranteeing sustainability and scalability of AT initiatives. Furthermore, we reflect on the potential of universal design for learning (UDL) principles as a blueprint in designing education environments that are inherently inclusive.

Collectively, the three parts try to present a broad and detailed image of both the revolutionary promise and persistent constraints inherent in utilizing assistive technologies within education. By examining contemporary circumstances, existing institutional obstacles, and tactical possibilities, this chapter aims to add to current scholarly and policy-driven debates regarding how technology may be harnessed to develop more equitable, inclusive, and fairer learning experiences for children with special education needs.

SITUATION OF ASSISTIVE TECHNOLOGY INTEGRATION IN SCHOOLS

AT encompasses a wide range of tools—from software, adaptive devices, mobile apps, and communication aids—that are designed to enable children with special education needs to access and participate in educational activities. Their use is key to developing inclusive learning environments, enhancing academic outcomes, and fostering independence in students with diverse needs, including those with physical, learning, and developmental disabilities (Zilz & Pang, 2019; Fernández-Batanero et al., 2022; Abdelwahab et al., 2025; Mandal et al., 2025; Mukhtarkyzyzy et al., 2025).

Assistive technology (AT) encompasses a continuum from simple aids to high-tech inventions, such as augmentative communication devices and robotic systems. They are utilized to reduce obstacles to learning and participation by compensating for the individual needs of users (Hemmingsson et al., 2009; Zilz & Pang, 2019). Notwithstanding their promise, effective use of AT in school settings remains hampered by some perennial challenges (Yenduri et al., 2023, Bi & Casper, 2023).

Challenges to integration consist of inadequate teacher preparation, lack of knowledge of existing tools, low technology acceptance, technical intricacy of the technology, and institutional support weakness (Park et al., 2021; Abdelwahab et al., 2025; Chandra et al., 2025; Fernández-Batanero et al., 2022). Such challenges highlight the need for continuous professional development (McNicholl, et al. 2021), cooperated planning between teachers, researchers, and technology developers, and long-term governmental support (McGregor & Pachuski, 1996; White & Robertson, 2015).

Successful implementation of assistive technology (AT) is critical to the provision of equal educational opportunities. By facilitating access to the curriculum for students, interaction with classmates, and involvement in classroom activities, AT supports academic and social inclusion. The guarantee of AT availability and use is a fundamental step toward ensuring every child's right to receive quality education alongside peers (Hemmingsson et al., 2009; Fernández-Batanero et al., 2022; Mandal et al., 2025).

Yet AT use in schools varies greatly in terms of region, school type, and resources. High-resource schools are typically equipped with advanced AT and expert support, while common or low-resource schools receive just basic tools. This unequal provision results in disparate opportunities for education.

Dedicated education centers and resource rooms usually provide a broader variety of assistive technology (AT), both simple and complex devices, and are augmented with organized support programs, such as occupational therapy services (Zilz & Pang, 2019; Abu-Alghayth, 2020; Visser et al., 2020; Khasawneh, 2024; Özdamar & Odluyurt, 2025). Examples of innovative technologies in these settings are tablet apps for individualized learning and communication (Khasawneh, 2024), robotic systems that support social interaction with classmates (Zilz & Pang, 2019), and programs such as text-to-speech and speech-to-text programs specially designed for learners with reading and writing challenges (Nordström et al., 2018). Physical adaptations, such as height-adjustable desks and mobility devices, are also required for inclusive engagement (Visser et al., 2020).

Conversely, conventional or low-equipped schools tend to rely on basic, combined accessibility features—such as simple speech tools and cellphone technology—rather than individualized complex assistive technologies (Ismaili & Ibrahimi, 2017; Widiyastono et al., 2023). Educators in these environments often report a sense of insufficiency in their use of assistive technology and indicate a desire for more training opportunities (Alsolami, 2022; Özdamar & Odluyurt, 2025).

These variations are typical inequities in the use of assistive technology within and between nations. Budget constraints, disparate levels of educator training, and sporadic institutional support create uneven implementation (Abu-Alghayth, 2020; Seiradakis, 2024). In most developing countries, affordability and access continue to be major obstacles, with mobile learning technologies such as smartphones being utilized as alternatives to high-cost assistive technology tools (Ismaili & Ibrahimi, 2017).

Put briefly, those schools with more resources and trained personnel are more likely to be in a position to implement a wider range of AT, while for many others, systemic and financial limitations act as a constraint. Reducing this disparity is key to forging more inclusive and equitable learning environments.

To better accentuate these disparities, Table 1 summarizes the stark contrasts between high-resource and low-resource learning settings based on existing assistive technologies as well as the challenges they face. The comparison emphasizes the pronounced differences in AT uptake among different learning settings.

As summarized in Table 1, the implementation of assistive technologies across different educational settings reveals significant variation in cost, support needs, and outcomes. This comparative operational matrix illustrates how technological, economic, and pedagogical factors intersect, influencing both accessibility and educational equity outcomes.

Table 1. Operational Matrix of Assistive Technology Implementation in Educational Settings

Setting	AT Exemplar	Pedagogical Use Case	Staffing / Support Requirements	Documented Outcomes (from cited literature)
Specialized/ High-resource Schools	Robotics, adaptive communication aids, screen readers	Used to support individualized instruction and foster independent learning for students with ASD or intellectual disabilities	Requires specialized staff training, ongoing technical support, and collaboration between educators and developers	Enhanced participation and autonomy in learning (Al Husaeni & Wahyudin, 2023); greater inclusion and accessibility (Bozkurt et al., 2021)
Typical/ Low-resource Schools	Basic accessibility features, mobile devices, standard apps	Supports general accessibility, communication, and engagement in heterogeneous classrooms	Requires teacher awareness and limited technical assistance	Improved access but inconsistent use due to limited training and policy gaps (Dermatini et al., 2020)
Policy and Systemic Contexts	Digital transformation frameworks, UDL-based systems	Guides inclusive curriculum design and equitable technology integration	Requires inter-sectoral collaboration and sustainable investment	Demonstrated potential to reduce digital divides and promote systemic inclusion (Bozkurt et al., 2021; Alakoç, 2003)

While high-resource schools may successfully implement advanced assistive technologies such as robotics or adaptive learning systems, the feasibility of large-scale deployment in low-resource settings remains limited. Infrastructure deficits, maintenance costs, and lack of long-term funding mechanisms often prevent the sustainable adoption of such tools (Fteiha, et al. 2024). In these contexts, scalable solutions tend to be those that leverage existing low-cost digital infrastructure—such as mobile devices and open-source accessibility software—rather than high-end proprietary systems. Therefore, the discussion around AT integration must move beyond technological innovation to consider financial and logistical sustainability in low-resource environments.

THE INFLUENCE OF INTERNATIONAL STANDARDS ON AT ADOPTION

While the table above illustrates the current landscape of assistive technology implementation across different educational settings, it is crucial to recognize that this implementation occurs within a broader framework of international standards and regulatory instruments. These standards increasingly shape not only what technologies are available but also how they are selected, implemented, and evaluated in educational contexts.

The United Nations Convention on the Rights of Persons with Disabilities represents the most comprehensive international framework affecting assistive technology implementation. Article 9 explicitly addresses accessibility, mandating that States Parties take appropriate measures to ensure persons with disabilities access information and communications technologies, including assistive devices, on an equal basis with others. This provision directly impacts educational contexts, where Article 24 guarantees the right to inclusive education without discrimination (United Nations, 2006). The disparities evident in the table above - between specialized high-resource schools and typical low-resource schools - reflect not only resource differences but also varying levels of compliance with these international obligations.

Technical standards provide the operational framework through which these broad principles translate into practical implementation. The ISO/IEC Guide 71 offers comprehensive guidance for addressing accessibility in standards development, establishing eleven accessibility goals that directly inform assistive technology design and evaluation. These goals, including perceivability, understandability, operability, and error tolerance, create a systematic approach to ensuring that assistive technologies meet diverse user needs across varying contexts (ISO/IEC, 2014). The Guide emphasizes that "accessibility goals provide one approach to the identification and development of specific accessibility-related requirements and recommendations to be included in standards" (ISO/IEC, 2014, p. 10). Educational institutions increasingly reference these goals when establishing procurement criteria, recognizing that ISO-compliant technologies typically demonstrate more rigorous attention to accessibility considerations.

Digital accessibility standards, particularly the Web Content Accessibility Guidelines formalized as ISO/IEC 40500, have transformed the landscape of technology-mediated learning. The four foundational principles of WCAG - perceivable, operable, understandable, and robust - establish clear criteria for ensuring that web-based educational content and digital learning platforms remain accessible to students using various assistive technologies. As noted in the ISO/IEC Guide 71, these principles have become integral to ensuring that "diverse users in diverse contexts can sense the information and functionalities" presented by digital systems (ISO/IEC, 2014, p. 15). Educational technology vendors now routinely design products with WCAG compliance as a baseline requirement, recognizing that institutional procurement often mandates such adherence.

The World Health Organization's Global Report on Assistive Technology introduces another critical dimension to standards implementation. The report emphasizes that effective assistive technology provision requires comprehensive service delivery systems beyond technical specifications. According to WHO, "assistive technology enables and promotes the inclusion, participation and engagement of persons with disabilities, ageing populations and people living with chronic conditions in the family, community and all areas of society" (WHO & UNICEF, 2022, p. xii). The report's framework, encompassing people, products, provision, personnel, and policy, underscores that standards must address the entire ecosystem supporting assistive technology use.

However, the relationship between standards and actual implementation reveals persistent challenges. While the UN Convention provides a robust legal framework and ISO standards offer technical guidance, their translation into practice encounters numerous obstacles. Many educators remain unaware of relevant standards or struggle to understand their practical implications. The ISO/IEC Guide 71 acknowledges this challenge, noting that standards documents must be made more accessible to diverse stakeholders, including those without technical expertise (ISO/IEC, 2014). Resource constraints further complicate compliance, particularly in low-resource settings where the costs of standards-compliant technologies may exceed available budgets.

These variations in AT provision and use are exacerbated by human factors, namely the willingness and mindset of the very teachers who are central to successful AT integration. The following section examines how teacher attitudes and awareness impact effective use of assistive technologies in schools.

Educators' Awareness and Attitudes Toward AT

One of the most significant factors in AT integration in schools is teachers' awareness, willingness, and attitude toward these devices. Access to AT in the school setting in most cases is to a great extent a factor of the awareness and comfort level of teachers regarding its usage.

Despite growing interest, the majority of teachers report low to moderate AT knowledge, skills, and confidence and, in most instances, a high level of need for further training (O'Sullivan et al., 2021; Alsolami, 2022). Teachers' perceptions of AT usefulness are contingent mainly on computer literacy and experience with specific tools, but many consider themselves unprepared due to having had inadequate pre-service training (Atanga et al., 2019; Lamond & Cunningham, 2019). For instance, fewer than one-third of undergraduate and post baccalaureate special education programs require coursework in AT, with even lower proportions at the master's level (Judge & Simms, 2009).

Nonetheless, positive attitudes towards assistive technology (AT) have been found to be boosted when teachers undergo hands-on training, witness live demonstrations, or engage in structured educational activities—particularly among instructors within regular education settings (Park et al., 2021, 2023; Arslan-Ari & Başer, 2022). Empirical research underscores that hands-on activity programs—such as Assistive and Instructional Technology Labs—can strongly increase educators' preparedness and mindsets (Jones et al., 2020; Park et al., 2021, 2023; Arslan-Ari & Başer, 2022). Training models such as the Student Environment Task Tools (SETT) model are similarly effective, assisting teachers in matching AT tools to individual student needs. Case-based courses based on actual classroom life settings also enable teachers to actively learn how AT facilitates learning, building knowledge and confidence (Arslan-Ari & Başer, 2022).

The provision of experiential and contextually relevant learning experiences for teachers significantly enhances teachers' awareness, skills, and readiness to use assistive technologies. Nevertheless, issues such as limited access to professional development, the absence of follow-up support, and constrained fiscal resources still impact implementation effectiveness (Copley & Ziviani, 2004; Fteiha, et al. 2024). These results reflect the present status of teacher readiness and illuminate the systemic concerns to be elaborated upon in Section 10.2.

CHALLENGES

Despite the development in technology, there are numerous hindrances to the successful implementation of assistive technologies into the educational system for children with special education needs. Such hindrances can be generally divided into technological, socioeconomic, and pedagogical hindrances, all of which pose distinct but related challenges to the attainment of inclusive education. Assistive technology is crucial in promoting the academic performance of children with special education needs by mitigating particular challenges and enhancing their strengths. Current research has focused on creating inclusive learning environments and tailored learning experiences (Morash-Macneil et al., 2018). Globally, educational institutions are increasingly recognizing the unique learning styles and capacities of children with special education needs. With ongoing developments in assistive technology, it presents the possibility for further enhancing the personalization of the learning experience, which responds dynamically to the changing needs of the individual learner. This responsive pedagogy in education not only helps children with special education needs but also creates a more inclusive, innovative, and varied society. However, there are certain issues that need to be resolved for effectively harnessing the potential of assistive technologies in the educational setting.

Technological Challenges

While AT holds enormous potential to aid individuals with special needs, its creation, acceptance, and availability are often slowed by a host of technological challenges. One of them is the minimal involvement of individuals with special needs in the development and design process. The lack of user-led or user-focused approaches creates products that do not meet actual demands, ultimately resulting in their rejection because of the lack of adequate personalization, usability issues, or general ineffectiveness (Dirks et al., 2022; Peters et al., 2023). Moreover, prevalent is the issue of a mismatch between technological possibilities and users' actual demands, especially where tools are not able to overcome sensory, cognitive, or communication-oriented barriers successfully (Verma & Maurya, 2024). The exorbitant price of high-tech assistive technology devices restricts access, particularly in impoverished communities, whereas insufficient financial support and development inhibits the availability of much-needed technologies. Dependence on imported products worsens accessibility, especially in economically disadvantaged environments (Chakabwata, 2025).

The challenge of incorporating end-user feedback extends beyond simple consultation to encompass fundamental questions about representation, communication, and power dynamics in the design process. Many individuals with disabilities face multiple barriers to participation, including physical accessibility of design spaces, lack of appropriate communication support during feedback sessions, and scheduling constraints that fail to accommodate diverse needs. Furthermore, traditional feedback methodologies often privilege certain forms of expression over others, potentially excluding individuals who communicate through alternative means or require additional processing time. The temporal demands of iterative design cycles frequently clash with the realities of users' lives, particularly for children who must balance participation with educational requirements and therapeutic interventions. These structural barriers are compounded by attitudinal challenges, where design teams may unconsciously prioritize feedback from more articulate or conventionally communicative users, thereby marginalizing perspectives from individuals with complex communication needs who often have the most innovative insights about technology requirements (Fteiha, et al. 2024).

Aside from issues of design and accessibility, there remain substantial systemic and organizational hurdles. Insufficient interdisciplinary cooperation between developers, educators, and policymakers constrains the creation and implementation of assistive technology solutions (Fineberga et al., 2019). Disjointed efforts in sectors like education, healthcare, and employment constrain the large-scale adoption of such technologies (Kobayashi et al., 2021).

In addition, most innovations created from assistive technology research do not make it into real-world applications within community settings. Even the most promising programs experience challenges related to non adoption and subsequent abandonment, which makes it difficult to maintain their impact. Moreover, the speed with which technology is changing can also cause problems for teachers. Technology's continually changing nature can get in the way of staying current with new developments. In addition, the rapid turnover rate as a result of technology can lead to substantial financial investments in the education sector (Felicia et al., 2014). The fast rate of technological advancement introduces other dilemmas of maintaining equipment updated, effective, and attentive to changing user requirements (Leahy & Lane, 2010). Moreover, the lack of long-term plans for public investment jeopardizes the sustainability and development of assistive technology programs.

Socioeconomic Challenges

Socioeconomic aspects account for both the availability and usability of assistive technology (AT), with a tendency to reproduce existing inequalities and social exclusion. Economic factors represent a significant barrier. The expense of AT devices restricts access in middle- and low-income nations (Verma & Maurya, 2024), whereas the lack of organized funding mechanisms deepens these disparities (Penton & Gustafson, 2014, Morelle & Matshidiso, 2024). Financial restrictions frequently hinder the implementation of AT in schools. These prohibitions restrict access to assistive technology (AT) for children who require it the most, for instance, children with special education needs. Consequently, such barriers frustrate and reduce the quality of education that can be provided to children with special education needs. The price of AT is in certain instances too expensive, particularly for complex technology like augmentative and alternative communication (AAC) devices. The cost of such technology is typically beyond affordability especially in developing nations. As a result, AT is not a priority and thus investment in supports that children with special education needs require is low.

AT access varies considerably by place and income (Hersh & Mouroutsou, 2019). English-speaking developed countries have more access, but low-income regions have ample limitations. Schools also lack the equipment and personnel trained to implement AT effectively, reducing its possible gains (Fernández-Batanero et al., 2022).

Inequitable distribution systems and a lack of public funding or insurance for AT cause a digital divide. Low-income schools and families are unable to pay for the technology children with special education needs demand, which leads to an evident disparity in the learning opportunities offered to these children.

Pedagogical Challenges

The incorporation and effective use of AT in the learning settings of students with special needs is faced with several pedagogical issues. They are predominantly related to the need for personalized support, curriculum adjustment, and the creation of genuinely inclusive learning settings that go beyond technology adoption.

The first pedagogical challenge is the intrinsic tension between standardized pedagogical approaches and the individualized process of AT implementation. As AT devices are introduced to address individualized needs, it is typically on the grounds of one-size-fits-all curricula in education systems. This creates a dilemma for teachers where they must reconcile meeting standardized learning outcomes and individualized AT support. Damyanov (2024) notes that this problem is particularly evident in the conventional classroom environments, wherein teachers lack the requisite time and resources to develop customized assistive technology plans for all students.

A second imperative challenge regards the pedagogical change required for effective AT integration. Traditional instructional approaches locate the instructor at the center as a knowledge source, but AT-supported classrooms require educators to move toward the position of facilitators of personalized learning pathways. This underlying pedagogical change requires more than just technical skills;it requires redefining the teacher's role itself. Most instructors are confronted with challenges in the process, especially without the examples of effective assistive technology-infused pedagogy (Macheque et al., 2024).

From the viewpoint of students, pedagogical difficulties arise from the disparity between the availability of assistive technology (AT) and the attainment of substantial learning outcomes. The mere provision of AT resources does not ensure enhanced educational experiences. Frequently, students encounter circumstances in which AT is accessible but remains unutilized in a significant manner within learning activities. Consequently, this results in what Dewi and Nurfaidah (2024) characterize as "technological presence without pedagogical purpose," whereby AT is perceived as an additional feature rather than a fundamental component of the educational process.

The collaborative challenge is not confined to the single classroom but is also reflective of systemic issues in the way AT is positioned in education systems. The divide between AT developers, curriculum developers, and classroom educators results in tools that are technically sophisticated but pedagogically limited. Oyedokun (2025) contends that in the absence of significant collaboration between these stakeholders, AT is a technological solution in pursuit of an educational problem, rather than a response to genuine pedagogical needs.

Furthermore, assessment and evaluation practices have lagged behind to incorporate AT-supported learning. Current assessment procedures may fail to capture AT-enabled learning gains, and this creates a scenario where student progress is minimally recognized or documented. This shortage of assessment undermines both student motivation and perceived value for AT investments in learning settings.

National and International Disparities

There are considerable inequalities in access to and usage of AT between countries, regions, and socio-economic settings. Most countries have no comprehensive, integrated policies for the evaluation and provision of AT, leading to patchy or uneven access. Where they exist, structured systems—e.g., national AT policy, product catalogs, and delivery systems—are beneficial to more open and fair access to AT (de Witte et al., 2018; MacLachlan et al., 2018; Ebuenyi et al., 2020; Aplin & Gustafsson, 2023; Domingues & Laplane, 2024). The absence of consolidated approaches is not the sole reason for inequality, though; the manner in which the systems are financed and delivered is also fundamental.

Provision and funding in other systems are dealt with by various schemes with varying criteria, which creates confusion, delay, and inequalities in AT access (Morelle & Matshidiso 2024). Clear, evidence-based policies and decision-making structures are advocated for to optimize efficiency and user satisfaction (Aplin & Gustafsson, 2023; Domingues & Laplane, 2024). Yet even where policies are in place, their application differs greatly between education systems.

There is considerable variation in the implementation of AT policy at the system and school levels. Whereas some schools or districts receive good support and have well-developed policy direction, others receive limited support, have few personnel with appropriate skills, and fragmented policy realization (MacLachlan et al., 2018; Aplin & Gustafsson, 2023; Guillén-Martínez et al., 2025). Disparities in funding, training, and infrastructure lead to uneven AT access across schools and geographical areas, thus exacerbating existing educational disparities for children with special education needs (Guillén-Martínez et al., 2025). Outside schools, disparities are also clear taking into account geographical variations in infrastructure and digital access.

Rural communities have historically had less access to sophisticated digital technology, high-speed internet, and AT compared to urban communities, restricting telemedicine, educational, and social interaction opportunities (Harris et al, 2016; Curtis et al., 2022). In low- and middle-income countries (LMICs), just 5–15% of individuals who require AT have access, which is extremely high in developed nations (Matter et al., 2016; Kumar & Vinita, 2023). Industrialized nations possess more extensive policies, stable financing, and data gathering on AT, whereas developing nations are faced with fragmented governance, unpredictable tariffs, and an absence of harmonized systems (MacLachlan et al., 2018; Olarewaju et al., 2021) These infrastructural and technological disparities are even more pronounced in low- and middle-income nations, where general systemic problems still exist.

Policy Environment and Implementation Gaps

AT policy is developing, with growing awareness at both the national and local levels. Yet, there are substantial disconnects between policy aspiration and actual delivery, frequently due to constraints in finance, infrastructure, and coordination. These disconnects become even more evident when taking into account the way national policies are developed and which international norms shape them.

The majority of countries are taking on or updating national AT policy, frequently following international standards like the UN Convention on the Rights of Persons with Disabilities as well as the World Health Organization's GATE program (MacLachlan et al., 2018; Ebuenyi et al., 2020; Domingues & Laplane, 2024). Successful AT policy must be context-sensitive, entail the engagement of AT users, and be sectoral-transcending, covering sectors such as health, education, and social services. There is a growing emphasis on evidence-based, inclusive policy development, and some countries (e.g., Norway) have provided sound examples of user-centered, holistic AT services. Notwithstanding all these, nevertheless, there is still a considerable gap between policy and practice—particularly in low-resource settings.

A critical dimension of policy implementation involves compliance with international accessibility standards. Despite the comprehensive framework provided by the UN Convention on the Rights of Persons with Disabilities, many educational institutions struggle to translate these standards into practice. The ISO/IEC Guide 71 acknowledges this gap, emphasizing the need for standards to be "written in a way that is understandable to the broadest possible range of readers" (ISO/IEC, 2014, p. 7). The technical complexity of standards such as WCAG creates barriers for educators who lack specialized training, while the costs of ensuring full compliance often exceed available budgets. As the WHO Global Report notes, "the costs of assistive products remain a major barrier" to access, and standards compliance requirements can further increase these costs (WHO & UNICEF, 2022, p. 110). This creates a situation where policy aspirations for standards-based AT implementation remain unrealized due to practical constraints.

Notwithstanding the technological gains in recent decades, there are scant rates of AT adoption by policymakers, educators, and service providers. An enabling policy environment is required for the promotion of the quality and safety of AT and their use on a large scale. Policies that enable activities at the national and international levels are necessary. For instance, the harmonization of AT policy in the EU would provide uniform standards, provision of services, and financing mechanisms for AT in Europe. Despite all these endeavors, a huge disparity exists between policy and practice—especially in resource-poor environments. Notwithstanding policy formulation, there remains a persistent demand and supply gap for AT, particularly in low- and middle-income countries (Garçon et al., 2016; MacLachlan et al., 2018; Tangcharoensathien et al., 2018; Ebuenyi et al., 2020; Domingues & Laplane, 2024). The main gaps in implementation are the lack of resourcing and funding, as most policies have no or inadequate funding or resourcing priorities, which hinders their implementation (Morelle & Matshidiso, 2024). Fragmented service systems, as well as shortages of trained personnel, also undermine effective AT delivery. Adding to these structural difficulties is the problem of limited awareness and counseling, especially in less conspicuous AT areas.

Limited awareness among policymakers, users, and service providers reduces demand and utilization of AT, especially in older people and low-resource environments (Garçon et al., 2016; Tangcharoensathien et al., 2018). Improved and consolidated guidelines for specific categories of AT, especially cognition and communication, are also lacking (Zhang & Borg, 2025).

These policy and implementation issues need to be addressed through a multifaceted strategy, such as investing in extensive teacher training, increasing the quantity of AT professionals, facilitating cooperation among stakeholders, and fostering the transmission of research into applied educational practices (Morelle & Matshidiso, 2024). Eliminating these barriers will enable AT to contribute more towards enhancing educational outcomes and advancing social inclusion for students with special needs.

STRATEGIES FOR ACCESSIBILITY

To tackle the obstacles delineated in the preceding section, it is imperative to employ evidence-informed strategies aimed at addressing the particular technological, socioeconomic, and pedagogical impediments that obstruct the effective integration of assistive technology within educational environments. This section presents strategic methodologies designed to improve accessibility through the deliberate application of assistive technologies, utilizing successful implementations and frameworks derived from global practices.

User-Centered Design and Development Methodologies

Successful implementation of assistive technology (AT) starts with user-led design principles that engage children with special education needs throughout all stages of the development and roll-out of the technology. Evidence from Loughborough's design process for assistive technology indicates that the high level of engagement of end-users in the design process greatly enhances both the effectiveness and acceptance levels (Torrens & Asghar, 2023). This approach extends beyond conventional top-down implementation methods to ensure AT solutions respond to actual needs rather than perceived requirements.

The SETT (Student Environment Tasks and Tools) model offers a framework for the use of user-centered assistive technology (AT) selection (Parette & Peterson-Karlan, 2007). The model describes four fundamental components: learning about the strengths and needs of the student, assessing the environments where AT will be used, determining specific tasks that must be performed, and choosing suitable tools. Enable Ireland's assistive technology (AT) assessment service statistics indicate that when the AT assessments are conducted through remote media with direct involvement of school staff, both the teachers and students become more active participants in the selection process. This involvement results in more suitable technology being chosen and greater adoption rates (Bergin, 2022).

Models of Professional Development and Capacity Building

The issue of poor teacher preparation demands systematic responses to professional development lasting longer than one-off training sessions. The ENTELIS+ project has offered a comprehensive Trainers Competence Framework with five primary domains: needs and barriers assessment, resource selection and utilization, inclusive pedagogical practices, creating inclusive learning environments, and building learners' digital competencies (Switters et al., 2022; Bi & Casper, 2023). The framework offers levels of progression to enable teachers to build AT competencies in a systematic way.

UDL principles are a fundamental framework for the incorporation of AT into teaching practices. Instead of retrofitting curricula that already exist, UDL encourages the proactive development of learning environments that render them accessible to all students in the first place (Bergin & Relihan, 2022). The application of UDL principles to AT training programs has reported great success,particularly when augmented with experiential learning activities. For example, Enable Ireland's online AT training course employs multiple modes of representation (text, audio, video), multiple modes of engagement (case studies, reflective exercises), and multiple modes of expression (forums, social media interaction), and participant satisfaction levels are high as is the level of practical application.

Technology-Mediated Autonomy and Skill Acquisition

AT implementation must emphasize the cultivation of independent learning capacities more than the cultivation of dependence on assistance from external sources. Studies of switch-operated devices and adaptive computer interfaces indicate that through the provision of relevant AT tools, students with motor disabilities can develop self-regulated interaction patterns that generalize beyond the classroom setting (Parette & Peterson-Karlan, 2007).

Speech recognition software and augmentative communication devices allow students to complete learning activities with less reliance on teacher assistance, thereby promoting both academic success and self-esteem. The underlying principle in this case is what Parette and Peterson-Karlan (2007) refer to as establishing a "floor of opportunity"- an initial point of accessibility that enables students to engage meaningfully in curriculum-based activities while simultaneously developing skills for more complex tasks.

Application of Models in Evidence-Based Assessment

Effective integration of assistive technology (AT) needs inclusive evaluation methods extending beyond initial device selection phases and including continued monitoring of their effectiveness. The Rapid Assistive Technology Assessment (rATA) method, implemented in various environments such as Mongolia, offers a systematic way of evaluating AT needs within various populations and resource environments (WHO Country Office Mongolia, 2021). The method aims to collect data on real use behavior, user satisfaction, and barriers to adoption, alongside theoretical appropriateness.

Evaluation should also address the gap between availability of devices and pedagogically meaningful use. Research indicates that providing AT devices without pedagogical integration usually results in "technological presence without pedagogical purpose" (Damyanov, 2024). Effective implementation models therefore evaluate not only if students can utilize AT devices, but if or how these devices enhance specific educational outcomes and support curriculum goals.

Resource Allocation and Sustainability Strategies

Easing financial constraints involves embracing innovative resource allocation measures beyond single-time investment in hardware. The focus on free and built-in access tools, as seen in Enable Ireland's training initiatives, provides a practical foundation for resource-poor schools (Bergin & Relihan, 2022). Built-in accessibility options within standard operating systems and software provide readily available solutions that can act as fundamental stepping-stones toward the introduction of more complex specialized assistive technology on an as-needed basis.

International frameworks concerned with the delivery of assistive technology (AT), as outlined by de Witte et al. (2018), emphasize the place of structured approaches to resource allocation and funding. Effective frameworks integrate governmental financing, insurance schemes, and multi-tiered support mechanisms that facilitate entry-level AT access with the progression toward more extended solutions. The evolution of AT service delivery systems needs to be coordinated across the health, education, and social services sectors to provide ongoing support across life domains.

Community Engagement and Stakeholder Collaboration

Effective AT implementation extends outside of the classroom to involve the community, and professionthe emphasis of the aSTEP project on collaborative development involving end-users, teachers, as well as technology developers, underscores the importance of multi-stakeholder collaboration (aSTEP Consortium, 2024). The collaboration model ensures AT solutions are feasible to apply and can be sustained in the long run.

Parent and family engagement is critical to the effective use of assistive technology (AT). Research shows that when families are educated and supportive of AT use at home, students show enhanced performance in academic settings (Parette & Peterson-Karlan, 2007). Professional development programs with family involvement and provision of resources for home implementation promote consistency between educational and home environments.

Policy and Systems-Level Integration

Aside from individual-level interventions, effective AT use relies on enabling policy contexts that break systemic barriers. Examples of effective AT policy incorporation in countries, as in Norway's coordinated user-centered AT services, underscore the importance of evidence-based and inclusive policy formulation (MacLachlan et al., 2018). These models emphasize context-tailored policy, involvement of AT users in decision-making, and intersectoral coordination of health, education, and social services.

Use of accessibility standards and guidelines, such as the WCAG and universal design principles, offers a model for uniform application of assistive technology to various learning settings (Torrens & Asghar, 2023). Policy effectiveness, though, is still contingent upon sufficient funding sources, trained staff, and continuous monitoring of implementation results (Morelle & Matshidiso, 2024).

STRENGTHENING STANDARDS IMPLEMENTATION FOR INCLUSIVE AT ADOPTION

Addressing the standards-related challenges identified in the previous sections requires coordinated strategies that translate international frameworks into actionable practices. Educational authorities must prioritize the development of coherent national frameworks that effectively interpret international standards for local contexts. The UN Convention on the Rights of Persons with Disabilities provides the overarching framework, but as the WHO Global Report emphasizes, "countries need to develop or update their national assistive technology policies" to ensure effective implementation (WHO & UNICEF, 2022, p. 115).

Systematic capacity building around standards awareness emerges as fundamental to sustainable progress. The ISO/IEC Guide 71 specifically recommends involving "representatives of various affected accessibility stakeholder groups and accessibility experts" in validation processes (ISO/IEC, 2014, p. 9). Training initiatives should target multiple stakeholder groups with differentiated approaches: administrators need understanding of how standards inform procurement decisions, teachers require practical guidance on leveraging standards-compliant technologies, and technical staff need skills for maintaining standards-based systems.

Procurement policies must evolve to explicitly incorporate accessibility standards as primary evaluation criteria. The WHO Global Report recommends that countries "develop a national list of priority assistive products that are affordable and cost-effective and meet minimum quality and safety standards" (WHO & UNICEF, 2022, p. 111). Institutions should develop comprehensive procurement frameworks requiring vendors to provide detailed documentation of standards compliance, including evidence of adherence to WCAG principles for digital tools and ISO accessibility goals for physical devices.

Regular accessibility auditing proves essential for ensuring standards implementation translates into meaningful access. The UN Convention requires States Parties to maintain "appropriate information on disability" to assess implementation (United Nations, 2006, Article 31), which should include systematic evaluation of assistive technology provision against established standards.

International cooperation can significantly accelerate standards adoption, particularly benefiting resource-constrained contexts. The WHO Global Report calls for countries to "encourage international and/or regional collaboration for the manufacturing, procurement and supply of priority assistive products" (WHO & UNICEF, 2022, p. 111). This cooperation might encompass developing open-source compliance assessment tools aligned with ISO/IEC Guide 71 principles, adapting training materials for different contexts, or establishing mentorship relationships between institutions at varying implementation stages.

CONCLUSION

This chapter has explored the complex interplay between assistive technologies and inclusive education for children with special education needs. By way of analysis of current implementation practices, ongoing challenges, and strategic responses, a number of important insights arise that are worthy of our consideration.

The present reality of schools betrays a worrying picture of inequity, as while some specialist schools make good use of high-level assistive technologies—stretching from robotics through to adaptive communications aids—many ordinary educational environments struggle with issues of basic accessibility features. This disparity goes beyond simple financial limitations; it highlights more systemic difficulties relating to teacher training, institutional culture, and policy implementation. The gap between the outcomes we know are possible and those seen in classrooms remains considerable.

Teacher preparedness continues to be a fundamental bottleneck. Although there is growing awareness of AT's potential, too many teachers report they don't have the preparation they need to easily integrate these tools into their classrooms. The problem isn't disinterest—research consistently shows that hands-on training sessions radically change teacher attitudes and aptitudes (Vanderpuye & Okai, 2023). Rather, it's the absence of ongoing, sustained professional development that goes beyond stand-alone workshops to instill AT know-how into everyday practice.

The challenges identified traverse numerous areas, and they do so in a reinforcing manner. The technological hurdles, specifically the mismatch between developers' offerings and actual user needs, are exacerbated by economic conditions that render advanced assistive technology unaffordable to most schools and families. Such practical limitations intersect with pedagogical challenges that frame our understanding of what education is. The tension between standardized curricula and individualized assistive technology provision prompts critical questions about how far our education systems are truly designed for inclusivity.

Most obvious to surface is that the implementation of assistive technology cannot be considered a technical problem requiring technical fixes. The evidence presented in this chapter shows that successful AT implementation requires coordinated approaches addressing technological, economic, and pedagogical aspects in tandem. User-centered design principles, systemic professional development, and evidence-based assessment models provide ways forward, but only with adequate resources and institutional commitment.

The global view demonstrates that economic and geographical location still influence access to fundamental educational resources. Although some nations have established overarching assistive technology policy and service delivery frameworks, others have limited basic frameworks in place to promote equitable access. These disparities are not simply regrettable situations; rather, they reflect profoundly entrenched obstacles to educational equity that require immediate redress.

For the future, the number one priority for most schools is transforming policy designs into actionable realities. That requires ongoing investment in teacher preparation, developing durable funding channels, and fostering genuine collaboration between technology developers, teachers, and policymakers. The approaches outlined in this chapter provide evidence-based direction, yet success will depend on recognizing that AT integration is really about creating learning environments where all students can participate meaningfully.

The path from assistive technology to inclusive education is a long one, but the payoff is enormous. In the right hands, AT has the potential to transform not just individualized learning environments but entire educational cultures, making a space where all learners belong. It requires understanding that assistive technology is not ancillary to education—it is a component of 21st-century educational equity.

Most critically, the integration of end-user feedback from individuals with disabilities must become a non-negotiable standard in assistive technology development and evaluation. This requires establishing formal feedback mechanisms at every stage of the technology lifecycle, from initial conceptualization through long-term impact assessment. Educational institutions should create permanent advisory roles for individuals with disabilities, ensuring their perspectives shape not only individual tools but institutional policies and practices. Furthermore, research funding bodies and policy makers must mandate meaningful user involvement as a prerequisite for support, recognizing that technologies developed without authentic user partnership perpetuate rather than address existing inequities. The transformation from designing for to designing with individuals with disabilities represents not merely a methodological shift but a fundamental reimagining of how we conceptualize expertise, innovation, and the very purpose of assistive technology in educational contexts.

In conclusion, advancing digital accessibility requires not only innovative assistive technologies but also coordinated action among researchers, industry leaders, and policymakers. Building on the insights discussed throughout this paper, it becomes evident that sustainable impact depends on bridging the gap between design and implementation. Collaborative research should prioritize user-centered frameworks that integrate end-user feedback from persons with disabilities, ensuring that solutions remain both effective and inclusive. At the same time, industry stakeholders must focus on developing cost-effective and interoperable technologies that align with international accessibility standards such as WCAG and ISO 9241. Finally, policymakers play a crucial role in establishing supportive funding mechanisms, monitoring accessibility compliance, and fostering knowledge exchange across sectors. By aligning these strategic efforts, the digital accessibility gap can be effectively narrowed, paving the way for a more equitable and inclusive digital future.

REFERENCES

Abdelwahab, M. M., Al-Karawi, K. A., & Semary, H. E. (2025). A Systematic Review of Assistive Technology for Enhancing the Students with Disabilities. *JDR*, *4*(2). Advance online publication. DOI: 10.57197/JDR-2024-0117

Abu-Alghayth, K. (2020). Teachers' use of assistive technology in Saudi special education schools: A mixed-methods enquiry. *International Journal of Developmental Disabilities*, *68*(4), 547–557. DOI: 10.1080/20473869.2020.1836943 PMID: 35937161

Al Husaeni, D. F., & Wahyudin, W. (2023). Digital transformation in special needs education: Computational bibliometrics. *ASEAN Journal of Community and Special Needs Education*, *2*(2), 97–110.

Alakoç, Z. (2003). Matematik öğretiminde teknolojik modern öğretim yaklaşımları. *The Turkish Online Journal of Educational Technology*, •••, 43–49. DOI: 10.17943/etku.341421

Alsolami, A. S. (2022). Teachers of Special Education and Assistive Technology: Teachers' Perceptions of Knowledge, Competencies and Professional Development. *SAGE Open, 12*(1). https://doi.org/ (Original work published 2022)DOI: 10.1177/21582440221079900

Aplin, T., & Gustafsson, L. (2023). Assistive technology funding and policy in Australia: Moving towards a healthier assistive technology ecosystem. *Australian Occupational Therapy Journal*, *70*(4). Advance online publication. DOI: 10.1111/1440-1630.12895 PMID: 37409610

Arslan-Ari, I., & Başer, D. (2022). Assistive technology training within an educational technology course: Perceptions of preservice special education teachers. *Journal of Digital Learning in Teacher Education*, *39*(1), 4–20. DOI: 10.1080/21532974.2022.2137606

aSTEP Consortium (2024). Report on Best Practices in Assistive Technologies for Social Inclusion. https://doi.org/DOI: 10.6084/m9.figshare.26039902.v2

Atanga, C., Jones, B. A., Krueger, L. E., & Lu, S. (2019). Teachers of Students With Learning Disabilities: Assistive Technology Knowledge, Perceptions, Interests, and Barriers. *Journal of Special Education Technology, 35*(4), 236-248. https://doi.org/ (Original work published 2020)DOI: 10.1177/0162643419864858

Bergin, J. (2022). Primary School Educators' Involvement in AT Assessment and Support. *ICCHP-AAATE 2022 Open Access Compendium" Assistive Technology, Accessibility and (e) Inclusion" Part II*. https://aaate.net/wp-content/uploads/sites/12/2023/08/OAC22_V1.0_Part_2.pdf

Bergin, J., & Relihan, M. (2022). Addressing Assistive Technology Training Needs in Education. *ICCHP-AAATE 2022 Open Access Compendium" Assistive Technology, Accessibility and (e) Inclusion" Part II*. https://aaate.net/wp-content/uploads/sites/12/2023/08/OAC22_V1.0_Part_2.pdf

Bi, D., & Casper, C. (2023). A Case Study on the Efficacy and Usage of Assistive Technologies in Howard County Schools, MD. *Journal of Student Research, 12*(3). Advance online publication. DOI: 10.47611/jsrhs.v12i3.4987

Bozkurt, A., Hamutoğlu, N. B., Kaban, A. L., Taşçı, G., & Aykul, M. (2021). Dijital bilgi çağı: Dijital toplum, dijital dönüşüm, dijital eğitim ve dijital yeterlilikler. *Açıköğretim Uygulamaları ve Araştırmaları Dergisi, 7*(2), 35–63. DOI: 10.51948/auad.911584

Chakabwata, W. (2025). The Role of Assistive Technology in Education: A Study of Four SADC States. In Çela, E., Fonkam, M., Vajjhala, N., & Eappen, P. (Eds.), *Advancing Adaptive Education: Technological Innovations for Disability Support* (pp. 163–192). IGI Global Scientific Publishing., DOI: 10.4018/979-8-3693-8227-1.ch007

Chandra, S., Fane, J., Azizi, N., McKenzie-Gray, M., Sager, M., & Dautenhahn, K. (2025). Integrating New Instructional Assistive Technology to Support Academic and Behavioural Instruction for Students with Learning Disabilities. *Journal of Special Education Technology, 0*(0). Advance online publication. DOI: 10.1177/01626434251314042

Copley, J., & Ziviani, J. (2004). Barriers to the use of assistive technology for children with multiple disabilities. *Occupational Therapy International, 11*(4), 229–243. DOI: 10.1002/oti.213 PMID: 15771212

Curtis, M. E., Clingan, S. E., Guo, H., Zhu, Y., Mooney, L. J., & Hser, Y. I. (2022). Disparities in digital access among American rural and urban households and implications for telemedicine-based services. *The Journal of Rural Health, 38*(3), 512–518. DOI: 10.1111/jrh.12614 PMID: 34355427

Damyanov, K. (2024). Effective Pedagogical Strategies and Support Mechanisms for Enhancing the Learning Outcomes of Students with Special Educational Needs: A Systematic Approach. [IJSRM]. *International Journal of Scientific Research and Management, 12*(10). Advance online publication. DOI: 10.18535/ijsrm/v12i10.el03 de Witte, L., Steel, E., Gupta, S., Ramos, V. D., & Roentgen, U. (2018). Assistive technology provision: Towards an international framework for assuring availability and accessibility of affordable high-quality assistive technology. *Disability and Rehabilitation. Assistive Technology*, *13*(5), 467–472. DOI: 10.1080/17483107.2018.1470264 PMID: 29741965

Dewi, A. E. R., & Nurfaidah, S. (2024). The Future of Inclusive Education: Preparing Students with Special Needs for the World of Work. *Journal of Pedagogi*, *1*(6), 65–72. DOI: 10.62872/c335h261

Dirks, S., Bühler, C., Heumader, P., & Miesenberger, K. (2022). Development, Evaluation and Assessment of Assistive Technologies. In Miesenberger, K., Kouroupetroglou, G., Mavrou, K., Manduchi, R., Covarrubias Rodriguez, M., & Penáz, P. (Eds.), Lecture Notes in Computer Science: Vol. 13342. *Computers Helping People with Special Needs. ICCHP-AAATE 2022*. Springer., DOI: 10.1007/978-3-031-08645-8_30

Domingues, C. dos A., & Laplane, A. L. F. (2024). Assistive technology in public policies: Trends in the international debate and implications for Brazil. *Disability and Rehabilitation. Assistive Technology*, *19*(8), 2761–2773. DOI: 10.1080/17483107.2024.2316896 PMID: 38372271

Ebuenyi, I. D., Smith, E. M., Kafumba, J., Jamali, M. Z., Munthali, A., & MacLachlan, M. (2020). Implementation of the Assistive Product List (APL) in Malawi through development of appropriate policy and systems: An action research protocol. *BMJ Open*, *10*(11), e040281. PMID: 33158833

Felicia, A., Sharif, S., Wong, W., & Marriappan, M. (2014). Innovation of assistive technologies in special education: A review. *Journal of Enhanced Research in Educational Development*, *2*(3), 25–38.

Fernández-Batanero, J. M., Montenegro-Rueda, M., Fernández-Cerero, J., & García-Martínez, I. (2022). Assistive technology for the inclusion of students with disabilities: A systematic review. *Educational Technology Research and Development*, *70*, 1911–1930. DOI: 10.1007/s11423-022-10127-7

Fineberga, A., Savageb, M., Austinc, A., Boitend, S., Droopd, J., Allen, M., Heydte, P., Sondergaard, D., & Mitra, G. (2019). ATscale – Establishing a Cross-Sector Partnership to Increase Access to Assistive Technology. https://discovery.ucl.ac.uk/id/eprint/10084647/

Fteiha, M., Al-Rashaida, M., Elsori, D., Khalil, A., & Bustami, G. (2024). Obstacles for using assistive technology in centres of special needs in the UAE. *Disability and Rehabilitation. Assistive Technology*, *19*(8), 2934–2944. DOI: 10.1080/17483107.2024.2323698 PMID: 38436086

Garçon, L., Nakatani, Y., Khasnabis, C., Berumen, A., Lapitan, J., Walker, L., Ross, A., & Borg, J. (2016). Medical and Assistive Health Technology: Meeting the Needs of Aging Populations. *The Gerontologist*, *56*, 293–302. DOI: 10.1093/geront/gnw005 PMID: 26994268

Guillén-Martínez, D., Alcázar-Espinoza, J. A., Rámirez-Sánchez, I., Samaniego-Cobo, T., & Villacís-Macias, C. (2025). Policies, Assistive Technologies, and Barriers in Inclusive Education: A Global Systematic Review (2019-2024). *Journal of Posthumanism*, *5*(2), 208–218. DOI: 10.63332/joph.v5i2.418

Harris, K., Burley, H., McLachlan, R., Bowman, M., Macaldowie, A., Taylor, K., & Chambers, G. M. (2016). Socio-economic disparities in access to assisted reproductive technologies in Australia. *Reproductive Biomedicine Online*, *33*(5), 575–584. DOI: 10.1016/j.rbmo.2016.07.012 PMID: 27595434

Hemmingsson, H., Lidström, H., & Nygård, L. (2009). Use of assistive technology devices in mainstream schools: Students' perspective. *The American Journal of Occupational Therapy*, *63*(4), 463–472. DOI: 10.5014/AJOT.63.4.463 PMID: 19708475

Hersh, M., & Mouroutsou, S. (2019). Learning technology and disability—Overcoming barriers to inclusion: Evidence from a multicountry study. *British Journal of Educational Technology*, *50*(6), 3329–3344. DOI: 10.1111/bjet.12737

Ismaili, J., & Ibrahimi, E. (2017). Mobile learning as alternative to assistive technology devices for special needs students. *Education and Information Technologies*, *22*, 883–899. DOI: 10.1007/s10639-015-9462-9

ISO/IEC. (2014). *ISO/IEC Guide 71:2014 Guide for addressing accessibility in standards*. International Organization for Standardization.

Jones, B. A., Peterson-Ahmad, M., Fields, M., & Williams, N. (2020). Training Preservice Teachers to Match Assistive Technology to Student Needs. *Journal of Special Education Technology, 36*(4), 271-283. https://doi.org/ (Original work published 2021)DOI: 10.1177/0162643420918337

Judge, S., & Simms, K. A. (2009). Assistive Technology Training at the Pre-Service Level: A National Snapshot of Teacher Preparation Programs. *Teacher Education and Special Education, 32*(1), 33-44. https://doi.org/ (Original work published 2009) DOI: 10.1177/0888406408330868

Khasawneh, M. A. S. (2024). Evaluating the efficacy of tablet-based assistive technology in Saudi special education settings. *International Journal of Learning. Teaching and Educational Research*, *23*(6), 547–561. DOI: 10.26803/ijlter.23.6.25

Kobayashi, K. M., Grenier, A., & Gontcharov, I. (2021). Learning Activity: Embedding Healthcare Technologies in Real-World Contexts—Developing the Scale-Up, Spread, and Sustainability of Assistive Technologies in Health Systems. In Sixsmith, A., Sixsmith, J., Mihailidis, A., & Fang, M. L. (Eds.), *Knowledge, Innovation, and Impact: A Guide for the Engaged Health Researcher. International Perspectives on Social Policy, Administration, and Practice*. Springer., DOI: 10.1007/978-3-030-34390-3_48

Kumar, A. & Vinita. (2023). Solution-focused approach towards improved access to assistive mobility technology and devices in low and middle-income countries: A narrative review. *Philippine Journal of Allied Health Sciences*, *7*(1), 11–17. DOI: 10.36413/pjahs.0701.003

Lamond, B., & Cunningham, T. (2019). Understanding Teacher Perceptions of Assistive Technology. *Journal of Special Education Technology, 35*(2), 97-108. https://doi.org/ (Original work published 2020)DOI: 10.1177/0162643419841550

Leahy, J. A., & Lane, J. P. (2010). Knowledge from Research and Practice on the Barriers and Carriers to Successful Technology Transfer for Assistive Technology Devices. *Assistive Technology Outcomes and Benefits*, *6*(1), 73–86.

Macheque, V., Kadyamatimba, A., & Ochara, N. (2024). Sociotechnical challenges faced by students with disability and factors influencing the integration of assistive technologies. *International Journal of Research In Business and Social Science*, *13*(6), 253–269. DOI: 10.20525/ijrbs.v13i6.3533

MacLachlan, M., Banes, D., Bell, D., Borg, J., Donnelly, B., Fembek, M., & Hooks, H. (2018). Assistive technology policy: A position paper from the first global research, innovation, and education on assistive technology (GREAT) summit. *Disability and Rehabilitation. Assistive Technology*, *13*(5), 454–466. DOI: 10.1080/17483107.2018.1468496 PMID: 29790393

Mandal, S., Ruidar, I., & Gope, L. (2025). Role of Assistive Technology to Enhance Learning and Participation in Inclusive Education. *International Journal of Scientific Research and Engineering Trends*, *11*(2), 1459–1464. DOI: 10.61137/ijsret.vol.11.issue2.238

Matter, R., Harniss, M., Oderud, T., Borg, J., & Eide, A. H. (2016). Assistive technology in resource-limited environments: A scoping review. *Disability and Rehabilitation. Assistive Technology, 12*(2), 105–114. DOI: 10.1080/17483107.2016.1188170 PMID: 27443790

McGregor, G., & Pachuski, P. (1996). Assistive Technology in Schools: Are Teachers Ready, Able, and Supported? *Journal of Special Education Technology, 13*(1), 4-15. https://doi.org/ (Original work published 1996)DOI: 10.1177/016264349601300102

McNicholl, A., Casey, H., Desmond, D., & Gallagher, P. (2021). The impact of assistive technology use for students with disabilities in higher education: A systematic review. *Disability and Rehabilitation. Assistive Technology, 16*(2), 130–143. DOI: 10.1080/17483107.2019.1642395 PMID: 31335220

Morash-Macneil, V., Johnson, F., & Ryan, J. B. (2018). A systematic review of assistive technology for individuals with intellectual disability in the workplace. *Journal of Special Education Technology, 33*(1), 15–26. DOI: 10.1177/0162643417729166

Morelle, M., & Matshidiso, T. (2024). Challenges in Implementing Assistive Devices in Teaching Learners who are Visually Impaired in full Service Classrooms. [IJISRT]. *International Journal of Innovative Science and Research Technology, 9*(3), 2509–2511. DOI: 10.38124/ijisrt/ijisrt24mar1819

Mukhtarkyzy, K., Smagulova, L., Tokzhigitova, A., Serikbayeva, N., Sayakov, O., Turkmenbayev, A., & Assilbayeva, R. (2025). A systematic review of the utility of assistive technologies for SEND students in schools. *Frontiers in Education, 10*. Advance online publication. DOI: 10.3389/feduc.2025.1523797

Nordström, T., Nilsson, S., Gustafson, S., & Svensson, I. (2018). Assistive technology applications for students with reading difficulties: Special education teachers' experiences and perceptions. *Disability and Rehabilitation. Assistive Technology, 14*(8), 798–808. DOI: 10.1080/17483107.2018.1499142 PMID: 30239256

O'Sullivan, K., McGrane, A., Long, S., Marshall, K., & Maclachlan, M. (2021). Using a systems thinking approach to understand teachers perceptions and use of assistive technology in the republic of Ireland. *Disability and Rehabilitation. Assistive Technology, 18*(5), 502–510. DOI: 10.1080/17483107.2021.1878297 PMID: 33573427

Olarewaju, T., Healy, A., & Chockalingam, N. (2021). Barriers to accessing assistive technology in Africa. *Assistive Technology, 35*(1), 116–117. DOI: 10.1080/10400435.2021.1985011 PMID: 34554890

Oyedokun, T. T. (2025). Assistive Technology and Accessibility Tools in Enhancing Adaptive Education. In Çela, E., Fonkam, M., Vajjhala, N., & Eappen, P. (Eds.), *Advancing Adaptive Education: Technological Innovations for Disability Support* (pp. 125–162). IGI Global Scientific Publishing., DOI: 10.4018/979-8-3693-8227-1.ch006

Özdamar, O., & Odluyurt, S. (2025). Determination of Teachers' Views on the Use of Assistive Technology in Special Education Classrooms. *E-Kafkas Journal of Educational Research, 12*(1), 146–160. DOI: 10.30900/kafkasegt.1585399

Parette, H. P., & Peterson-Karlan, G. R. (2007). Facilitating Student Achievement with Assistive Technology. *Education and Training in Developmental Disabilities, 42*(4), 387–397. https://www.jstor.org/stable/23879844

Park, J., Bagwell, A. F., Bryant, D. P., & Bryant, B. R. (2021). Integrating Assistive Technology Into a Teacher Preparation Program. *Teacher Education and Special Education, 45*(2), 141-159. https://doi.org/ (Original work published 2022)DOI: 10.1177/08884064211001447

Park, J., Gremp, M., & Ok, M. W. (2023). Effects of Assistive Technology Instruction on Pre-Service Teachers: A Systematic Review. *Journal of Special Education Technology, 39*(3), 349-362. https://doi.org/ (Original work published 2024)DOI: 10.1177/01626434231210988

Penton, V., & Gustafson, D. L. (2014). Access to Assistive Technology and Single Entry Point Programs. *Canadian Journal of Disability Studies, 3*(1), 93–120. DOI: 10.15353/cjds.v3i1.90

Peters, J., Bleakney, A., Sornson, A., Hsiao-Wecksler, E., & McDonagh, D. (2023). User-driven product development: Designed *by,* not designed *for. The Design Journal, 27*(1), 133–152. DOI: 10.1080/14606925.2023.2275868

Seiradakis, E. (2024). *Investigating the barriers to using assistive technologies in Greek special education classrooms: EFL teachers' perspectives.* European Journal of Special Education Research., DOI: 10.46827/ejse.v10i1.5151

Switters, J., Verma, A. K., Mavrou, K., Boland, S., Franz, L., Karfitsa, E., ... & Valoti, I. (2022). Bridging the Digital Divide: A Review of the ENTELIS+ Project on the Development of Digital Accessibility Training Addressing the EU and Global Disability Policy Agendas. *ICCHP-AAATE 2022 Open Access Compendium" Assistive Technology, Accessibility and (e) Inclusion" Part II.*

Tangcharoensathien, V., Witthayapipopsakul, W., Viriyathorn, S., & Patcharanarumol, W. (2018). Improving access to assistive technologies: Challenges and solutions in low- and middle-income countries. *WHO South-East Asia Journal of Public Health*, *7*(2), 84–89. PMID: 30136666

Torrens, G. E., & Asghar, S. (2023). 20 years of the Loughborough user centered assistive technology design process: Has it made a difference? *Assistive Technology*, *35*(5), 425–434. DOI: 10.1080/10400435.2022.2113477 PMID: 36040847

United Nations. (2006). *Convention on the Rights of Persons with Disabilities*. United Nations Department of Economic and Social Affairs.

Vanderpuye, I., & Okai, M. (2023). Effective use of assistive technology in inclusive classroom: Views of teachers on resources and challenges in a developing economy. *Support for Learning*, *38*(3), 68–82. DOI: 10.1111/1467-9604.12433

Verma, A., & Maurya, M. C. (2024). Addressing the Challenges to Accessibility and Research Gaps in Assistive Technology. Advances in Medical Technologies and Clinical Practice Book Series, 89–116. https://doi.org/DOI: 10.4018/979-8-3693-6308-9.ch005

Visser, M., Nel, M., de Klerk, M., Ganzevoort, A., Hubble, C., Liebenberg, A., Snyman, M., & Young, M. (2020). The use of assistive technology in classroom activities for learners with motor impairments at a special school in South Africa. *South African Journal of Occupational Therapy*, *50*(2), 11–22. DOI: 10.17159/2310-3833/2020/vol50no2a3

White, D. H., & Robertson, L. (2015). Implementing assistive technologies: A study on co-learning in the Canadian elementary school context. *Computers in Human Behavior*, *51*, 1268–1275. DOI: 10.1016/j.chb.2014.12.003

WHO Country Office Mongolia. (2021). Rapid Assistive Technology Assessment (rATA) Survey Implementation. https://cdn.who.int/media/docs/default-source/assistive-technology-2/rata-master-training/20201021-rata-enumerator-manual-final.pdf?sfvrsn=3864b5f8_12

Widiyastono, H., Rejeki, D. S., Supratiwi, M., Gunarhadi, G., Yuwono, J., & Hermawan, H. (2023). Utilization of Assistive Technology in Special Needs Children's Learning (Inclusive Education). *Journal of Disability*, *3*(1), 1–6. DOI: 10.20961/jod.v3i1.80244

World Health Organization & UNICEF. (2022). *Global report on assistive technology*. World Health Organization.

Yenduri, G.. (2023). From Assistive Technologies to Metaverse—Technologies in Inclusive Higher Education for Students With Specific Learning Difficulties: A Review. *IEEE Access : Practical Innovations, Open Solutions*, *11*, 64907–64927. DOI: 10.1109/ACCESS.2023.3289496

Zhang, W., & Borg, J. (2025). Global availability of guidelines related to assistive technology: A scoping review. *Frontiers in Rehabilitation Sciences*, *6*. Advance online publication. DOI: 10.3389/fresc.2025.1581104 PMID: 40342299

Zilz, W., & Pang, Y. (2019). Application of assistive technology in inclusive classrooms. *Disability and Rehabilitation. Assistive Technology*, *16*(7), 684–686. DOI: 10.1080/17483107.2019.1695963 PMID: 31814471

Compilation of References

Ab Rahman, R., Ahmad, S., & Hashim, U. R. (2019). A Study on Gamification for Higher Education Students' Engagement Towards Education 4.0. In Piuri, V., Balas, V. E., Borah, S., & Syed Ahmad, S. S. (Eds.), *Intelligent and Interactive Computing* (Vol. 67, pp. 491–502). Springer Singapore., DOI: 10.1007/978-981-13-6031-2_5

Abbas, H. A. (2024). Transforming education: The role of Artificial Intelligence. *Studies in Engineering and Exact Sciences*, *5*(3), e12579. DOI: 10.54021/seesv5n3-041

Abbas, N., Ali, I., Manzoor, R., Hussain, T., & Hussain, M. H. A. i. (2023). Role of artificial intelligence tools in enhancing students' educational performance at higher levels. *Journal of Artificial Intelligence. Machine Learning and Neural Network*, (35), 36–49. DOI: 10.55529/jaimlnn.35.36.49

Abbasoğlu, B. (2020). Predicting academic achievement of secondary school students using educational data mining methods. *Data Science*, *3*(1), 1–10.

Abdelwahab, M. M., Al-Karawi, K. A., & Semary, H. E. (2025). A Systematic Review of Assistive Technology for Enhancing the Students with Disabilities. *JDR*, *4*(2). Advance online publication. DOI: 10.57197/JDR-2024-0117

Abernathy, P. C. (2024). *AI Tools as Supplementary Support in Language Acquisition*. https://doi.org/DOI: 10.20944/preprints202407.2213.v1

Abu-Alghayth, K. (2020). Teachers' use of assistive technology in Saudi special education schools: A mixed-methods enquiry. *International Journal of Developmental Disabilities*, *68*(4), 547–557. DOI: 10.1080/20473869.2020.1836943 PMID: 35937161

Adair, A. (2023). Teaching and learning with AI: How artificial intelligence is transforming the future of education. *XRDS Crossroads the ACM Magazine for Students*, *29*(3), 7–9. DOI: 10.1145/3589252

Aggarwal, D. (2023). Exploring the Scope of Artificial Intelligence (AI) for Life-long Education through Personalised & Adaptive Learning. *Journal of Artificial Intelligence. Machine Learning and Neural Network*, *41*, 21–26. DOI: 10.55529/jaimlnn.41.21.26

Aghaziarati, A., Nejatifar, S., & Abedi, A. (2023). Artificial intelligence in education: Investigating teacher attitudes. *AI and Tech in Behavioral and Social Sciences*, *1*(1), 35–42. DOI: 10.61838/kman.aitech.1.1.6

Ahmad, W., Shokeen, R., & Raj, R. (2024). Artificial intelligence. *Advances in Educational Technologies and Instructional Design*, •••, 459–520. DOI: 10.4018/979-8-3693-5538-1.ch017 PMID: 38274052

Ajuwon, O. A., Animashaun, E. S., & Chiekezie, N. R. (2024). *Integrating AI and technology in educational administration: Improving efficiency and educational quality*. Open Access Research Journal of Science and Technology., DOI: 10.53022/oarjst.2024.11.2.0102

Akçayır, M., & Akçayır, G. (2017). Advantages and challenges associated with augmented reality for education: A systematic review of the literature. *Educational Research Review*, *20*, 1–11. DOI: 10.1016/j.edurev.2016.11.002

Akgün, S., & Greenhow, C. (2021). Artificial intelligence in education: Addressing ethical challenges in k-12 settings. *AI and Ethics*, *2*(3), 431–440. DOI: 10.1007/s43681-021-00096-7 PMID: 34790956

Akseki, B., Meydaneri, S., & Taşdemir, C. (2023). Cyber security and information securıty studies in Turkey. [Smart Journal]. *Social Mentality and Researcher Thinkers Journal*, *9*(73), 3902–3909. DOI: 10.29228/smryj.70755

Akyel, Y., & Tur, E. (2024). Prospects, challenges, and future directions in the research and investigation of artificial intelligence's potential and applications in educational sciences. *Ahi Evran Üniversitesi Kırşehir Eğitim Fakültesi Dergisi*, *25*(1), 645–711. DOI: 10.29299/kefad.1322341

Al Hasani, S. H. S., & Husin, N. A. (2021). A REVIEW OF DIGITAL TRANSFORMATION OF EDUCATION IN OMAN. *Journal of Business Management and Accounting*, *11*(2), 41–59. DOI: 10.32890/jbma2021.11.2.3

Al Husaeni, D. F., & Wahyudin, W. (2023). Digital transformation in special needs education: Computational bibliometrics. *ASEAN Journal of Community and Special Needs Education*, *2*(2), 97–110.

Al Nabhani, F., Hamzah, M. B., & Abuhassna, H. (2025). The role of artificial intelligence in personalizing educational content: Enhancing the learning experience and developing the teacher's role in an integrated educational environment. *Contemporary Educational Technology, 17*(2), ep573. DOI: 10.30935/cedtech/16089

Alakoç, Z. (2003). Matematik öğretiminde teknolojik modern öğretim yaklaşımları. *The Turkish Online Journal of Educational Technology*, •••, 43–49. DOI: 10.17943/etku.341421

Alemanno, A., Carmone, M., & Priore, L. (2025). Prompting for healthcare professionals: Enhancing clinical Decision-Making with artificial intelligence. *Infermieristica Journal, 4*(1), 33–39. DOI: 10.36253/if-3198

Alkaissi, H., & McFarlane, S. I. (2023). Artificial hallucinations in ChatGPT: Implications in scientific writing. *Cureus*. Advance online publication. DOI: 10.7759/cureus.35179 PMID: 36811129

Allen, R. R., & Rott, R. K. (1969). *The nature of critical thinking*. Report from the Concepts in Verbal Argument Project. Theoretical Paper No. 20.

Alpizar-Chacon, I., & Keuning, H. (2025). Students' use of generative AI as a support tool in an advanced web development course. In *Proceedings of the 30th ACM Conference on Innovation and Technology in Computer Science Education*, Vol. 1 (pp. 312-318).

Alsawaier, R. S. (2018). The effect of gamification on motivation and engagement. *The International Journal of Information and Learning Technology, 35*(1), 56–79. DOI: 10.1108/IJILT-02-2017-0009

Alsolami, A. S. (2022). Teachers of Special Education and Assistive Technology: Teachers' Perceptions of Knowledge, Competencies and Professional Development. *SAGE Open, 12*(1). https://doi.org/ (Original work published 2022)DOI: 10.1177/21582440221079900

Anand, A., Gupta, A., Yadav, N., & Bajaj, S. (2024). A comprehensive survey of AI-driven advancements and techniques in automated program repair and code generation. *arXiv (Cornell University)*. https://doi.org//arxiv.2411.07586DOI: 10.48550

Anderson, L. W., & Krathwohl, D. R. (Eds.). (2021). *A Taxonomy for Learning, Teaching, and Assessing: A Revision of Bloom's Taxonomy of Educational Objectives*. Addison Wesley Longman, Inc.

Anisimova, A. N., & Efremova, Yu. I. (2022). Digital Transformation of Vocational Education: Challenges of Modern Society. In Ashmarina, S. I., & Mantulenko, V. V. (Eds.), *Digital Technologies in the New Socio-Economic Reality* (Vol. 304, pp. 773–781). Springer International Publishing., DOI: 10.1007/978-3-030-83175-2_95

Anuyahong, B., Rattanapong, C., & Patcha, I. (2023). Analyzing the impact of artificial intelligence in personalized learning and adaptive assessment in higher education. *International Journal of Research and Scientific Innovation*, *X*(IV), 88–93. DOI: 10.51244/ijrsi.2023.10412

Anwar, R. W., Abdullah, T., & Pastore, F. (2021). Firewall best practices for securing smart healthcare environment: A review. *Applied Sciences (Basel, Switzerland)*, *11*(19), 9183.

Apetorgbor, M., Narad, S., Akpabio, E., Dhawale, C., Konto, A., & Verma, P. (2024). *Leveraging Artificial Intelligence for Effective Assessment and Evaluation in Education: A Comprehensive Review*. 1–6. https://doi.org/DOI: 10.1109/idic-aiei61867.2024.10842940

Aplin, T., & Gustafsson, L. (2023). Assistive technology funding and policy in Australia: Moving towards a healthier assistive technology ecosystem. *Australian Occupational Therapy Journal*, *70*(4). Advance online publication. DOI: 10.1111/1440-1630.12895 PMID: 37409610

Arendes, K., Kerkhoff, S., & Adhikari, B. (2024). Engaging Students to Learn Coding in the AI Era with Emphasis on the Process. *Edukasiana Jurnal Inovasi Pendidikan*, *3*(2), 257–268. DOI: 10.56916/ejip.v3i2.728

Arf, C. (1959). *Makine düşünebilir mi ve nasıl düşünebilir?* [Can machines think, and how do they think?]. [Conference session]. Atatürk Üniversitesi 19581959 Öğretim Yılı Halk Konferansları (1), 91-103.

Arslan-Ari, I., & Başer, D. (2022). Assistive technology training within an educational technology course: Perceptions of preservice special education teachers. *Journal of Digital Learning in Teacher Education*, *39*(1), 4–20. DOI: 10.1080/21532974.2022.2137606

Arslan, E. (2014). Yabancı dil öğretiminde robot öğretmenler. *Ondokuz Mayıs Üniversitesi Eğitim Fakültesi Dergisi*, *33*(1), 15–26. DOI: 10.7822/egt181

Arslan, K. (2020). Eğitimde yapay zekâ ve uygulamaları. *Batı Anadolu Eğitim Bilimleri Dergisi*, *11*(1), 71–88.

Astakhova, L. V. (2020). Issues of the culture of information security under the conditions of the digital economy. *Scientific and Technical Information Processing, 47*(1), 56–64. https://link.springer.com/article/10.3103/S0147688220010062

aSTEP Consortium (2024). Report on Best Practices in Assistive Technologies for Social Inclusion. https://doi.org/DOI: 10.6084/m9.figshare.26039902.v2

Atanga, C., Jones, B. A., Krueger, L. E., & Lu, S. (2019). Teachers of Students With Learning Disabilities: Assistive Technology Knowledge, Perceptions, Interests, and Barriers. *Journal of Special Education Technology, 35*(4), 236-248. https://doi.org/ (Original work published 2020)DOI: 10.1177/0162643419864858

Athaluri, S. A., Manthena, S. V., Kesapragada, V. S. R. K. M., Yarlagadda, V., Dave, T., & Duddumpudi, R. T. S. (2023). Exploring the boundaries of Reality: Investigating the phenomenon of artificial intelligence hallucination in scientific writing through ChatGPT references. *Cureus*. Advance online publication. DOI: 10.7759/cureus.37432 PMID: 37182055

Authentication. (2017). In *Guide to Computer Network Security* (pp. 207–225). Springer.

Avcı, Ü., & Oruç, O. (2020). Investigation of the students' personal cyber security behaviour and information security awareness. İnönü University Journal of the Faculty of Education, 21(1), 284-303. doi: DOI: 10.17679/inuefd.526390

Aydın, Ö. (2022). *Security and privacy in computer systems*. Efeakademi Press.

Ayeni, O. O., Hamad, N. M. A., Chisom, O. N., Osawaru, B., & Adewusi, O. E. (2024). Ai in education: A review of personalized learning and educational technology. *GSC Advanced Research and Reviews, 18*(2), 261–271. DOI: 10.30574/gscarr.2024.18.2.0062

Azzam, A., & And Charles, T. (2024). A review of artificial ıntelligence in K-12 education. *Open Journal of Applied Sciences, 14*, 2088–2100. DOI: 10.4236/ojapps.2024.148137

Babu, C. V. S., & Suruthi, G. (2024). Unravelling the evolution of generative ai in communication education. *Advances in Educational Technologies and Instructional Design*, •••, 55–71. DOI: 10.4018/979-8-3693-0831-8.ch003

Bahroun, Z., Anane, C., Ahmed, V., & Zacca, A. (2023). Transforming education: A comprehensive review of generative artificial intelligence in educational settings through bibliometric and content analysis. *Sustainability, 15*(17), 12983. DOI: 10.3390/su151712983

Baïdoo-Anu, D., & Ansah, L. O. (2023). Education in the era of generative artificial intelligence (AI): Understanding the potential benefits of ChatGPT in promoting teaching and learning. *Journal of AI*, *7*(1), 52–62. DOI: 10.61969/jai.1337500

Baker, R. S. (2016). Stupid tutoring systems, intelligent humans. *International Journal of Artificial Intelligence in Education*, *26*(2), 600–614. DOI: 10.1007/s40593-016-0105-z

Baker, R. S. J. D., & Yacef, K. (2009). The state of educational data mining in 2009: A review and future visions. *Journal of Educational Data Mining*, *1*(1), 3–17.

Baker, R. S., & Hawn, A. (2022). Algorithmic bias in education. *International Journal of Artificial Intelligence in Education*, *32*(4), 1052–1092. DOI: 10.1007/s40593-021-00285-9

Barua, P. D., Vicnesh, J., Gururajan, R., Oh, S. L., Palmer, E. E., Azizan, M. M., & Acharya, U. R. (2022). Artificial intelligence enabled personalised assistive tools to enhance education of children with neurodevelopmental disorders—A review. *International Journal of Environmental Research and Public Health*, *19*(3), 1192. DOI: 10.3390/ijerph19031192 PMID: 35162220

Batey, M., & Furnham, A. (2006). Creativity, intelligence, and personality: A critical review of the scattered literature. *Genetic, Social, and General Psychology Monographs*, *132*(4), 355–429. DOI: 10.3200/MONO.132.4.355-430 PMID: 18341234

Bayne, S. (2015). Teacherbot: Interventions in automated teaching. *Teaching in Higher Education*, *20*(4). Advance online publication. DOI: 10.1080/13562517.2015.1020783

Bayrakcı, E., & Koçman, M. A. (2023). Information security and electronic warfare. [NEUSBF]. *Journal of the Faculty of Political Science*, *5*(Special Issue), 184–206. DOI: 10.51124/jneusbf.2023.56

Begum, I. U. (2024). Role of artificial intelligence in higher education- an empirical investigation. [IRJAEM]. *International Research Journal on Advanced Engineering and Management*, *2*(03), 49–53. DOI: 10.47392/irjaem.2024.0009

Begum, R. (2025). A systematic literature review on how artificial intelligence (AI) is revolutionizing education 4.0. *Journal of Scientific Reports*, *9*(1), 60–79. DOI: 10.58970/jsr.1096 PMID: 39747217

Beiting-Parrish, M., & Whitmer, J. (2023). Lessons learned about evaluating fairness from a data challenge to automatically score naep reading items. https://doi.org/DOI: 10.35542/osf.io/j9c5g

Belousova, M. N., Belousov, V. A., & Narkevich, L. V. (2021). Digital Transformation of the Educational Process in University in the Context of Globalization. In Popkova, E. G., Ostrovskaya, V. N., & Bogoviz, A. V. (Eds.), *Socio-economic Systems: Paradigms for the Future* (Vol. 314, pp. 1267–1277). Springer International Publishing., DOI: 10.1007/978-3-030-56433-9_133

Belpaeme, T., Kennedy, J., Ramachandran, A., Scassellati, B., & Tanaka, F. (2018). Social robots for education: A review. *Science Robotics*, *3*(21), eaat5954. https://www.science.org/doi/10.1126/scirobotics.aat5954 PMID: 33141719

Benitti, F. B. V. (2012). Exploring the educational potential of robotics in schools: A systematic review. *Computers & Education*, *58*(3), 978–988. DOI: 10.1016/j.compedu.2011.10.006

Benjamin, L. T. (1988). A history of teaching machines. *The American Psychologist*, *43*(9), 703.

Benzakour, A., Altsitzioglou, P., Lemée, J. M., Ahmad, A., Mavrogenis, A. F., & Benzakour, T. (2023). Artificial intelligence in spine surgery. *International Orthopaedics*, *47*(2), 457–465. DOI: 10.1007/s00264-022-05517-8 PMID: 35902390

Bergin, J. (2022). Primary School Educators' Involvement in AT Assessment and Support. *ICCHP-AAATE 2022 Open Access Compendium" Assistive Technology, Accessibility and (e) Inclusion" Part II*. https://aaate.net/wp-content/uploads/sites/12/2023/08/OAC22_V1.0_Part_2.pdf

Bergin, J., & Relihan, M. (2022). Addressing Assistive Technology Training Needs in Education. *ICCHP-AAATE 2022 Open Access Compendium" Assistive Technology, Accessibility and (e) Inclusion" Part II*. https://aaate.net/wp-content/uploads/sites/12/2023/08/OAC22_V1.0_Part_2.pdf

Beri, G., & Srivastava, V. (2025). *Advanced techniques in prompt engineering for large language models: A comprehensive study*. IEEE., DOI: 10.1109/ictbig64922.2024.10911672

Bernacki, M. L., Greene, M. J., & Lobczowski, N. G. (2021). A Systematic review of research on personalized learning: Personalized by whom, to what, how, and for what purpose(s)? *Educational Psychology Review*, *33*(4), 1675–1715. DOI: 10.1007/s10648-021-09615-8

Bers, M. U. (2018). *Coding as a playground: Programming and computational thinking in the early childhood classroom*. Routledge.

Beyer, B. K. (1991). *Teaching thinking skills: A hand book for secondary school teachers*. Allyn and Bacon.

Bianchi, A., & Phillips, J. G. (2005). Psychological predictors of problem mobile phone use. *Cyberpsychology & Behavior*, *8*(1), 39–51. DOI: 10.1089/cpb.2005.8.39

Bi, D., & Casper, C. (2023). A Case Study on the Efficacy and Usage of Assistive Technologies in Howard County Schools, MD. *Journal of Student Research*, *12*(3). Advance online publication. DOI: 10.47611/jsrhs.v12i3.4987

Bienkowski, M., Feng, M., & Means, B. (2012*). Enhancing teaching and learning through educational data mining and learning analytics: an issue brief.* https://files.eric.ed.gov/fulltext/ED611199.pdf

Bilyalova, A. A., Salimova, D. A., & Zelenina, T. I. (2020). Digital Transformation in Education. In Antipova, T. (Ed.), *Integrated Science in Digital Age* (Vol. 78, pp. 265–276). Springer International Publishing., DOI: 10.1007/978-3-030-22493-6_24

Birthriya, S. K., Ahlawat, P., & Jain, A. K. (2025). a. A comprehensive survey of social engineering attacks: Taxonomy of attacks, prevention, and mitigation strategies. *Journal of Applied Security Research*, *20*(2), 244–292.

Birthriya, S. K., Ahlawat, P., & Jain, A. K. (2025). b. Detection and prevention of spear phishing attacks: A comprehensive survey. *Computers & Security*, *104317*. Advance online publication. DOI: 10.1016/j.cose.2025.104317

Bloom, B. S. (1968). *Learning for mastery. Evaluation Comment*, 1(2), 1–12. University of Chicago, Department of Education. https://eric.ed.gov/?id=eD053419

Boden, M. A. (2014). Creativity and artificial intelligence: A contradiction in terms. *The philosophy of creativity: New essays*, 224-246.

Borate, V., Adsul, A., Dhakane, R., Gawade, S., Ghodake, S., & Jadhav, M. P. (2024). A comprehensive review of phishing attack detection using machine learning techniques. *International Journal of Advanced Research in Science* [IJARSCT]. *Tongxin Jishu*, *4*(3).

Borocki, J., Jovanović, A., Vekić, A., Đaković, V., & Ćović, M. (2023). Empowering content creation with generative ai in metaverse. *19th International Scientific Conference on Industrial Systems,* 554-559. https://doi.org/DOI: 10.24867/is-2023-vp1.1-14_07941

Boston Consulting Group. (2022, September). *Why children are unsafe in cyberspace*. https://web-assets.bcg.com/ec/76/4d06204a4f8e9f90428a3d992373/bcg-why-children-are-unsafe-in-cyberspace-sep-2022.pdf

Bouslama, F., & Kalota, F. (2013). Creating smart classrooms to benefit from innovative technologies and learning space design. *2013 International Conference on Current Trends in Information Technology (CTIT)*, 102–106. https://doi.org/DOI: 10.1109/CTIT.2013.6749486

Bower, M., Howe, C., McCredie, N., Robinson, A., & Grover, D. (2014). Augmented Reality in education – cases, places and potentials. *Educational Media International, 51*(1), 1–15. DOI: 10.1080/09523987.2014.889400

Bozkurt, A. (2016). Learning analytics: E-learning, big data and personalized learning. *Journal of Open Education Applications and Research, 2*(4), 55–81.

Bozkurt, A., Hamutoğlu, N. B., Kaban, A. L., Taşçı, G., & Aykul, M. (2021). Dijital bilgi çağı: Dijital toplum, dijital dönüşüm, dijital eğitim ve dijital yeterlilikler. *Açıköğretim Uygulamaları ve Araştırmaları Dergisi, 7*(2), 35–63. DOI: 10.51948/auad.911584

Brantly, A. (2017). Innovation and adaptation in jihadist digital security. *Survival Global Politics and Strategy, 59*(1), 79–102. DOI: 10.1080/00396338.2017.1282678

Breazeal, C. (2002). *Designing sociable robots*. MIT Press.

Bron, D. (April 2023). *The Emergence of Holographic Telepresence: Disrupting Communication and Collaboration in the Digital Age.* https://medium.com/chain-reaction/the-emergence-of-holographic-telepresence-disrupting-communication-and-collaboration-in-the-cd3461811e

Broussard, M. (2018). *Artificial unintelligence: How computers misunderstand the world*. MIT Press.

Buchanan, M. B., & Farrell, S. J. (2025). The editorial word: Binary balancing the binary—AI, expertise, and the future of gifted education. *Journal of Advanced Academics, 36*(4), 593–600. DOI: 10.1177/1932202X251373093

Bulathwela, S., Pérez-Ortiz, M., Holloway, C., Cukurova, M., & Shawe-Taylor, J. (2024). Artificial intelligence alone will not democratise education: On educational inequality, techno-solutionism and inclusive tools. *Sustainability, 16*(2), 781. DOI: 10.3390/su16020781

Cai, C., Zhu, G., & Ma, M. (2025). A systematic review of AI for interdisciplinary learning: Application contexts, roles, and influences. *Education and Information Technologies*. Advance online publication. DOI: 10.1007/s10639-024-13193-x

Calatayud, V. G., Espinosa, M. P. P., & Vila, R. R. (2021). Artificial intelligence for student assessment: A systematic review. *Applied Sciences (Basel, Switzerland)*, *11*(12), 5467. DOI: 10.3390/app11125467

Carbonell, J. R. (1970). AI in CAI: An artificial-intelligence approach to computer-assisted instruction. *IEEE Transactions on Man-Machine Systems*, *11*(4), 190–202. DOI: 10.1109/TMMS.1970.299942

Carless, D. (2007). Learning-oriented assessment: Conceptual bases and practical implications. *Innovations in Education and Teaching International*, *44*(1), 57–66. https://www.tandfonline.com/doi/abs/10.1080/14703290601081332

Carney, P. A., Mejicano, G. C., Bumsted, T., & Quirk, M. (2018). Assessing learning in the adaptive curriculum. *Medical Teacher*, *40*(8), 813–819. DOI: 10.1080/0142159X.2018.1484083 PMID: 30106597

Cavus, N. (2010). The evaluation of Learning Management Systems using an artificial intelligence fuzzy logic algorithm. *Advances in Engineering Software*, *41*(2), 248–254. DOI: 10.1016/j.advengsoft.2009.07.009

Çetin, H. (2014). Personal data security and determination of its users' awareness level. *Akdeniz İİBF journal, 14*(29), 86-105. https://dergipark.org.tr/en/pub/auiibfd/issue/32333/359291

Chai, C. S., Chiu, T. K. F., Wang, X., Jiang, F., & Lin, X. (2022). Modeling chinese secondary school students' behavioral intentions to learn artificial intelligence with the theory of planned behavior and self-determination theory. *Sustainability*, *15*(1), 605. DOI: 10.3390/su15010605

Chakabwata, W. (2025). The Role of Assistive Technology in Education: A Study of Four SADC States. In Çela, E., Fonkam, M., Vajjhala, N., & Eappen, P. (Eds.), *Advancing Adaptive Education: Technological Innovations for Disability Support* (pp. 163–192). IGI Global Scientific Publishing., DOI: 10.4018/979-8-3693-8227-1.ch007

Chandra, S., Fane, J., Azizi, N., McKenzie-Gray, M., Sager, M., & Dautenhahn, K. (2025). Integrating New Instructional Assistive Technology to Support Academic and Behavioural Instruction for Students with Learning Disabilities. *Journal of Special Education Technology*, *0*(0). Advance online publication. DOI: 10.1177/01626434251314042

Chang, J., & Lu, X. (2019, August). The study on students' participation in personalized learning under the background of artificial intelligence. *In 10th International Conference on Information Technology in Medicine and Education (ITME)* (pp. 555-558). IEEE

Chaudhary, N., Jain, P., & Sharma, C. (2024). From traditional to technological. *Advances in Educational Marketing, Administration, and Leadership*, •••, 79–108. DOI: 10.4018/979-8-3373-1692-5.ch004

Chedrawi, C., Kazoun, N., & Kokkinaki, A. (2024). The role of ai agents in fostering inclusivity for heis' students with special needs against backdrops of the accreditation trend. *Quality Assurance in Education*, *32*(4), 582–596. DOI: 10.1108/qae-01-2024-0010

Chen, L., Chen, P., & Lin, Z. (2020). Artificial intelligence in education: A review. *IEEE Access : Practical Innovations, Open Solutions*, *8*, 75264–75278. DOI: 10.1109/access.2020.2988510

Chen, L., Chen, P., & Lin, Z. (2020). Artificial Intelligence in Education: A Review. *IEEE Access: Practical Innovations, Open Solutions*, *8*, 75264–75278. DOI: 10.1109/ACCESS.2020.2988510

Choi, W. C., Choi, I. C., & Chang, C. (2025). *The Impact of Artificial Intelligence on Education: The Applications, Advantages, Challenges and Researchers' Perspective.* https://doi.org/DOI: 10.20944/preprints202501.1420.v1

Clark, B. (2002). *Growing up gifted: Developing the potential of children at home and at school* (6th ed.). Pearson College Div. Council of Europe (2016). *Competencies for democratic culture: Living together as equals in culturally diverse democratic societies*. Council of Europe. https://rm.coe.int/16806ccc07

Collins, A. (2006). Cognitive apprenticeship. In Sawyer, R. K. (Ed.), *The Cambridge Handbook of the Learning Sciences* (pp. 109–127). Cambridge University Press.

Copley, J., & Ziviani, J. (2004). Barriers to the use of assistive technology for children with multiple disabilities. *Occupational Therapy International*, *11*(4), 229–243. DOI: 10.1002/oti.213 PMID: 15771212

Corrêa, N. K., Galvão, C., Santos, J. W., Del Pino, C., Pinto, E. P., Barbosa, C., Massmann, D., Mambrini, R., Galvão, L., Terem, E., & De Oliveira, N. (2023). Worldwide AI ethics: A review of 200 guidelines and recommendations for AI governance. *Patterns (New York, N.Y.)*, *4*(10), 100857. DOI: 10.1016/j.patter.2023.100857 PMID: 37876898

Cortes-Camarillo, C. A., Alor-Hernández, G., Sánchez-Morales, L. N., Rosales-Morales, V. Y., Rodríguez-Mazahua, L., & Sánchez-Cervantes, J. L. (2019). EduGene: A UIDP-Based Educational App Generator for Multiple Devices and Platforms. *International Journal of Human-Computer Interaction, 35*(3), 274–296. DOI: 10.1080/10447318.2018.1459347

Costa, C., Sousa, C., Rogado, J., & Henriques, S. (2017). Playing digital security: Youth voices on their digital rights. [IJGBL]. *International Journal of Game-Based Learning, 7*(3), 11–25. DOI: 10.4018/IJGBL.2017070102

Crompton, H., & Burke, D. (2023). Artificial intelligence in higher education: The state of the field. *International Journal of Educational Technology in Higher Education, 20*(1). Advance online publication. DOI: 10.1186/s41239-023-00392-8

Csikszentmihalyi, M. (1996). *Creative aging*. Harper Collins.

Cukurova, M. (2025). The interplay of learning, analytics, and artificial intelligence in education: A vision for hybrid intelligence. *British Journal of Educational Technology*. Advance online publication. DOI: 10.1111/bjet.13514

Curtis, M. E., Clingan, S. E., Guo, H., Zhu, Y., Mooney, L. J., & Hser, Y. I. (2022). Disparities in digital access among American rural and urban households and implications for telemedicine-based services. *The Journal of Rural Health, 38*(3), 512–518. DOI: 10.1111/jrh.12614 PMID: 34355427

Da Silva, C. A. G., Ramos, F. N., De Moraes, R. V., & Santos, E. L. D. (2024). ChatGPT: Challenges and benefits in software programming for higher education. *Sustainability, 16*(3), 1245. DOI: 10.3390/su16031245

Dai, Y., Chai, C., Lin, P., Jong, M. S., Guo, Y., & Qin, J. (2020). Promoting students' well-being by developing their readiness for the Artificial Intelligence age. *Sustainability, 12*(16), 6597. DOI: 10.3390/su12166597

Damyanov, K. (2024). Effective Pedagogical Strategies and Support Mechanisms for Enhancing the Learning Outcomes of Students with Special Educational Needs: A Systematic Approach. [IJSRM]. *International Journal of Scientific Research and Management, 12*(10). Advance online publication. DOI: 10.18535/ijsrm/v12i10.el03

Davis, G. A. (2006). *Gifted children and gifted education*. Grest Potential Press.

Daxenberger, F., Deußing, M., Eijkenboom, Q. L., Gust, C., Thamm, J., Hartmann, D., & Sattler, E. (2023). Innovation in actinic keratosis assessment: Artificial intelligence-based approach to lc-oct pro score evaluation. *Cancers (Basel), 15*(18), 4457. DOI: 10.3390/cancers15184457 PMID: 37760425 de Witte, L., Steel, E., Gupta, S., Ramos, V. D., & Roentgen, U. (2018). Assistive technology provision: Towards an international framework for assuring availability and accessibility of affordable high-quality assistive technology. *Disability and Rehabilitation. Assistive Technology*, *13*(5), 467–472. DOI: 10.1080/17483107.2018.1470264 PMID: 29741965

Değirmenci, N., & Demiral, D. G. (2023). Research on information security awareness among university students. *BlackSea Journal of Social Sciences*, 15(29), 613-635. https://dergipark.org.tr/en/pub/ksbd/article/1347428

Deri, M. N., Singh, A., Zaazie, P., & Anandene, D. (2024). Leveraging Artificial Intelligence in Higher Educational Institutions: A Comprehensive Overview. *Revista de Educación y Derecho*, *30*. Advance online publication. DOI: 10.1344/reyd2024.30.45777

Dewi, A. E. R., & Nurfaidah, S. (2024). The Future of Inclusive Education: Preparing Students with Special Needs for the World of Work. *Journal of Pedagogi*, *1*(6), 65–72. DOI: 10.62872/c335h261

Dey, S., & Sahoo, B. B. (2024). Ai integration in education 5.0. *Advances in Educational Technologies and Instructional Design*, •••, 77–92. DOI: 10.4018/979-8-3693-8191-5.ch003

Dhirani, L. L., Mukhtiar, N., Chowdhry, B. S., & Newe, T. (2023). Ethical dilemmas and privacy issues in emerging technologies: A review. *Sensors (Basel)*, *23*(3), 1151. DOI: 10.3390/s23031151 PMID: 36772190

Diehl, J. J., Schmitt, L. M., Villano, M., & Crowell, C. R. (2012). The clinical use of robots for individuals with autism spectrum disorders: A critical review. *Research in Autism Spectrum Disorders*, *6*(1), 249–262. DOI: 10.1016/j.rasd.2011.05.006 PMID: 22125579

Dignum, V. (2021). The role and challenges of education for responsible ai. *London Review of Education*, *19*(1). Advance online publication. DOI: 10.14324/lre.19.1.01

Dirks, S., Bühler, C., Heumader, P., & Miesenberger, K. (2022). Development, Evaluation and Assessment of Assistive Technologies. In Miesenberger, K., Kouroupetroglou, G., Mavrou, K., Manduchi, R., Covarrubias Rodriguez, M., & Penáz, P. (Eds.), Lecture Notes in Computer Science: Vol. 13342. *Computers Helping People with Special Needs. ICCHP-AAATE 2022*. Springer., DOI: 10.1007/978-3-031-08645-8_30

Domingo-Alejo, J. (2024). *AI Integrated Administration tool design with ML Technology for Smart Education System. 42*, 1423–1428. https://doi.org/DOI: 10.1109/icacite60783.2024.10616455

Domingues, C. dos A., & Laplane, A. L. F. (2024). Assistive technology in public policies: Trends in the international debate and implications for Brazil. *Disability and Rehabilitation. Assistive Technology*, *19*(8), 2761–2773. DOI: 10.1080/17483107.2024.2316896 PMID: 38372271

Dong, Z., & Sha, N. (2023). Research on the current situation and countermeasures of cultivating talents in recreational sports under the perspective of artificial intelligence. *Applied Mathematics and Nonlinear Sciences*, *9*(1). Advance online publication. DOI: 10.2478/amns.2023.2.00161

Dron, J. (2018). Smart learning environments, and not so smart learning environments: A systems view. *Smart Learning Environments*, *5*(1), 25. DOI: 10.1186/s40561-018-0075-9

Eager, B., & Brunton, R. (2023). Prompting higher education towards AI-augmented teaching and learning practice. *Journal of University Teaching & Learning Practice*, *20*(5). Advance online publication. DOI: 10.53761/1.20.5.02

Ebuenyi, I. D., Smith, E. M., Kafumba, J., Jamali, M. Z., Munthali, A., & MacLachlan, M. (2020). Implementation of the Assistive Product List (APL) in Malawi through development of appropriate policy and systems: An action research protocol. *BMJ Open*, *10*(11), e040281. PMID: 33158833

Ecker, J., Eckert, G., & Cummings, E. (2025). Augmenting gifted education through artificial intelligence: A four-dimensional framework for AI tutoring integration. *Journal of Advanced Academics*, *36*(4), 879–896. DOI: 10.1177/1932202X251356326

Ekin, S. (2023). *Prompt Engineering for ChatGPT: A quick guide to techniques, tips, and best practices. TechRxiv*. https://doi.org/DOI: 10.36227/techrxiv.22683919

Erbaşı, Z., Tural, B., & Çoşkuner, İ. (2023). The role and potential of artificial intelligence and gamification in education: The example of vakıf participation bank. *Orclever Proceedings of Research and Development*, *3*(1), 243–254. DOI: 10.56038/oprd.v3i1.329

European Commission Directorate-General for Education Youth Sport Culture. (2022). Ethical Guidelines on the Use of Artificial Intelligence (AI) and Data in Teaching and Learning for Educators. *Publications Office of the European Union* https://op.europa.eu/en/publication-detail/-/publication/d81a0d54-5348-11ed-92ed-01aa75ed71a1/language-en

European Commission. (2023). Proposal for a Regulation laying down additional procedural rules relating to the enforcement of GDPR. https://commission.europa.eu/publications/proposal-regulation-laying-down-additional-procedural-rules-relating-enforcement-gdpr_en

European Commission. (2024). *Artificial Intelligence Act.* https://data.europa.eu/eli/reg/2024/1689/oj

Facione, P. A. (1990). *Critical thinking: A statement of expert consensus for purposes of educational assessment and instruction.* The California Academic Press.

Fadel, C., Bialik, M., & Trilling, B. (2015). *Four dimension education. The competence learner need to succeed.* The Center For Curriculum Redesign.

Farid, G., Warraich, N. F., & Iftikhar, S. (2023). Digital information security management policy in academic libraries: A systematic review (2010–2022). *Journal of Information Science*, •••, 1–15. DOI: 10.1177/01655515231160026

Farooqi, M. T. K., Amanat, I., & Awan, S. M. (2024). Ethical Considerations and Challenges in the Integration of Artificial Intelligence in Education. *Systematic Reviews*, *3*(4), 35–50. DOI: 10.69565/jems.v3i4.314

Felicia, A., Sharif, S., Wong, W., & Marriappan, M. (2014). Innovation of assistive technologies in special education: A review. *Journal of Enhanced Research in Educational Development*, *2*(3), 25–38.

Fernández-Batanero, J. M., Montenegro-Rueda, M., Fernández-Cerero, J., & García-Martínez, I. (2022). Assistive technology for the inclusion of students with disabilities: A systematic review. *Educational Technology Research and Development*, *70*, 1911–1930. DOI: 10.1007/s11423-022-10127-7

Fineberga, A., Savageb, M., Austinc, A., Boitend, S., Droopd, J., Allen, M., Heydte, P., Sondergaard, D., & Mitra, G. (2019). ATscale – Establishing a Cross-Sector Partnership to Increase Access to Assistive Technology. https://discovery.ucl.ac.uk/id/eprint/10084647/

Fırat Güner, D. (2021). Protection of children's personal data. (Unpublished doctoral dissertation). Istanbul Bilgi University.

Fırat, M. (2015). A new field in educational technology research: learning analytics. *Mersin University Faculty of Education Journal, 11*(3), 870-882

Floridi, L., Cowls, J., Beltrametti, M., Chatila, R., Chazerand, P., Dignum, V., Luetge, C., Madelin, R., Pagallo, U., Rossi, F., Schafer, B., Valcke, P., & Vayena, E. (2018). AI4People—An Ethical Framework for a Good AI Society: Opportunities, risks, principles, and recommendations. *Minds and Machines*, *28*(4), 689–707. DOI: 10.1007/s11023-018-9482-5 PMID: 30930541

Fong, T., Nourbakhsh, I., & Dautenhahn, K. (2003). A survey of socially interactive robots. *Robotics and Autonomous Systems*, *42*, 143–166. DOI: 10.1016/S0921-8890(02)00372-X

Forsell, K., Tibshirani, R., & Brunskill, E. (2023). *White Paper: The science behind the scootpad mastery-based adaptive learning platform.* https://learningexplorer.com/wp-content/uploads/2024/04/ScootPad-Mastery-Research-White-Paper.pdf

Fortino, G., Mangione, F., & Pupo, F. (2025). Intersezione tra intelligenza artificiale generativa e educazione: Un'ipotesi. *Journal of Educational. Cultural and Psychological Studies*, *30*. Advance online publication. DOI: 10.7358/ecps-2024-030-fort

Fteiha, M., Al-Rashaida, M., Elsori, D., Khalil, A., & Bustami, G. (2024). Obstacles for using assistive technology in centres of special needs in the UAE. *Disability and Rehabilitation. Assistive Technology*, *19*(8), 2934–2944. DOI: 10.1080/17483107.2024.2323698 PMID: 38436086

Fussell, R. S. (2005, October). Protecting information security availability via self-adapting intelligent agents. In *MILCOM 2005-2005 IEEE Military Communications Conference* (pp. 2977–2982). IEEE.

Gabor, D. (December 1971). Holography, 1948-1971. *Nobel Lecture*, December 11, 1971. https://www.nobelprize.org/uploads/2018/06/gabor-lecture.pdf

Gabor, D. (1948). A new microscopic principle. *Nature*, *161*(4098), 777–778. https://scispace.com/pdf/a-new-microscopic-principle-2a06oi3wvh.pdf PMID: 18860291

Garçon, L., Nakatani, Y., Khasnabis, C., Berumen, A., Lapitan, J., Walker, L., Ross, A., & Borg, J. (2016). Medical and Assistive Health Technology: Meeting the Needs of Aging Populations. *The Gerontologist*, *56*, 293–302. DOI: 10.1093/geront/gnw005 PMID: 26994268

Gaur, A., Sharan, H. O., & Kumar, R. (2024). *AI in Education*. IGI Global., DOI: 10.4018/979-8-3693-2964-1.ch003

Ghosh, M. (2024). *Using AI for Student Success*. 236–243. https://doi.org/DOI: 10.1201/9781032694375-13

Gillpatrick, T. (2020). Innovation and the Digital Transformation of Education. *Sınırsız Eğitim ve Araştırma Dergisi*, *5*(3), 194–201. DOI: 10.29250/sead.797372

Ginsberg, M. (2012). *Essentials of artificial intelligence*. Morgan Kaufmann Publishers.

Giri, A. K. (2024). Revolutionizing Student Evaluation. *Advances in Educational Technologies and Instructional Design Book Series*, 333–362. https://doi.org/DOI: 10.4018/979-8-3693-6170-2.ch012

Gligorea, I., Cioca, M., Oancea, R., Gorski, A., Gorski, H., & Tudorache, P. (2023). *Adaptive Learning Using Artificial Intelligence in e-Learning: A Literature Review*. Neveléstudomány., DOI: 10.3390/educsci13121216

Göçen, A., & Aydemir, F. (2020). Artificial intelligence in education and schools. *Research on Education and Media*, *12*(1), 13–21. DOI: 10.2478/rem-2020-0003

Goh, Y., & Abdul Rahman, N. A. (2024). Personalized Language Learning With AI for Pedagogical and Andragogical Approaches. *Advances in Educational Technologies and Instructional Design Book Series*, 153–174. https://doi.org/DOI: 10.4018/979-8-3693-6130-6.ch007

Goodfellow, I., Bengio, Y., & Courville, A. (2016). *Deep learning*. MIT Press.

Google. (2024). *Generative AI for Educators*. Grow With Google. Retrieved June 20, 2025, from https://grow.google/ai-for-educators/

Grandbastien, M., Luckin, R., Mizoguchi, R., & Aleven, V. (2016). Preface to the ijaied 25th anniversary issue. *International Journal of Artificial Intelligence in Education*, *26*(1), 1–3. DOI: 10.1007/s40593-015-0092-6

Grassegger, T., & Nedbal, D. (2021). The role of employees' information security awareness on the intention to resist social engineering. *Procedia Computer Science*, *181*, 59–66. DOI: 10.1016/j.procs.2021.01.103

Grimaud, L. M., & Gathu, C. (2024). Integrating artificial intelligence ethics education into the undergraduate medical curriculum - a scoping review. (preprint). https://doi.org/DOI: 10.2196/preprints.57746

Grissom, J. A., Egalite, A. J., & Lindsay, C. A. (2021). *How principals affect students and schools: A systematic synthesis of two decades of research*. The Wallace Foundation. Retrieved June 23, 2025, from http://www.wallacefoundation.org/principalsynthesis

Guan, C., Mou, J., & Jiang, Z. (2020). Artificial intelligence innovation in education: A twenty-year data-driven historical analysis. *International Journal of Innovation Studies*, *4*(4), 134–147. DOI: 10.1016/j.ijis.2020.09.001

Guillén-Martínez, D., Alcázar-Espinoza, J. A., Rámirez-Sánchez, I., Samaniego-Cobo, T., & Villacís-Macias, C. (2025). Policies, Assistive Technologies, and Barriers in Inclusive Education: A Global Systematic Review (2019-2024). *Journal of Posthumanism*, *5*(2), 208–218. DOI: 10.63332/joph.v5i2.418

Güler, C., & Furat, F. (2022). The contribution of records management and archival practices to information security principles. *Turkish Librarianship*, *36*(1), 74–89.

Gültekin, V., & Özel, N. (2023). Information security awareness of university students: Example of ankara university. *Journal of International Management*, *6*(2), 310–331. https://dergipark.org.tr/tr/pub/by/issue/81900/1366855

Gümüş, H. T., & Eyüpoğlu, C. (2022). Anonymization techniques and attack types in big data: Application examples. *İstanbul Commerce University. Journal of Science*, *21*(42), 422–441.

Gündüzalp, C. (2021). University employees' awareness of digital data and personal cyber security (a case study of IT departments). *Journal of Computer and Education Research*, *9*(18), 598–625.

Güngör, M. (2015). *National information security: Strategy and institutional structuring*. Republic of Turkey Ministry of Development.

Guo, H., Johnson, M., Saldivia, L., Worthington, M., & Ercikan, K. (2024). Human-centered AI for discovering student engagement profiles on large-scale educational assessments. *Egitimde ve Psikolojide Ölçme ve Degerlendirme Dergisi*. Advance online publication. DOI: 10.21031/epod.1532846

Gupta, T. R. (2024). Adaptive Learning Systems: Harnessing AI to Personalize Educational Outcomes. *International Journal For Science Technology And Engineering*, *12*(11), 458–464. DOI: 10.22214/ijraset.2024.65088

Gutiérrez, L. (2023). Artificial intelligence in language education: Navigating the potential and challenges of chatbots and nlp. *Research Studies in English Language Teaching and Learning*, *1*(3), 180–191. DOI: 10.62583/rseltl.v1i3.44

Gyawali, Y. P., & Mehandroo, M. (2022). Artificial intelligence in english language teaching: Navigating the future with emerging perspectives. *Journal of Language and Linguistics in Society*, *26*, 21–27. DOI: 10.55529/jlls.26.21.27

HaeJin., L., Frank, S., Ruohan, Z., Hannah, V., Dong, W., & Nigel, B. (2025). *Learning behaviors mediate the effect of AI-powered support for metacognitive calibration on learning outcomes*. In CHI Conference on Human Factors in Computing Systems (CHI '25), April 26–May01, 2025. https://doi.org/DOI: 10.1145/3706598.3713960

Halkiopoulos, C., & Gkintoni, E. (2024). Leveraging AI in e-learning: Personalized learning and adaptive assessment through cognitive neuropsychology—A systematic analysis. *Electronics (Basel)*, *13*(18), 3762. DOI: 10.3390/electronics13183762

Hamarat, E. (2019). *21.yüzyıl becerileri odağında Türkiye'nin eğitim politikaları* [Türkiye's education policies focused on 21st century skills]. Seta Analiz. https://www.setav.org/assets/uploads/2019/04/272A.pdf

Hamdi, M. (2024). *How AI is Transforming and Shaping the Future of Education*. 000115–000116. https://doi.org/DOI: 10.1109/ines63318.2024.10629089

Hardaker, G., & Glenn, L. E. (2025). Artificial intelligence for personalized learning: A systematic literature review. *International Journal of Information and Learning Technology*. https://doi.org/DOI: 10.1108/ijilt-07-2024-0160

Harris, K., Burley, H., McLachlan, R., Bowman, M., Macaldowie, A., Taylor, K., & Chambers, G. M. (2016). Socio-economic disparities in access to assisted reproductive technologies in Australia. *Reproductive Biomedicine Online*, *33*(5), 575–584. DOI: 10.1016/j.rbmo.2016.07.012 PMID: 27595434

Haseski, H. I. (2019). What do Turkish pre-service teachers think about artificial intelligence? *International Journal of Computer Science Education in Schools*, *3*(2). Advance online publication. DOI: 10.21585/ijcses.v3i2.55

Hashimoto, T., Kato, N., & Kobayashi, H. (2011). Development of educational system with the android robot SAYA and evaluation. *International Journal of Advanced Robotic Systems*, *8*(3), 51–61. DOI: 10.5772/10667

Hattie, J., & Timperley, H. (2007). The power of feedback. *Review of Educational Research*, *77*(1), 81–112. DOI: 10.3102/003465430298487

Haug, C. J., & Drazen, J. M. (2023). Artificial intelligence and machine learning in clinical medicine. *The New England Journal of Medicine*, *388*(13), 1201–1208. DOI: 10.1056/nejmra2302038 PMID: 36988595

Hekim, H. (2015). *Phishing attacks*. Retrieved from academia: http://www.academia.edu/35136881/Oltalama_Phishing_Saldirilari

Hemmingsson, H., Lidström, H., & Nygård, L. (2009). Use of assistive technology devices in mainstream schools: Students' perspective. *The American Journal of Occupational Therapy, 63*(4), 463–472. DOI: 10.5014/AJOT.63.4.463 PMID: 19708475

Hendler, J. (2009). Web 3.0 emerging. *Computer, 42*(1), 111–113. DOI: 10.1109/MC.2009.30

Hersh, M., & Mouroutsou, S. (2019). Learning technology and disability—Overcoming barriers to inclusion: Evidence from a multicountry study. *British Journal of Educational Technology, 50*(6), 3329–3344. DOI: 10.1111/bjet.12737

High-Level Expert Group on Artificial Intelligence [HLEG]. (2019). *A definition of Artificial Intelligence: Main capabilities and scientific disciplines*. European Commission. Retrieved June 19, 2025, from https://digital-strategy.ec.europa.eu/en/library/definition-artificial-intelligence-main-capabilities-and-scientific-disciplines

Hinojo-Lucena, F., Díaz, I. A., Reche, M. P. C., & Rodríguez, J. M. R. (2019). Artificial intelligence in higher education: A bibliometric study on its impact in the scientific literature. *Education Sciences, 9*(1), 51. DOI: 10.3390/educsci9010051

Hirschberg, J., & Manning, C. D. (2015). Advances in natural language processing. *Science, 349*(6245), 261–266. DOI: 10.1126/science.aaa8685 PMID: 26185244

Hitchcock, C., & Stahl, S. (2003). Assistive technology, universal design, universal design for learning: Improved learning opportunities. *Journal of Special Education Technology, 18*(4), 45–52. DOI: 10.1177/016264340301800404

Holmes, W., Bialik, M., & Fadel, C. (2019). *Artificial intelligence in Education: Promises and implications for teaching & learning*. The Center for Curriculum Redesign.

Holmes, W., Bialik, M., & Fadel, C. (2019). *Artificial intelligence in education: Promises and implications for teaching and learning*. Center for Curriculum Redesign., http://bit.ly/AIED-BOOK

Holmes, W., & Tuomi, I. (2022). State of the art and practice in AI in education. *European Journal of Education, 57*(4), 542–570. DOI: 10.1111/ejed.12533

Hong, Y., Nguyen, A., Dang, B., & Nguyen, B.-P. T. (2022). Data ethics framework for artificial intelligence in education (AIED). In the *2022 International Conference on Advanced Learning Technologies (ICALT)* (pp. 297–301). IEEE. https://doi.org/DOI: 10.1109/ICALT55010.2022.00095

Hossain, S. B., Jiang, N., Zhou, Q., Li, X., Chiang, W., Lyu, Y., Nguyen, H., & Tripp, O. (2024). A deep dive into large language models for automated bug localization and repair. In *Proceedings of the ACM on Software Engineering*. (Vol. 1, Issue FSE, pp. 1471–1493). Association for Computing Machinery. https://doi.org/DOI: 10.1145/3660773

Hosseinkhani, N. T. (2025). Evaluating the economic impact, equity implications, and long-term prospects of AI-powered personalized learning in education by mid-century. https://doi.org/DOI: 10.31219/osf.io/j8kh4_v1

Huang, Y.-M., Lin, Y.-T., & Cheng, S.-C. (2009). An adaptive testing system for supporting versatile educational assessment. *Computers & Education*, *52*(1), 53–67. DOI: 10.1016/j.compedu.2008.06.007

Hwang, I., Wakefield, R., Kim, S., & Kim, T. (2021). Security awareness: The first step in information security compliance behavior. *Journal of Computer Information Systems*, *61*(4), 345–356.

Iatsyshyn, A. V., Kovach, V. O., Lyubchak, V. O., Zuban, Y. O., Piven, A. G., Sokolyuk, O. M., Iatsyshyn, A. V., Popov, O. O., Artemchuk, V. O., & Shyshkina, M. P. (2020). *Application of augmented reality technologies for education projects preparation*. [б. в.]. https://doi.org/DOI: 10.31812/123456789/3856

İçen, M. (2022). The future of education utilizing artificial intelligence in Turkey. *Humanities & Social Sciences Communications*, *9*, 268. DOI: 10.1057/s41599-022-01284-4

Ifenthaler, D., & Schumacher, C. (2023). Reciprocal issues of artificial and human intelligence in education. *Journal of Research on Technology in Education*, *55*(1), 1–6. DOI: 10.1080/15391523.2022.2154511

Iman, M. Z., Asis, A. A., & Rahma, A. U. Z. (2024). Enhancing Personalized Learning: The Impact of Artificial Intelligence in Education. *Edu Spectrum.*, *1*(2), 101–112. DOI: 10.70063/eduspectrum.v1i2.55

Inagaki, K., Bradshaw, T., Murgia, M., & Garrahan, M. (2023, September 28). OpenAI and Jony Ive in talks to raise “bn from SoftBank for AI device venture. *Financial Times*. https://www.ft.com/content/4c64ffc1-f57b-4e22-a4a5-f9f90a7419b7

International Federation of Robotics. (2017). *Executive Summary World Robotics 2017 Industrial Robots.* Retrieved from https://ifr.org/downloads/press/Executive_Summary_WR_2017_Industrial_Robots.pdf

Isaacs, M., Majeed, A. P. P. A., Moussa, K. H., & Shodipo, D. (2024). Design and implementation of an ethical ai-based teaching assistant for iot security education. *African Journal of Inter/Multidisciplinary Studies, 6*(1). https://doi.org/DOI: 10.51415/ajims.v6i1.1586

Ishaq, M., Abid, K., Farooq, U., Ishaq, K., Safie, N., & Abid, A. (2025). A Framework for Designing Courses by Synergizing Project-Based Learning With Gamification. *Human Behavior and Emerging Technologies*, *2025*(1), 9915839. DOI: 10.1155/hbe2/9915839

İşler, B., & Kılıç, M. (2021). Eğitimde yapay zekâ kullanımı ve gelişimi. *Yeni Medya Elektronik Dergisi*, *5*(1), 1–11. DOI: 10.17932/IAU.EJNM.25480200.2021/ejnm_v5i1001

Ismaili, J., & Ibrahimi, E. (2017). Mobile learning as alternative to assistive technology devices for special needs students. *Education and Information Technologies*, *22*, 883–899. DOI: 10.1007/s10639-015-9462-9

ISO/IEC. (2014). *ISO/IEC Guide 71:2014 Guide for addressing accessibility in standards*. International Organization for Standardization.

ISTE. (2017). *ISTE Standards.* International Society for Technology in Education. https://www.iste.org/standards

Jensen, P. E. (2005). A Contextual Theory of Learning and the Learning Organization. *Knowledge and Process Management*, *12*(1), 53–64.

Ji, Z., Lee, N., Frieske, R., Yu, T., Su, D., Xu, Y., Ishii, E., Bang, Y. J., Madotto, A., & Fung, P. (2022). Survey of hallucination in natural language generation. *ACM Computing Surveys*, *55*(12), 1–38. DOI: 10.1145/3571730

Jobin, A., Ienca, M., & Vayena, E. (2019). The global landscape of ai ethics guidelines. *Nature Machine Intelligence*, *1*(9), 389–399. DOI: 10.1038/s42256-019-0088-2

Johnson, D. W., Johnson, R. T., & Holubec, E. J. (1990). *Cooperation in the Classroom*. Interaction Book Co.

Johnson, M., Liu, X., & McCaffrey, D. F. (2022). Psychometric methods to evaluate measurement and algorithmic bias in automated scoring. *Journal of Educational Measurement*, *59*(3), 338–361. DOI: 10.1111/jedm.12335

Jones, B. A., Peterson-Ahmad, M., Fields, M., & Williams, N. (2020). Training Preservice Teachers to Match Assistive Technology to Student Needs. *Journal of Special Education Technology, 36*(4), 271-283. https://doi.org/ (Original work published 2021)DOI: 10.1177/0162643420918337

Jordan, M. I., & Mitchell, T. M. (2015). Machine learning: Trends, perspectives, and prospects. *Science, 349*(6245), 255–260. DOI: 10.1126/science.aaa8415 PMID: 26185243

Josué, A., Bedoya-Flores, M. C., Mosquera-Quiñonez, E. F., Mesías-Simisterra, Á. E., & Bautista-Sánchez, J. V. (2023). Educational Platforms: Digital Tools for the teaching-learning process in Education. *Ibero-American Journal of Education & Society Research*, *3*(1), 259–263.

Judge, S., & Simms, K. A. (2009). Assistive Technology Training at the Pre-Service Level: A National Snapshot of Teacher Preparation Programs. *Teacher Education and Special Education, 32*(1), 33-44. https://doi.org/ (Original work published 2009) DOI: 10.1177/0888406408330868

Junaid, M., Arslan, S., Lee, T., & Kim, H. (2022). Optimal architecture of Floating-Point arithmetic for neural network training processors. *Sensors (Basel), 22*(3), 1230. DOI: 10.3390/s22031230 PMID: 35161975

Jurafsky, D., & Martin, J. H. (2024). *Speech and language processing*. Retrieved 19 June 2025, from https://web.stanford.edu/~jurafsky/slp3/

Kadaruddin, K. (2023). Empowering education through generative ai: Innovative instructional strategies for tomorrow's learners. *International Journal of Business, Law, and Education*, *4*(2), 618–625. DOI: 10.56442/ijble.v4i2.215

Kaiser, G., & Kaiser, S. (2024). AI in Education. *Advances in Educational Technologies and Instructional Design Book Series*, 241–260. https://doi.org/DOI: 10.4018/979-8-3693-6130-6.ch010

Kalseth, K., & Cummings, S. (2001). Knowledge management: Development strategy or business strategy? *Information Development*, *17*(3), 163–172.

Kamalov, F., Calonge, D. S., & Gurrib, I. (2023). New era of artificial intelligence in education: Towards a sustainable multifaceted revolution. *Sustainability*, *15*(16), 12451. DOI: 10.3390/su151612451

Kamenskih, A. (2022). The analysis of security and privacy risks in smart education environments. *Journal of Smart Cities and Society*, *1*(1), 17–29. DOI: 10.3233/SCS-210114

Kamphuis, C., Barsom, E., Schijven, M., & Christoph, N. (2014). Augmented reality in medical education? *Perspectives on Medical Education*, *3*(4), 300–311. DOI: 10.1007/s40037-013-0107-7 PMID: 24464832

Kanero, J., Geçkin, V., Oranç, C., Mamus, E., Küntay, A. C., & Göksun, T. (2018). Social Robots for Early Language Learning: Current Evidence and Future Directions. *Child Development Perspectives*, *12*, 146–151. DOI: 10.1111/cdep.12277

Kaplan, A., & Haenlein, M. (2018). Siri, Siri, in my hand: Who is the fairest in the land? On the interpretations, illustrations, and implications of artificial intelligence. *Business Horizons*, *62*(1), 15–25. DOI: 10.1016/j.bushor.2018.08.004

Karaibrahimoğlu, A., İnce, F., Hassanzadeh, G., Alizadeh, A. M., Bagheri, K., Yucel, I., & Shariat, A. (2024). Ethical considerations in telehealth and artificial intelligence for work related musculoskeletal disorders: A scoping review. *Work (Reading, Mass.)*, *79*(3), 1577–1588. DOI: 10.3233/wor-240187 PMID: 39093108

Karaoğlan Yılmaz, D. F. G., Yılmaz, D. R., & Sezer, B. (2014). Secure information and communication technology usage behavior of university students and an overview to information security training. *Bartın University Journal of Faculty of Education*, *3*(1), 176–199. DOI: 10.14686/BUEFAD.201416213

Karayel, T., & Akbıyık, A. (2023). A global perspective of cybersecurity research: Publication trends and research directions. *Journal of Information Technology*, *16*(3), 221–235. https://dergipark.org.tr/en/pub/gazibtd/issue/79101/1291783

Karmakar, S., & Das, T. K. (2024). *Effect of artificial intelligence on education*. 198–211. https://doi.org/DOI: 10.1201/9781003536796-8

Karsenti, T. (2019). Artificial Intelligence in Education: The Urgent Need to Prepare Teachers for Tomorrow's Schools. *Formation et Profession*, 27(1), 112-116. https://doi.org/. 2019.a166DOI: 10.18162/fp

Kasneci, E., Sessler, K., Küchemann, S., Bannert, M., Dementieva, D., Fischer, F., Gasser, U., Groh, G., Günnemann, S., Hüllermeier, E., Krusche, S., Kutyniok, G., Michaeli, T., Nerdel, C., Pfeffer, J., Poquet, O., Sailer, M., Schmidt, A., Seidel, T., & Kasneci, G. (2023). ChatGPT for good? On opportunities and challenges of large language models for education. *Learning and Individual Differences*, *103*, 102274. DOI: 10.1016/j.lindif.2023.102274

Kasneci, E., Seßler, K., Küchemann, S., Bannert, M., Dementieva, D., Fischer, F., & Kasneci, G. (2023). Chatgpt for good? on opportunities and challenges of large language models for education. https://doi.org/DOI: 10.35542/osf.io/5er8f

Kaufman, J. C., & Beghetto, R. A. (2009). Beyond big and little: The four c model of creativity. *Review of General Psychology*, *13*(1), 1–12. DOI: 10.1037/a0013688

Kaur, S., Budhraja, K., Pahuja, A., Nayyar, V., & Saluja, S. (2024). Leveraging Artificial Intelligence in Education. *Advances in Marketing, Customer Relationship Management, and e-Services Book Series*, 125–140. https://doi.org/DOI: 10.4018/979-8-3693-6660-8.ch010

Kayabaş, İ. (2010). *Yapay zekâ sohbet ajanlarının uzaktan eğitimde öğrenci destek hizmeti olarak kullanılabilirliği*. Anadolu Üniversitesi Sosyal Bilimler Enstitüsü Uzaktan Eğitim Anabilim Dalı, Yüksek Lisans Tezi.

Kayyali, M. (2025). AI in Higher Education. *Advances in Educational Technologies and Instructional Design Book Series*, 31–62. https://doi.org/DOI: 10.4018/979-8-3693-7949-3.ch002

Keser, H., & Güldüren, C. (2015). Development of information security awareness scale. *K.U. Kastamonu Education Journal*, *23*(3), 1167–1184. DOI: 10.17051/io.2016.27218

Khademi, A. (2023). Can chatgpt and bard generate aligned assessment items? a reliability analysis against human performance. *Journal of Applied Learning &Amp. Teaching*, *6*(1). Advance online publication. DOI: 10.37074/jalt.2023.6.1.28

Khan, I., Ahmad, A. R., Jabeur, N., & Mahdi, M. N. (2021). An artificial intelligence approach to monitor student performance and devise preventive measures. *Smart Learning Environments*, *8*(1), 17. DOI: 10.1186/s40561-021-00161-y

Khasawneh, M. A. S. (2024). Evaluating the efficacy of tablet-based assistive technology in Saudi special education settings. *International Journal of Learning. Teaching and Educational Research*, *23*(6), 547–561. DOI: 10.26803/ijlter.23.6.25

Khosravi, H., Shum, S. B., Chen, G., Conati, C., Tsai, Y., Kay, J., Knight, S., Martinez-Maldonado, R., Sadiq, S., & Gašević, D. (2022). Explainable Artificial Intelligence in education. *Computers and Education Artificial Intelligence*, *3*, 100074. DOI: 10.1016/j.caeai.2022.100074

Khosravizadeh, O. (2023). Analysis of the impact of vygotsky's collaborative learning theory on the development of group skills. *Journal of Study and Innovation in Education and Development*, *3*(1), 1–14. DOI: 10.61838/jsied.3.1.1

Khotamov, I. S., Umarov, E. G., Kuznetsov, V. P., Smirnova, Z. V., & Kutepov, M. M. (2023). Digital Transformation in the Modern Educational System. In Popkova, E. G., & Sergi, B. S. (Eds.), *Anti-Crisis Approach to the Provision of the Environmental Sustainability of Economy* (pp. 195–199). Springer Nature Singapore., DOI: 10.1007/978-981-99-2198-0_20

Kiemde, S. M. A., & Kora, A. D. (2021). Towards an ethics of ai in Africa: Rule of education. *AI and Ethics*, *2*(1), 35–40. DOI: 10.1007/s43681-021-00106-8

Kılıç, T. (2021). *Yeni bilim: Bağlantısallık – Yeni kültür: Yaşamdaşlık: "Beyin Nedir?"den, "Yaşam Nedir?"e bir bilim serüveni* [New science: Interconnectedness – New culture: Coexistence: A scientific journey from 'What is the brain?' to 'What is life?']. Ayrıntı Yayınları.

Kınacı, B. F., Güven, E. Y., Seyyarer, E., Biçek, E., Kına, E., Ayata, F., & Yiner, Z. (2023). *Information and information systems security*. Nobel Academic Publishing.

Klímová, B., Pikhart, M., & Kacetl, J. (2023). Ethical issues of the use of AI-driven mobile apps for education. *Frontiers in Public Health, 10*, 1118116. DOI: 10.3389/fpubh.2022.1118116 PMID: 36711343

Kobayashi, K. M., Grenier, A., & Gontcharov, I. (2021). Learning Activity: Embedding Healthcare Technologies in Real-World Contexts—Developing the Scale-Up, Spread, and Sustainability of Assistive Technologies in Health Systems. In Sixsmith, A., Sixsmith, J., Mihailidis, A., & Fang, M. L. (Eds.), *Knowledge, Innovation, and Impact: A Guide for the Engaged Health Researcher. International Perspectives on Social Policy, Administration, and Practice*. Springer., DOI: 10.1007/978-3-030-34390-3_48

Koblyakov, P. (2024). ChatGPT in the Educational Landscape: A Comprehensive Guide.

Konishi, E., Saiki, T., Kamiyama, H., Nishiya, K., Tsunekawa, K., Imafuku, R., & Suzuki, Y. (2020). Improved cognitive apprenticeship clinical teaching after a faculty development program. *Pediatrics International*, *62*(5), 542–548. DOI: 10.1111/ped.14095 PMID: 31834972

Korucu, O. (2021). Effects of the new normal world order to cyber and information security. *Journal of Management Information Systems, 7*(1), 2021, 44-60, Issn: 2148-3752

Kotsi, S., Handrinou, S., Iatraki, G., & Soulis, S.-G. (2025). A Review of Artificial Intelligence Interventions for Students with Autism Spectrum Disorder. *Disabilities*, *5*(1), 7. DOI: 10.3390/disabilities5010007

Kotsis, K. T. (2025). Issues between artificial intelligence and personal data in education. *International Review of Education*, *13*(1), 45. DOI: 10.5296/ire.v13i1.22850

Kretzschmar, V., Sailer, A., Wertenauer, M., & Seitz, J. (2024). Enhanced educational experiences through personalized and AI-based learning. *International Journal on Studies in Education*, *6*(2), 191–209. DOI: 10.46328/ijonse.206

Krombholz, K., Hobel, H., Huber, M., & Weippl, E. (2015). Advanced social engineering attacks. *Journal of Information Security and Applications*, *22*, 113–122.

Küçükvardar, M., & Tıngöy, Ö. (2018). Investigation of technology addiction based on symptoms. AJIT-e. *Online Academic Journal of Information Technology*, *9*(35), 111–123. DOI: 10.5824/1309-1581.2018.5.008.x

Kuddus, K. (2022). Artificial Intelligence in Language Learning: Practices and Prospects. In Mire, A., Malik, S., & Tyagi, A. K. (Eds.), *Advanced Analytics and Deep Learning Models* (1st ed., pp. 1–17). Wiley., DOI: 10.1002/9781119792437.ch1

Kumar, A. & Vinita. (2023). Solution-focused approach towards improved access to assistive mobility technology and devices in low and middle-income countries: A narrative review. *Philippine Journal of Allied Health Sciences*, *7*(1), 11–17. DOI: 10.36413/pjahs.0701.003

Kumar, D., Haque, M. A., Mishra, K., Islam, F., Mishra, B. K., & Ahmad, S. (2023). Exploring the transformative role of artificial intelligence and metaverse in education: A comprehensive review. *Metaverse Basic and Applied Research*, *2*, 55. DOI: 10.56294/mr202355

Kumar, J., Jieyao, Z., & Soeiro, J. D. (2024). *Empowering Lifelong Learning*. IGI Global., DOI: 10.4018/979-8-3693-6955-5.ch003

Kumar, S. (2023). Impact of Digitalization in Higher Education and Smart Learning Techniques. In Nadda, V., Tyagi, P. K., Moniz Vieira, R., & Tyagi, P. (Eds.), *Advances in Hospitality, Tourism, and the Services Industry* (pp. 198–207). IGI Global., DOI: 10.4018/979-8-3693-0650-5.ch013

Kumar, S. (2024). Impact of Assessment on Childhood Education Theories and Practice. In Badea, M., & Suditu, M. (Eds.), *Advances in Early Childhood and K-12 Education* (pp. 84–101). IGI Global., DOI: 10.4018/979-8-3693-0956-8.ch004

Kumar, S., & Bayram, G. E. (2025). The effect on education and training. In *Greening Our Economy for a Sustainable Future* (pp. 177–185). Elsevier., DOI: 10.1016/B978-0-443-23603-7.00014-5

Kumar, S., Talukder, M. B., & Pego, A. (Eds.). (2024). *Utilizing Smart Technology and AI in Hybrid Tourism and Hospitality*. IGI Global., DOI: 10.4018/979-8-3693-1978-9

Kurniawan, Y., & Halim, E. (2013). *Data Warehouse and Data Mining to Predict Student Academic Performance in Schools: A Case Study (Perspective Application and Benefits)*. 2013 IEEE International Conference on Teaching, Assessment and Learning for Engineering (TALE), Kuta/Indonesia.

Kurzweil, R. (2005). The singularity is near. In *Ethics and emerging technologies* (pp. 393–406). Palgrave Macmillan UK., https://link.springer.com/chapter/10.1057/9781137349088_26

Laaziri, M., Khoulji, S., Benmoussa, K., & Kerkeb, M. L. (2018). Outlining an intelligent tutoring system for a university cooperation information system. *Engineering, Technology &. Applied Scientific Research*, *8*(5), 3427–3431. DOI: 10.48084/etasr.2158

Lamond, B., & Cunningham, T. (2019). Understanding Teacher Perceptions of Assistive Technology. *Journal of Special Education Technology, 35*(2), 97-108. https://doi.org/ (Original work published 2020)DOI: 10.1177/0162643419841550

Leahy, J. A., & Lane, J. P. (2010). Knowledge from Research and Practice on the Barriers and Carriers to Successful Technology Transfer for Assistive Technology Devices. *Assistive Technology Outcomes and Benefits*, *6*(1), 73–86.

Lee, A. V. Y. (2023). Supporting students' generation of feedback in large-scale online course with artificial intelligence-enabled evaluation. *Studies in Educational Evaluation*, *77*, 101250. DOI: 10.1016/j.stueduc.2023.101250

Lee, S. S., & Moore, R. L. (2024). Harnessing Generative AI (GenAI) for Automated Feedback in Higher Education: A Systematic Review. *Online Learning : the Official Journal of the Online Learning Consortium*, *28*(3). Advance online publication. DOI: 10.24059/olj.v28i3.4593

Leonard, S. N., & Fitzgerald, R. N. (2018). Holographic learning: A mixed reality trial of Microsoft HoloLens in an Australian secondary school. *Research in Learning Technology*, *26*. Advance online publication. DOI: 10.25304/rlt.v26.2160

Leong, W. Y., Leong, Y. Z., & Leong, W. S. (2025). Artificial Intelligence in education. *IET Conference Proceedings.,* 2024(22), 183–184. https://doi.org/DOI: 10.1049/icp.2024.4341

Leta, F. M., & Vancea, D.-P. (2023). Ethics in Education: Exploring the Ethical Implications of Artificial Intelligence Implementation. *Ovidius University Annals: Economic Sciences Series*. https://doi.org/DOI: 10.61801/ouaess.2023.1.54

Liang, Y., & Lu, J. (2025). How school support influences the content creation of pre-service teachers' instructional design. *Behavioral Sciences (Basel, Switzerland)*, *15*(5), 568. DOI: 10.3390/bs15050568 PMID: 40426346

Li, K. C., & Wong, B. T. M. (2023). Artificial intelligence in personalised learning: A bibliometric analysis. *Interactive Technology and Smart Education*, *20*(3), 422–445. DOI: 10.1108/itse-01-2023-0007

Lim, T., Gottipati, S., & Cheong, M. (2023). *Artificial Intelligence in Today's Education Landscape: Understanding and Managing Ethical Issues for Educational Assessment*. In Review. https://doi.org/DOI: 10.21203/rs.3.rs-2696273/v1

Lin, C.-C., Huang, A. Y. Q., & Lu, O. H. T. (2023). Artificial intelligence in intelligent tutoring systems toward sustainable education: A systematic review. *Smart Learning Environments, 10*(1), 41. DOI: 10.1186/s40561-023-00260-y

Linder, A. L., & Webb, C. L. (2022). Educational technology: A systematic review of the literature. In Webb, C. L., & Linder, A. L. (Eds.), *Preparing pre-service teachers to integrate technology in K-12 classrooms: Standards and best practices* (pp. 1–45). IGI Global., DOI: 10.4018/978-1-6684-5478-7.ch001

Lin, P., Brummelen, J. V., Lukin, G., Williams, R., & Breazeal, C. (2020). Zhorai: designing a conversational agent for children to explore machine learning concepts. Proceedings of the *AAAI Conference on Artificial Intelligence, 34(*09), 13381-13388. https://doi.org/DOI: 10.1609/aaai.v34i09.7061

Liu, M. (2023). Exploring the application of artificial intelligence in foreign language teaching: challenges and future development. *SHS Web of Conferences,* 168, 03025. https://doi.org/DOI: 10.1051/shsconf/202316803025

Liu, M., Wang, Y., Xu, W., & Liu, L. (2017). Automated scoring of chinese engineering students' english essays. *International Journal of Distance Education Technologies, 15*(1), 52–68. DOI: 10.4018/ijdet.2017010104

Liu, P., Yuan, W., Fu, J., Jiang, Z., Hayashi, H., & Neubig, G. (2022). Pre-train, prompt, and predict: A systematic survey of prompting methods in natural language processing. *ACM Computing Surveys, 55*(9), 1–35. DOI: 10.1145/3560815

Liu, Y.-Z., Pang, X.-N., Jiang, S., & Dong, J.-W. (2013). Viewing-angle enlargement in holographic augmented reality using time division and spatial tiling. *Optics Express, 21*(10), 12068. DOI: 10.1364/oe.21.012068 PMID: 23736427

Lo, L. S. (2023). The art and science of prompt engineering: A new literacy in the information age. *Internet Reference Services Quarterly, 27*(4), 203–210. DOI: 10.1080/10875301.2023.2227621

Luckin, R., & Holmes, W. (2016). Intelligence unleashed: An argument for AI in education. https://www.pearson.com/content/dam/corporate/global/pearson-dot-com/files/innovation/Intelligence-Unleashed-Publication.pdf

Luckin, R., Holmes, W., Griffiths, M., & Forcier, L. B. (2016). *Intelligence unleashed: An argument for AI in education*. Pearson.

Lukwaro, E. A. E., Kalegele, K., & Nyambo, D. G. (2024). A review on nlp techniques and associated challenges in extracting features from education data. *International Journal of Computing and Digital Systems*, *15*(1), 961–979. DOI: 10.12785/ijcds/160170

Lumsdaine, A. A. (1959). Teaching machines and self-instructional materials. *AVCR*, *7*, 163–181. DOI: 10.1007/BF02767482

Luo, Y. (2024). Innovative research on ai-assisted teaching models for college english listening and speaking courses. *Applied and Computational Engineering*, *69*(1), 155–160. DOI: 10.54254/2755-2721/69/20241493

Machado, A., Tenório, K., Santos, M. M., Barros, A. P., Rodrigues, L., Mello, R. F., Paiva, R., & Dermeval, D. (2025). Workload perception in educational resource recommendation supported by artificial intelligence: A controlled experiment with teachers. *Smart Learning Environments*, *12*(1). Advance online publication. DOI: 10.1186/s40561-025-00373-6

Macheque, V., Kadyamatimba, A., & Ochara, N. (2024). Sociotechnical challenges faced by students with disability and factors influencing the integration of assistive technologies. *International Journal of Research In Business and Social Science*, *13*(6), 253–269. DOI: 10.20525/ijrbs.v13i6.3533

MacKinnon, D. W. (1978). *In search of human effectiveness*. Creative Education Foundation.

MacLachlan, M., Banes, D., Bell, D., Borg, J., Donnelly, B., Fembek, M., & Hooks, H. (2018). Assistive technology policy: A position paper from the first global research, innovation, and education on assistive technology (GREAT) summit. *Disability and Rehabilitation. Assistive Technology*, *13*(5), 454–466. DOI: 10.1080/17483107.2018.1468496 PMID: 29790393

MacLeod, J., Yang, H. H., Zhu, S., & Li, Y. (2018). Understanding students' preferences toward the smart classroom learning environment: Development and validation of an instrument. *Computers & Education*, *122*, 80–91. DOI: 10.1016/j.compedu.2018.03.015

Maconachy, W. V., Schou, C. D., Ragsdale, D., & Welch, D. (2001, June). A model for information assurance: an integrated approach. In *Proceedings of the 2001 IEEE workshop on information assurance and security* (Vol. 310, pp. 5-6). United States Military Academy, West Point. IEEE.

Mahamuni, A. J., & Tonpe, S. S. (2024). Enhancing Educational Assessment with Artificial Intelligence. *Challenges and Opportunities.*, *112*, 1–5. DOI: 10.1109/ickecs61492.2024.10616620

Maker, C. J., & Schiever, S. W. (2010). *Curriculum development and teaching strategies for gifted learners.* Pro.ed An International Publisher

Mandal, S., Ruidar, I., & Gope, L. (2025). Role of Assistive Technology to Enhance Learning and Participation in Inclusive Education. *International Journal of Scientific Research and Engineering Trends*, *11*(2), 1459–1464. DOI: 10.61137/ijsret.vol.11.issue2.238

Marcus, G., & Davis, E. (2019). *Rebooting AI: Building artificial intelligence we can trust.* Vintage.

Masters, K., Correia, R., Nemethy, K., Benjamin, J., Carver, T., & MacNeill, H. (2024). Online learning in health professions education. Part 2: Tools and practical application: AMEE Guide No. 163. *Medical Teacher*, *46*(1), 18–33. DOI: 10.1080/0142159X.2023.2259069 PMID: 37740948

Matter, R., Harniss, M., Oderud, T., Borg, J., & Eide, A. H. (2016). Assistive technology in resource-limited environments: A scoping review. *Disability and Rehabilitation. Assistive Technology*, *12*(2), 105–114. DOI: 10.1080/17483107.2016.1188170 PMID: 27443790

McCarthy, J. (2007). *What is artificial intelligence?* Retrieved from https://www-formal.stanford.edu/jmc/whatisai.pdf

McCarthy, J., Minsky, M. L., Rochester, N., & Shannon, C. E. (1955). A proposal for the Dartmouth summer research project on artificial intelligence. http://jmc.stanford.edu/articles/dartmouth.html

McCorduck, P., Minsky, M., & Selfridge, O. ve Simon, H. (1977). History of artificial intelligence. *IJCAI Proceedings* (951-954). https://www.ijcai.org/Proceedings/77-2/Papers/083.pdf

McCumber, J. (1991, October). *Information systems security: a comprehensive model. 14th National Computer Security Conference*, Baltimore, MD, Washington D.C.

McCumber, J. (2005). *Assessing and managing security risk in IT systems.* CRC Press.

McGovern, E., Moreira, G., & Luna-Nevarez, C. (2020). An application of virtual reality in education: Can this technology enhance the quality of students' learning experience? *Journal of Education for Business*, *95*(7), 490–496. DOI: 10.1080/08832323.2019.1703096

McGregor, G., & Pachuski, P. (1996). Assistive Technology in Schools: Are Teachers Ready, Able, and Supported? *Journal of Special Education Technology, 13*(1), 4-15. https://doi.org/ (Original work published 1996)DOI: 10.1177/016264349601300102

McMahon, D., & Firestone, J. B. (2024). Remixing special education practices with artificial intelligence: Udl, ebp, and hlps. *Journal of Special Education Preparation*, *4*(2), 66–76. DOI: 10.33043/3dq2d32d

McNicholl, A., Casey, H., Desmond, D., & Gallagher, P. (2021). The impact of assistive technology use for students with disabilities in higher education: A systematic review. *Disability and Rehabilitation. Assistive Technology*, *16*(2), 130–143. DOI: 10.1080/17483107.2019.1642395 PMID: 31335220

Meng, L., & Meng, L. Q. (2014). Application of Big Data in Higher Education. *2nd International Conference on Teaching and Computational Science*. Shenzhen/ China.

Messer, M., Brown, N. C. C., Kölling, M., & Shi, M. (2024). Automated grading and feedback tools for programming education: A systematic review. *ACM Transactions on Computing Education*, *24*(1), 1–43. DOI: 10.1145/3636515

Michels, J. D., Ruiz, J., & Worsley, M. (2023). Computer vision in education: A survey. *IEEE Transactions on Learning Technologies*, *16*(3), 304–323. DOI: 10.1109/TLT.2023.3273898

Milgram, P., & Kishino, F. (1994). A taxonomy of mixed reality visual displays. *IEICE Transactions on Information and Systems*, *E77-D*(12), 1321–1329. https://globals.ieice.org/en_transactions/information/10.1587/e77-d_12_1321/_p

Miller, W. T. (2024). Adapting to ai: reimagining the role of assessment professionals. Intersection: *A Journal at the Intersection of Assessment and Learning, 5*(4). https://doi.org/DOI: 10.61669/001c.121439

Milli Eğitim Bakanlığı (MEB). (2025). *Eğitimde Yapay Zekâ Politika Belgesi ve Eylem Planı (2025-2029)*. https://yegitek.meb.gov.tr/meb_iys_dosyalar/2025_06/17092340_egitimdeyapayzekapolitikabelgesiveeylemplani202520291.pdf

Mills, S., Lucas, S., Irakliotis, L., Ruppa, M., Carlson, T., & Perlowitz, B. (2012). Demystifying big data: A practical guide to transforming the business of government. Available at http://breakinggov.com/documents/demystifying-big-data-a-practical -guide-to- transforming-the-bus/

Minsky, M. (Ed.). (1969). *Semantic information processing*. The MIT Press.

Mishra, S. (2024). Transformative Impact of AI on Education: Personalizing Learning and Addressing Challenges. *International Journal For Science Technology And Engineering, 12*(8), 1183–1189. DOI: 10.22214/ijraset.2024.63891

Mohammed, M., Khan, M. B., & Bashier, E. B. M. (2016). Machine learning: Algorithms and applications. In *CRC Press eBooks* (1st ed.). CRC Press., DOI: 10.1201/9781315371658

Mollick, E. R., & Mollick, L. (2023). Using AI to implement effective classroom teaching strategies: Five strategies, including prompts. SSRN *Electronic Journal*. https://doi.org/DOI: 10.2139/ssrn.4391243

Morash-Macneil, V., Johnson, F., & Ryan, J. B. (2018). A systematic review of assistive technology for individuals with intellectual disability in the workplace. *Journal of Special Education Technology, 33*(1), 15–26. DOI: 10.1177/0162643417729166

Morelle, M., & Matshidiso, T. (2024). Challenges in Implementing Assistive Devices in Teaching Learners who are Visually Impaired in full Service Classrooms. [IJISRT]. *International Journal of Innovative Science and Research Technology, 9*(3), 2509–2511. DOI: 10.38124/ijisrt/ijisrt24mar1819

Mpu, Y. (2024). *Bridging the knowledge gap on special needs learner support: the use of artificial intelligence (ai) to combat digital divide post-covid-19 pandemic and beyond – a comprehensive literature review*. Education and Human Development., DOI: 10.5772/intechopen.113054

Msambwa, M., Wen, Z., & Kangwa, D. (2025). The Impact of <scp>AI</scp> on the Personal and Collaborative Learning Environments in Higher Education. *European Journal of Education, 60*(1). Advance online publication. DOI: 10.1111/ejed.12909

Mubin, O., Stevens, C. J., Shahid, S., Al Mahmud, A., & Dong, J. J. (2013). A review of the applicability of robots in education. *Journal of Technology in Education and Learning, 1*(1), 1–7. DOI: 10.2316/Journal.201.2013.1.201-0002

Muggleton, S. (2014). Alan Turing and the development of Artificial Intelligence. *AI Communications, 27*(1), 3–10. DOI: 10.3233/AIC-130579

Muhtar, F. (n.d.). Navigating AI Integration for Inclusive Development: A Case Study of Sabah's Socio-Economic Landscape. *Social Science Research Network*. https://doi.org/DOI: 10.2139/ssrn.4807268

Mukhtarkyzy, K., Smagulova, L., Tokzhigitova, A., Serikbayeva, N., Sayakov, O., Turkmenbayev, A., & Assilbayeva, R. (2025). A systematic review of the utility of assistive technologies for SEND students in schools. *Frontiers in Education, 10*. Advance online publication. DOI: 10.3389/feduc.2025.1523797

Mukul, E., & Büyüközkan, G. (2023). Digital transformation in education: A systematic review of education 4.0. *Technological Forecasting and Social Change, 194*, 122664. DOI: 10.1016/j.techfore.2023.122664

Mulyana, E., Hakimi, R., & Hendrawan. (2018). Bringing Automation to the Classroom: A ChatOps-Based Approach. *2018 4th International Conference on Wireless and Telematics (ICWT)*, 1–6. https://doi.org/DOI: 10.1109/ICWT.2018.8527810

Mumford, M. D. (2003). Where have we been, where are we going? Taking stock in creativity research. *Creativity Research Journal, 15*(2-3), 107–120. DOI: 10.1207/S15326934CRJ152&3_01

Murwaningsih, T., Rahardjo, S. S., Suwandi, S., Saddhono, K., & Nurhasanah, F. (2024). *A Well Structured Strategy Development via AI Integrated Analytics Systems to Improve Performance of Education*. 873–878. https://doi.org/DOI: 10.1109/icacite60783.2024.10617260

Mustafa, M. Y., Tlili, A., Lampropoulos, G., Huang, R., Jandrić, P., Zhao, J., Salha, S., Xu, L., Panda, S., Kinshuk, N., López-Pernas, S., & Saqr, M. (2024). A systematic review of literature reviews on artificial intelligence in education (AIED): A roadmap to a future research agenda. *Smart Learning Environments, 11*(1). Advance online publication. DOI: 10.1186/s40561-024-00350-5

Nabiyev, V., & Erümit, A. K. (2020). Yapay zekanın temelleri. Nabiyev, V. & Erümit, A.K. (Eds.), *Eğitimde Yapay Zeka: Kuramdan Uygulamaya* (s.2-34). Pegem Akademi.

Nabiyev, V. V. (2010). *Yapay zekâ: İnsan bilgisayar etkileşimi*. Seçkin Yayıncılık.

Nagy, E., Sík, D., Biczó, Z., Zimányi, K., Pörzse, G., & Molnár, G. (2024). *Advanced Digital and Artificial Intelligence-Based Solutions for Interactive, Collaborative Learning Support*. 103–108. https://doi.org/DOI: 10.1109/candoepe65072.2024.10772869

Nair, B. R., Loon, J. v., Lierop, M. v., & Govaerts, M. (2024). Leveraging narrative feedback in programmatic assessment: The potential of automated text analysis to support coaching and decision-making in programmatic assessment. *Advances in Medical Education and Practice, 15*, 671–683. DOI: 10.2147/amep.s465259 PMID: 39050116

Neumann, M. M., Keioskie, M. K., Patterson, D., & Neumann, D. L. (2022). Virtual, Augmented, and Mixed Reality: Benefits and Barriers for Early Childhood Education. *Childhood Education, 98*(4), 68–79. DOI: 10.1080/00094056.2022.2108298

Nevin, C. R., Westfall, A. O., Rodriguez, J. M., Dempsey, D. M., Cherrington, A., Roy, B., Patel, M., & Willig, J. H. (2014). Gamification as a tool for enhancing graduate medical education. *Postgraduate Medical Journal*, *90*(1070), 685–693. DOI: 10.1136/postgradmedj-2013-132486 PMID: 25352673

Ng, D. T. K., Leung, J. K. L., Chu, S. K. W., & Qiao, M. S. (2021). Conceptualizing AI literacy: An exploratory review. *Computers and Education Artificial Intelligence*, *2*, 100041. DOI: 10.1016/j.caeai.2021.100041

Nguyen, A., Kremantzis, M., Essien, A., Petrounias, I., & Hosseini, S. (2024). Enhancing Student Engagement Through Artificial Intelligence (AI): Understanding the Basics, Opportunities, and Challenges. *Journal of University Teaching & Learning Practice*, *21*(06). Advance online publication. DOI: 10.53761/caraaq92

Ninaus, M., & Sailer, M. (2022). Closing the loop – the human role in artificial intelligence for education. *Frontiers in Psychology*, *13*. Advance online publication. DOI: 10.3389/fpsyg.2022.956798 PMID: 36092115

Niu, W., Zhang, W., Zhang, C., & Chen, X. (2024). The role of artificial intelligence autonomy in higher education: A uses and gratification perspective. *Sustainability*, *16*(3), 1276. DOI: 10.3390/su16031276

Nordström, T., Nilsson, S., Gustafson, S., & Svensson, I. (2018). Assistive technology applications for students with reading difficulties: Special education teachers' experiences and perceptions. *Disability and Rehabilitation. Assistive Technology*, *14*(8), 798–808. DOI: 10.1080/17483107.2018.1499142 PMID: 30239256

Nwana, H. S. (1990). Intelligent tutoring systems: An overview. *Artificial Intelligence Review*, *4*, 251–277. DOI: 10.1007/BF00168958

O'Malley, C., Vavoula, G., Glew, J. P., Taylor, J., Sharples, M., Lefrere, P., . . . Waycott, J. (2005). Guidelines for learning/teaching/tutoring in a mobile environment. *MOBIlearn*. https://hal.science/hal-00696244v1

O'Neil, C. (2016). *Weapons of math destruction: How big data increases inequality and threatens democracy*. Crown Publisher.

O'Sullivan, K., McGrane, A., Long, S., Marshall, K., & Maclachlan, M. (2021). Using a systems thinking approach to understand teachers perceptions and use of assistive technology in the republic of Ireland. *Disability and Rehabilitation. Assistive Technology*, *18*(5), 502–510. DOI: 10.1080/17483107.2021.1878297 PMID: 33573427

Oberdieck, T., & Moch, E. (2024). Lifelong learning with artificial intelligence: Potentials, challenges and future perspectives. *International Journal of Advanced Research*, *12*(06), 545–555. DOI: 10.21474/ijar01/18915

OECD. (2023), AI and the Future of Skills, Volume 2: Methods for Evaluating AI Capabilities, Educational Research and Innovation, OECD Publishing, Paris, https://doi.org/DOI: 10.1787/a9fe53cb-en

OECD. (2025). *Empowering learners for the age of AI: An AI literacy framework for primary and secondary education (Review draft).* https://ailiteracyframework.org/

Okonkwo, C. W., & Ade-Ibijola, A. (2021). Chatbots in education: A systematic review. *Computers and Education: Artificial Intelligence*, *2*, 100023. DOI: 10.1016/j.caeai.2021.100023

Olarewaju, T., Healy, A., & Chockalingam, N. (2021). Barriers to accessing assistive technology in Africa. *Assistive Technology*, *35*(1), 116–117. DOI: 10.1080/10400435.2021.1985011 PMID: 34554890

Oleet, J. B., & Yu, C. (2025). Ai and the future of education. *Advances in Computational Intelligence and Robotics*, •••, 407–440. DOI: 10.4018/979-8-3693-7873-1.ch015

Ometov, A., Bezzateev, S., Mäkitalo, N., Andreev, S., Mikkonen, T., & Koucheryavy, Y. (2018). Multi-factor authentication: A survey. *Cryptography*, *2*(1), 1.

Oppenlaender, J., Linder, R., & Silvennoinen, J. (2024). Prompting AI Art: An investigation into the creative skill of prompt engineering. *International Journal of Human-Computer Interaction*, •••, 1–23. DOI: 10.1080/10447318.2024.2431761

Orcos, L., & Magreñán, A. (2018). The hologram as a teaching medium for the acquisition of STEM contents. *International Journal of Learning Technology*, *13*(2), 163–177. DOI: 10.1504/IJLT.2018.092097

Organization for Economic Co-operation and Development. (2023). OECD Digital Education Outlook 2023. In *the Digital Education Outlook*. https://doi.org/DOI: 10.1787/c74f03de-en

Ouyang, F., Dinh, T. A., & Xu, W. (2023). A systematic review of AI-driven educational assessment in STEM education. *Journal for STEM Education Research*, *6*(3), 408–426. DOI: 10.1007/s41979-023-00112-x

Ouyang, F., Zheng, L., & Jiao, P. (2022). Artificial intelligence in online higher education: A systematic review of empirical research from 2011 to 2020. *Education and Information Technologies*, *27*(6), 7893–7925. DOI: 10.1007/s10639-022-10925-9

Owan, V. J., Idika, D. O., & Bassey, B. A. (2023). Exploring the potential of artificial intelligence tools in educational measurement and assessment. *Eurasia Journal of Mathematics, Science and Technology Education*, *19*(8), em2307. Advance online publication. DOI: 10.29333/ejmste/13428

Owoc, M. L., Sawicka, A., & Weichbroth, P. (2021). Artificial Intelligence Technologies in Education: Benefits, Challenges and Strategies of Implementation. In Owoc, M. L., & Pondel, M. (Eds.), *Artificial Intelligence for Knowledge Management* (Vol. 599, pp. 37–58). Springer International Publishing., DOI: 10.1007/978-3-030-85001-2_4

Özdamar, O., & Odluyurt, S. (2025). Determination of Teachers' Views on the Use of Assistive Technology in Special Education Classrooms. *E-Kafkas Journal of Educational Research, 12*(1), 146–160. DOI: 10.30900/kafkasegt.1585399

Öztezcan, B. A., & Çetinkaya, A. (2018). A research on information security awareness: The example of Marmara University. *National Multidisciplinary Refereed Journal of Social Sciences and Research*, 56-71. doi: DOI: 10.17373/MSBAD.2017.1.3

Özünlü Pekyavaş, N., Yürük, Z. Ö., & Saygılı, F. (2020). Pain syndrome caused by increased mobile technology use: "Text Neck". *Adnan Menderes University Journal of Health Sciences, 4*(3), 251–257. DOI: 10.46237/amusbfd.713569

Padmaja, C. V. R. and Lakshminarayana, S. (2024). The rise of ai: a comprehensive research review. *IAES International Journal of Artificial Intelligence (IJ-AI), 13*(2), 2226. https://doi.org/DOI: 10.11591/ijai.v13.i2.pp2226-2235

Pagliara, S. M., Bonavolontà, G., Pia, M. G., Falchi, S., Zurru, A. L., Fenu, G., & Mura, A. (2024). The integration of artificial intelligence in inclusive education: a scoping review. https://doi.org/DOI: 10.20944/preprints202410.1386.v1

Pallathadka, H., Sonia, B., Sanchez, D. T., De Vera, J. V., Godinez, J. A. T., & Pepito, M. T. (2022). Investigating the impact of artificial intelligence in the *education sector by predicting student performance. Materials Today: Proceedings, 51*, 2264–2267. DOI: 10.1016/j.matpr.2021.11.395

Pane, J. F., Steiner, E. D., Baird, M. D., Hamilton, L. S., & Pane, J. D. (2017). *Informing progress: Insights on personalized learning implementation and effects*. The RAND Corporation. Retrieved June 23, 2025, from https://www.rand.org/content/dam/rand/pubs/research_reports/RR2000/RR2042/RAND_RR2042.pdf

Pang, T. Y., Kootsookos, A., & Cheng, C.-T. (2024). Artificial Intelligence Use in Feedback: A Qualitative Analysis. *Journal of University Teaching & Learning Practice*. Advance online publication. DOI: 10.53761/40wmcj98

Papadakis, S. (2021). Tools for evaluating educational apps for young children: A systematic review of the literature. *Interactive Technology and Smart Education, 18*(1), 18–49. DOI: 10.1108/ITSE-08-2020-0127

Papert, S. (1980). *Mindstorms: Children, computers, and powerful ideas*. Basic Books.

Pappas, M. A., & Drigas, A. (2016). Incorporation of artificial intelligence tutoring techniques in mathematics. [iJEP]. *International Journal of Engineering Pedagogy, 6*(4), 12. DOI: 10.3991/ijep.v6i4.6063

Parette, H. P., & Peterson-Karlan, G. R. (2007). Facilitating Student Achievement with Assistive Technology. *Education and Training in Developmental Disabilities, 42*(4), 387–397. https://www.jstor.org/stable/23879844

Park, J., Bagwell, A. F., Bryant, D. P., & Bryant, B. R. (2021). Integrating Assistive Technology Into a Teacher Preparation Program. *Teacher Education and Special Education, 45*(2), 141-159. https://doi.org/ (Original work published 2022)DOI: 10.1177/08884064211001447

Park, J., Gremp, M., & Ok, M. W. (2023). Effects of Assistive Technology Instruction on Pre-Service Teachers: A Systematic Review. *Journal of Special Education Technology, 39*(3), 349-362. https://doi.org/ (Original work published 2024)DOI: 10.1177/01626434231210988

Park, J., & Choo, S. (2024). Generative AI prompt engineering for educators: Practical strategies. *Journal of Special Education Technology*. Advance online publication. DOI: 10.1177/01626434241298954

Park, K., Kim, D., & Han, S. H. (2020). Usability of the size, spacing, and operation method of virtual buttons with virtual hand on head-mounted displays. *International Journal of Industrial Ergonomics, 76*, 102939. DOI: 10.1016/j.ergon.2020.102939

Parsons, K., Calic, D., Pattinson, M., Butavicius, M., & McCormac, A., & Zwaans, T. (2017). The human aspects of information security questionnaire (HAIS-Q): Two further validation studies. *Computers & Security, 66*, 40–51. DOI: 10.1016/j.cose.2017.01.004

Partnership for 21st Century Skills. (2019). *P21 framework definitions.* https://files.eric.ed.gov/fulltext/ED519462.pdf

Pea-Assounga, J. B. B., Yao, H., Bahizire, G. M., Bambi, P. D. R., & Ngapey, J. D. N. (2024). Effect of financial innovation and stakeholders' satisfaction on investment decisions: Does internet security matter? *Heliyon, 10*(6).

Penton, V., & Gustafson, D. L. (2014). Access to Assistive Technology and Single Entry Point Programs. *Canadian Journal of Disability Studies, 3*(1), 93–120. DOI: 10.15353/cjds.v3i1.90

Pereira, R., Reis, A., Barroso, J., Sousa, J., & Pinto, T. (2022). Virtual Assistants Applications in Education. In Reis, A., Barroso, J., Martins, P., Jimoyiannis, A., Huang, R. Y.-M., & Henriques, R. (Eds.), *Technology and Innovation in Learning, Teaching and Education* (Vol. 1720, pp. 468–480). Springer Nature Switzerland., DOI: 10.1007/978-3-031-22918-3_38

Peters, J., Bleakney, A., Sornson, A., Hsiao-Wecksler, E., & McDonagh, D. (2023). User-driven product development: Designed *by,* not designed *for. The Design Journal, 27*(1), 133–152. DOI: 10.1080/14606925.2023.2275868

Petruse, R. E., Grecu, V., Chiliban, M. B., & Tâlvan, E. T. (2024). Comparative analysis of mixed reality and powerpoint in education: Tailoring learning approaches to cognitive profiles. *Sensors (Basel), 24*(16), 5138. DOI: 10.3390/s24165138 PMID: 39204835

Pfeiffer, S. I. (2012). *Serving the gifted: Evidence-based clinical and psychoeducational practice.* Routledge.

Plucker, J. A., Runco, M. A., & Hegarty, C. B. (2011). Enhancement of creativity. In Runco, M. A., & Pritzker, S. R. (Eds.), *Encyclopedia of creativity* (2nd ed., pp. 456–460). Academic Press., DOI: 10.1016/B978-0-12-375038-9.00090-X

Popenici, Ş., & Kerr, S. (2017). Exploring the impact of artificial intelligence on teaching and learning in higher education. *Research and Practice in Technology Enhanced Learning, 12*(1). Advance online publication. DOI: 10.1186/s41039-017-0062-8 PMID: 30595727

Portilla, J. E. N., Cedeño, J. K. Z., Jácome, G. O. L., & Gallegos, L. A. M. (2025). Systematic Review: Artificial Intelligence (AI) in Education 4.0. *The Journal of Educators Online, 22*(3), n3.

Preckel, F., Golle, J., Grabner, R., Jarvin, L., Kozbelt, A., Müllensiefen, D., Olszewski-Kubilius, P., Schneider, W., Subotnik, R., Vock, M., & Worrell, F. C. (2020). Talent development in achievement domains: A psychological framework for within- and cross-domain research. *Perspectives on Psychological Science, 15*(3), 691–722. DOI: 10.1177/1745691619895030 PMID: 32196409

Prepare, S. (2025). *Research on future of education for U.S. educators* https://skillprepare.com/research-on-future-of-education-for-u-s-educators/

Qian, Y., & Lehman, J. D. (2019). Using targeted feedback to address common student misconceptions in introductory programming: A data-driven approach. *SAGE Open, 9*(4). Advance online publication. DOI: 10.1177/2158244019885136

Qin, L. (2024). Adaptive system of english-speaking learning based on artificial intelligence. *Journal of Electrical Systems, 20*(6s), 267–275. DOI: 10.52783/jes.2637

Radanliev, P. (2024). Digital security by design. *Security Journal*, 1–40. DOI: 10.1057/s41284-024-00435-

Radu, I. (2012). Why should my students use AR? A comparative review of the educational impacts of augmented-reality. *2012 IEEE International Symposium on Mixed and Augmented Reality (ISMAR)*, 313–314. https://doi.org/DOI: 10.1109/ISMAR.2012.6402590

Rahwan, I., Cebrian, M., Obradovich, N., Bongard, J., Bonnefon, J., Breazeal, C., Crandall, J. W., Christakis, N. A., Couzin, I. D., Jackson, M. O., Jennings, N. R., Kamar, E., Kloumann, I. M., Larochelle, H., Lazer, D., McElreath, R., Mislove, A., Parkes, D. C., & Pentland, A. '., . . . Wellman, M. (2019). Machine behavior. *Nature, 568*(7753), 477–486. DOI: 10.1038/s41586-019-1138-y PMID: 31019318

Rakshit, S. (2025). Edtech 5.0: The role of immersive technologies and ai tutors in shaping future classrooms. *International Journal of Recent Innovations, 01*(01), 24–31. DOI: 10.63665/ijri.v1i1.04

Ramesh, D., & Sanampudi, S. K. (2022). An automated essay scoring system: A systematic literature review. *Artificial Intelligence Review, 55*(3), 2495–2527. DOI: 10.1007/s10462-021-10068-2 PMID: 34584325

Ramesh, S. (2021). Unleashing the future: The dynamic impacts of artificial intelligence on education. *Journal of Artificial Intelligence. Machine Learning and Neural Network*, (12), 27–31. DOI: 10.55529/jaimlnn.12.27.31

Ramos, J. G., & Wilson-Kennedy, Z. S. (2024). Promoting equity and addressing concerns in teaching and learning with artificial intelligence. *Frontiers in Education, 9*. Advance online publication. DOI: 10.3389/feduc.2024.1487882

Rasheed, T., Bhatti, J. A., Hashim, A., & Fauz, F. (2025). Teacher-AI collaboration: How educators can harness artificial ıntelligence without losing pedagogical control. *Review of Applied Management and Social Sciences, 8*(2), 697–709. DOI: 10.47067/ramss.v8i2.509

Rayati, M. (2021). Neuro-linguistic programming and its applicability in efl classrooms: Perceptions of nlp-trained english teachers. *Language Teaching Research Quarterly, 24*, 44–64. DOI: 10.32038/ltrq.2021.24.03

Reidenberg, J. R., & Schaub, F. (2018). Achieving big data privacy in education. *Theory and Research in Education, 16*(3), 263–279. DOI: 10.1177/1477878518805308

Resnick, L. B., & Klopher, L. E. (1989). *Toward the thinking curriculum: Current cognitive research.* ASCD Yearbook. Association for Supervision and Curriculum Development.

Rimm, S. B., Siegle, D., & Davis, G. A. (2018). *Education of the gifted and talented* (7th ed.). Pearson.

Rojas Contreras, M., & Portilla Jaimes, J. O. (2024). *AI Ethics in the Fields of Education and Research: A Systematic Literature Review.* 1–6. https://doi.org/DOI: 10.1109/icacit62963.2024.10788651

Romero, C., & Ventura, S. (2013). Data mining in education. *Wiley Interdisciplinary Reviews. Data Mining and Knowledge Discovery*, *3*(1), 12–27.

Roshanaei, M., Olivares, H., & Lopez, R. R. (2023). Harnessing AI to foster equity in education: Opportunities, challenges, and emerging strategies. *Journal of Intelligent Learning Systems and Applications*, *15*(04), 123–143. DOI: 10.4236/jilsa.2023.154009

Rumbaugh, D., King, J. E., Berman, M. L., Washburn, D. A., Gould, K., Kornell, N., Scaturo, D. J., Haig, B., Schvaneveldt, R., Barton, B. K., Ulrich, T. A., Robinson, P., Schuelke, M. J., Day, E. A., Chase, H. W., Carayannis, E. G., Flemming, T. M., Mitchelmore, M., White, P., … Reznikova, Z. (n.d.). *Adaptive learning.* https://doi.org/DOI: 10.1007/978-1-4419-1428-6_3075

Runco, M. (2007). *Encouraging creativity in education.* Creativity a Handbook for Teachers. Stallion.

Russell, S. J., & Norvig, P. (2003). *Artificial intelligence: A modern approach* (2nd ed.). Pearson.

Russell, S., & Norvig, P. (2021). *Artificial Intelligence: A Modern Approach* (4th ed.). Pearson.

Ružić, I., & Balaban, I. (2024). The use of social robots as teaching assistants in schools: Implications for research and practice. [*RED*]. *Revista de Educación a Distancia*, *24*(78). Advance online publication. DOI: 10.6018/red.600771

Saborío-Taylor, S., & Rojas-Ramírez, F. (2024). Universal design for learning and artificial intelligence in the digital era: Fostering inclusion and autonomous learning. *International Journal of Professional Development Learners and Learning*, *6*(2), ep2408. Advance online publication. DOI: 10.30935/ijpdll/14694

Saini, M. K., & Goel, N. (2020). How Smart Are Smart Classrooms? A Review of Smart Classroom Technologies. *ACM Computing Surveys*, *52*(6), 1–28. DOI: 10.1145/3365757

Sak, U. (2014). Üstün zekâlılar: Özellikleri, tanılanmaları, eğitimleri [Giftedness: Characteristics, identification, education] (4th ed). Vize Yayıncılık.

Salahdine, F., & Kaabouch, N. (2019). Social engineering attacks: A survey. *Future Internet*, *11*(4), 89.

Salloum, S. A. (2024). *AI Perils in Education: Exploring Ethical Concerns*. Springer International Publishing., DOI: 10.1007/978-3-031-52280-2_43

Sari, H., Tumanggor, B., & Efron, D. (2024). Improving Educational Outcomes Through Adaptive Learning Systems using AI. *International Transactions on Artificial Intelligence*, *3*(1), 21–31. DOI: 10.33050/italic.v3i1.647

Sarker, I. H. (2021). Machine learning: Algorithms, Real-world applications, and research directions. *SN Computer Science*, *2*(3). Advance online publication. DOI: 10.1007/s42979-021-00592-x PMID: 33778771

Saylam, S., Duman, N., Yildirim, Y., & Satsevich, K. (2023). *Empowering education with AI: Addressing ethical concerns*. London Journal of Social Sciences., DOI: 10.31039/ljss.2023.6.103

Scassellati, B., Admoni, H., & Matarić, M. (2012). Robots for use in autism research. *Annual Review of Biomedical Engineering*, *14*, 275–294. DOI: 10.1146/annurev-bioeng-071811-150036 PMID: 22577778

Schmuck, V., Spiess, T., & Ploder, C. (2024). Augmented reality glasses in class–blessing or curse. *Education and New Developments*, *2024*(2), 366–370. DOI: 10.36315/2024v2end083

Schulze, M. (2025). Icall and AI: Seven lessons from seventy years. *Insights Into AI and Language Teaching and Learning,* 11-31. https://doi.org/DOI: 10.29140/9781763711600-02

Seiradakis, E. (2024). *Investigating the barriers to using assistive technologies in Greek special education classrooms: EFL teachers' perspectives*. European Journal of Special Education Research., DOI: 10.46827/ejse.v10i1.5151

Sen, P. C., Hajra, M., & Ghosh, M. (2020). Supervised classification algorithms in machine learning: A survey and review. In *Emerging technology in modeling and graphics* (pp. 99–111). Springer.

Sergeyuk, A., Golubev, Y., Bryksin, T., & Ahmed, I. (2024). Using AI-based coding assistants in practice: State of affairs, perceptions, and ways forward. *Information and Software Technology*, *178*, 107610. DOI: 10.1016/j.infsof.2024.107610

Sevinç, M., & Avcı, İ. (2024). Analysis of security vulnerabilities caused by human error in iot devices. *Journal of Engineering Sciences and Design*, *12*(2), 403–415. doi: DOI: 10.21923/jesd.1231326

Shao, J., & Sun, S. (2025). Teacher identity in the era of intelligence. *Journal of Educational Theory and Practice*, *2*(1). Advance online publication. DOI: 10.62177/jetp.v2i1.141

Shen, S. (2024). Application of large language models in the field of education. *Theoretical and Natural Science*, *34*(1), 147–154. DOI: 10.54254/2753-8818/34/20241163

Shute, V., & Rahimi, S. (2017). Review of computer-based assessment for learning in elementary and secondary education. *Journal of Computer Assisted Learning*, *33*(1), 1–19. DOI: 10.1111/jcal.12172

Siemens, G. (2013). Learning analytics: The emergence of a discipline. *The American Behavioral Scientist*, *57*(10), 1380–1400.

Sihite, M. R., Meisuri, M., & Sibarani, B. (2023). Examining the validity and reliability of chatgpt 3.5-generated reading comprehension questions for academic texts. *Randwick International of Education and Linguistics Science Journal*, *4*(4), 937–944. DOI: 10.47175/rielsj.v4i4.835

Silva, G., Godwin, G., & Jayanagara, O. (2024). *The Impact of AI on Personalized Learning and Educational Analytics*. https://doi.org/DOI: 10.33050/itee.v3i1.669

Silver, D., Huang, A., Maddison, C. J., Guez, A., Sifre, L., Van Den Driessche, G., Schrittwieser, J., Antonoglou, I., Panneershelvam, V., Lanctot, M., Dieleman, S., Grewe, D., Nham, J., Kalchbrenner, N., Sutskever, I., Lillicrap, T., Leach, M., Kavukcuoglu, K., Graepel, T., & Hassabis, D. (2016). Mastering the game of Go with deep neural networks and tree search. *Nature*, *529*(7587), 484–489. DOI: 10.1038/nature16961 PMID: 26819042

Singh, A., & Kumar, S. (2024). Effective Talent Management Practices Implemented in the Hospitality Sector. In Christiansen, B., Aziz, M. A., & O'Keeffe, E. L. (Eds.), (pp. 126–144). Advances in Human Resources Management and Organizational Development. IGI Global., DOI: 10.4018/979-8-3693-1938-3.ch008

Sisman-Ugur, S., & Kurubacak, G. (Eds.). (2019). *Handbook of Research on Learning in the Age of Transhumanism*. IGI Global., DOI: 10.4018/978-1-5225-8431-5

Skinner, B. F. (1958). Teaching machines. *The Review of Economics and Statistics, 42*(3), 189–191. PMID: 13592277

Sleeman, D. (1984). *Intelligent Tutoring Systems: A Review.* https://files.eric.ed.gov/fulltext/ED257450.pdf

Sleeman, D., & Brown, J. S. (Eds.). (1982). *Intelligent tutoring systems.* Academic Press.

Smith, G., Haworth, R., & Žitnik, S. (2020). Computer science meets education: Natural language processing for automatic grading of open-ended questions in ebooks. *Journal of Educational Computing Research, 58*(7), 1227–1255. DOI: 10.1177/0735633120927486

Sofi-Karim, M., Bali, A. O., & Rached, K. (2023). Online education via media platforms and applications as an innovative teaching method. *Education and Information Technologies, 28*(1), 507–523. DOI: 10.1007/s10639-022-11188-0 PMID: 35791317

Soliman, M., Pesyridis, A., Dalaymani-Zad, D., Gronfula, M., & Kourmpetis, M. (2021). The Application of Virtual Reality in Engineering Education. *Applied Sciences (Basel, Switzerland), 11*(6), 2879. DOI: 10.3390/app11062879

Somers, R., Cunningham, S., & Boles, W. (2021). Applying natural language processing to automatically assess student conceptual understanding from textual responses. *Australasian Journal of Educational Technology, 37*(5), 98–115. DOI: 10.14742/ajet.7121

Sourati, J., & Evans, J. A. (2023). Accelerating science with human-aware artificial intelligence. *Nature Human Behaviour, 7*(10), 1682–1696. DOI: 10.1038/s41562-023-01648-z PMID: 37443269

Sperling, K., Stenberg, C., McGrath, C., Åkerfeldt, A., Heintz, F., & Stenliden, L. (2024). In search of artificial intelligence (AI) literacy in teacher education: A scoping review. *Computers and Education Open, 6*, 100169. DOI: 10.1016/j.caeo.2024.100169

Stallings, W. & Brown, L. (2015*). Computer security: Principles and practice* (3. bs.). Pearson Education, Inc.

Steenis, van M. (2025). Social Robots in education: Should we prepare for social robots in education? *Surf Responsible Tech Reports.* https://www.surf.nl/files/2025-03/20250303-social-robots-in-education-v1.0.pdf

Sternberg, R. J., & Lubart, T. I. (1995). *Defying the crowd: Cultivating creativity in a culture of conformity.* Free Press.

Suleski, T., Ahmed, M., Yang, W., & Wang, E. (2023). A review of multi-factor authentication in the Internet of Healthcare Things. *Digital Health*, *9*, 20552076231177144.

Sullivan, M., Kelly, A., & McLaughlan, P. (2023). Chatgpt in higher education: Considerations for academic integrity and student learning. *Journal of Applied Learning & Teaching*, *6*(1). Advance online publication. DOI: 10.37074/jalt.2023.6.1.17

Sumbera, B. G. (2024). The Ethical Use of AI in Education. *Advances in Educational Technologies and Instructional Design Book Series*, 175–210. https://doi.org/DOI: 10.4018/979-8-3693-6130-6.ch008

Suvacı, B., & Yamacı, A. (2024, February). *Bibliometric analysis of thesis studies on knowledge security*. International AEGEAN Conferences On Social Sciences & Humanities IX, İzmir, Türkiye.

Switters, J., Verma, A. K., Mavrou, K., Boland, S., Franz, L., Karfitsa, E., ... & Valoti, I. (2022). Bridging the Digital Divide: A Review of the ENTELIS+ Project on the Development of Digital Accessibility Training Addressing the EU and Global Disability Policy Agendas. *ICCHP-AAATE 2022 Open Access Compendium" Assistive Technology, Accessibility and (e) Inclusion" Part II*.

Sych, T. V., Khrykov, Y. M., & Ptakhina, O. M. (2021). Digital transformation as the main condition for the development of modern higher education. *Educational Technology Quarterly*, *2021*(2), 293–309. DOI: 10.55056/etq.27

Tangcharoensathien, V., Witthayapipopsakul, W., Viriyathorn, S., & Patcharanarumol, W. (2018). Improving access to assistive technologies: Challenges and solutions in low- and middle-income countries. *WHO South-East Asia Journal of Public Health*, *7*(2), 84–89. PMID: 30136666

Tannenbaum, A. J. (2003) Nature and nurture of giftedness. In Colangelo, N. & Davis, G. A. (Eds.) *Handbook of gifted education* (3rd ed.), 45-59. Pearson Education.

Tardif, T. Z., & Sternberg, R. J. (1988). What do we know about creativity? In Sternberg, R. J. (Ed.), *The nature of creativity. Contemporary psychological perspectives* (pp. 429–440). Cambridge University.

Taşkın, M. (2025). Artificial Intelligence in Personalized Education: Enhancing Learning Outcomes Through Adaptive Technologies and Data-Driven Insights. *Human-Computer Interaction*, *8*(1), 173. DOI: 10.62802/ygye0506

Tegmark, M. (2017). *Life 3.0: Being human in the age of artificial intelligence*. Alfred A. Knopf.

Tekerek, M. (2008). Information Security Management. *KSÜ Journal of Natural Sciences, 11*(1), 132-137. https://dergipark.org.tr/en/pub/ksudobil/issue/35406/393310

Temur, S. (2025). Eğitimde yapay zekâ kullanımı: Etik sorunlar ve çözümler. *Mehmet Akif Ersoy University Journal of Education Faculty*, (74), 568–595. DOI: 10.21764/maeuefd.1516576

Teoh, C. S., & Mahmood, A. K. (2017). National cyber security strategies for digital economy. *Journal of Theoretical and Applied Information Technology, 95*(23), 6510–6522. doi: DOI: 10.1109/ICRIIS.2017.8002519

Thangaraj, J. (2021). Automated assessment & feedback system for novice programmers. *Proceedings of the 26th ACM Conference on Innovation and Technology in Computer Science Education* v. 2, 672-673. https://doi.org/DOI: 10.1145/3456565.3460021

The International Educational Data Mining Society. (2025, 10 August). Educational Data Mining. Retrieved August 10 from https://educationaldatamining.org/

Thrun, S., Burgard, W., & Fox, D. (2005). *Probabilistic robotics.* The MIT Press. https://docs.ufpr.br/~danielsantos/ProbabilisticRobotics.pdf

Timotheou, S., Miliou, O., Dimitriadis, Y., Sobrino, S. V., Giannoutsou, N., Cachia, R., Monés, A. M., & Ioannou, A. (2023). Impacts of digital technologies on education and factors influencing schools' digital capacity and transformation: A literature review. *Education and Information Technologies, 28*(6), 6695–6726. DOI: 10.1007/s10639-022-11431-8 PMID: 36465416

Tiwari, C. K., Bhaskar, P., & Pal, A. (2023). Prospects of augmented reality and virtual reality for online education: A scientometric view. *International Journal of Educational Management, 37*(5), 1042–1066. DOI: 10.1108/IJEM-10-2022-0407

Tomlinson, C. A. (2001). *How to differentiate instruction in mixed-ability classrooms.* Pearson Education.

Torrance, E. P. (1998). *The Torrance Tests of Creative Thinking Norms—technical manual figural (streamlined) forms* (Vol. A & B). Scholastic Testing Service.

Torrens, G. E., & Asghar, S. (2023). 20 years of the Loughborough user centered assistive technology design process: Has it made a difference? *Assistive Technology, 35*(5), 425–434. DOI: 10.1080/10400435.2022.2113477 PMID: 36040847

Trivedi, N. (2018). ProblemPal: Generating autonomous practice content in real-time with voice commands and amazon alexa. In *Proceedings of E-Learn: World Conference on E-Learning in Corporate, Government, Healthcare, and Higher Education*, (s. 80-82). https://www.learntechlib.org/primary/p/184950/

Trivedi, N. B. (2023).. . *AI in Education-A Transformative Force.*, *1*, 1–4. DOI: 10.1109/idicaiei58380.2023.10406541

Tsang, P. W. M., & Poon, T. C. (2016). Review on the state-of-the-art technologies for acquisition and display of digital holograms. *IEEE Transactions on Industrial Informatics*, *12*(3), 886–901. DOI: 10.1109/TII.2016.2550535

Tsarapkina, J. M., Anisimova, A. V., Gadzhimetova, B. D., Kireycheva, A. M., & Mironov, A. G. (2021). The impact of digital education transformation on technical college teachers. *Journal of Physics: Conference Series*, *2001*(1), 012030. DOI: 10.1088/1742-6596/2001/1/012030

Tseng, E., Sabet, M., Bellini, R., Sodhi, H. K., Ristenpart, T., & Dell, N. (2022, April). *Care infrastructures for digital security in intimate partner violence*. In *Proceedings of the 2022 CHI Conference on Human Factors in Computing Systems* (pp. 1-20).

Türkmen, G. (2024). The review of studies on Explainable Artificial Intelligence in educational research. *Journal of Educational Computing Research*. Advance online publication. DOI: 10.1177/07356331241310915

U.S. Department of Education, Office of Educational Technology. (2023). *Artificial intelligence and the future of teaching and learning: Insights and recommendations*. U.S. Department of Education.

U.S. Department of Education. Office of Educational Technology, *Artificial Intelligence and Future of Teaching and Learning: Insights and Recommendations*, Washington, DC, 2023. Retrieved from https://www.ed.gov/sites/ed/files/documents/ai-report/ai-report.pdf

Ünal, N. E., & Davis, G. (2023). Eleştirel düşünme becerilerinin geliştirilmesine yönelik stratejiler. In B. B., & N. N. Ateşgöz (Eds.) *Üst düzey düşünme becerilerini geliştirme stratejileri* (pp. 88-139). Anı Yayıncılık.

UNESCO World Commission on the Ethics of Scientific Knowledge and Technology (COMEST). (2019). Preliminary study on the ethics of artificial intelligence. United Nations Educational, Scientific, and Cultural Organization. https://unesdoc.unesco.org/ark:/48223/pf0000367823

UNESCO. (2023). *UNESCO survey: Less than 10% of schools and universities have formal guidance on AI.* Retrieved June 16, 2025, from https://www.unesco.org/en/articles/unesco-survey-less-10-schools-and-universities-have-formal-guidance-ai

UNESCO. 2023. *Recommendation on the ethics of artificial intelligence.* Retrieved from https://www.unesco.org/en/articles/recommendation-ethics-artificial-intelligence

Unicef (2021). Convention on the Rights of the Child. General comment No. 25 (2021) on children's rights in relation to the digital environment. https://www.unicef.org/bulgaria/en/media/10596/file

United Nations Educational, Scientific and Cultural Organization [UNESCO] (2023). *ChatGPT and artificial intelligence in higher education-quick start guide.* Retrieved from https://etico.iiep.unesco.org/en/chatgpt-and-artificial-intelligence-higher-education-quick-start-guide

United Nations. (2006). *Convention on the Rights of Persons with Disabilities.* United Nations Department of Economic and Social Affairs.

Ünsal, H. (2024). Yapay zekâ ve yapay zekânın eğitimin geleceğine ilişkin olası doğurguları. *Journal of Social. Humanities and Administrative Sciences, 10*(5), 674–682. DOI: 10.5281/zenodo.13 851822

Vachkova, S. N., Petryaeva, E. Yu., Milyaeva, D. A., Ageeva, N. S., & Mikhailova, S. V. (2022). *Analytical Review of Education Policies on Digital Transformation of School Education Worldwide*. 248–270. https://doi.org/DOI: 10.15405/epes.22043.23

van den Berghe, R., Verhagen, J., Oudgenoeg-Paz, O., van der Ven, S., & Leseman, P. (2019). Social robots for language learning: A review. *Review of Educational Research, 89*(2), 259–295. DOI: 10.3102/0034654318821262

Vanderpuye, I., & Okai, M. (2023). Effective use of assistive technology in inclusive classroom: Views of teachers on resources and challenges in a developing economy. *Support for Learning, 38*(3), 68–82. DOI: 10.1111/1467-9604.12433

Vashishth, T. K., Sharma, V., Sharma, K. K., Kumar, B., Panwar, R., & Chaudhary, S. (2024). *AI-Driven Learning Analytics for Personalized Feedback and Assessment in Higher Education.* IGI Global., DOI: 10.4018/979-8-3693-0639-0.ch009

Velásquez-Henao, J. D., Franco-Cardona, C. J., & Cadavid-Higuita, L. (2023). Prompt Engineering: A methodology for optimizing interactions with AI-language models in engineering. *Dyna, 90*(230), 9–17. DOI: 10.15446/dyna.v90n230.111700

Velki, T., & Romstein, K. (2018). User risky behavior and security awareness through lifespan. *International Journal of Electrical and Computer Engineering Systems*, *9*(2), 53–60.

Verma, A., & Maurya, M. C. (2024). Addressing the Challenges to Accessibility and Research Gaps in Assistive Technology. Advances in Medical Technologies and Clinical Practice Book Series, 89–116. https://doi.org/DOI: 10.4018/979-8-3693-6308-9.ch005

Vetrivel, S. C., Vidhyapriya, P., & Arun, V. P. (2024). The Role of AI in Transforming Assessment Practices in Education. *Advances in Educational Marketing, Administration, and Leadership Book Series*, 43–70. https://doi.org/DOI: 10.4018/979-8-3693-5443-8.ch003

Visser, M., Nel, M., de Klerk, M., Ganzevoort, A., Hubble, C., Liebenberg, A., Snyman, M., & Young, M. (2020). The use of assistive technology in classroom activities for learners with motor impairments at a special school in South Africa. *South African Journal of Occupational Therapy*, *50*(2), 11–22. DOI: 10.17159/2310-3833/2020/vol50no2a3

Viswanathan, N. P. S. (2025). Prompt engineering for conversational AI systems: A systematic review of techniques and applications. *International Journal of Scientific Research in Computer Science Engineering and Information Technology*, *11*(1), 733–741. DOI: 10.32628/cseit25111276

Vodafone Foundation. (2024). *AI in European schools: A European report comparing seven countries*. Retrieved June 23, 2025, from https://skillsuploadjr.eu/docs/contents/AI_in_European_schools.pdf

Vootukuri, N. S. R., & Jyothi, J. (2024). Harnessing the potential of AI applications in Education: Opportunities, challenges, and future directions. *Magna Scientia Advanced Research and Reviews*, *11*(2), 405–410. DOI: 10.30574/msarr.2024.11.2.0139

Wagner, A. E., & Brooke, C. (2007). Wasting time: The mission impossible with respect to technology-oriented security approaches electronic. *Journal of Business Research Methods*, *5*(2), 117–124. https://academic-publishing.org/index.php/ejbrm/issue/view/147

Wang, C., Wang, Y., Chen, Y., Liu, H., & Liu, J. (2020). User authentication on mobile devices: Approaches, threats and trends. *Computer Networks*, *170*, 107118.

Wang, D., & Han, Y. (2023). Exploration of the path for school principals to promote the construction of artificial intelligence curriculum – based on case study. *Fuzzy Systems and Data Mining*, *IX*. Advance online publication. DOI: 10.3233/faia231092

Wang, H., Fu, T., Du, Y., Gao, W., Huang, K., Liu, Z., Chandak, P., Liu, S., Van Katwyk, P., Deac, A., Anandkumar, A., Bergen, K., Gomes, C. P., Ho, S., Kohli, P., Lasenby, J., Leskovec, J., Liu, T., Manrai, A., & Zitnik, M. (2023). Scientific discovery in the age of artificial intelligence. *Nature*, *620*(7972), 47–60. DOI: 10.1038/s41586-023-06221-2 PMID: 37532811

Wang, P. (2019). On defining artificial intelligence. *Journal of Artificial General Intelligence*, *10*(2), 1–37. DOI: 10.2478/jagi-2019-0002

Wang, X., Huang, R., Sommer, M., Pei, B., Shidfar, P., Rehman, M. S., Ritzhaupt, A. D., & Martin, F. (2024). The efficacy of artificial intelligence-enabled adaptive learning systems from 2010 to 2022 on learner outcomes: A meta-analysis. *Journal of Educational Computing Research*, *62*(6), 1568–1603. DOI: 10.1177/07356331241240459

Webb, N. M. (1982). Student interaction and learning in small groups. *Review of Educational Research*, *52*(3), 421–445. DOI: 10.3102/00346543052003421

Wei, S. (2024). Research on the disruptive transformation and future development of american teaching models in the context of intelligent transformation. *Advances in Economics. Management and Political Sciences*, *72*(1), 201–210. DOI: 10.54254/2754-1169/72/20240696

Wells, R. E. (2023). Strong AI vs. weak AI: What's the difference? Strong AI can do anything a human can do, while weak AI is limited to a specific task. *LifeWire*. Retrieved from https://www.lifewire.com/strong-ai-vs-weak-ai-7508012

White, J., Fu, Q., Hays, S., Sandborn, M., Olea, C., Gilbert, H., Elnashar, A., Spencer-Smith, J., & Schmidt, D. C. (2023). *A Prompt Pattern Catalog to Enhance Prompt Engineering with ChatGPT*. arXiv.org. https://arxiv.org/abs/2302.11382v1

White, D. H., & Robertson, L. (2015). Implementing assistive technologies: A study on co-learning in the Canadian elementary school context. *Computers in Human Behavior*, *51*, 1268–1275. DOI: 10.1016/j.chb.2014.12.003

WHO Country Office Mongolia. (2021). Rapid Assistive Technology Assessment (rATA) Survey Implementation. https://cdn.who.int/media/docs/default-source/assistive-technology-2/rata-master-training/20201021-rata-enumerator-manual-final.pdf?sfvrsn=3864b5f8_12

Widiyastono, H., Rejeki, D. S., Supratiwi, M., Gunarhadi, G., Yuwono, J., & Hermawan, H. (2023). Utilization of Assistive Technology in Special Needs Children's Learning (Inclusive Education). *Journal of Disability*, *3*(1), 1–6. DOI: 10.20961/jod.v3i1.80244

Woodrow, J., Malik, A., & Piech, C. (2024). *AI teaches the art of elegant coding: Timely, fair, and helpful style feedback in a global course*. In *Proceedings of the 55th ACM Technical Symposium on Computer Science Education (SIGCSE 2024)*, Vol. 1 (pp. 1442–1448). Association for Computing Machinery. https://doi.org/DOI: 10.1145/3626252.3630773

World Economic Forum. (2015). *The skills needed in the 21st century*. https://widgets.weforum.org/nve-2015/chapter1.html

World Economic Forum. (2025). *Future of jobs report*. https://reports.weforum.org/docs/WEF_Future_of_Jobs_Report_2025.pdf

World Health Organization & UNICEF. (2022). *Global report on assistive technology*. World Health Organization.

Wu, H.-K., Lee, S. W.-Y., Chang, H.-Y., & Liang, J.-C. (2013). Current status, opportunities and challenges of augmented reality in education. *Computers & Education*, *62*, 41–49. DOI: 10.1016/j.compedu.2012.10.024

Wu, P., Su, J., Hong, L., Ren, J., Chien, C., Chen, H., Ke, C., Hsiao, H., Li, S., Sheu, S., Lo, W., Chang, S., Lo, C., Liu, R., Hsieh, C., Tang, K., & Chang, M. (2023). A floating-point 6T SRAM in-Memory-Compute macro using Hybrid-Domain structure for advanced AI edge chips. *IEEE Journal of Solid-State Circuits*, *59*(1), 196–207. DOI: 10.1109/jssc.2023.3309966

Xiao, N., Pei, Y., Yuan, C., Bu, Y., & Cai, Z. (2025). Transforming Education with Artificial Intelligence: A Comprehensive Review of Applications. *Challenges, and Future Directions.*, *2*(1), 337–356. DOI: 10.70693/itphss.v2i1.211

Xie, X. (2023). Influence of ai-driven inquiry teaching on learning outcomes. [iJET]. *International Journal of Emerging Technologies in Learning*, *18*(23), 59–70. DOI: 10.3991/ijet.v18i23.45473

Xu, W., & Ouyang, F. (2022). The application of ai technologies in stem education: A systematic review from 2011 to 2021. *International Journal of STEM Education*, *9*(1). Advance online publication. DOI: 10.1186/s40594-022-00377-5

Y, M. N., H, L. P., & N, S. (2024). Revolutionizing Education: Harnessing AI for Personalized Learning Pathways and Student Success. *International Journal For Multidisciplinary Research*. https://doi.org/DOI: 10.36948/ijfmr.2024.v06i05.28371

Yadav, S. (2024). Advancing Education With AI-Driven Education for Diverse Learners. *Advances in Educational Technologies and Instructional Design Book Series*, 49–80. https://doi.org/DOI: 10.4018/979-8-3693-6130-6.ch003

Yang, Z. (2022). Natural language enhancement for english teaching using character-level recurrent neural network with back propagation neural network based classification by deep learning architectures. *JUCS -. Journal of Universal Computer Science*, *28*(9), 984–1000. DOI: 10.3897/jucs.94162

Yenduri, G.. (2023). From Assistive Technologies to Metaverse—Technologies in Inclusive Higher Education for Students With Specific Learning Difficulties: A Review. *IEEE Access : Practical Innovations, Open Solutions*, *11*, 64907–64927. DOI: 10.1109/ACCESS.2023.3289496

Yeşilbaş Özenç, Y., & Başaran, R. (2024). Lifelong learning and artificial intelligence. *Sinop Üniversitesi Eğitim Fakültesi Dergisi*, *1*(1), 101–125.

Yıldırım, A. (2024). Analysis of turkey's cyber security policy through action plans. *Journal of Organization and Management Sciences*, *16*(1), 23–47.

Yılmaz, E., Şahin, Y. L., & Akbulut, Y. (2015). Development of the digital data security awareness scale. *AJIT-e: Academic Journal of Information Technology, 6*(21), 23-40. https://dergipark.org.tr/en/pub/ajit-e/article/740906

Yılmaz, E., Şahin, Y. L., & Akbulut, Y. (2016). Digital data security awareness of teachers. *Sakarya University Journal of Education*, 6(2), 26-45. https://dergipark.org.tr/tr/pub/suje/issue/24692/261095

Yılmaz, H. (2014). Establishment of information security management system and information security risk analysis within the scope of TS ISO/IEC 27001 information security management standard. *Denetişim*, (15), 45–59.

Yılmaz, Ö. (2024). *Personalised learning and artificial intelligence in science education: current state and future perspectives*. Educational Technology Quarterly., DOI: 10.55056/etq.744

Yilmaz, R., Yurdugül, H., Yilmaz, F. G. K., Şahin, M., Sulak, S., Aydin, F., Tepgeç, M., Müftüoğlu, C. T., & Oral, N. Ö. (2022). Smart MOOC integrated with intelligent tutoring: A system architecture and framework model proposal. *Computers and Education Artificial Intelligence*, *3*, 100092. DOI: 10.1016/j.caeai.2022.100092

Yoo, H., Jang, J., Oh, H., & Park, I. (2022). The potentials and trends of holography in education: A scoping review. *Computers & Education*, *186*, 104533. DOI: 10.1016/j.compedu.2022.104533

Yuen, S. C.-Y., Yaoyuneyong, G., & Johnson, E. (2013). Augmented Reality and Education: Applications and Potentials. In R. Huang, Kinshuk, & J. M. Spector (Eds.), *Reshaping Learning* (pp. 385–414). Springer Berlin Heidelberg. https://doi.org/DOI: 10.1007/978-3-642-32301-0_17

Yu, H., & Guo, Y. (2023). Generative artificial intelligence empowers educational reform: Current status, issues, and prospects. *Frontiers in Education*, *8*, 1183162. DOI: 10.3389/feduc.2023.1183162

Yu, Y., Han, L., Du, X., & Yu, J. (2022). An oral english evaluation model using artificial intelligence method. *Mobile Information Systems*, •••, 1–8. DOI: 10.1155/2022/3998886

Zaman, B. U. (2024). *Transforming Education Through AI Benefits Risks and Ethical Considerations*. https://doi.org/DOI: 10.20944/preprints202407.0859.v1

Zawacki-Richter, O., Marín, V. I., Bond, M., & Gouverneur, F. (2019). Systematic review of research on artificial intelligence applications in higher education–where are the educators? *International Journal of Educational Technology in Higher Education*, *16*(1), 1–27. DOI: 10.1186/s41239-019-0171-0

Zeng, W., & Koutny, M. (2019). Modelling and analysis of corporate efficiency and productivity loss associated with enterprise information security technologies. *Journal of Information Security and Applications*, *49*, 102385.

Zhai, X., & Nehm, R. H. (2023). ai and formative assessment: The train has left the station. *Journal of Research in Science Teaching*, *60*(6), 1390–1398. DOI: 10.1002/tea.21885

Zhang, C. (2024). AI in Education: Opportunities, Challenges, and Pathways for Equitable Learning. *Journal of Education. Humanities and Social Sciences*, *45*, 723–728. DOI: 10.54097/kfgp6j07

Zhang, C., Zheng, X., & Wan, J. (2024). Research on the construction of a curriculum system of asset appraisal major under the background of artificial intelligence. *International Journal of Education and Humanities*, *15*(3), 357–360. DOI: 10.54097/e7yprc40

Zhang, H., Lee, I., Ali, S., DiPaola, D., Cheng, Y., & Breazeal, C. (2022). Integrating ethics and career futures with technical learning to promote ai literacy for middle school students: An exploratory study. *International Journal of Artificial Intelligence in Education*, *33*(2), 290–324. DOI: 10.1007/s40593-022-00293-3 PMID: 35573722

Zhang, L., Fu, K., & Liu, X. (2022). Artificial Intelligence in Education: Ethical Issues and its Regulations. *Proceedings of the 5th International Conference on Big Data and Education*, 1–6. https://doi.org/DOI: 10.1145/3524383.3524406

Zhang, Q. (2024). Harnessing Artificial Intelligence for Personalized Learning Pathways: A Framework for Adaptive Education Management Systems. *Applied and Computational Engineering*, *82*(1), 167–172. DOI: 10.54254/2755-2721/82/20241102

Zhang, W., & Borg, J. (2025). Global availability of guidelines related to assistive technology: A scoping review. *Frontiers in Rehabilitation Sciences*, *6*. Advance online publication. DOI: 10.3389/fresc.2025.1581104 PMID: 40342299

Zhao, N., & Zhang, J. (2021). The "change" and "constancy" of teacher's role in the age of artificial intelligence. *Proceedings of the 6th International Conference on Education Reform and Modern Management (ERMM 2021)*. https://doi.org/DOI: 10.2991/assehr.k.210513.098

Zheng, R., & Badarch, T. (2022). Research on applications of artificial intelligence in education. *American Journal of Computer Science and Technology*, *5*(2), 72. DOI: 10.11648/j.ajcst.20220502.17

Zhu, C. (2022). Reflections on the reform of curriculum ideological and political teaching mode in the era of artificial intelligence. *International Symposium on Robotics, Artificial Intelligence, and Information Engineering* (RAIIE 2022), 114. https://doi.org/DOI: 10.1117/12.2660041

Zhu, Q. (2023). Natural language processing in teacher training: A systematic review. *Lecture Notes in Education Psychology and Public Media*, *18*(1), 83–90. DOI: 10.54254/2753-7048/18/20231293

Zilz, W., & Pang, Y. (2019). Application of assistive technology in inclusive classrooms. *Disability and Rehabilitation. Assistive Technology*, *16*(7), 684–686. DOI: 10.1080/17483107.2019.1695963 PMID: 31814471

Zins, C. (2007). Conceptual approaches for defining data, information, and knowledge. *Journal of the American Society for Information Science and Technology*, *58*(4), 479–493.

Zviel-Girshin, R. (2024). The good and bad of AI tools in novice programming education. *Education Sciences*, *14*(10), 1089. DOI: 10.3390/educsci14101089

Zwilling, M., Klien, G., Lesjak, D., Wiechetek, Ł., Cetin, F., & Basim, H. N. (2022). Cyber security awareness, knowledge and behavior: A comparative study. *Journal of Computer Information Systems*, *62*(1), 82–97.

About the Contributors

Nihal Dulkadir Yaman earned her Ph.D. in Computer Education and Instructional Technologies from Anadolu University in 2019, following a Master's degree in Distance Education (2018) and a Bachelor's degree in Computer Education and Instructional Technologies (2008) from the same institution. Currently, she serves as a faculty member in the Department of Management Information Systems at Kırşehir Ahi Evran University. Her academic journey includes faculty positions at Muş Alparslan University and Burdur Mehmet Akif Ersoy University, as well as research assistant roles at Anadolu University and Burdur Mehmet Akif Ersoy University. Throughout her career, Dr. Yaman has made significant contributions to integrating technology into education, focusing on digital literacy, distance education, and the application of artificial intelligence in learning environments. Her research interests span educational technology, database management systems, and computer networks. Dr. Yaman has an extensive teaching portfolio, offering undergraduate courses such as instructional technologies, database management systems, computer networks, programming languages, and web design. She has authored numerous publications in respected journals and conferences, contributing to the academic discourse in her areas of expertise. Dr. Yaman's work is dedicated to advancing educational practices through technology, bridging the gap between theoretical knowledge and practical application in modern learning environments.

Fatih Yaman earned his Ph.D. in Computer Education and Instructional Technologies from Anadolu University in 2018, following a Bachelor's degree in Computer Education and Instructional Technologies from Marmara University in 2008. Currently, he serves as a faculty member in the Department of Information Systems and Technologies at Kırşehir Ahi Evran University. Dr. Yaman has extensive teaching experience in undergraduate courses, including instructional technologies, database management systems, web design, and software engineering. His academic contributions span a variety of research areas, including digital literacy, the integration of artificial intelligence in education, and distance learning methodologies. He has previously held positions as a faculty member at Muş Alparslan University and as a research assistant at Anadolu University, where he actively engaged in both teaching and research activities. Dr. Yaman has authored numerous publications in peer-reviewed journals and presented his work at international conferences, significantly contributing to the academic discourse in educational technology. Dr. Yaman is committed to leveraging technology to enhance educational practices and to fostering innovative solutions that address the challenges of modern learning environments.

***

Fatma Akgün is an Associate Professor at Trakya University (Turkey), within the Department of Computer and Instructional Technologies Education. She earned her B.Sc. (2002), M.Sc. (2004), and Ph.D. (2010) in Computer Engineering — all from Trakya University. Her academic career includes appointments as research assistant (from 2002), lecturer (from 2008), and full-time faculty member since 2012. She was promoted to Associate Professor in 2021. Her main research interests are educational technology integration, internet-based educational applications, instructional technologies, and multimedia applications. Over the years, she has published numerous peer-reviewed journal articles and book chapters. Among her recent research topics are digital citizenship, technology-mediated learning, cyberbullying sensitivity in secondary schools, and parental attitudes toward children's technology use. In addition to her research, Dr. Akgün has extensive experience teaching courses such as Information Technology, Instructional Technology Design, Internet Applications in Education, Multimedia Design, E-learning Foundations, and Material Design for Distance Education.

Gülşah Avcı Doğan earned her Ph.D. in Gifted Education from Anadolu University. She conducts research in the field of mathematics education, the characteristics of gifted individuals, their identification and education. She is a faculty member in the Department of Special Education at Ordu University, teaching undergraduate and postgraduate level courses.

Şenay Ozan Deniz is an assistant professor in the Faculty of Education at Trakya University. She earned BA degree at 2010 from Computer Education and Instructional Technologies (CEIT) Department, Faculty of Education, Ege University, Turkey. She graduated from Ph.D. program at CEIT Department by Anadolu University at 2018. Her research interests include technology integration, material design and instructional design, teacher education, information ethics,

Artificial ethics and, new possibilities in education. She has taken part in many projects and has published book chapters and articles.

Selin Göçen is a research assistant at Dicle Üniversitesi, within the Ziya Gökalp Eğitim Fakültesi (Faculty of Education), Temel Eğitim (Basic Education) Department — working specifically in the Division of Primary / Classroom Education. Her academic background includes undergraduate training in Classroom Teaching (Sınıf Öğretmenliği) at Hacettepe Üniversitesi, followed by a master's in Education Management, Inspection, Planning and Economics at Dicle University. As of her profile on DergiPark, she is pursuing her doctoral studies in Distance Education at another institution. Selin Göçen's research spans issues in basic education, teacher education, and distance / open learning. Her publications include studies on prospective teachers' intercultural sensitivity, perceptions of the role of research assistants, evaluations of open and distance learning technologies (e.g. digital twin technologies), and broader analyses of educational programs and the role of universities in addressing social problems.

Merita Hoxha is a university lecturer, researcher, and teacher trainer at the University of Elbasan "Aleksandër Xhuvani" in Albania. She holds a Ph.D. in pedagogy and is deeply committed to advancing inclusive education as a means of promoting equity in learning. She has been actively engaged with AAATE, serving as the national contact point for Albania, and has contributed to its conferences and collaborative outputs—including white papers, reports, and peer-reviewed articles focused on assistive technology, methodology of teaching and learning, and inclusion. Her international experience includes leading roles in European research initiatives, most notably as a Working Group Leader and Management Committee member in COST Action CA19104 – "advancing Social inclusion through Technology and EmPowerment (a-STEP)", from 2020 to 2024. She is currently a research assistant at the University of Oslo, working on projects funded by the Research Council of Norway. Beyond academia, she actively contributes to her local community as a member of the Rotary Club of Elbasan. One of her most recent volunteer initiatives was recording an audiobook for individuals with visual impairments, in collaboration with the Institute VISUM for the Blinds as part of the project "Donate Your Voice."

Sanjeev Kumar Is a Professor in Lovely Professional University Punjab India. He received Undergraduate in Hotel Management from Osmania University, Postgraduate in Tourism Management from Madurai Kamaraj University. He completed Doctor of Philosophy in Hospitality Management in 2019 from Amity University Jaipur India. His research areas lies in food Service Industry, his research focuses on Alcoholic beverages, Event management and Sustainable Management Practices, Metaverse, AI Machine Learning and Artificial Intelligence. He published more than 80 research papers, articles and chapters in Scopus Indexed, UGC Approved and peer reviewed Journals and books. Dr. Sanjeev Kumar participated and acted as resource person in various National and International conferences, seminars, session chair, research workshops and industry talks and his work has been widely cited. Dr. Sanjeev also edited more than 20 books with various International Publishers such as IGI Global, Cambridge Scholars, Emerald, CABI, Bentham Science, Taylor & Francis. Dr Sanjeev is an active researcher and has published numerous research articles in prestigious National and International journals and books.

Gülsün Kurubacak Çakır is a distinguished expert in open and distance education, currently serving as a Professor at Anadolu University (Open Education Faculty, Distance Education) and, since 2023, at Ankara Hacı Bayram Veli Üniversitesi (Faculty of Communication). Her academic background includes a B.A. from Ankara University, an M.A. in Educational Technology from Anadolu University, and an Ed.D. in Curriculum & Instruction from University of Cincinnati, USA. With over three decades of experience, Prof. Dr. Kurubacak Çakır has significantly contributed to the fields of online and distance learning, educational technology, instructional design, and media/communication studies. She has published numerous peer-reviewed articles and book chapters, and led many R&D projects exploring innovative and flexible e-learning environments — including adaptive e-assessment systems, augmented reality in education, mobile learning, and strategic design of open education systems.

Ozge Misirli is a faculty member of the Department of Computer Education and Instructional Technology at Eskisehir Osmangazi University. She has an MA in Primary Math Teaching and a Ph.D. in Computer Education and Instructional Technology. She has offered several undergraduate courses such as Information Technologies and media literacy. She conducts researches on social media, effective use of social media by children and families, ICT integration, and gender balance in ICT. She is still working at Eskisehir Osmangazi University.

Zeynep Şahin Timar is a senior lecturer in the Department of Software Engineering at Karadeniz Technical University's Technology Faculty in Turkey. She holds a Ph.D. in Computer and Instructional Technologies Education, with her doctoral research focusing on emotional design in multimedia assessment materials and their effects on cognitive load and motivation. Dr. Şahin Timar's research centers on multimedia learning, computer-based assessment, gender balance in informatics, assistive technologies, and AI in education. She is actively involved in promoting gender diversity in computing through her leadership roles in international initiatives, including co-leading Working Group 1 of the EUGAIN COST Action (European Network for Gender Balance in Informatics) and serving as vice-chair of the a-STEP COST Action (advancing Social inclusion through Technology and EmPowerment). Her work has been recognized with multiple EU awards, including the Horizon Europe Seal of Excellence Award (2025) and TUBITAK Horizon 2020 Above-Threshold Awards. She has presented her research at prestigious international conferences and has been an invited speaker at events such as the European Computer Science Summit and UN General Assembly Science Summit. Dr. Şahin Timar is committed to advancing social inclusion through technology and empowering underrepresented groups in STEM fields, particularly focusing on strategies to encourage girls' participation in informatics and computing from school to university level.

Sohel Rana Sarkar, an accomplished educator and scholar, has cleared NET-JRF and excelled at TMB University and Ramakrishna Mission Sikshanamandira. He has authored and edited 10 books and published 25 research papers and chapters, including Scopus and UGC-CARE. Currently, he is an Assistant Professor in Education at Hingalganj Mahavidyalaya, West Bengal State University with research interests in education, AI and sustainability.

Sirajun Tahura is a distinguished author and educator known for her outstanding achievements in the field of academics. She achieved the rare distinction of “First class first” in both her B. Sc. and M. Sc. in Mathematics from the esteemed University of Calcutta. Notably, Sirajun Tahura's dedication and expertise extend to her success in various examinations, including UGC NET-JRF. She has also made a significant impact in the world of research by publishing 1 Book, 4 Edited Books and so many research papers with national and international recognition. Presently, she holds the position of an Assistant Teacher (PG) in Mathematics at Kumarpukur High School, WB, India.

Betül Tonbuloğlu is a faculty member at the Distance Education Application and Research Center of Yıldız Technical University. She holds a Master's degree in Computer and Instructional Technologies Education and a Ph.D. in Educational Programs and Instruction, with a focus on distance education programs. Her research interests include distance education, educational technologies, e- learning, ai in education, e- assessment, usability evaluation, computer science education, quality standards and program evaluation.

Index

A

Accessibility 1, 2, 3, 12, 13, 39, 58, 99, 121, 127, 128, 132, 133, 138, 140, 144, 156, 160, 165, 167, 169, 171, 177, 225, 248, 249, 251, 253, 254, 255, 258, 262, 263, 265, 266, 267, 268, 269, 271, 272, 273, 276, 277
Adaptive Learning Systems 2, 3, 42, 97, 102, 110, 139, 160, 175, 183, 185, 192, 249, 254
Administrative Efficiency 53, 68, 80, 87, 102, 159
AI in Education 4, 13, 26, 28, 29, 32, 33, 34, 53, 54, 55, 87, 93, 101, 103, 140, 141, 143, 144, 146, 149, 152, 157, 159, 160, 161, 164, 168, 170, 171, 172, 174, 177, 179, 180, 181, 183, 185, 186, 187
Algorithmic Bias 4, 13, 42, 53, 54, 77, 83, 89, 126, 140, 141, 145, 150, 159, 160, 161, 163, 168, 180
Artificial intelligence 1, 2, 3, 4, 5, 7, 8, 13, 14, 15, 19, 20, 21, 22, 23, 25, 26, 27, 29, 44, 45, 46, 47, 48, 49, 50, 53, 54, 55, 67, 83, 89, 90, 91, 92, 93, 94, 95, 96, 97, 98, 99, 146, 147, 148, 149, 150, 151, 152, 153, 154, 155, 156, 157, 159, 160, 161, 164, 168, 174, 179, 182, 183, 184, 185, 186, 187, 189, 191, 192, 193, 196, 197, 200, 206, 211, 213, 214, 217, 220, 248
Assistive Technologies 247, 248, 249, 250, 251, 253, 254, 255, 256, 257, 263, 268, 269, 270, 271, 272, 273, 274, 275, 276, 277, 278
Authentication 15, 228, 231, 235, 239, 240, 244, 245
Authorization 234

B

Big Data 22, 23, 47, 191, 206, 219, 221, 237, 241, 242, 243

C

CIA Triangle 223
Content Creation 53, 68, 69, 70, 87, 101, 104, 127, 131, 132, 144, 147, 151
Creativity 14, 16, 44, 54, 63, 67, 68, 77, 126, 127, 163, 164, 172, 181, 194, 195, 199, 200, 201, 202, 203, 208, 213, 214, 215, 216, 217
Critical Thinking 14, 16, 68, 71, 72, 77, 85, 87, 102, 116, 125, 126, 127, 142, 169, 194, 195, 196, 197, 198, 199, 204, 208, 209, 214, 217, 220
Cyber Security Threats 229

D

Data Ethics 54, 92, 181
Data Privacy 2, 4, 8, 13, 15, 17, 22, 53, 54, 84, 87, 126, 141, 145, 159, 160, 162, 166, 168, 173, 180, 219, 222, 223
Data Protection 15, 41, 84, 168, 219, 230, 232, 236, 239
Digital Inequality 159
Digital Transformation 1, 3, 17, 18, 19, 20, 21, 22, 23, 219, 220, 221, 222, 247, 248, 249, 254, 270

E

Educational Assessment 19, 21, 94, 166, 184, 214
Educational Data Mining 219, 221, 222, 223, 240, 245
Educational Equity 141, 145, 181, 253, 269
Educational Technology 2, 22, 44, 49, 50, 60, 61, 90, 97, 98, 103, 146, 154, 155, 175, 186, 215, 241, 255, 270, 272, 273
Education Systems 1, 3, 5, 29, 31, 32, 33, 142, 192, 222, 251, 260, 261, 268
Effective AI Prompts 59
Equity and Access 180

Ethical AI 140, 144, 150, 157, 170
Ethical Challenges 55, 146, 159, 160, 168, 171, 180
Ethical Considerations 8, 13, 72, 83, 87, 132, 150, 162, 166, 182, 186
Ethics 54, 55, 90, 92, 96, 120, 126, 132, 139, 141, 142, 143, 146, 149, 150, 151, 155, 156, 168, 171, 180, 181, 184, 185

G

Gifted 189, 193, 194, 206, 207, 208, 210, 211, 213, 214, 215, 216, 217

H

High Intelligence 190, 217
Human-AI Partnership 63

I

Inclusion 55, 74, 95, 171, 179, 210, 249, 251, 252, 254, 256, 263, 270, 271, 272, 273, 276
Inclusive Education 12, 76, 153, 157, 161, 247, 248, 250, 255, 257, 268, 269, 272, 273, 274, 277
Innovation 5, 7, 17, 19, 22, 54, 69, 89, 91, 145, 146, 148, 150, 152, 153, 155, 160, 163, 171, 180, 189, 194, 195, 200, 202, 203, 217, 241, 244, 249, 254, 269, 272, 274
Intelligent Learning Environments 159, 160, 174, 175

L

Lifelong Learning 9, 50, 159, 160, 163, 164, 174, 176, 178, 179, 180, 184, 185, 191, 192, 217

M

Malware 227, 233, 234
Meta-Learner 189
Multi-Factor Authentication 15, 231, 235, 239, 244

P

Personalized Learning 1, 2, 3, 4, 5, 13, 14, 29, 32, 53, 55, 68, 74, 75, 76, 87, 90, 91, 95, 99, 101, 103, 104, 105, 106, 109, 110, 111, 112, 125, 127, 128, 129, 131, 132, 133, 138, 139, 142, 144, 146, 147, 149, 157, 160, 161, 169, 174, 177, 183, 185, 186, 187, 192, 219, 241, 249, 260
Problem Solving 55, 106, 190, 195, 200, 203, 204, 209

R

Reality Technology 39

S

Security Threats 219, 227, 229, 239
Social Engineering 229, 230, 240, 242, 243, 244
Social Robot 25, 26, 35, 41, 42, 51
Special Education 6, 36, 95, 101, 104, 133, 137, 138, 139, 140, 144, 152, 215, 247, 248, 249, 250, 251, 256, 257, 259, 261, 263, 268, 270, 271, 272, 273, 274, 275, 276
Special Education Needs 247, 248, 249, 250, 251, 257, 259, 261, 263, 268
Strategies 3, 8, 22, 53, 55, 59, 63, 64, 65, 69, 83, 94, 95, 103, 105, 115, 129, 139, 145, 150, 162, 163, 166, 168, 170, 174, 175, 176, 181, 196, 198, 202, 209, 210, 213, 215, 219, 226, 227, 235, 238, 240, 245, 248, 263, 265, 266, 271

T

Talented 189, 206, 208, 216, 217

V

Virtual Classrooms 1, 2, 3

www.ingramcontent.com/pod-product-compliance
Lightning Source LLC
LaVergne TN
LVHW080901300926
849162LV00003B/510